Z. 40 036

This book is dedicated to
the Leslie Price Memorial
Library by

Stephen and Pamela Kraft

The
ULTIMATE
ENCYCLOPEDIA OF

Classical
music

CARLTON

The ULTIMATE ENCYCLOPEDIA OF Classical music

General Editor: **Robert Ainsley**

THIS IS A CARLTON BOOK

Text and Design copyright © 1995 Carlton Books Limited

First published in 1995 by Carlton Books Limited

10 9 8 7 6 5 4 3 2 1

A CIP catalogue record for this book is available from the British Library

ISBN 0 74752 380 0

Project editor: Tessa Rose **Copy editor:** Diana Vowles **Indexer:** Peter Barber
Art direction: Robert Fairclough **Design:** Jon Lucas, Carol Wright **Picture research:** Emily Hedges
Production: Garry Lewis, Angela Davies

Printed and bound in Spain

Carlton Books Limited 20 St Anne's Court Wardour Street London W1V 3AW

Contents

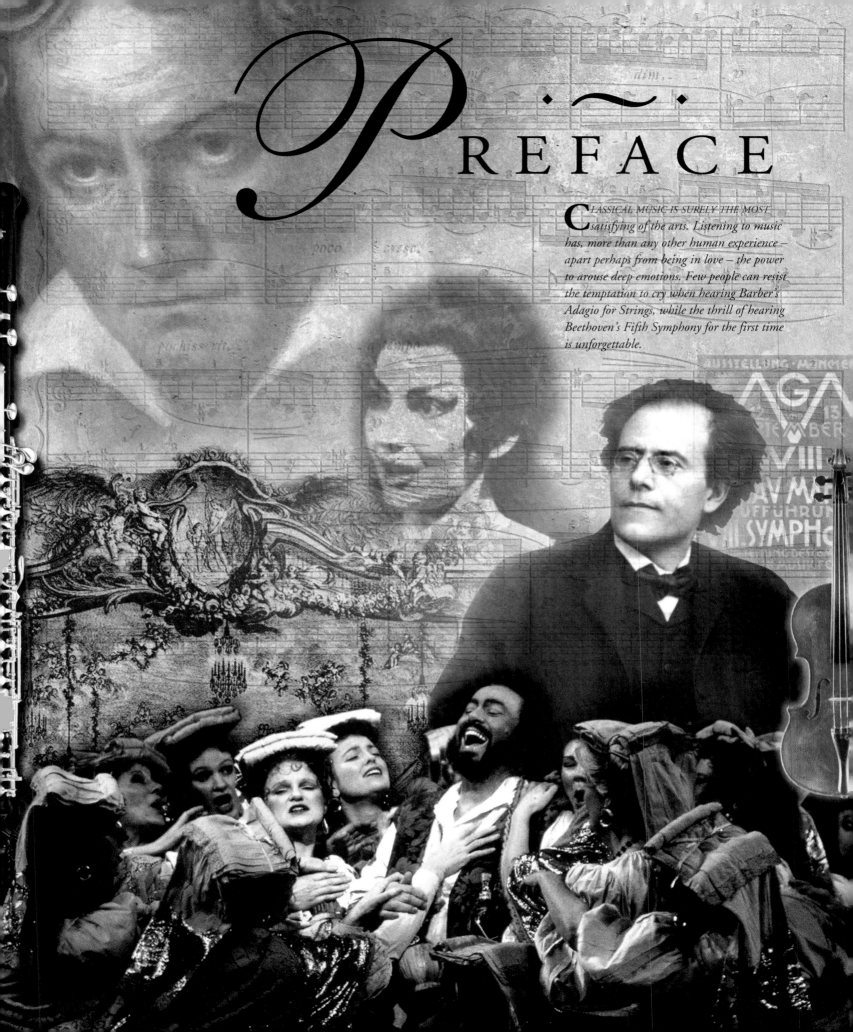

PREFACE

CLASSICAL MUSIC IS SURELY THE MOST satisfying of the arts. Listening to music has, more than any other human experience – apart perhaps from being in love – the power to arouse deep emotions. Few people can resist the temptation to cry when hearing Barber's Adagio for Strings, while the thrill of hearing Beethoven's Fifth Symphony for the first time is unforgettable.

AND THERE IS A RANGE OF STYLES AND TYPES of music to suit everyone. Lovers of tunes will find an inexhaustible supply in the works of Schubert, Chopin or Dvořák; Bach's 'absolute music', on the other hand, is so irresistibly satisfying for its stand-alone structure that it's tempting to write 'QED' at the end of his great works. The music of Mahler or Britten explores the darker human moods in penetrating depth, while Vivaldi's glorious concertos provide the light to balance the shadows. Great opera, by masters such as Puccini or Verdi, reflects human psychology and society, while those by Wagner serve for many as deep philosophical and spiritual guides. Many religious pieces – some of the most effective written by atheists! – can provide great comfort and inspiration; even non-believers will be uplifted by Handel's *Messiah*. Where Schoenberg and Webern can be daunting, complex and challenging, the brief and humorous piano pieces of Erik Satie are delightfully simple – at least on the surface.

Music can paint a portrait of a country. Smetana's music could only have beeen written by a Czech; Vaughan Williams wrote symphonies from the language of English folk-song; Copland's orchestral works suggest wide-open American plains; Rodrigo's Guitar Concerto captures the essence of what we expect Spain to be.

And it can paint an even deeper portrait of the composer. Haydn's wit, love of jokes and unflappable nature is clear from his symphonies and string quartets, while Mozart's raucous love of life and great understanding of human nature comes across in his operas. Sometimes the portrait isn't totally flattering. Beethoven's towering genius, bar-room humour and belief in the brotherhood of man is in virtually all his music – as well as the bad-tempered bully in him. Beneath Elgar's noble tunes is a disturbing melancholy that reminds us of his depressions. Tchaikovsky's highly emotional symphonies show a man desperate about his fate: that of being homosexual in an era that regarded such a disposition as a mortal sin.

The great works can also give us insight into the way life and society worked in ages gone by. Listen to any sacred vocal works by Hildegard of Bingen, Palestrina or Allegri, and you can easily picture yourself in a medieval church, trembling under the eye of God. Shostakovich's earlier music, on the other hand, draws a grim picture of Stalin's depersonalized, mechanized Russia.

The wonderful thing about music is its unpredictable nature. There are always new surprises: new composers, new sounds, new musical languages, whole new types of music to discover. You could spend a lifetime exploring the works of any one of the great names mentioned above: the descriptions of them are only a fraction of the whole story!

The cost of recorded classical music has never been lower, so building up a classical library can be a very inexpensive affair. Budget- and mid-price labels have mushroomed in the last few years, and you can quite easily build up a collection of excellent recordings of the pieces mentioned in this book with modest outlay. There are several music magazines on the market which offer detailed reviews and buying recommendations, some with cover CDs to let you hear samples of the music under review.

The aim of this book is to guide your exploration of the vast world of classical music. We wanted it to be a reference which you can turn to for explanation or reinforcement; but also an enjoyable read in its own right, which you can dip into anywhere and always find something interesting and stimulating – hence the unique structure. Each double-page section is able to stand alone as a topic in itself, but is also part of a sequence of articles which together give a complete overview of one major subject area of music.

Planning, organizing and compiling it has been a daunting job, made easier thanks to the help of some of the very best writers on classical music today. In the course of it all I've encountered several composers, dozens of pieces of music, and hundreds of fascinating facts I'd never heard or seen before, and my life is richer for it. I hope the same goes for you. ♪

Robert Ainsley, May 1995

• CONTRIBUTORS •

∾ JEREMY J. BEADLE
is a broadcaster and writer. His books including *The Age of Romanticism* and a guide to classical music.

∾ BRYAN CRIMP
has written a biography of the pianist Solomon and has contributed to most of the major music magazines in Britain and the United States.

∾ BOB DEARLING
is a musicologist. His books include *The Guinness Book of Music* (with Celia Dearling) and *Mozart – The Symphonies*.

∾ SOPHIE FULLER
is the editor of the *Pandora Guide to Women Composers* and a contributor to the *New Grove Dictionary of Women Composers*.

∾ STEPHEN JOHNSON
is a broadcaster and writer and contributor to *The Independent* newspaper and several major music magazines.

∾ PATRICK O'CONNOR
is consultant editor to *The New Grove Dictionary of Opera*, a regular broadcaster and contributor to *The Gramophone*.

∾ ATES ORGA
is a record producer and former music lecturer, and has written biographies of Beethoven and Chopin.

∾ RODERICK SWANSTON
is a Fellow of the Royal College of Music in London, where he is Principal Lecturer, and a regular broadcaster.

∾ MICHAEL TANNER
lectures at Corpus Christi College, Cambridge and writes on opera for a number of major music magazines.

∾ SIMON TREZISE
lectures in music at Trinity College, Dublin and writes for several music magazines. His researches include Schoenberg and Debussy.

$\mathcal{M}$OVEMENTS
in MUSIC

Early Music

THERE ARE REFERENCES TO MUSIC IN
many of the earliest literary sources, but
we have little idea what any of it would have
sounded like. The oldest music we have any
definite knowledge about is plainchant, or
plainsong, which is the first organized, dominant musical 'style' in the Western world.

PLAINCHANT WAS A RELIGIOUS MUSICAL
form, based around the liturgy and calendar
of the Catholic Church. The first
systematized scheme to emerge was
'Gregorian' chant, which was the dominant
musical style from about 550 to the end of
the 12th century. Plainchant consisted of a
single line of music to be sung by one voice
or many, possibly with instrumental
accompaniment – although this would not
have consisted of independent melodic
lines, merely the same tune with perhaps a
rhythm or a drone. Originally plainchant
would have been fairly simple; one note for
each syllable of text, with the occasional

• MUSICAL DEVELOPMENTS •

➢ A free-flowing single line of melody, for one voice or many, with the rhythm primarily dictated by the natural rhythm of the texts.

➢ The principal stylistic ornament was 'melisma' – one syllable sung to more than one note.

➢ As chant develops, melisma becomes more dominant, but plainchant may not have sounded smooth and tuneful as it is performed nowadays; medieval singing was probably quite nasal and probably involved falsetto singing as well.

➢ With two- and more- part vocal music, melisma dominates entirely, reducing the role of text.

➢ Léonin and Pérotin's polyphony is not based on harmony in the modern sense; some

of the effect is therefore surprisingly harsh and strong, using bold intervals.

➢ The interweaving sounds surprisingly complex. Part of the aim was to give an impression of eternity and there are no rests (breaks) in the middle of vocal lines, which move independently and inexorably. Early polyphony makes much use of triple time, although the effect is still free-flowing.

➢ Music of this period is predominantly vocal, with instruments restricted to a supporting role.

➢ Religious music is intended to serve a functional purpose and is not for pleasure.

➢ Entertainment in courtly circles is provided by troubadours singing love songs, constructed along the same lines as plainchant.

{ The Catholic Church was the nurturing place for the greatest early contributors to Western music. Léonin's influential *Book of Organum* enabled two-, three-, four- and even five-part works for the voice.

'melisma' (several notes to one syllable) on significant words. As time went on, melisma came to dominate the melody, giving the music a spacier, more ethereal feel. Gregorian chant took its name from Pope Gregory the Great, but it is unlikely that he actually wrote any. The first person to make an individual mark on the world of plainchant was the poet and mystic Abbess Hildegard of Bingen (see page 78), who created a highly personal tone with extended melismas.

The secular music of the time was the province of the troubadours, the wandering minstrel bands who sang love songs aimed largely at courtly audiences; troubadour music probably employed stronger rhythms and noisier accompaniment, but it certainly did not involve music with more than one single melodic line.

Around the beginning of the 12th century, someone came up with the idea of writing music with two melodic lines to be performed simultaneously. At first this idea seems to have belonged only to wealthy churches like Notre Dame in Paris or Santiago in Compostela, Spain (a church with a healthy income from the pilgrimage

trade), and it was at Notre Dame that the first major composers of this new style emerged – Léonin and Pérotin. Léonin provided the first major collection of 'polyphony', as this new style was called, contributing many two-part works to Notre Dame's *Book of Organum* (organum came to

mean vocal music). The younger Pérotin provided the first surviving written work for four separate voices – *Viderunt Omnes*, composed for Christmas 1198.

Léonin's and Pérotin's music was not 'harmonic' in the modern sense of the term; although the different lines were designed to complement each other, they were also independent and free-flowing. These composers had no idea of chords, nor of music where a line of melody is supported by harmonies which do not necessarily have much melody in themselves (as in a hymn tune). Each line was virtuosic and complete in itself; the music was usually highly based on melisma, with syllables often being extended to vanishing point. Where plainchant employed no rhythm beyond that of the liturgical words being set, this early polyphony tended to organize itself around fairly straightforward triple rhythms. The style is often labelled 'Ars Antiqua' ('Ancient Art'). It was dominant for about a century, until the more sophisticated 'Ars Nova' was developed by some of Western music's first theoreticians. ♪

GREGORIAN CHANT

Gregorian Chant was designed to be sung in all religious foundations throughout the Christian world. There was a Gregorian Chant prescribed for every liturgical text for every feast day and ordinary day of the Church. Doubtless some of the simpler parts of prayer settings and Mass settings were intended to be sung by congregations as a whole, as perhaps were some of the plainchant hymns; quite a lot of Gregorian chant, though, was of sufficient complexity that it could only have been meant to be sung by trained choirs (who were probably priests or members of religious orders).

S·GREGORIVS·I·MAGNVS·ROMAN

There was a tradition that Gregorian Chant had been dictated by the Holy Spirit to Pope Gregory the Great (who reigned from 590 to 604), but in fact much of the structure of the Chant was developed after his time, and went on evolving in complexity for nearly 400 years, reaching its maturity some time in the century before 1000. Quite why it was named after Gregory is not really known. Its development seems to have had as much to do with the Frankish court of Charlemagne (742–814), the first Holy Roman Emperor, as with the Roman Papal establishment.

The New Art

ARS NOVA, A BOOK BY THE COMPOSER AND writer, Philippe de Vitry, and published in 1320, suggested new ideas for rhythm in music, allowing for greater complexity and interplay between different vocal lines. De Vitry's contemporary Guillaume de Machaut, a polymath who was a diplomat and a canon of Rheims, took up his ideas and, as well as pushing even further with rhythmic complexity, became the first composer to create a complete Mass setting. Prior to his *Messe de Notre Dame*, written around 1370, the different parts of the service – Kyrie, Gloria, Credo and so on – would not have been composed as a single unit with any sense of unity. Machaut introduced unified Mass settings, a concept which the next two generations of polyphonic composers were to embrace and which became the established pattern.

Other features of 'Ars Nova' included the use of short breaks between notes in a phrase in order to enliven the rhythm (this was known as the 'hocket') and the use of phrases from pre-existing melodies in one vocal line (usually the tenor) as a framework for a new piece. This became a particularly popular device for Mass settings, and from the 15th century onwards was the main way that composers showed their ingenuity, as they recycled popular songs, religious motets by others and chansons (secular songs, often bawdy) and motets of their own. One of the last of the great French-trained composers, Guillaume Dufay (c. 1400–74), may well have begun the trend for using a popular Burgundian song 'L'Homme armé,' which almost every major composer between the mid-15th century and the Baroque era employed as the basis for a Mass setting, the settings becoming ever more daring and inventive – running a rhythmically adapted snatch of the original tune backwards, upside down, half back and half forwards simultaneously meeting in the middle – and each composer

The interior of the great Gothic cathedral of Notre Dame in Paris. Notre Dame was the centre of all the earliest musical advances, from the organum of Léonin and Pérotin to the 'Ars Nova' of Philippe de Vitry and Guillaume de Machaut.

An illustration of a priest with the Christ-child from the 13th-century Mass Book of King Ludwig – an early example of a musical manuscript.

produced music which was quite baldly dissonant and of which the rhythmic complexities were obvious and sometimes unsettling. Dufay laid more stress on mellifluousness and 'proportion', as well as paying more attention to the meaning of the words he was setting and trying to make the music reflect something of it. This trend continued when musical power shifted to the Netherlands in the latter part of the century. Johannes Ockeghem and his pupil Josquin des Près became the most celebrated composers in the whole of Europe; in their music, under a calm, flowing surface, many ingenious things are taking place which become evident only on detailed study of the piece. This is particularly the case in Josquin's use of the tune 'L'Homme armé' in his *Missa Sexti Toni*.

Inevitably, as rhythmic and melodic skills became more and more subtle, composers tested their skill by expanding the number of different vocal lines, so that by 1500 works for six or more voices were common, with Antoine Brumel, one of the later Flemish composers, even producing a Mass for 12 voices.

imitating and capping his predecessors.

Dufay's music, like that of other mid-15th century composers from other parts of Europe – the Italian Francesco Landini and the Englishman John Dunstable – showed a shift towards a greater preoccupation with melody and sweetness of sound. The pioneers of the French school had often

EARLY SCORES

The earliest music scores were written by hand, some as carefully wrought as the illuminated literary manuscripts produced by monasteries in the Middle Ages. Musically, they offered minimal information, giving note-pitches and word syllables under the relevant note. There was no indication of expression, softness or loudness, and no bar lines to indicate rhythm. It required scholarship to write such manuscripts, so they tended to be collected at wealthy and important musical and religious centres like Notre Dame or Venice; most European courts had their own collections, too.

Music printing was invented in 1501 by Ottaviano Petrucci. His system was not much less laborious than the old manuscripts and it was around 1528 that the Parisian Pierre Attaignant developed a system more suited to mass production, which caught on in Italy ten years later. These early printed manuscripts still lack expression marks, dynamic instructions and bar lines. Even with the new technology it was still cost-effective only to produce collections of Mass settings, motets and so on, sometimes by a single composer, sometimes by several; and the technology was more readily available in continental centres like Venice, Rome and Paris than in England, where manuscript continued to be the main currency of written music well into the 16th century.

The Return to Simplicity

The Sistine Chapel, Rome. Palestrina held the top musical position in the Vatican and redefined the role of music in liturgy.

THE 16TH CENTURY PRODUCED SOME OF the greatest and best-known composers of polyphony. It was also in the 16th century that the technology of musical instruments developed sufficiently for purely instrumental music to become a lively sphere of activity. Secular music became much more sophisticated, too, with the chansons of composers like Josquin early in the century and Orlando Lassus in the later 1500s (some of Lassus's chansons were extremely bawdy). Most leading composers were attached to one of the influential courts or held important posts at a religious institution like St Mark's in Venice or St Peter's in Rome.

The religious upheavals of the Reformation and the Catholic backlash of the Counter-Reformation had a significant impact on music. Mass settings and motets had become more and more ambitious and elaborate as time wore on; more voices were used and movements became longer and longer, cleverer and cleverer, and as much concerned with letting the composer show off as with putting forward any significant religious message. The later Masses of Josquin, of his Flemish contemporary

Antoine Brumel and of the great Scottish composer Robert Carver were typical of this tendency, as were many of the works written by the best-known of all 16th-century composers Giovanni Perluigi da Palestrina, up to a certain point in his career.

That point was the Council of Trent, the Catholic Church's great and lengthy council of war which launched the Counter-Reformation. Ferocious debate went on about the role of music in liturgical life and a large section of opinion held that settings of the Mass and some motets had become too elaborate, and that far too many of them were making use of chansons of dubious moral content as the basis for their musical structure. Some senior figures demanded a return to plainchant, but a warning was sent out to leading composers to make their music more of a vehicle for the words of the liturgy and less a showpiece for their own talent. This marked the end of

the free-flowing independent lines of polyphony and pointed the way towards something more tightly organized, in which all the parts moved together to underline the text; the beginning, in fact, of chordally structured music. The European composers who straddled the 16th and 17th centuries, like the Spaniard Tomás Luis de Victoria, show a shift towards this new technique. English composers such as Thomas Tallis and William Byrd showed an ease with both styles; Tallis created the enormous 40-voice motet *Spem in Alium* as well as several Catholic Masses but, like Byrd, he also wrote simpler, more direct music for use in the new Church of England (although both were, in fact, Catholics).

The rise of instrumental music was due partly to the development of the viol (the ancestor of violins, violas and cellos), the popularity of the lute, and refinements in brass instruments so that they became less raucous than in the Middle Ages. Venetian composers such as the Gabrielis (an uncle and nephew) specialized in instrumental works for brass ensembles. Keyboard writing expanded, too, as it became common for monarchs and nobles to play music themselves and to sustain musical ensembles (usually called 'consorts'). ♪

• MUSICAL DEVELOPMENTS •

➤ For the first 60 to 70 years of the 16th century polyphonic vocal music becomes more and more ambitious, using larger numbers of voices and technical tricks, but always remaining mellifluous and melodic.

➤ Composers of religious music also write a lot of secular chansons, mainly about love, drinking and popular pastimes, and many of them quite bawdy.

➤ Melodies of these chansons often find their way into settings of the Mass; this enrages dignitaries of the Church, as does the increasingly elaborate virtuosity of the singing. Consequently, from the 1570s, the Council of Trent demands simpler, more straightforward religious music.

➤ Palestrina creates a blueprint in his functional, direct *Missa Papae Marcelli.*

➤ Vocal writing tends to become less based on independent melodic lines and more on chordal progression.

➤ In secular vocal music also, more stress is laid upon the meaning of the words, something which ultimately characterizes the Baroque era.

➤ There is a great growth of instrumental music: consorts of viols and brass, keyboard pieces (for instruments like the virginals and early organs) and lute music. Harmonic organization of all types of music sounds much more like standard Western structure of major and minor keys.

This 1596 painting by Hans Vredeman de Vries shows that instrumental music in secular venues was established by the late 16th century.

GLOSSARY

A key to the technical words often used in articles, books and record notes about early or Renaissance music.

ARS ANTIQUA *The first style of writing with more than one melodic line, exemplified by Léonin and Pérotin.*

ARS NOVA *Succeeded Ars Antiqua in the early 14th century; its pioneers included de Vitry and de Machaut. Notable for greater rhythmic complexity.*

CANON *One musical line imitating another; standard in vocal polyphony.*

CHANSON *A song for one or two vocal lines and sometimes instrumental accompaniment.*

CONDUCTUS *Entirely newly composed music used to set verse of a religious nature, though not necessarily drawn from the liturgy.*

HOCKET *A rhythmic device which enlivens rhythm by putting rests in the middle of vocal lines.*

ISORHYTHM *Putting parts of a melody into a repeated rhythmic pattern to form one strand in a polyphonic work, usually a motet.*

MADRIGAL *A 16th-century secular piece for four or more voices which emphasized the meaning of words.*

MASS *The Catholic liturgy; in a musical context, the Kyrie, Gloria, Credo, Sanctus, Benedictus and Agnus Dei.*

MELISMA *Several notes sung to a single syllable.*

MOTET *A sacred piece for several voices.*

NEUMA *A sign in very early manuscripts indicating pitch.*

ORGANUM *Liturgical music, based on existing plainsong, used to set prose.*

POLYPHONY *Music which uses several independent vocal lines simultaneously; the predominant early music style, replaced by homophony, in which the music moves chordally (for example, like a hymn).*

Baroque

BY THE END OF THE 18TH CENTURY 'Baroque' had come to mean something unnatural, contorted and highly decorated. In fact, one of the main preoccupations of the earliest composers we now label 'Baroque' was to produce something expressive and more emotionally communicative. The revolutionary who inaugurated the Baroque was Claudio Monteverdi. His music took new risks, did exciting things with rhythms like stressing weaker beats, and introduced new dissonances to make the music more expressive. Monteverdi's career coincided with the rise of solo singing, as well as some Florentine noblemen's experiments to re-create the musical texture of Greek drama. These experiments resulted in a form called 'opera' and although Monteverdi did not write the very first opera (that was the creation of Jacopo Peri), within a decade of Peri's foray into this dramatic form Monteverdi had produced Orfeo, a musical retelling of a mythological legend full of outrageously expressive devices, demanding singing of some virtuosity.

A NUMBER OF OLDER MUSICIANS ATTACKED Monteverdi for doing violence to the beauty of music, but his madrigals, his sacred works (such as the celebrated Vespers of 1610) and his operas swept all before them. His music also required a high level of virtuosity from both string and brass players on account of the dramatic musical effects.

The new style demanded new musical forms. It was in the Baroque era that some of the forms we know today began to take shape; opera, the instrumental sonata, the cantata (Italian and French taste favoured secular cantatas for solo voice, German cantatas tended to have a primarily religious function) and the concerto. To begin with, most of these terms were bandied about fairly freely, but in Italy and German the sonata and the concerto developed as a vehicle for musicians to show off their virtuosity, and by the time figures like Handel, J S Bach and Vivaldi were learning their trade at the end of the 17th century, the terms bore some relation to the meanings they carry today.

Although there was a fair amount of movement around continental Europe by musicians at this time, France remained a rather insular culture and developed its own

---

• MUSICAL DEVELOPMENTS •

➤ Baroque music is more directly expressive. There is greater use of harsh dissonance to express extremes of emotion, especially in vocal music.

➤ There is more use of ornament, especially in French music; trills and grace-notes, little twists on notes, all find their way into musical notation. There are more overt rhythmic tricks (stresses on unnatural beats being a particular feature).

➤ Choral and instrumental music usually moves chordally by now. There is much more virtuosic instrumental music, which leads to the appearance of sonatas for solo instruments and concertos in which soloists or groups of soloists get a chance to show off their skill.

➤ Choral music makes a greater feature of instrumental sounds to create a more exuberant sense of celebration (for example Monteverdi's Vespers of 1610).

➤ Opera is invented.

➤ Solo singing becomes more common in both sacred and secular music.

➤ In France, the dance becomes central to musical composition.

➤ Harmonic organization around major and minor key structures develops; the idea of a top line melody becomes much more the fulcrum of a musical work; the independent melodic lines of polyphony are mainly a thing of the past, except where different parts imitate each other (out of this the fugue develops).

Claudio Monteverdi towards the end of his life (c. 1640). One of the most revolutionary figures in the history of music, he introduced devices that inaugurated the Baroque era.

A print depicting part of the action in Lully's opera *Thesée*. Like most of Lully's operas, *Thesée* uses a mythological story involving a great deal of spectacle and ornament; dance would have been an integral part of the action, too, as in all French Baroque opera.

BAROQUE COMPOSERS – WORKING CONDITIONS

To be a composer in the Baroque era, you also had to be a practising musician, quite often to a high level of virtuosity. Composers were generally employed either by princely courts or by religious institutions and were expected to produce music to order. Monteverdi spent years trying to escape from Mantua to a much more attractive job at St Mark's Venice; when J S Bach tried to leave a job in Weimar a hundred years later, the Duke threw him into prison.

Court composers would write mainly secular music for courtly entertainments, much of which was intended as background music; courtly employment also afforded the opportunity for masques and operas, too. An endless thirst for concertos developed, especially in Dresden and Venice, and many Baroque composers (like Telemann, Heinichen and Vivaldi) spent much of their time churning them out. Composers attached to a large church or cathedral would be expected to turn out reams of music for use in services; in Catholic churches like St Mark's in Venice or those in Rome this meant Masses and motets, but in Lutheran churches like St Thomas's in Leipzig it meant providing a new cantata for every Sunday of the year.

unique Baroque style, which eventually reached out and influenced composers in other countries – especially many of the Germans and J S Bach in particular. French music was centred on dance and dance forms, and it was in 17th-century France that ballet became the crucial art form. Even French opera depended hugely on a large ballet quotient. The leading French composers of the time – Jean-Baptiste Lully in the middle of the century, followed by François Couperin and Jean-Philippe Rameau in the 18th century – wrote music, whether operas, orchestral or instrumental suites, heavily dependent on dance forms. It was French Baroque music which developed an instrumental style involving huge amounts of ornamentation – the kind of frilliness which became synonymous with the word 'Baroque'. It was also in France that people began to publish collections of pieces organized around the principle of major and minor keys – the basis of the harmonies which were to prevail over the next 300 years.

The Concerto Factories

IN THE 150 YEARS WHICH ROUGHLY COVER the Baroque era (up to about 1750), music took on some of the features of an industry. The popularity of the concerto form turned composers into 'concerto factories'. This was much easier for Baroque composers than it would have been for their Romantic counterparts; Baroque composers were not interested in baring their souls for their listeners, just in producing a pleasing sound with interesting effects that might make their pieces stand out a little, but always playing by established formulaic rules.

The concerto was developed in the second half of the 17th century by Italian-based composers like Torelli, Alessandro Scarlatti and Corelli, but it quickly spread and within the first 25 years of the 18th century, most German musical centres had their resident concerto composer – Telemann in Hamburg, Heinichen in Dresden, J S Bach in Cöthen. Concertos sometimes featured soloists, sometimes groups of soloists; there was a lot of technical skill in writing four different violin parts interweaving with each other. The most famous of all Baroque concertos, though, were for solo violin and orchestra; Vivaldi's *Four Seasons* was particularly notable for its descriptive quality, this being something which Baroque music could achieve to which the abstract polyphony of early music was not so suited. However, it was not meant as an internal personal mode of expression. Vivaldi was simply following the musical rhetoric of his age, which is why he provided sonnets of dubious literary quality to accompany the music.

Descriptive music of this kind was all part of the ornate expressiveness of the Baroque. It found another outlet in the solo cantatas popular in France and Italy at the end of the 17th century and beginning of the 18th, which often centred on the characters of abandoned lovers in extreme states of mind. There was no attempt to

• MUSICAL DEVELOPMENTS •

➢ **The concerto becomes the dominant instrumental form of the late 17th and early 18th centuries.**

➢ **Concertos can feature either solo instrumentalists (usually violins) and orchestra or groups of instruments and orchestra.** If a solo instrument, look for dazzling virtuosity, numerous runs, leaps, ornaments (for example trills) and vibrato (wobbly tone, designed to be expressive). A group of instruments will have all these virtuosic features plus a lot of subtle interweaving of lines, while the main orchestra (which will not be large) simply plays the same passage over and over again at regular intervals while the soloist(s) draw breath.

➢ **An orchestra always has a keyboard player** underpinning the bass line and no conductor in the modern sense.

➢ **Instrumental music seeks to be descriptive** (as in the *Four Seasons*) so that the ornamentation can be justifiably elaborate.

➢ **Vocal music takes more and more interest in extreme figures** – abandoned lovers, the deranged – but this is not a sympathetic interest; these are freaky people given freaky vocal effects.

➢ **Operas become ever more spectacular** both vocally and visually; lead roles are often allotted to castrati and women playing men ('trouser roles').

➢ **In all, elaborate ornamentation and seeking after effect are very much the order of the day.**

MUSIC PRINTING

By the 18th century printing was commonplace, yet some musicians still preferred working with manuscripts; typed music was sometimes hard to read, especially the values of the shorter notes, and opera houses preferred manuscripts because they were easier to amend. Some composers also believed that it was easier to avoid piracy if their music remained in manuscript. So Italian composers usually had their music printed outside the Italian states, if they had it printed at all. By contrast, J S Bach in Germany scarcely had any of his music printed in his lifetime.

Composers who did want to make money by having their music printed and published had to make sure pirate publishers didn't get their hands on it. Most ingenious of all was Telemann, who ran his own imprint, engraved all his own plates and produced all his own editions. When he discovered pirate copies of his music on a trip to Paris, he paid to buy the 'privilege', which gave him the sole right to print and publish his music in that city.

Not everyone went to such elaborate lengths as Telemann; Handel made a deal with a London printer and publisher, John Walsh, to make sure that all the royalties went into his own pocket.

probe or sympathize with the deranged mind, just to find ornate musical ways in which it could be depicted. There was a trend in England for miniature versions of such works, often known today as 'mad songs', in which composers like Purcell and Blow would use the most grotesque

techniques at their disposal to exhibit someone like 'Bess of Bedlam'.

This vocal spectacle was quite common in the opera of the period and found a reflection in stage techniques. As the Baroque era wore on, no opera was likely to find an audience if it could not offer special

effects (like real floods on stage); and that was true whether the opera was serious, some great mythological tragedy (the genre which became known as 'opera seria'), or farcical comedy ('opera buffa'). By the early 18th century the Baroque ethic, born of a desire to clarify emotion and present something realistic, had acquired the rococo flamboyance for which it is remembered, whether in opera, religious and secular vocal music or in instrumental works such as the concerto. ♪

Georg Philipp Telemann, the German composer of concertos, trio sonatas and overture suites, went to ingenious lengths to prevent his music from being pirated.

A 17th-century German printing shop. Piracy was such a problem that many composers preferred not to have their music printed at all.

Ornament Restrained

THE LAST YEARS OF THE BAROQUE ERA were dominated by two of music's greatest giants – Johann Sebastian Bach and Handel. In many ways they are the key figures in the transition to the more restrained, formal Classical period, and there are those who would object to their appearing in pages devoted to the Baroque. Yet at the time, Bach was regarded as a curiously old-fashioned figure, and many of his compositions were a final summation of the theorizing side of the Baroque; in collections like *The Well-Tempered Clavier* and *The Art of Fugue* he set out to show just what could be done with certain forms – especially the fugue – in every single key of the Western musical system. His adherence to fugue was in itself regarded as old-fashioned; it was the last hangover from polyphonic composition and it allowed for elaborate contrapuntal display, always, in Bach's hands, with a fair amount of ornamentation, at a time when this was going out of fashion. Bach was fond of exhaustively exploring forms; this was partly why he grouped together the six concertos known as the 'Brandenburgs' (not all of which had been written for the Margrave of Brandenburg, whose commission gave the concertos their name). These set the standards which the concerto form was to follow in the Classical period as well as inventing the keyboard concerto.

Bach's music always remains essentially Baroque in its heavy reliance on ornamentation, its determined backward glance to polyphonic method. However, Bach is very different from many Baroque composers in that his music is intellectual and abstract, often seeming like an academic exercise given a spiritual twist.

The interior of the Thomaskirche in Leipzig, where J S Bach held an appointment.

• MUSICAL DEVELOPMENTS •

➤ Bach and Handel both make extensive use of keyboards and develop works designed to exhibit keyboard virtuosity.

➤ Keyboards at this stage are mainly the organ (slightly lighter in tone than its modern counterpart) and the harpsichord (development of the piano's forerunners belongs to the Classical period).

➤ Bach's music possesses abundant ornamentation but at the same time is highly 'philosophical' and often gives a sense of almost spiritual abstraction, especially in solo keyboard pieces like the *Goldberg Variations*.

➤ Bach's oratorios and cantatas remain firmly rooted in German Lutheran tradition, often built around popular chorale tunes by figures such as Luther; Handel's oratorios are closer to the spirit of Italian opera.

➤ Orchestral sound becomes denser, closer to the compact, concentrated sound familiar in later 18th-century music.

➤ As the 18th century progresses, a perceptible shift in public opinion makes the ornamental style of Bach less fashionable and Vivaldi falls out of favour.

➤ Opera remains dominated by spectacle and vocal gymnastics; the concerto remains popular throughout the period; and the orchestral overture to operas (sometimes known as a 'sinfonia' or 'symphony') begins to take on a life of its own, developing a basic shape and form along the same lines as the concerto.

Handel's music, on the other hand, is much more concrete, which is why he was so comfortable with dramatic forms like opera and oratorio. Handel elaborated on both forms, making the choral content of oratorio more extensive and filling in the instrumental lines to give a denser sound with more impact than some 17th-century Italian works in the same field. His serious operas also partly foreshadow the Classical period, although vocal extravagance was still at a premium. Handel made an enormous contribution to concerto writing and his works for organ remain among the most powerful and influential concerto pieces for that instrument.

Bach and Handel dominated the first half of the 17th century, both surviving fluctuating fortunes in a world where the public were increasingly restless in search of novelty. However, the English public stubbornly went against the trend; the ornate French operatic style never caught on in the 17th century, the semi-operas of Purcell and Blow or shorter all-music dramas like *Dido and Aeneas* and *Venus and Adonis* being preferred instead, and in the 18th century Handel's Italian operas were chased out of London's opera houses by the folk-based *Beggar's Opera*. Whether this means that English taste was ahead of its time or non-existent, it is hard to say. ♪

An engraving by Hogarth entitled 'The Beggar's Opera Burlesqued'. The popularity of *The Beggar's Opera*, with its realistic depiction of low-life and use of popular street-tunes, shows how British taste was not for the high-minded.

·WHERE BAROQUE MUSIC WAS COMPOSED·

ENGLAND
LONDON	Blow, Jeremiah Clarke, Purcell, Handel

FRANCE
PARIS	Marc-Antoine Charpentier, Louis Couperin, François Couperin ('le Grand'), Marin Marais, Lully, Monteclair, Rameau

GERMANY AND AUSTRIA
NORTH GERMANY AND BERLIN	Buxtehude, Michael Praetorius, Tunder
HAMBURG	Telemann
DRESDEN	Schütz, Heinichen, Veracini, Zelenka
LEIPZIG	J S Bach, Schein
SALZBURG	Biber
VIENNA	Caldara; Vivaldi tried (and failed) to make an impact on Vienna and died there in poverty

ITALY
MANTUA	The city where Monteverdi began to compose
VENICE	Monteverdi from about 1610; Albinoni, Galuppi, Lotti, Tartini and Vivaldi
ROME	Allegri, Carissimi, Corelli, Alessandro Scarlatti, Stradella, Handel (in his early days)
NAPLES	Pergolesi, Gesualdo

LOW COUNTRIES
AMSTERDAM	Locatelli, Sweelinck

SPAIN
MADRID	Domenico Scarlatti (who went there to get away from his father, Alessandro)

Classical

A general artistic interest in Classicism was kindled by the discovery of the remains of Pompeii in 1748, which led to writers, painters and sculptors trying to imitate Greek and Roman models. Composers, of course, were not in any position to do this, as no one knows what Greek and Roman music really sounded like; instead they attempted to imitate Classicism by precise formality and avoiding extravagant excess.

A**S ALWAYS WITH THESE CONVENIENT** labels, deciding where one era ends and another begins can be a bit arbitrary. There is a strong argument for saying that much of J S Bach's and Handel's music should properly be called 'Classical', though the generally accepted start of the Classical period is somewhere in the 1740s, when a new, more restrained style of Italian opera swept through Europe.

IN SOME WAYS THE AIMS OF THE NEW musical style were the same as those of Monteverdi in the first half of the previous century – to make the music more directly expressive and simpler for the audience to follow. Instrumental music was severely disciplined and excessive ornamentation was abandoned for more tightly organized formal design; the result was that a new instrumental form, the 'sinfonia' or 'symphony' very quickly developed and became a firm favourite with both composers and audiences. Although the term 'sinfonia' had been around throughout the Baroque, referring to any instrumental interlude or introduction, it came to signify a three-part piece in which two fast sections bracketed a brief slower segment. By the 1760s, the symphony was an important, widespread form, being pioneered by C P E Bach (who was *the* Bach, as far as the late 18th century was concerned) and Haydn.

The musicians of the Classical period concentrated on making music clearer. They went even further than the earlier Baroque writers in making the top melodic line the main point of listening; music was intended to gratify the sense of hearing, not be a means for the composer to show off. Although Classical composers still went in for writing fugues and other hangovers from polyphony, they did so in the context of sure, clear melodic lines that could be followed by all and that did not baffle public taste ('taste' was an important matter in the Classical period).

The reform of opera was one of the

The title page of the Paris edition of the libretto to Gluck's *Orfeo ed Euridice*.

A 19th-century engraving of the ruins of Pompeii. Their discovery inspired interest in Classicism.

most immediate Classical missions; out went Baroque extravagance and indulgence, and in came a simpler, melody-led style which concentrated (as had early Baroque writing) on the meaning of the texts; of course, the texts also had to embody decent Classical restraint and tastefulness and usually be morally uplifting. The great Classical opera reformer was Christoph Willibald Gluck, who dominated the operatic world in Germany, Austria and France; for Parisian taste he would usually rewrite his works with a greater emphasis on dance, which remained

Carl Philipp Emanuel Bach, one of the fathers of the symphony.

• MUSICAL DEVELOPMENTS •

➤ Fewer ornaments, frills, vocal gymnastics or anything distracting from the main thrust of the music.

➤ Music is much more dominated by a top-line of melody; there is less use of dissonance, and a more compact, restrained sound.

➤ The symphony develops as instrumental music which offers melody without the distraction of a soloist showing off virtuosic skill; in the early part of the Classical period it is a three-section piece, quite short (often no longer than the operatic overture from which it has developed) with two longer fast sections bracketing a fairly short slower section.

➤ Opera is severely pruned; special effects become less significant and melody. becomes the key factor in arias, which try to give greater psychological realism about the plight of characters.

➤ Opera is also designed to be morally and spiritually uplifting; there is even more emphasis on Classical myths, and stories are nicely rounded to give a message.

➤ 'Taste' becomes significant; music is designed first and foremost to appeal to the listener and for gratification of the sense of hearing, so that purity and clarity become the key elements.

---

fundamental to French musical enjoyment. Gluck's operas were more realistic and more dramatic; they also employed more memorable melodies, which were not upstaged by orchestral effects or vocal gymnastics. Like Monteverdi before him, Gluck set out his operatic stall with a version of the story of Orpheus although, in keeping with the Classical ethos, it had a happy ending with the lovers reunited.

Enlightenment Ideals vs Romantic Expressionism

THE PEAK OF THE CLASSICAL PERIOD SAW the expansion of forms like the symphony and concerto into more or less what they were to remain until the 20th century. Haydn's symphonies had eventually settled on the four-movement form – Fast-Slow-Minuet-Fast – and Mozart had defined the ideal of the concerto, above all in his piano concertos, which showed a new, dramatic touch, turning the form into a kind of operatic dialogue between soloist and orchestra.

Although the civilized restraint of the Enlightenment remained the musical order of the day, a new literary and artistic movement called *Sturm und Drang* had its impact on music, and it became fashionable to write works that were slightly more turbulent and hinted at emotional depths. However, the music of the Classical period remained an embodiment of

Enlightenment ideals; these centred on the idea that the reason of man could ultimately unlock every mystery, that civilization was heading onward and upward, and that extremes of emotion were undesirable.

During this period, German and Austrian courts became important musical centres, although all performers and composers (the one would usually also be the other) would put in some time at Paris. The court of the Elector of Mannheim in Germany became a haven for

The writer Goethe, c. 1791. One of the prime movers of *Sturm und Drang*, he went on to define Romanticism.

composers; its young ruler, Carl Theodor, epitomized Enlightenment virtues, and he built up an impressive orchestra with technical accomplishments beyond almost every other ensemble of the day. Many of Mozart's first mature works were written for the Mannheim orchestra, exploiting its highly proficient brass section (the first to resemble that of a modern symphony orchestra, although much smaller than came to be the custom) and its ability to cover a wide range of dynamics. The 'Mannheim crescendo' became a distinct feature of music in the 1760s and 1770s. In Vienna, Maria Theresia and her son Josef II turned the city, over 50 years, into the most prestigious musical centre in Europe.

The wedding of Josef II, the emperor depicted in Milos Forman's film *Amadeus*, and Isabella of Parma in 1760. The four-year-old Mozart can be seen in the centre of the painting.

• MUSICAL DEVELOPMENTS •

➤ *Sturm und Drang* comes into being. This movement allows a certain amount of emotional expression, but nothing which truly unsettles proportion and order; the Enlightenment, with its belief in 'reason', remains the guiding spirit for 18th-century composers.

➤ There is a shift in the musical balance towards German centres; while Italy remains the main source for opera, the various courts in Germany provide the more up-to-date orchestras.

➤ Technological improvements in instruments lead to a greater role for oboes, clarinets, brass and timpani in ensembles with strings; instruments are now sounding a little more like those of today, although string playing has a thinner texture.

➤ The symphony expands into its now accepted four-movement form with movements being self-sufficient pieces.

➤ The concerto develops into a dialogue between soloist and orchestra and with Mozart's keyboard concertos the modern piano begins to emerge, although the sound made at this time is less resonant and still bears traces of the harpsichord's timbre.

➤ The technological advances in instruments mean that a greater range of expression becomes possible in purely orchestral works; composers favour the use of the 'Mannheim crescendo.

➤ Contemporary taste in opera demands that highborn and lowborn characters do not occupy the same stage; lofty idealistic stories related like tableaux are still preferred, but Mozart's mature works point the way forward.

{ Henry Fuseli's picture *The Nightmare,* painted in 1781, shows evidence of the new, darker sensibility that prevailed in the arts.

The technology of musical instruments developed, allowing new sounds that can still be heard today; the oboe reached something like its present form, and the new clarinet proved particularly attractive to Mozart, who incorporated it in the score of some of his symphonies and concertos, as well as writing a clarinet concerto. Both symphony and concerto form expanded, so that each movement became self-contained, a small self-sufficient unit. Opera maintained the lofty ideals of Enlightenment Classicism, although Mozart caused something of a stir with both the Singspiel *Die Entführung aus dem Serail* (The abduction from the harem) and the Italian *Le nozze di Figaro* by depicting lowly characters alongside the nobility and mixing noble sentiments and farce. This was something that did not immediately catch on – especially in Vienna, where the 'true' Italian serious opera, as composed by musicians such as Salieri, remained preferable to the public. ♪

STURM UND DRANG

Sturm und Drang – 'Storm and Stress' – was a German artistic movement, primarily literary, which set out to present emotional extremity from a subjective point of view. Its name came from a 1777 play by the German writer Klinger. One of the principal figures in the movement was Goethe, who went on to become one of the greatest of all Romantic writers. Literary *Sturm und Drang* aimed to overcome the reader with emotion. Its musical counterpart, which preceded the literary by almost a decade, rather held back from that extreme. Key moments of musical *Sturm und Drang* include the presentation of the Furies in Gluck's opera *Orfeo ed Euridice* (1762) – which may be macabre, but is not especially realistic – and also the more melodramatic episodes in Mozart's operas. There is also a whole series of Haydn symphonies which have been labelled *Sturm und Drang*; these are predominantly minor-key works, the most famous of which is probably the *Farewell,* and any emotional extremity is kept well under control.

Some of C P E Bach's symphonies also evoke the same kind of brooding, minor key mood, as indeed do works like Mozart's 40th Symphony and the 20th and 24th Piano Concertos, but there is no suggestion that these works are descriptive of any anguish of the inner soul. Still, *Sturm und Drang* was an early move away from the sweet reason of Enlightenment.

New Patronage for Old Values

MOZART BROKE FROM HIS PATRON, Cardinal Colloredo of Salzburg, in 1781, amid considerable acrimony. Although the split was largely for personal – even selfish – reasons and not especially intended to disrupt the traditional system of patronage, a sea-change was taking place during the Classical period. A rising middle class throughout Europe began to take more interest in music as a social activity, and there was money to be made away from princely courts and religious institutions. This was something in which England had been slightly ahead of the game, because the upheavals of the 17th century and the Civil

War had given the mercantile middle classes a good deal of financial clout; for example, for almost 40 years from the late 1670s there were regular concerts above a coal merchant's shop in Clerkenwell. Social and political changes in continental Europe over

the latter part of the 18th century began to take music into public halls and to change the nature of patronage; through events like 'subscription concerts', which were financed by the purchase of season tickets in advance, anyone could become a patron. Mozart

• MUSICAL DEVELOPMENTS •

➤ Elegance and formality remain the order of the day; music can be heard in more venues as the public concert – as opposed to the private court or salon performance – begins to take off all around Europe as a means of composing music.

➤ Wind instruments become a regular fixture in orchestras; a craze for 'Turkish' music means that jingling percussion is frequently included; this interest in pseudo-martial music was probably prolonged by the French Revolution and the subsequent Napoleonic campaigns.

➤ In the opera house, Italian styles rule supreme; melody, nothing too demanding, is dominant.

➤ In the 1810s and 1820s, Rossinimania sweeps Europe in the form of opera, his works combining Classical elegance with an amount of vocal showing off.

➤ The early works of Beethoven appear; the orchestral and chamber works are rather rough-hewn and perhaps not as effortlessly melodic as popular taste, especially in Vienna, would like them to be.

➤ The piano continues to develop, becoming closer in sound to the modern instrument, but not nearly as full-toned.

➤ There is no sense as yet that music is about personal expression, except in the music of Beethoven, and composers still produce works to order, as they had in the Baroque 'concerto factories' of Telemann, Heinichen and Vivaldi.

made quite a nice living in Vienna by subscription concerts when he was not able to find a court appointment.

At the end of the Classical period Haydn remained the dominant musical figure; he was able to travel to England and present new works there, and well into the 19th century he remained an ideal model for orchestral (and to some extent operatic) composers. He was no less a model for Beethoven, for all that Beethoven's ideas about composition were profoundly different almost from the very start of his career in the 1790s. The ideal of the late Classical period was still elegance, aural pleasure, music which was not self-advertising; however, there arose a craze for 'Turkish' sounds, which involved using lots of jingly percussion, which persisted from Mozart's music, through Rossini's in the 1810s and into Beethoven's 9th Symphony in the mid-1820s.

Even at this stage of musical history there was no concept of the great 'masterpiece' over which a composer sweated while giving expression to his innermost thoughts. This idea belonged exclusively to the Romantics, although it begins with the pivotal figure of Beethoven, whose music was from the outset rougher-

A poster advertising a public concert by Mozart in 1789.

hewn and less melodic than that of his contemporaries; his first chamber works alarmed Haydn, on whose music they had supposedly been modelled.

Effortless melody remained the prime objective in late Classical opera, too, and Italy and the Italians remained the model for all operatic composition. A whole host of now-forgotten figures kept the Italian flag flying, and in the 1810s Europe went mad for Rossini, who in his civilized comedies (like *The Barber of Seville*) and his serious pieces (*William Tell*) created a style entirely dependent on melody and importing just enough opportunity for vocal display to appease the less 'pure' tastes of some audiences. Rossini's music was so popular that he set back the cause of German opera by some 30 years, and made the Viennese forget about Beethoven; he even won over the French and eventually became one of the dominant figures in Parisian musical life, living well into the Romantic age. ♪

Picture of a Turkish hunting party. The jingly percussion of Turkish music enjoyed a great vogue in the last part of the Classical period.

CONCERT-GOING IN THE CLASSICAL PERIOD

The Classical period saw the rise of the public concert. In Catholic cities like Vienna, public concerts were held in Lent, when the theatres were closed. Then the imperial court would allow musicians to use the theatres for instrumental concerts, often financed by public subscription; people would be asked to pay for a block booking in advance, to allow the orchestra, hire of instruments, heating and lighting to be paid for. It was at such concerts in the 1780s that most of Mozart's mature piano concertos were first performed.

The most developed concert life, though, was in London. By 1780 there were several large-scale venues like the York Rooms in the Strand and the Hanover Square Rooms, where Haydn presented new works in the 1790s. There were also Promenade concerts in Ranelagh Gardens and Vauxhall Pleasure Gardens (illustrated right). Tickets could cost as much as half a guinea (equivalent to £100/$140–£150/$200 today), but you got a lot of music for your money. Today three or four works are the norm; a typical Hanover Square concert would feature two overtures, two concertos, usually some arias, and a series of instrumental duets. It was also commonplace to applaud in the middle of movements, to encore movements before a piece was ended (unthinkable today), and, if the composer was present, to rush forward and mob the stage.

Romanticism

TO A VERY LARGE EXTENT OUR IDEAS about music and musicians are still very much conditioned by the ideals of Romanticism. It is perhaps easier to relate to the Romantic ideal than the Classical one, because in Romanticism the personality of the artist moves centre stage and so pieces of music (and novels, poems and paintings) come to be about the artist's struggles and feelings rather than about something abstract. One of the fundamental novelties about pure Romanticism was that it was music designed to be 'about' something rather than being purely abstract, like Bach's, Haydn's or Mozart's. Of course, there had been descriptive music before, during the Baroque period – Vivaldi's Four Seasons is one example – but Romantic music was not meant to be merely descriptive; it was about subjective response to the external world. So the pastoral scenes in Beethoven's Sixth Symphony (the Pastoral), Berlioz's Symphonie fantastique or Liszt's piano works The Years of Pilgrimage are more about Beethoven or Berlioz or Liszt than about rural picture-painting.

ALTHOUGH ARGUMENTS RAGE ABOUT whether Beethoven's music is Classical or Romantic, there is no doubt that his Third Symphony – the Eroica – was a major break with the Classical symphony. It was much longer than any previous symphony, to start with, and demanded a larger orchestra to play it; and it also depicted some kind of personal struggle, possibly to do with Beethoven's attitude to Napoleon (whom he hero-worshipped until Napoleon declared himself Emperor). Later symphonies like the Fifth, the Seventh and the Ninth (the Choral) all told of inner turmoil, and the Ninth, with its concluding huge movement including the 'Ode to Joy', set new standards for symphonic length, complexity and orchestral resources.

There is no doubt, though, that Berlioz's 1830 Symphonie fantastique gave a fully Romantic twist to music; it told a highly personal story, with lots of macabre, extreme emotional fantasizing induced by opium, and the music existed first and foremost to tell the story. The music too abandoned any notion of restraint or proportion, going in for strange effects and unusual combinations of instruments. This tendency continued in the orchestral works of Liszt, a flamboyant personality who loved to reflect himself in his music, whether it was piano music (written for his own formidable performing talents) or orchestral pieces, usually based on literary works or Greek legends. Liszt and Berlioz allowed what they wanted to say to determine the form of the music – when Liszt wrote a concerto, a symphony or a sonata, he modified the forms to suit himself, and Berlioz's music too always went for the grand gesture. Not all major Romantics in the first stage of the movement were quite

• MUSICAL DEVELOPMENTS •

➤ Orchestral works get longer, starting with Beethoven's Third Symphony (Eroica), his Ninth (Choral) and Schubert's Ninth (The Great C Major).

➤ Music becomes more overtly emotional (critics thought that Beethoven's Fifth was the work of a lunatic).

➤ With the arrival of Berlioz's Symphonie fantastique a whole new idea of orchestral colouring appears.

➤ Wind instruments (some bizarre and now obsolete, such as the serpent) dominate and are used in much more daring combinations.

➤ The emotional extremes of the music become much more turbulent.

➤ There is also a story of some kind to follow (Berlioz had a short story about his unhappy love affair printed to go with the Symphonie), and it helps to be well read when you listen to Liszt's orchestral music.

➤ Flamboyant music requires a flamboyant personality, leading to the personality cult of Liszt, while the more intimate style of Chopin is highly suitable for smaller salon performances.

➤ Piano music becomes a major vehicle of personal expression, exemplified by Liszt, Chopin, Schumann (and later Brahms).

➤ The concerto returns to being a vehicle for extravagant virtuoso showing-off, with a few exceptions (notably Schumann, whose piano concerto got a very cool reception).

ROMANTICISM VERSUS THE ENLIGHTENMENT

Romanticism was a reaction against the Enlightenment philosophy which dominated much of the late 18th century. Enlightenment dictated that the mind of man could ultimately master everything; Romanticism delighted in the unpredictable power of Nature. Enlightenment gloried in civilization; Romanticism revived folk traditions, ballads, medieval sagas and so on (even going to the lengths of inventing them) and made heroes of backward rural figures. Enlightenment condemned excess; Romanticism praised emotional extremes and seems to have been dependent on opium and laudanum. Enlightenment believed in princely rule of a benevolent kind; Romanticism believed in democracy, and many Romantics saw first the French Revolution and then Napoleon (until he proclaimed himself Emperor) as a source of inspiration and liberation. Enlightenment believed in a generally positive approach to life and the abandonment of superstition; Romanticism developed an obsession with death as an 'other kingdom' and paid great attention to the supernatural (hence the whole 'Gothic' streak in literature, which found its way into music). Enlightenment believed that the discipline of formal structure was beneficial to artistic expression; Romanticism believed that the emotional demands of the particular work should dictate form.

Napoleon Buonaparte was at first seen as a republican liberator – the embodiment of Romantic political ideals – and when he declared himself Emperor it provoked mass disillusion. Most famously, Beethoven destroyed the original dedication of the *Eroica* Symphony.

so overtly flamboyant; Chopin delighted in working in restrained miniatures and had no taste for the flamboyant style of Liszt. As a consequence, his sonatas and concertos are much more formal. Composers such as Schubert and Schumann, both admirers of Beethoven, did not want to abandon traditional sonata structures. This set up one of the major dichotomies of Romanticism, which was to lead to the divide in German music that dominated the second half of the 19th century.

Romantic Music

THE MIDDLE 50 YEARS OF THE 19TH century saw two schools of musical Romanticism grow apart from each other, so that by the 1870s the Germanic musical establishment – which, as far as instrumental music and much operatic repertoire went, was *the* musical establishment – was split between the 'New German School', who all followed Liszt and his devotee and protégé Wagner, and a more traditional group, who lined up behind Brahms. And when it came to opera, the division was basically between Wagner and Verdi.

Liszt, of course, had developed a new personal, almost confessional, style of

• MUSICAL DEVELOPMENTS •

➤ Pieces get longer. Whether it is Wagner's operas or Bruckner's symphonies and concertos, forms lengthen as musical arguments get more complex.

➤ Orchestras become larger and musical instruments are capable of more precise intonation, allowing composers to produce music which has more chromatic sliding around.

➤ Instruments also produce a much fuller sound and pianos sound more like their modern counterparts, meaning that all music – even small-ensemble music such as quartets and trios – sounds chunkier and more powerful; wind instruments are refined close to modern standards.

➤ Opera divides into two: Verdi and his Italian followers produce works which cling to the traditional format of big tune arias, duets, choruses and so on, interspersed by periods of recitative (although with full orchestral accompaniment throughout); while Wagner's operas are a carefully woven texture based around the 'significant' leitmotifs without easily separable arias and so on. They also give much more prominence to the orchestral part, allowing it at times almost to swamp the singers, and Wagner demands larger resources than ever before – seven separate horn parts, lots of harps, new instruments.

➤ Large-scale orchestras are not solely required for Wagnerian music, though; Brahms, Dvořák, Tchaikovsky and other composers use forces on a scale unimaginable to Haydn or Mozart.

music. Wagner wanted to recast the whole nature of music; he concentrated on opera, as he believed that it came closest to a merging of all art forms, which was one ideal of a certain type of Romanticism (the earliest manifestation of this was some

THE LITERARY CONNECTION

*M*any Romantic composers were heavily influenced and inspired by writers. Here are some of the main writers and their key works:

GOETHE — *His Sorrows of Young Werther* was the basic Romantic text; artist-centred, deeply emotional, a model for Berlioz's *Symphonie fantastique*; *Faust* inspired almost everyone, especially Liszt – *Faust-Symphony* – and Mahler, who set vast chunks of Goethe's text in his Symphony No. 8. Countless lyrics written by Goethe were set by Schubert, Liszt, Brahms and Wolf, among others.

SCHILLER — Beethoven used his 'Ode to Joy' in the Ninth Symphony; many of his plays were the basis for Verdi's operas

MÜLLER — Not a front-rank poet but he provided the texts for Schubert's *Die schöne Müllerin* and *Die Winterreise*.

HEINE — Despite a cynical edge, the emotional turmoil of his short lyrics made him an obsessive subject for Schumann

EICHENDORFF — Like Heine, Eichendorff was part of a 'New German School' of Romantics. He provided the texts for Schumann's *Liederkreis*, Op 39.

RUCKERT — Another member of the New German School. Mahler set five of his poems to music (the *Ruckert Lieder*)

BYRON — *Childe Harold's Pilgrimage* inspired Berlioz's *Harold In Italy* (and had some bearing on Liszt's *Years of Pilgrimage*); his poem 'Tasso' inspired one of Liszt's Tone Poems; *Manfred* was the basis for an Overture by Schumann.

SCHOPENHAUER — His ideas about reality, illusion and eternity were the basis of much of Wagner's later work (especially *Tristan und Isolde*).

SCOTT — His descriptions of Scotland in books such as *Ivanhoe* had a great impact on Mendelssohn's imagination.

Liszt at the piano, watched by Victor Hugo, George Sand, Paganini, Rossini and Marie d'Agoult. Note, too, the bust of Beethoven.

composers' reliance on literary sources). Wagner wanted everything writ large; from a very early point in his career he was incapable of composing on a small scale and the central work of his life was the great four-opera *Ring* cycle, an epic tale of the creation and destruction of the world, packed with gods, giants, dwarves and magic, drawn from medieval legend but rewritten in Wagner's inimitable style. He based his work around leitmotifs – musical phrases which signified ideas, objects or emotions.

This was not a new idea, as Beethoven had used motivic phrases in his symphonies, Berlioz had depicted his 'beloved' by a phrase (an 'idée fixe') in his *Symphonie fantastique*, and Liszt used motivic phrases in many of his 'narrative' orchestral works. Wagner took the whole idea further than ever before, building huge structures around it. His music also demanded a larger orchestra than ever before, with vast amounts of brass (in one case, the 'Wagner Tuba', specially designed for the event) and designed a new style of opera house, eventually built at Bayreuth. As if this was not enough, he explored a new kind of harmony, creating for those who followed him in the next generation a crisis in the traditional key structure.

The Classical Romantics were entirely happy with traditional key signatures, even if they did exploit the development in instrumental technology to achieve a more luscious orchestral sound. The school of composers such as Schubert, Mendelssohn, Schumann and Brahms clung to the Classical forms, exploring new sound textures within them. Occasionally there would be a twist – a fourth movement in a concerto, for instance – and some were more interested in the idea of using musical motifs as unifying devices than others (Brahms was, Mendelssohn was in some works, but not in others). This tradition saw form as a useful discipline for expression, and above all believed that music could not 'mean' anything in the way that Liszt and Wagner wanted it to. Followers of Verdi believed that Wagner's abandoning of the separation between solo arias or duets and recitative, and his long declamatory passages, were alien to the whole idea of opera. ♪

An illustration from Goethe's Faust, one of the most influential works of Romantic literature.

The Last Romantics

THE FINAL PHASE OF PURE ROMANTICISM saw the continuation of that streak of 'gigantism' so marked in Wagner's music and the rise of one of the most colourful figures of late 19th/early 20th century music – Richard Strauss. But all the time there was a sense of old certainties being lost as composers searched for new ways forward, for new elements to import into their music; some (such as Grieg, Tchaikovsky and Dvořák) opted to combine the predominantly Germanic tradition with their own individual national culture, while others looked to other artistic media for new techniques.

The gigantic symphony continued to be an important form for some – principally

Bruckner and Mahler, who used their music to express very different messages, yet both of whom were heavily in thrall to Wagnerian ideas about texture and harmony. Bruckner clung more closely to traditional form, even though he probably idolized Wagner the more; he imported

Wagner Tubas into the symphonic orchestra and sought to reproduce Wagnerian orchestral textures in the concert hall. Mahler's symphonies were generally massive, and in his earlier works he showed a great deal of interest in incorporating folk tunes; his works were usually based on some

ROMANTIC
TRAVELS

Romantic composers travelled extensively and were often inspired by their tourism.

AUSTRIA Brahms – who feared sea travel – was fond of a Carpathian resort called Pörtschach, where he composed his Second Symphony and Violin Concerto (he later complained that the place was too full of tourists).

ITALY Nearly all composers visited Italy and brought home some music. Mendelssohn's *Italian* Symphony (No. 4) was inspired by Naples, while Liszt's visit provided a great deal of his *Years of Pilgrimage* (including his portrait of the fountains in the gardens of the Villa d'Este at Tivoli) as well as a Gondolier's Song. Brahms spent a winter in Italy. Tchaikovsky was inspired to write his string sextet *Souvenirs de Florence*. Wagner was very fond of Venice and wrote much of *Parsifal* there. Richard Strauss's trip to Naples provoked *Aus Italien*.

MAJORCA George Sand took Chopin to Majorca, but the journey almost killed him and certainly shortened his life.

SCOTLAND The novels of Walter Scott made Scotland seem a glamorous destination. Mendelssohn was inspired by the mists of Edinburgh and the ruins of Holyrood to produce his Third Symphony – the *Scottish*.

SWITZERLAND Mountains and lakes provided inspiration. The first volume of Liszt's *Years of Pilgrimage* is about his travels in Switzerland; the sights depicted include the Chapel of William Tell and the Lake at Wallenstadt. Tchaikovsky wrote his Violin Concerto on the shores of Lake Geneva.

story, as was Berlioz's *Symphonie fantastique*, and most frequently connected with a hero figure (himself) and fear of mortality. However, Mahler suppressed these stories and those that have survived have done so in purely private correspondence. In this he is unlike Richard Strauss, who composed bombastic, colourful tone poems, taking on Liszt's personal form to tell stories about Richard Strauss himself, his great genius, his fights against his enemies, and even, in one (the *Symphonia Domestica*), what life was like in the Strauss household, with a graphic description of bathing the baby. Both Strauss and Mahler added a sardonic edge to Romantic musical gestures; Mahler particularly went in for brass passages which seemed inspired by inept military bands. The idea that artistic expression must always be lofty and noble – something to which all Romantics had subscribed – was beginning to fade. Mahler also expanded the orchestral percussion range enormously. Sometimes his music (and that of Strauss) seems to head away from melody, into the atonal pastures of the 20th century, though this threat is never quite realized.

Verdi and Wagner were both dominant in the operatic field, each producing late masterpieces in his own particular style; the scramble in Italy during the 1890s to be the 'new Verdi' shows that enthusiasm for his music had not diminished. The winner of this accolade was eventually deemed to be Puccini, who added to a natural melodic lyricism a taste for describing 'ordinary life' (known as *verismo*, which became a major operatic trend of the time) and a certain sadistic inclination to dwell on pain; both Tosca and Turandot have torture scenes.

Of course, the most popular composer of the late 19th century was probably Johann Strauss II, the famous 'Waltz King', which shows that composers need not be part of the great ideological tendencies of their time to make a living and to compose enduringly popular music. ♪

The Villa d'Este at Tivoli, near Rome, 1839. The fountains and cypresses in the villa's famous gardens provided the inspiration for several piano pieces by Liszt.

Johann Strauss II and Brahms in 1894. Strauss was probably then the most popular composer alive, while Brahms was the acknowledged leader of 'traditional' German music.

Nationalism

ONE OF THE ELEMENTS OF ROMANTICISM
was a fascination with folk legends and nationalistic culture. Inevitably, one of the by-products of Romanticism was that some composers developed an interest in their own musical folk traditions, especially in countries whose identity was being suppressed, or where the national culture was completely dominated by a narrow Franco-Germanic tradition. In the 19th century countries like the Czech Republic, Poland, Finland, even to an extent Hungary (which won itself a limited autonomy in the middle of the century) had no separate identity; they had all been swallowed up by gigantic imperial neighbours. Music was a useful tool in rediscovering a sense of national identity and often served as a propaganda weapon.

TWO TRAIL-BLAZING ROMANTICS WERE, to some extent, nationalist composers: Liszt used the folk rhythms and 'gypsy' style of his native Hungary in his music (the *Hungarian Rhapsodies*, for example) and Chopin, half-Polish, used his music to assert his country's rights, turning the folk-dances the polonaise and mazurka into small piano art-forms. The first major nationalist schools of composers were Eastern European, too. In Russia, Mikhail Glinka tried to break the domination of French and

German styles in his operas *Kamarinskya* (the first Nationalist piece of all) and *Ruslan and Ludmilla.* His ideas were taken up by a group who called themselves 'The Five,' the most significant of whom were Rimsky-Korsakov (who eventually taught Stravinsky) and Mussorgsky,

Top: The title page to Glinka's opera *Ruslan and Ludmilla.*

Left: Glinka, the father of Russian Nationalism. His opera *Kamarinskya* was the first to establish a definitive Russian style independent of French and German tradition.

MUSICAL DEVELOPMENTS

➤ The determination to be distinctive leads to more colourful harmonies; Russian harmonies tend to be starker, bolder, more open (the music of Mussorgsky, for instance), while Czech music has more minor keys.

➤ 'Hungarian' music, particularly characterized by gipsy violin sound, gains popularity. It is especially pioneered in Brahms's music (finale of the Violin Concerto and the *Hungarian Dances*).

➤ There is a greater use of dance rhythms – for example, in Chopin's polonaises and mazurkas, the Finale of Grieg's Piano Concerto, Tchaikovsky's symphonies, Dvořák's scherzos.

➤ Music often has a strong sense of pastoral and orchestral textures will involve more woodwind in an attempt to sound more rural and folk-like; folk tunes are frequently incorporated, for example by Liszt, Chopin, Tchaikovsky, Dvořák.

➤ Melody is of supreme importance, at a time when melody is becoming more elusive and hidden beneath chromatics in mainstream Western music.

➤ There is simplicity of harmony (within constraints of national tradition) in direct conrtrast to the music of Wagner.

➤ Passion is given free rein, as in Grieg's Piano Concerto, Tchaikovsky's last three symphonies, Mussorgsky's Mad Scene in *Boris Godunov*.

➤ Nationalism becomes popular subject matter for opera, for example Glinka's *Kamarinskya*, Mussorgsky's *Boris Godunov* and Dvořák's *Rusalka*.

➤ The most successful and lasting nationalist music adopts Classical forms such as the symphony and concerto.

NATIONALIST SCHOOLS OF COMPOSERS

~

*R*USSIA Alexander Borodin, Cesar Cui, Mily Balakirev, Modest Mussorgsky and Nikolai Rimsky-Korsakov are collectively known as 'The Five'. They were influenced by the slightly earlier music of Glinka; in turn they influenced Tchaikovsky, and Rimsky-Korsakov taught Stravinsky.
FRANCE Les Six – Arthur Honegger (who was born in Switzerland), Darius Milhaud, Francis Poulenc, Germaine Tailleferre, Georges Auric and Louis Durey – developed their style after the establishment of a distinctive French idiom by Debussy and Ravel, and followed the whimsical dictates of Satie.
BOHEMIA (Czech Republic and Slovakia) Although there was no organized Bohemian nationalist school, composers promulgating the Bohemian musical tradition include Smetana, Dvořák and his pupil (and son-in-law) Josef Suk.
HUNGARY Again no organized school; after Hungarian themes evoked by Liszt and Brahms, major composers are Béla Bartók and Zoltán Kodály.
ENGLAND The derisive name of 'the cowpat school' was applied to such composers of typically pastoral English music as Ralph Vaughan Williams, Frederick Delius, Gustav Holst, Herbert Howells and Gerald Finzi.
SPAIN Although a lot of the most famous Spanish music was actually written by French and Russian composers, there was a Spanish nationalist tradition, begun by Felipe Pedrell and continued by Manuel de Falla, Isaac Albéniz, Enrique Granados and Joaquín Turina.

who in such Russian works on Russian subjects as *Boris Godunov* gave expression to a particular national voice. The Five had a major influence on the most famous Russian composer of all, Tchaikovsky, and he tried throughout his whole career to blend the traditional Western forms with Russian folk influence and Russian harmonies, succeeding in this aim best, perhaps, in his ballets. Ballet became of central importance to Russian music at this time.

Smaller countries had their champions also; Antonin Dvořák was to Bohemia what Tchaikovsky was to Russia, blending Western forms like the symphony, concerto and string quartet with Czech melodies and textures. Dvořák followed in the footsteps of Bedřich Smetana, whose *Má vlast (My Country)* was a great nationalist celebration. It was because of his reputation as a composer with an interest in national folk traditions that Dvořák was invited to America to take charge of the newly-founded New York Conservatory, in the hope that he would help American composers to find their own 'tradition'; this, of course, led to the composition of the famous *New World* Symphony.

The first great Scandinavian nationalist to make a splash outside his own country was the Norwegian Edvard Grieg, whose Piano Concerto, using Norwegian dance rhythms in its Finale, won praise from Liszt; Grieg hoped to encourage an individual style of Norwegian music, but none of his protégés ever quite achieved the same level of fame. Other Scandinavian nationalists included the Finn Sibelius and the Dane Carl Nielsen, two of the 20th century's greatest symphonists and part of the second wave of nationalist Romantics. ♪

An illustration of a 19th-century Russian village fête. It was from this kind of folk tradition that Glinka, Borodin, Mussorgsky, Rimsky-Korsakov and to an extent Tchaikovsky tried to refine a distinctive 'Russian' musical voice.

Distinctive Echoes in the West

MUSICAL NATIONALISM WAS NOT CONFINED to Eastern Europe and Scandinavia. One of the most political examples of nationalist music was the early work of Giuseppe Verdi, who had the luck to have a name which served as a useful acronym for the Italian Unification movement and its candidate for the overall monarchy of the state it wished to create ('Vittorio Emanuele, Re D'Italia' – 'Victor Emmanuel, King of Italy'). Verdi's music did not make any particular use of folk song or folk rhythms, but by taking plots about enslaved people fighting to overcome tyrants, as in *Nabucco*, with its famous 'Chorus of the Hebrew Slaves', he provided rallying points for the Unifiers which often provoked riots.

French composers at the end of the 19th century and well into the 20th tried to establish a stronger concept of French music; some did so through new techniques, but others, for example Canteloube, turned to regional folk traditions. In his *Songs of the Auvergne*, Canteloube mixed a little orchestral

The title page to Bartók's 32 Piano Pieces. Bartók developed a unique style from his researches.

• MUSICAL DEVELOPMENTS •

➤ Italian nationalism, embodied by Verdi's early operas, is not so interested in folk tradition as in using plots and stories to depict the plight of the people and provide rousing choric anthems (for example the 'Chorus of the Hebrew Slaves').

➤ Such French nationalism as there is goes in for deceptively simple arrangements of folk songs from different regions; more a regionalism than a nationalism.

➤ Many French composers are actually writing 'Spanish' music.

➤ Spanish nationalism draws on an energetic, rhythmic gipsy tradition, rather like flamenco, characterized by slightly 'Eastern' harmonies.

➤ The English national voice looks to a native folk tradition, but becomes distinctive first through grave, stately measure, fitting the pomp of Empire, then through a lush, densely woven harmonic style which becomes known as the 'cowpat' style.

➤ Composers after Debussy seeking to establish a national style also embrace jazz rhythms and employ pastiche of other styles, so that French music becomes characterized by a cosmopolitan good humour a long way from the rural simplicity of the folk song; this gives essentially two 'French' styles, that exemplified by, for example, Canteloube's *Songs of the Auvergne*, and that of smart Parisian society.

sophistication into the folk world of his particular part of France to great effect; he also arranged folk songs from other parts of France (the Pays Basque and Languedoc, to name two). Another influential French group was 'Les six', formed in the 1920s, who attempted to blend the simplicity of Satie with new jazz influences to create a distinctive French music.

It was in the early 20th century, too, that English music began to find a distinctive voice; Elgar wrote several pieces which were to become representatively 'English', above all his *Enigma* Variations and the 'Pomp and Circumstance March' which has come down to posterity as 'Land of Hope and Glory'. The English composers who followed him also looked to a native folk tradition and to the past; Vaughan Williams wrote lush fantasias around 16th-century works like 'Greensleeves' and in so doing created a 'rural' strain of English music which has unkindly been labelled 'cowpat music' by its detractors. But this interest in older British traditions was not confined to the late-flowering English Romantics; Benjamin Britten made arrangements of British folk songs.

Far left: Bartók collecting Slovak folk songs in 1907. This village is now in the Czech Republic.

Left: Giuseppe Garibaldi, the leader of the Italian Nationalist Movement, in 1850.

A Spanish musical voice began to emerge in the early 20th century, too, which looked very much to the folk rhythms, strongly dance based, of that country. Manuel de Falla and Enrique Granados wrote music that captured the passion and mystery of Spain, deriving partly from the African influence in Spanish folk music and partly from the gipsy flamenco tradition, which was more authentic than its somewhat invented Hungarian counterpart. It is ironic, though, that an appetite for Spanish music had been whetted by Frenchmen – Bizet's opera *Carmen* and several works by Debussy, Ravel and Chabrier – and one of the great Russian nationalists, Rimsky-Korsakov, whose *Capriccio espagnol* remains one of his most popular works.

Musical nationalism remained a preoccupation well into the 20th century, with some of the most progressive of composers drawing inspiration from finding a 'native voice'. The Hungarian Béla Bartók, one of the greatest of all 20th-century composers, forged a uniquely personal style out of his research into Hungarian folk songs. ♪

◆ FAMOUS WORKS USING FOLK SONGS ◆

CANTELOUBE *Songs of the Auvergne* (more or less straight arrangements).

DEBUSSY *Gigues* (the first part of *Images*) uses the Northumbrian folk tune 'The Keel Row', which Debussy heard in Soho during a visit to London.

TCHAIKOVSKY Some folkish touches in the earlier, less popular symphonies; the Piano Concerto No. 1 uses Ukrainian folk tunes in its outer movements and a French tune in the slow movement.

DVORAK Although Dvořák liked to bring a folk-like texture and folk rhythms to his music, he did not use many authentic folk songs; exceptions are the Finale of the *Czech Suite* and several of the *Slavonic Dances*.

BIZET Much of the Spanish-style music in *Carmen* is also original, but one of Carmen's first-act arias is based on a genuine Spanish folk song, and the famous 'Habañera' uses a song by a Spanish-American composer called Iradier, which Bizet thought was a real folk song.

LISZT His 15 *Hungarian Rhapsodies* are all folk song-based, although Bartók's research discovered that much Hungarian folk music was not genuine (he harmonized some of the 'real thing' himself).

STRAVINSKY *Petrushka* uses a lot of Russian folk tunes (and some old Orthodox religious music) in its fair scenes

BORODIN The 'Polovtsian Dances' in *Prince Igor* are also folk-based.

Into the 20th Century

Erik Satie – a self-caricature. Satie's music, which was both playful and simple, had a great influence upon 20th-century French composers. It could be called the fore-runner of modern minimalism.

Igor Stravinsky, whose music for the ballet *The Rite of Spring* sounded one of the most exciting notes of modernism – colourful music resounding with powerful primitive rhythms.

B Y THE END OF THE CENTURY, SOME people felt that Romanticism had gone too far. Music had become longer, more complex, more harmonically dense; and a whole generation of composers were producing works with intense hothouse chromatic harmonies that slithered all over the place. Part of the problem stemmed from the crisis surrounding the whole system of tonality – major and minor keys with familiar do-re-mi scales – which Wagner had provoked in the advanced harmonic system of Tristan; part was caused by the sense of a new age, with all its technological advancements leading to a new spirit of modernism which infused all the arts, resulting in Cubism in painting and the experimental writing of Joyce in literature.

SOME COMPOSERS had already departed from the mainstream of Romanticism. Nationalist composers sought a solution in the folk traditions of their own countries (often making a political point into the bargain) and many came up with a folk-tinged form of Romanticism. A new generation of French composers, too, had looked for a new style, and had found it in poetry – the Symbolist writings of Baudelaire and Mallarmé – and painting, in the Impressionism of Monet. Debussy and Ravel and their followers tried to create a music which made its impact through colouring and orchestral texture, creating moods and impressions, and clarity of line was not the most immediate principle of the music (although it was very precisely orchestrated). In works like *La Mer* and *L'Après-midi d'un faune* Debussy came close

• MUSICAL DEVELOPMENTS •

➤ There is a desire to shock, exemplified in Richard Strauss's operas and Stravinsky's ballets.

➤ Music becomes very vivid, scoring very dense, with plenty of noise within noise.

➤ Melody becomes more and more abstruse and in some cases – Debussy, Stravinsky in *Rite of Spring* – not really the point.

➤ Composers look to exploit every element of the orchestra. Quite a lot of music is sumptuous – for example that of Mahler, Richard Strauss, early Schoenberg, some Debussy – with numerous chromatic harmonies.

➤ Some composers trying to change style place great emphasis on the use of percussion.

➤ One final dying gasp of Romanticism is Expressionism, where extremity of emotion should be described in the most effective way possible, regardless of aesthetic beauty, pleasantness of sound and so on.

➤ Symphony and concerto, as solid old-fashioned forms, do not have quite the central supremacy they once did.

➤ An ironic use of forms, especially dance forms and folk forms, is common (especially in Mahler).

➤ It is in this period that Schoenberg and his pupils finally break with tonality.

❖ DIFFERENT DIRECTIONS ❖

ELGAR, Delius and Vaughan Williams produced English Romanticism a century late.

MAHLER apparently stayed with Wagnerian Romanticism, but there are potentially atonal passages in his later symphonies (especially the completed movement of the unfinished Tenth).

RACHMANINOV remained a full-blooded Romantic.

RICHARD STRAUSS wrote deeply retro-Romantic works like *Rosenkavalier* and *Intermezzo* (the 18th century reinterpreted by the 19th) and wrote the funeral march of German Romanticism (*Metamorphosen,* 1945).

SATIE wrote whimsical simplistic music which inspired a generation of French composers and also modern American minimalists.

SIBELIUS AND NIELSEN crossed Romanticism with nationalist traditions of Finland and Denmark respectively to become great national composers.

STRAVINSKY returned to primitive rhythms with *Rite of Spring* and subsequently explored Neo-Classical 'Back to Bach' principles.

---

to realizing his ideal. But another Frenchman whom Debussy championed had very different ideas; Erik Satie believed in reducing music almost to a bare, childishly simple minimum, which had the status of wallpaper (essentially he invented the idea of Muzak).

Many German composers tried to plod along the old paths; Richard Strauss made a name for himself as a modern composer with his operas *Salome* and *Elektra*, and in the latter's extreme tortuous harmonies he anticipated the techniques of a movement called Expressionism (in which beauty of sound or image was secondary to the depiction of deranged emotions). But he never abandoned tonality; instead, with the delicious, glutinous harmonies of *Der Rosenkavalier*, he opted defiantly for the Romantic fold. Mahler hovered between Romantic and modern; there are hints in his unfinished Tenth Symphony that he was reaching beyond the old harmonies, and he was impressed enough with the new experiments of his pupil Schoenberg to lend him substantial sums of money.

The first modern style both to succeed commercially and to outrage the old guard was born partly of nationalism; Igor Stravinsky had been taught by one of Russia's leading nationalist composers, Rimsky-Korsakov, and he collaborated with the impresario Diaghilev to produce a series of ballets with colourful scores, daring harmonies and – in the case of *The Rite of Spring* – such powerful primitive rhythms that audiences were delighted and shocked. The old order was suitably shaken. But where would it all lead?

Meanwhile, as Europe pondered all these paths, Britain produced its first great Romantic composer – Edward Elgar. As German Romanticism floundered into the new century, English Romanticism finally found a distinctive voice. ♪

Monet's painting *Les Nympheas*. Debussy attempted to re-create Impressionism in sound.

Atonality

ARNOLD SCHOENBERG'S EARLIER WORKS were all masterpieces of sumptuous late Romanticism, very much in the style of Wagner at his most chromatic. However, he became convinced that the old idea of tonality was finished and so he set out to change the face of music. First he abandoned tonality and opted for atonal music in which there were no dominant key structures, no do-re-mi scale to dictate how harmonies or indeed melodies should progress. Atonality was not in itself a new idea; Liszt had written a specifically atonal piano work, and other theorists like the Italian Ferruccio Busoni also felt music needed a radical overhaul (Busoni even wanted to introduce quarter-tones, as used in Eastern music). Schoenberg took the idea further and also rebelled against the scale of late Romantic music, working on a severely miniature scale, writing pieces of extremely brief duration for chamber ensembles.

SCHOENBERG WON TWO FERVENT disciples, Alban Berg and Anton Webern, and the three formed the Second Viennese School. Both Berg and Webern followed

Schoenberg was a noted teacher as well as composer. After leaving Nazi Germany he settled in Los Angeles where he taught at the University of California from 1936 until 1944.

• THE CONCEPT OF ATONALITY •

➢ There are no key structures, so there is no logical starting harmony, no logical ending harmony.

➢ Harmony is unconventionally dissonant and does not have to sound sweet.

➢ There is no logical harmonic path for the music to follow, so traditional ideas of melody are abandoned.

➢ With the introduction of the 'twelve-note' system, melodies become even more angular. Lines have to go through every note of the chromatic scale, in any order which appeals to the composer, and usually employ huge leaps and intervals.

➢ This form of construction is akin to old-fashioned polyphony, as the different instru-mental or vocal lines run variations, such as retrogrades or inversions, on the original line.

➢ Pieces become significantly shorter, some composers taking this to extremes.

➢ Rhythms become extremely complex; the old structure of straightforward beats in a bar is almost impossible to maintain (except where the composer is being ironic, as Berg occasionally is in his longer works like operas and the Violin Concerto).

➢ Not all composers committed to the new faith embrace all its tenets; Berg did not systematically use twelve-note sets.

See also: Tonality and Harmony, pp 257–59; and Twelve-note Music, pp 259–60

Schoenberg's rules most strictly. He used other, more recognizably Romantic techniques and harmonies. It eventually transpired that most of his greatest works were inspired by a secret love affair and crammed with coded messages.

Schoenberg's music was not allowed to flourish for long in Germany; the advent of the Nazis in 1933 led to its condemnation as 'cultural Bolshevism' (ironically, the Soviet authorities also found it offensive). In the new musical era after 1945 atonality and the twelve-tone system were embraced with enthusiasm; indeed, when Schoenberg died in 1951, one of the leading spirits of the new age, Pierre Boulez, declared that he had not gone far enough. Over the next twenty to thirty years this spirit dominated the musical establishment. ♪

Schoenberg in abandoning traditional tonality and melody, and in writing concentrated short pieces; Berg also wrote very short works using large orchestras of Wagnerian-Brucknerian dimensions.

In the 1920s Schoenberg articulated the rules of 'twelve-tone' music, which, he claimed, 'would keep German music on top for 100 years'. Twelve-note composition took atonality to its logical extreme: with no keys to make certain notes more important than others, each of the 12 notes of the chromatic scale was of equal importance; music was to be formed from phrases which used each note of the chromatic scale once in turn and then progressed by taking that phrase and inverting it, or running it backwards and so on.

Not everyone reacted favourably to atonality; Paul Hindemith came out strongly against the whole concept, and Richard Strauss was uncomplimentary. Even other modernist composers like Stravinsky were dubious; although no particular devotee of tonality, he preferred to combine the rhythms of folk music and jazz with the techniques of J S Bach.

Schoenberg had not intended that his new style should remain permanently concerned with miniatures, and wrote two twelve-tone concertos and two twelve-tone operas. But only Berg seemed at ease with these longer forms, even when following

Composers on Atonality

"Upon the major key and the minor key, the whole of music has been established; one limitation leads to another." – **Busoni, 1906**

"The only person who can help poor Schoenberg now is a psychiatrist... I think he'd do much better to shovel snow . . . " – **Richard Strauss, 1913**

"The method of composing with 12 tones grew out of necessity. In the last 100 years the concept of harmony has changed tremendously through the development of chromaticism . . . It became doubtful whether a basic tone root remained the centre to which every harmonic and harmonic succession must be referred." – **Schoenberg, 1950**

"Tonality is a natural force, like gravity ... Music ... will always take its departure from the major triad and return to it. The musician cannot escape it any more than the painter his primary colours or the architect his three dimensions." – **Hindemith, 1937**

"The expression [atonality] is very fashionable. But that doesn't mean to say that it is very clear. And I should like to know just what those persons who use the term mean by it." – **Stravinsky, 1939**

"There is only one important thing in music and that is ideas plus feeling. The various tonalities and sound mean nothing unless they grow out of ideas. Not many composers have ideas . . ." – **George Gershwin, 1933**

"Harmony! Harmony!" – **Schoenberg's dying words, 1951**

Minimalism

WITH THE BOULEZ TENDENCY IN *control in Europe, music became ever more cerebral, dominated by mathematical constructs. However much composers and people inside the music establishment praised each other, the general public stubbornly retained a taste for melody and emotion. Some composers continued to write unfashionably Romantic music in the old large forms; and even some hailed as leaders of the avant-garde, such as Britain's Michael Tippett, experimented in combining popular forms like the blues or even rap with direct quotations from Beethoven and Bach.*

THE REACTION CAME, EVENTUALLY, FROM America in the shape of minimalism. A group of composers spearheaded by Steve Reich, Terry Riley, Philip Glass and John Adams developed a style in which simple small units of melody would be repeated over a long period of time, usually allied to detailed rhythms put through subtle variations. Some minimalism created a spacy, ambient sound (this was very much Glass's territory); other composers went for a more tense, highly motored sound with dense harmonies (the approach of both Reich and Adams). Surprisingly,

minimalism proved to be a fruitful method for opera.

As the grip of the purist avant-garde waned in Europe, minimalism caught on – with certain refinements. The most adventurous exponent has, arguably, been Dutchman Louis Andriessen; like the British composer Michael Nyman, he has thrown older music and popular music styles into the minimalist blender to come up with something much punchier than most of his American counterparts and on occasions quite disturbing. Nyman's pastiche 'eclectic minimalism' has proved immensely popular, especially when used for movie soundtracks. But the most striking popular success of minimalism has come with the so-called 'holy minimalists', composers who have combined the techniques of minimalism with a passion and lyricism born of spiritual belief; the Scot James MacMillan, Estonian Arvo Pärt

OTHER MODERN TRENDS AND MEMORABLE FIGURES

The original modern radical was probably the American John Cage, who tried to change the way composers thought about music and to introduce attitudes based on Eastern philosophies. His most famous work is arguably the minimalist piece to end all minimalism; *4 Minutes, 33 Seconds* is a piano piece in which the soloist is required to sit at the piano for precisely 4 minutes and 33 seconds and play – nothing at all.

One of Cage's philosophical imports, eagerly seized on by Boulez and Stockhausen, was the notion that chance should play a greater part in music and that the order in which sections or even pages of a work are played should be determined by the throw of a dice, by the I Ching or by the performer's mood; this is 'aleatoric' music.

Electronic music really started in the 1920s with Edgard Varèse, who tried to change our ideas about what musical sound really is. Radical figures like Stockhausen, Xenakis, Ligeti, Berio and Benjamin have all used new technology.

Many composers try to combine the methods of the East with the traditions of the West; Takemitsu, Tan Dun and Priti Paintal all use techniques and instrumental sounds from non-European traditions, which often offer smaller, more intricate intervals than the Western scale – a kind of modern version of Nationalism, it could be said.

and British convert to the Orthodox religion John Tavener have all managed to write new works which have instant appeal. The leading light of this tendency must be Henryk Górecki, the Pole whose Third Symphony inspired partly by the sufferings of his countryman during the World War II became a major 'crossover' chart hit. Their music is characterized by its simplicity, a slow-moving viscerally aimed and usually dense orchestral sound which consciously avoids complex harmonies and very often features a strong – but extremely plain – melodic line.

Minimalism has been a particularly fashionable style in the reaction to the intellectual mathematical serialist and serialist-derived techniques of Boulez and his disciples; but the radical forces of music still keep going. Boulez, Stockhausen, and, in the younger generation, figures like George Benjamin have kept that flag flying. Computer technology and chaos theory have also influenced composition, as have the growing interest in world music and the

• MUSICAL DEVELOPMENTS •

➤ Simple phrases, usually easily graspable melodic units, are repeated over and over again to perhaps slightly shifting harmony; the harmony is always simple, fairly easy on the ear – often just a straightforward major or minor chord, and never much more complicated than that.

➤ Underlying rhythms may shift more subtly to introduce tension to the effect, although some minimalists (especially Philip Glass) often prefer a fairly spacy, unstressed sound.

➤ Minimalism often involves electronic instruments in addition to normal orchestral instruments, although the 'holy minimalism' of various European composers usually makes do with traditional orchestral forces.

➤ 'Holy minimalists' (for example Górecki,

Tavener) aim to produce visceral emotional impact, often with quite large forces, and employ soaring but simple melodies over relatively static, uncomplicated chords.

➤ 'Eclectic minimalists' (Nyman, Andriessen) often throw bits of other composers' music into the blend and come up with something where rhythm is more direct, driven and tension-provoking; it can also involve more jazzy instrumentation, with rather more complicated harmonies.

➤ Minimalism is instantly accessible to the listener and does not demand some higher degree in mathematics and musical theory for enjoyment – but it can seem like too much of a good thing, an endless loop stretching out to eternity.

continuing influence of jazz and popular forms. The emotion, passion and melody of Romanticism have their modern counterparts, and, of course, there are always a few good, old-fashioned mavericks doing things no one might have expected.

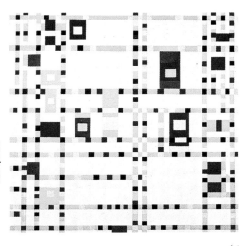

Steve Reich in the Music Center, Los Angeles, in 1983. Reich, one of the leading figures in minimalism, has had immense influence upon European musicians such as Louis Andriessen.

Piet Mondrian's painting *Broadway Boogie-Woogie* (1942/3). Mondrian's love of boogie-woogie is a driving force in Louis Andriessen's *De Stijl*.

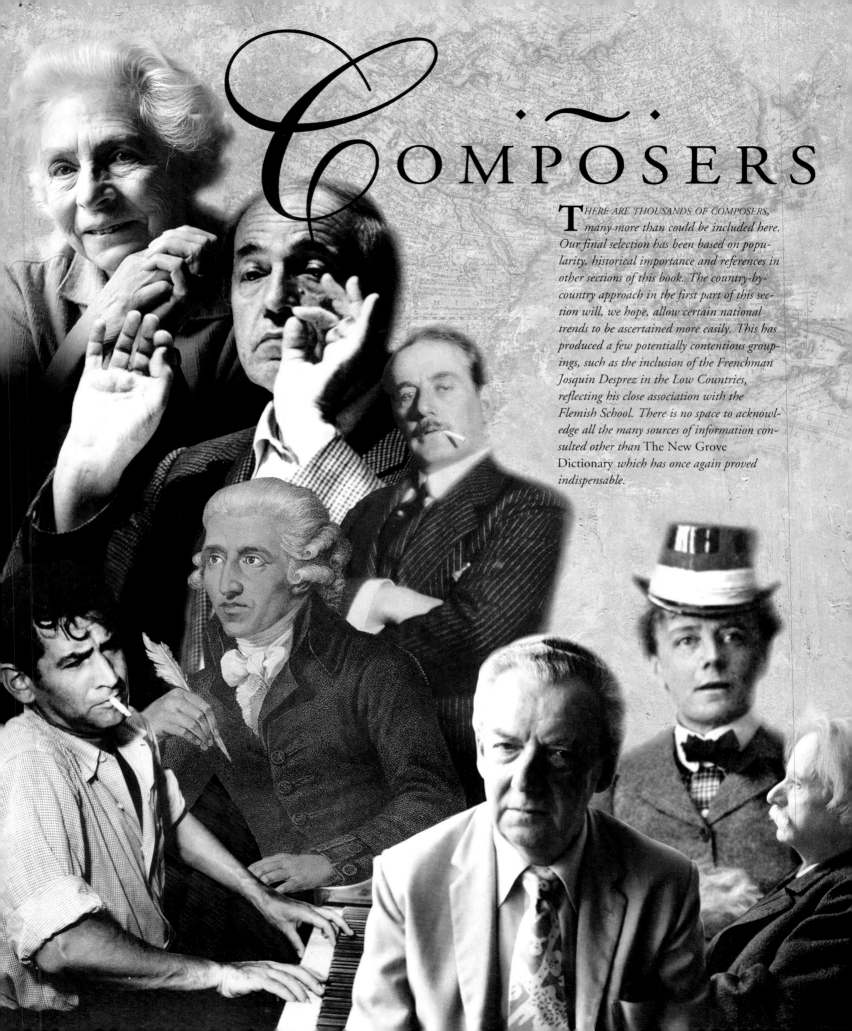

COMPOSERS

THERE ARE THOUSANDS OF COMPOSERS, many more than could be included here. Our final selection has been based on popularity, historical importance and references in other sections of this book. The country-by-country approach in the first part of this section will, we hope, allow certain national trends to be ascertained more easily. This has produced a few potentially contentious groupings, such as the inclusion of the Frenchman Josquin Desprez in the Low Countries, reflecting his close association with the Flemish School. There is no space to acknowledge all the many sources of information consulted other than The New Grove Dictionary which has once again proved indispensable.

France

GUILLAUME DE MACHAUT (c. 1300–77)
Born Rheims; died ? Rheims

∞ Machaut was by far the most prestigious composer of his day. A learned priest and accomplished poet, he followed troubadour tradition by writing his own texts for his songs. His accessible and very beautiful music is representative of the Ars Nova style, which he enriched in many ways, not least in his rhythmic innovations; he fully exploited the new potential for binary rhythms. Little is known of his life save that he was first employed by John of Luxembourg, King of Bohemia, until the King's death in 1346, after which he served France's most illustrious nobility. An ostensibly autobiographical poem *Voir dit* may well reflect real events; it describes Machaut's love for a 19-year-old girl who, while supposedly only interested in his verse and music, seems to have extended her favours to him as well.

FRANCOIS COUPERIN (1668–1733)
Born Paris; died Paris

∞ While several colourful anecdotes survive concerning his contemporaries, François Couperin is something of a mystery. Even his letters to J S Bach were lost, allegedly being used to wrap jam pots! From his pictures and other shreds of evidence, he seems to have been a fastidious, open-minded individual. He came of a musical family, so to distinguish him and acknowledge his greatness, he is known as *le grand*. His greatest achievement lies in his 27 *ordres* (suites), published in four books, which were among the finest keyboard works of the age, and greatly influenced J S Bach. At first, these were standard dance suites (gavotte, sarabande, and so on) but as he developed his style, so he chose exotic titles for these short compositions, making them into evocative character pieces. His writing is highly elaborate with numerous ornaments – appropriate for the rituals of Louis XIV's Versailles court – and in common with other French composers, his

music is more harmonic, less contrapuntal than that of the Germans. Emotions are usually kept at a courteously low level, but in the magnificent passacaille (a rondo rather than a conventional passacaglia which would use a repeated bass figure) of the eighth *ordre* (c. 1717), something akin to passion seems to erupt.

JEAN-PHILIPPE RAMEAU (1683–1764)
Born Dijon; died Paris

∞ An independent spirit, Rameau extricated himself from the last of a series of contracts as an organist at Clermont Cathedral by at first refusing to play on a feast day, then playing discords and using the ugliest stops on the instrument. In fact, the harpsichord figured more prominently than the organ in his output. At the age of 50 he teamed up with the Abbé Simon-Joseph Pellegrin to produce the first of his operas, *Hippolyte et Aricie* (1733), which were to be his most significant contributions to the French Baroque. His music is remarkable for its melodic diversity, and the operas contain a prodigious variety of orchestral effects. The dance movements have tended to attract most attention, yet his meticulous attention to the declamation of the text is also impressive. In spite of his obvious brilliance as a composer, Rameau preferred his career as a theorist. In 1722 he published his *Traité de l'harmonie*, which

Couperin: baroque master of highly ornate keyboard and vocal music.

laid out, often for the first time, the principles of harmony. This initiated a revolution – unwelcome to some – in the way music was perceived, which for years theorists had explained as a primarily contrapuntal activity. Rameau declared harmony to form the basis of music.

HECTOR BERLIOZ (1803–69)
Born near Grenoble; died Paris

∞ In spite of his genius, Berlioz remained for many years a misunderstood and underrated genius. Even now musicians still criticize him for his 'mistakes', failing to acknowledge the very great originality of his music. Unlike almost every other composer, he did not play the piano; his instrument was the guitar, which was held to account for his unorthodox harmony. He was a paradigm of nascent French Romanticism, portraying himself in his fanciful memoirs as a lovelorn youth wandering Europe for amorous fulfilment. His *Symphonie fantastique* (1830) goes so far as to represent, in its programme at least, the opium-induced delusions of the symphony's hero regarding his beloved. Yet his melodies show the influence of Gluck, and one of his greatest achievements is an opera, *Les troyens* (1858), on the great classical theme of the

Berlioz: unorthodox genius whose works epitomize Romantic ideals.

Trojans and the fall of Troy. He was frequently frustrated in his career as a composer at home, but he achieved some fame abroad, not least in Germany where his case was taken up by Liszt and Schumann. His voice is also heard in Wagner's music, Wagner having learnt a great deal about orchestration from him.

ALEXANDRE CESARE LEOPOLD (GEORGES) BIZET (1838–75)
Born Paris; died Bougival, near Paris

∞ Bizet joined the ranks of a handful of very distinguished composers and countless mediocrities when he won the august Grand Prix de Rome in 1857. Evidence of his early facility in composition is the infectiously tuneful Symphony in C, which was only rediscovered in 1935. On returning to Paris after his obligatory spell in Rome, he resumed his operatic activities, producing the uneven but often inspired *Les Pêcheurs de perles* (1863). While he wrote very successfully in various genres, his abiding achievement is the opera *Carmen* (1875), which now ranks among the five or so most popular operas of all, even inspiring a jazzed-up version, *Carmen Jones*. After Bizet's death *Carmen* had its dialogue replaced by recitative in a fairly humdrum manner by Debussy's teacher Ernest Guiraud, but now the original is back in favour. Bizet's music boasts a superabundance of whistlable tunes, brightly lit orchestration, and dashes of Spanish colour.

ACHILLE-CLAUDE DEBUSSY (1862–1918)
Born St Germaine-en-Laye; died Paris

∞ Debussy has been burdened with the title 'Impressionist composer', in spite of his distaste for the term and the Symbolist influence on works like *Prélude à l'après-midi d'un faune*. Accepting that a few works by him do indeed show similarities with Impressionist painting, we do best to accept him on his own terms as the founder of the modern school of composition that led directly to Stravinsky, Varèse, Messiaen and many others. He rejected his traditional musical training, following instead his own exquisite tastes in matters harmonic, tonal,

and formal. Sonata form he almost consigned to the dustbin, preferring instead a fluid unfolding of his material that has been likened to post-war electronic music. His range of works was considerable, though he had a marked fondness for music drama, evident in one completed opera, *Pelléas et Mélisande* (1902), and numerous attempts at others. As a man he was much given to the good life: he relished a good whisky, liked the then very trendy *mode anglaise*, and bought fine oriental *objets d'art* in preference to mundanities such as food.

MAURICE RAVEL (1875–1937)
Born Ciboure; died Paris

∞ Unlike Debussy's fluid forms, Ravel's have sharply etched outlines, many of which fall into sonata and other traditional forms. His music has been compared to a complex clockwork mechanism, a description that fits some of his music but not the dark fantasy *La valse* (1920) or the ecstatic lyricism of the great ballet *Daphnis et Chloë* (1912). Nevertheless, the strains of childhood are crucial in works such as *Ma mère l'oye* (1910). His soundworld is utterly distinctive in its slightly astringent dissonances, judicious use of bitonality, and ravishing orchestration. He did not found a school, yet in developing a piano style for the modern generation of French composers, he had a notable influence on Debussy and his successors. Ravel was an intensely private man whose emotional life is shrouded in mystery; certainly his music sheds little light on it.

EDGARD VARESE (1883–1965)
Born Paris; died New York

∞ Varèse managed to lose almost all his early works in a Berlin warehouse fire and destroyed one or two others himself. So when we finally catch his 'Opus 1', *Amériques* (1921), we already hear the composer in full flight, having thrown off tonality and the traditional reliance on

melody. Instead he became fascinated by sound itself and its movement through space. The idea of sound masses interacting and colliding that he speaks of in his lectures can be heard in the extraordinary series of works he produced in America in the 1920s and 1930s, including *Intégrales* (1925) (this music is performed by standard ensembles without specific spatial arrangements). He was fascinated by the possibilities of electronic music and was among the first major composers to incorporate it into a composition, *Ecuatorial* (1934), for voices, brass, and two theremins (an early predecessor of the ondes martenot). Finally, he was given a tape recorder after the war and began to collect sounds for the electro-acoustic masterpiece *Déserts* (1954), in which Edvard Munch's painting *The Scream* finds its musical analogue. He was in every sense a pioneer who physically and artistically discarded the old world of Europe and attempted to create a music appropriate to the skyscrapers of New York where he lived.

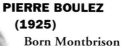

Boulez: a brilliant leader of the post-war avant garde.

PIERRE BOULEZ (1925)
Born Montbrison

∞ Stockhausen and Boulez seemed for many years to be the leaders of the avant-

Ravel: fastidious exponent of various genres.

garde, both of them producing works of great integrity and intellectual calibre. Unfortunately, Boulez has found it difficult to sustain his creative work and has for many years been more prominent as a conductor, a great deal of his music having been written very early in life and then revised or extended afterwards. Boulez's music embraced elements of total serialism early on and has always been tightly organized in the various domains of rhythm, pitch, and so on. Nevertheless, listening to works of the quality of *Pli selon pli* (1962), it is the larger gestures and their subsequent transformations that guide one through and arrest the attention. He has remained one of the most intriguing figures in the post-war generation of composers, influencing many younger men.

the *Low* countries

GUILLAUME DUFAY (c. 1400–74)
Born ?Hainaut; died Cambrai

∾ Although the map of medieval Europe may appear very fragmented, Dufay was, in fact, as well known around the countries of Europe in his century as Haydn and Wagner in theirs. His fame was so great that his music would have been copied and

studied in any centre of contrapuntal music. In common with many other composers of the time, his career grew up around the Church: he was a choirboy at Cambrai Cathedral and seems to have become a deacon at St Géry in Cambrai. He also worked for some of the wealthiest families of the time. The quantity of wine sent to him in later years – 36 lots on the feast day of St John the Evangelist – gives some indication of his fame. In his music we hear a consummately poised control of contrapuntal textures using a mixture of canon and imitation, often in four voices rather than the three of the preceding century, and his melodies are handsomely conceived with broad, arching phrases. He was not much given to innovation, but he did help to consolidate new features such as the cyclic integration of movements in the Mass. He was widely active as a teacher, his most famous pupil being Ockeghem.

JOHANNES OCKEGHEM (c. 1410–97)
Born ?; died Tours ?

∾ Ockeghem is one of the most significant composers of the Franco-Flemish School (his name might also have been included in the French section). He was highly regarded in his lifetime for his beautiful voice, his moral character, his kindness, and the outstanding quality of his music. His importance as a composer is primarily founded upon his refinement of the cyclic Mass. The idea that the movements of the Ordinary should be united by a common tune or chant had been established by the previous generation, but Ockeghem took things further, increasingly imbuing the other voices with the melodic and rhythmic character of the *cantus firmus,* and using secular tunes as well as liturgical chants. (A *cantus firmus* is the plainsong or other melody on which a Mass is based.) He

Josquin: one of the most accomplished of Renaissance polyphonists.

wrote the earliest extant Requiem. There are three through-composed Masses, one of which contains a veritable *tour de force* in its counterpoint: the *Missa prolationum* uses four different rhythmic modes (prolations) simultaneously in a series of canons. In spite of the immense intellectual effort this involved, the work sounds surprisingly straightforward and accessible. Continuity is a hallmark of Ockeghem's music, with few breaks in the inexorable flow of counterpoint.

JOSQUIN DESPRES (c. 1440–1521)
Born ?; died Condé-sur-l'Escaut, near Valenciennes

∾ It is a mistake to assume that Renaissance composers such as Josquin (a Frenchman, though usually grouped with the Flemish composers) fell into obscurity after their deaths only to be rediscovered in the 20th century. In fact, Burney in the 18th century studied Josquin closely and in the following century other scholars were similarly enlightened. All of them recognized in him one of the greatest figures in the entire history of Western music, one equally at home in motet, Mass, and secular song. He had a superb compositional technique, especially in the application of abstruse contrapuntal devices to the music, which never cloud its immediate sensual appeal; rather, it is like discovering intimate details in the adornment of the rich sweep of a Renaissance portico. A breathtaking example – one of many – occurs in the final Agnus Dei of the *Missa 'l'homme armé' sexti*

toni, where the two lowest voices sing the tune in long notes backwards and forwards at the same time as the four upper voices are paired up into two canons with rapid flowing lines brilliantly decorating the *cantus firmus*; it brings the Mass to an elated conclusion.

JACOB OBRECHT (c. 1450–1505)
Born ? Bergen-op-Zoom; died Ferrara

∾ A whiff of scandal attaches to Obrecht's early career, when he was dismissed from his post as choirmaster at Cambrai for inadequate care of the choristers and financial malpractice. He was, however, far too much in demand as a composer for his evident unreliability to prevent him assuming prestigious posts, which he fulfilled with a great number of fine sacred compositions. In his vitally important Masses he used a great deal of borrowed material, as did all his contemporaries. Drawing primarily on chant he developed the borrowed material in a formidable variety of ways. The sort of thematic unity that distinguishes comparable works by Josquin is less in evidence, Obrecht preferring to coin new ideas and embark upon free flights of contrapuntal development based on them. He was also less inclined to use elaborate devices such as crab canon, in which the imitating voice goes backwards. For these and other reasons, he was less influential than Josquin.

ORLANDE DE LASSUS (ORLANDO DI LASSO, 1532–94)
Born Mons, Hainaut; died Munich

∾ Lassus is one of the great trio of composers (the others were Palestrina and Victoria) who brought the music of the Renaissance to its culmination. All three wrote in long flowing melismas, producing carefully wrought counterpoint in their Masses and motets, but there are clear differences between them. Lassus valued the sound of the triad more than Palestrina, for his bassline often jumps around in a far from contrapuntal manner to produce pleasing harmonic sonorities. He was in this sense progressive, as was his adoption of the chromatic, highly expressive style of the Italian and Flemish madrigalists in his own

madrigals. More than Palestrina, he was concerned with the texts he set, adopting a declamatory style. He was enormously prolific: his output includes around 2,000 works. In his own time he became the most famous musician in Europe, in demand in numerous courts and cities.

CESAR FRANCK (1822–90)
Born Liège; died Paris

∾ The British composer Peter Warlock gracelessly sent up Franck's only symphony (1888) in a witty piano duet entitled 'The Old Codger'. This reflected the image of the composer aloof in his organ loft at Sainte-Clotilde composing austere chorale preludes. Reality was rather different, for Franck was

heavily influenced by Liszt and Wagner whose harmony and formal procedures find their way into much of his music. Some of his later works, especially the Piano Quintet (1879), are overtly erotic and caused a sensation at their first performances. Long winding chromatic melodies, vigorous contrapuntal developments and rich harmony distinguish the work of a musician who was posthumously responsible for a whole movement in France (led by his pupil Vincent d'Indy, a founder of the Schola Cantorum in Paris).

Franck was considered a saintly man given over to a modest subsistence and periods of meditation, but his was a cheerful personality.

Quantum exit melica reliquos Orlandus in arte,
Ætheriis propior tantum abit ille choris.

*B*ritain

JOHN DUNSTABLE (c. 1390–1453)
Born ?; died ?

∞ One epitaph described Dunstable as 'prince of music', and another as 'an astrologer, a musician, and what not'. Along with Dufay, he was one of the key figures in developing the contrapuntal style of the Renaissance (the absurd notion that he invented counterpoint, circulated many centuries ago, has long been forgotten). His music sounds more euphonious than that of his contemporaries due to his predilection for major thirds, which yielded what is referred to as the 'pan-consonant' style in which consonant harmonies based on thirds are the norm. Another important new feature was the linking of parts of the Mass with the use of a single tenor (to produce the 'cyclic mass'), an enterprise undertaken jointly with Power, another famous English composer of the period. The processional anthem *Quam pulchra es* is among his most popular works and is remarkable for its close attention to the rhythms of the text. This was a time when English music was as highly regarded as that of any other country, and the great beauty of Dunstable's contribution still has much to offer music-lovers today.

THOMAS TALLIS (c. 1505–85)
Born ?; died Greenwich

∞ Tallis's career spans the dissolution of the monasteries and adoption of the Protestant prayer book after the abolition of the Sarum Rite in 1559. His career was prosperous, almost certainly leading to personal acquaintance with Archbishop Cranmer and service under Henry VIII, Edward VI, Mary Tudor and Elizabeth I. His output reflects the uneasy transition to Protestantism, for he contributed several English services as well as anthems and motet adaptations. The most famous part of his output, however, is the Latin church music, including the spectacular motet *Spem in alium* for 40 voices, which begins with successive entries for no fewer than 20

parts. As this suggests, he was a master of Renaissance counterpoint, filling his works with remarkable feats of ingenuity and rivalling the achievements of contemporaries abroad. One of Tallis's 'tunes' written for *The Whole Psalter*, published 1567, became famous through its use by Vaughan Williams in his sublime *Tallis Fantasia* (1910).

WILLIAM BYRD (1543–1623)
Born Lincoln?; died Stondon Massey

∞ Byrd's Catholicism in a country fairly recently converted to Protestantism hindered his activity as a composer of liturgical music: he wrote only three Masses to the hundreds of his contemporaries. Nevertheless, he continued to write for the Church and was so famous in England that he was not persecuted; this, along with a few legal suits over property, is all that is known about the man. His music ranks with that of his great continental contemporaries for its beauty and emotional depth. He is closer to Lassus in the freedom of his counterpoint and its rich colouring. Among other major publications, he printed a collection of motets entitled *Cantiones, quae ab argumento sacrae vocantur* with his tutor Tallis in 1575. Among his miscellaneous compositions, the *Psalmes, Sonets, and Songs of Sadness* (1588) for all-vocal ensemble are of great interest; they were originally songs with instrumental accompaniment.

ORLANDO GIBBONS (1583–1625)
Born Oxford; died Canterbury

∞ Spend any evening in the company of madrigalists and sooner of later they will start singing the sublime madrigal 'The Silver Swanne' (1612), one of Gibbons' most memorable compositions; so it is worth noting that he published few madrigals, preferring instead the burgeoning lute song that partly replaced the older genre in the 17th century.

Alongside Tomkins and Weelkes, Gibbons was responsible for the early flowering of Anglican church music, especially in the form of the anthem (the approximate equivalent of the motet in Catholic church music). The anthem was developed by Gibbons into the verse anthem, whose cultivation was brought to its zenith in the following century by Purcell. Gibbons' works are often highly expressive through the use of imitation and other Renaissance contrapuntal techniques. He contributed prolifically to the keyboard repertoire and was one of the pioneers of violin music. With Coprario and Thomas Lupo, he was one of the first composers to develop the trio sonata.

HENRY PURCELL (1659–95)
Born ?; died London

∞ Purcell was well grounded in the arts of the French and Italians, from whom he gained familiarity with operatic and instrumental traditions. With this knowledge he developed a style that is both distinctly English and cosmopolitan in an output that embraced the widest imaginable range of compositions and idioms. Purcell almost single-handedly managed to create an English opera, but sadly the impetus was not matched by librettos or public demand; his masterpiece *Dido and Aeneas* (1689) therefore remains a frustrating taste of what might have been. We also have many examples of Purcell's incidental music, which was often composed for plays of little substance; yet somehow he found inspiration in them. Purcell contributed a great deal to English Church music, and his chamber and instrumental works are among the finest of the Baroque. Listening to his vast output, one is constantly struck by the inventiveness of the counterpoint, the originality of his harmony, and his unerring sense for whatever forces he was writing for. After Purcell, it was 200 years before England produced another great native composer.

EDWARD ELGAR (1857–1934)
Born Broadheath, near Worcester; died Worcester

∞ English music had been in the doldrums for much of the 19th century, producing few composers of above-average talent and arguably none of genius. The arrival of Elgar afforded great relief, and happily the English system of music festivals enabled his music to be performed. The success of the *Enigma Variations* (1899), his superlative grasp of the orchestra – which often seems to rival that of Strauss – and his complete absorption of the harmonic innovations of Liszt and Wagner led Elgar to success in Germany, especially with the First Symphony (1908) and the oratorio *The Dream of Gerontius* (1900). It seemed that he would rapidly become an international figure, but this was not to happen for many years; instead he seemed to epitomize the aspirations of Edwardian England, with its huge empire and prosperity.

Today, with many recordings of his works by conductors and orchestras of several nationalities, this trend seems to have been reversed and his symphonic music is established as part of the international musical scene. Elgar was a pioneer in his recognition of the importance of the gramophone and was the first composer to record a substantial part of his output. For all his public triumphs he was a private and often melancholy man; devastated by World War I and the death of his wife, he was largely unproductive in his last years.

Purcell, the father of English opera.

RALPH VAUGHAN WILLIAMS (1872–1958)
Born Down Ampney; died London

∞ Like Elgar, Vaughan Williams was a key figure in the renaissance of English music after many years of foreign domination. Unlike Elgar, who was largely influenced by the German school, Vaughan Williams drew nourishment from the large heritage of British folk song, which he did much to collect and notate. His music is permeated by it, including the *London* Symphony No. 2 (1914), which combines many such elements with Debussyian orchestration. The pastoral feel in the symphonies No. 3 and 5 is counterbalanced by striking use of dissonance in the Fourth and Sixth (1934, 1947), as if he was reflecting grim contemporary events such as the rise of Nazism and World War II. He benefited greatly from the services of many distinguished conductors, including Wood, Barbirolli, and Boult.

WILLIAM WALTON (1902–83)
Born Oldham; died Ischia, Italy

∞ Although a few English composers were won over to the radical innovations of Schoenberg and his school, many were of a more conservative disposition, perhaps flirting with Stravinsky's rhythmic style but not much else. One such was Walton, who throughout his life cherished traditional triadic harmony while giving his music terrific energy through

Vaughan Williams drew on English folk traditions in many of his works.

syncopated rhythms that often recall jazz. Like Elgar he was a natural orchestrator, producing a wonderful panoply of sound in works such as the First Symphony (1935), and he too could command the pomp-and-circumstance idiom so important to English music at the time. He started off as an *enfant terrible*, epitomized by *Façade* (1923) in which he collaborated with Edith Sitwell of the Bloomsbury set. Its brittle harmonies and ironic tone make it an English parallel to Schoenberg's *Pierrot Lunaire* (1912). Some have attributed his later decline to too much involvement with film music, but it may just be that as he grew older ideas came more slowly or he simply could not face the huge effort involved in composition.

Britten revived English musical fortunes, notably in opera, after 1945.

BENJAMIN BRITTEN (1913–76)
Born Lowestoft; died Aldeburgh

∞ Britten was another conservative in the healthy burgeoning of composition that occurred in 20th-century England; even the acerbic harmonies of Tippett's opera *King Priam* (1961) are rarely encountered in his superbly crafted works. Although he was hailed by some as England's greatest composer since Purcell, others have been less complimetary and the criticism is made that after the success of *Peter Grimes* (1945) Britten rarely opened his soul to the world in the way that made his early works so powerful. If this is the case, it is still possible to value the craftsmanship, the meticulous orchestration, and

the often very beautiful melodic ideas of the composer's later works. Britten's greatest achievement is single-handedly to have placed English opera centre of the world stage in the now legendary success of *Peter Grimes*. There is little in *Grimes* to support the view that he was interested in composing his homosexuality into his music; only later, in *Death in Venice* (1973), did he adopt such a theme, and there it is not in the context of a story concerned primarily with sexual love.

MICHAEL TIPPETT (1905)
Born London

∞ If Benjamin Britten's genius frequently sought constraints and turned in on itself, Tippett's sought to embrace the world. Strongly influenced by Jungian psychology, Tippett has invested his music with an openness and desire to grasp all avenues of communication. This has led him down a crooked path that can be sublime one moment and then embarrassingly crude the next (both are found in profusion in his fourth opera, *The Icebreak*, 1976). His works of the 1950s (including the superb *Fantasia Concertante on a Theme of Corelli*, 1953) have an almost classical control and

balance that still manages to embrace the elevated flights of fantasy central to his musical expression.

PETER MAXWELL DAVIES (1934)
Born Manchester

∞ Along with Birtwistle and Goehr, Peter Maxwell Davies was one of the Manchester New Music Group in the 1950s, the most important group of post-war English composers. His early works are enthralling in their diverse range of colours, the complex but never obtruse rhythmic structures, and fascination with music theatre, which produced the strangely compelling *Eight Songs for a Mad King* (1969). A by-product of this period is the wonderfully fresh orchestration of *The Boyfriend* for the Ken Russell film (1971). In recent years Maxwell Davies has lived in the relative isolation of Orkney, drawing inspiration from the stark landscape and sea. His compositions have become rather conservative, and he is currently producing a series of works in concerto and symphonic forms which are widely known thanks to recordings and his involvement in education.

GIOVANNI PIERLUIGI DA PALESTRINA (c. 1525–94)
Born ?Palestrina; died Rome

∞ Palestrina seems to have been a relatively spontaneous, worldly man, quite unlike the

chaste world suggested by his music. After the death of his brother, wife, and two sons in an epidemic he considered entering the priesthood, only to remarry just eight months after his wife's demise. His second wife was a very wealthy woman connected with the fur trade, and Palestrina became a keen businessman, accruing sufficient funds to publish 16 collections of his music. In earlier years he ran into difficulties with the Church, his main employer, for although he supported the Counter-Reformation – indeed Pfitzner (in his opera *Palestrina*, 1917) depicted him as the saviour of Catholic music – in reality he was irritated by such diverse problems as inadequate food for choirboys and the banning of secular melodies in Mass settings, which had been such a vital part of the Renaissance cyclic Mass. Palestrina's music stands beside that of Lassus and Victoria as the most perfect embodiment of the principles of vocal counterpoint; his works have a purity of sound, a musical perfection that has rarely been matched. Palestrina's counterpoint is so consistent it is possible to codify almost every aspect of it, which has meant that numerous music students have had to reproduce it (in pastiche composition) for their music degrees.

CLAUDIO MONTEVERDI (1567–1643)
Born Cremona; died Venice

∞ Monteverdi stands astride the great divide between the 'old practice' of the Renaissance and 'new practice' of the Baroque. He is indisputably one of the seminal figures in the history of music. Taking over the reins of opera from the Florentine Camerata, he fostered its growth in his 40 or so operatic works, only three of which have survived. He established the Baroque method of declamation with continuo accompaniment, imbuing it with an eloquence rarely surpassed, and moved from the Renaissance ensemble of diverse instruments in *Orfeo* (1607) to something approaching a standard Baroque ensemble based on strings with concertante parts. One glimpses a high dramatic ideal in moments such as the closing duet of the opera *L'Incoronazione di Poppea* (1642), his final masterwork, as the far from saintly lovers embrace each other in fluid, ecstatic melody – this is the very stuff of opera. In addition to his dramatic works, Monteverdi wrote numerous madrigals, the early ones *a cappella*, the later ones in the revolutionary concerted style; they are of outstanding quality.

ARCHANGELO CORELLI.

ARCANGELO CORELLI (1653–1713)
Born Fusignano, near Milan; died Rome
∞ Hawkins described Corelli as "remarkable for the mildness of his temper and the modesty of his deportment". This serenity seems to have departed when he was playing the violin (the instrument whose development he did so much to encourage): "his eyes rolled as if in agony". As well as establishing and directing string ensembles (as had Lully), and so assisting the development of the modern orchestra, Corelli taught widely and was in constant demand. His career, however, centred on Rome where he was found upon his death to have accumulated many paintings and a sizeable fortune. His compositions are not large in number, yet their influence was vast and their dissemination a key factor in the growth of Baroque instrumental music. Many of his works were repeatedly reprinted: the Trio Sonatas, Op. 1 (1681) went through 35 known editions.

Numerous composers have based works on his trio sonatas and concertos, including Rachmaninov and Tippett in the 20th century.

ANTONIO VIVALDI (1678–1741)
Born Venice; died Vienna
∞ Known as 'Il prete rosso' (the red priest) on account of his red hair, Vivaldi was best known for many years as an astonishing violin virtuoso whose antics on the instrument seem to anticipate those of Paganini a century later. He was a man of superabundant energy whose vanity was notorious, as was his fanatical interest in money. He had plenty to boast of, for he consolidated the use of ritornello form in the fast movements of the Baroque concerto and standardized many other features as well. His influence on his exact contemporary J S Bach was profound; the German master even recomposed works by him. Indeed, it was the revival of interest in Bach that led to Vivaldi's resurgence in popular esteem, which snowballed after the last war following a recording of four violin concertos fancifully named after the four seasons. For several years from 1703 he taught in a conservatory for orphaned or abandoned girls (Pio Ospedale della Pietà), for whom he wrote concertos for a wide range of instruments. Stravinsky's quip that Vivaldi had written the same concerto 500 times seems unjust now that we know the full extent of his inventiveness.

DOMENICO SCARLATTI (1685–1757)
Born Naples; died Madrid
∞ Scarlatti suffered from the ambitions of his famous father, Alessandro Scarlatti, who persuaded his son to take up various onerous appointments composing opera and church music. All his early work is eclipsed by his tuition of, and compositions for, Princess Maria Barbara of Portugal, whom he accompanied to Spain when she married the Spanish crown prince. This appointment enabled Scarlatti to devote himself to his first love, the harpsichord. He composed 550 single-movement sonatas that cover a breathtaking range of moods and

techniques. Their harmony is often quite unlike that of any other Baroque composer – he even uses clusters – and they have startling rhythmic vitality. Some even hear his influence in Haydn's music; certainly he anticipated many of the developments of the Classical period.

GIOACHINO ANTONIO ROSSINI (1792–1868)
Born Pesaro; died Paris
∞ The image of Rossini as a corpulent gourmet amid the wealthy salons of Second Empire Paris can only apply – if at all – to the later, mainly unproductive part of his life; that is, from 1829 when he retired from operatic composition. Up to this point he was phenomenally hard-working, turning out masterpiece after masterpiece at an extraordinary rate. He created and developed the basic vocabulary of Italian opera for the entire first half of the 19th century: without him the evolution of Romantic Italian opera in the hands of Donizetti and Bellini is unthinkable. He is best known for his comic operas, especially *The Barber of Seville* (1816), so admired by Beethoven and Wagner. These

Rossini: brilliantly inventive composer of *opera seria* and *opera buffa*.

sparkling works are full of irresistible ideas, often based on a handful of notes that look unpromising on paper but blossom under Rossini's brilliant orchestration and virtuoso vocal writing, which represents the very pinnacle of *bel canto* style. At climaxes Rossini often uses his famous crescendo to build up tension, bringing his 'geometric' forms (a sequence of small blocks continually rearranged and varied) to exhilarating conclusions. The serious operas are also fascinating for their many innovations, which emphasized dramatic values over the static conventions of the venerable *opera seria*.

GAETANO DONIZETTI (1797–1848)
Born Bergamo; died Bergamo

∾ As the low brass and darker reeds set the scene for the tragic conclusion of *Lucia di Lammermoor* (1835), we can hear the sounds of nascent Italian Romanticism. Alongside this innovative side we still find the popular two-part arias (slow-fast), while many scenes progress inexorably to the 'rabble-rousing' final *stretta*; many have wondered how Lucia's mad scene could be allowed to culminate in such an apparently cheerful melody. Perhaps here the traditional need for a singer to show off took priority over the demands of the drama. Underneath, however, this is a new sensibility, committed to expression and dramatic truth; no matter how often Donizetti lapses into the commonplace,

Verdi devoted himself almost entirely to opera.

there is always a melody, a sudden modulation, or some other means of restoring credibility. Donizetti's reputation is in the ascendant now, with revivals of many of his serious operas alongside the ever-popular *L'elisir d'amore* (1832), *La favorite* (1840) and *Don Pasquale* (1843).

VINCENZO BELLINI (1801–35)
Born Catania, Sicily; died near Paris

∾ A quick comparison between the output of Bellini and Donizetti is revealing, for while they both died young Donizetti produced over 60 works to Bellini's 11. This is partly due to the much stronger individual character of each of Bellini's operas: one could never mistake a fragment of *Beatrice di Tenda* (1833) for *Norma* (1831), for example. Alongside the ever-growing variety of harmonies and orchestral colours brought to bear on his Romantic subject matter, Bellini's operas have some of the most individual melodies of the 19th century. It is not for nothing that Chopin and Wagner both admired the refined, often very poignant lines that Bellini crafted for the voice; their subtle arches and curves are embellished with myriad coloratura devices that make his operas a continuing delight and challenge for singers. In his final opera, *I puritani* (1835), Bellini drew many threads of the early Romantic period to a climax with invention of overwhelming richness and long scenes that challenge the very basis of 'number' opera (the formal division into aria and recitative); there is even an extensive use of 'reminiscence motifs' which give the work an unusually integrated feel.

GIUSEPPE VERDI (1813–1901)
Born Le Roncole, Parma; died Milan

∾ Verdi was not just one of the supreme operatic geniuses of the 19th century – and the only one seriously to rival Wagner – he was also the greatest composer Italy had produced since Monteverdi. His arrival on the scene was opportune, for both Donizetti and Bellini had already

Puccini created a distinctive style out of many different influences.

done much to develop Romantic Italian opera. Part of the appeal of Verdi is his realism: in *La traviata* (1853) he depicted real characters in often shocking (for the period) circumstances. Violetta is not only a courtesan in theory, she actually 'lives in sin' during the opera; no wonder Verdi fell foul of the censors (who were already suspicious of his support for the nationalist movement). In his last operas (*Otello* and *Falstaff*, 1886, 1893) Verdi created a more continuous musical fabric, the result of years of experimentation and patient adaptation of existing operatic forms. He was another master tune-smith, more varied than Donizetti and Bellini: the gorgeous opening of *Simon Boccanegra* (1857/81) is just one of numerous examples of his genius. He used the orchestra to dramatic effect, allowing it near equality with the voices, and evolved a new style of dramatic vocal writing that replaced the elaborate ornamentation of Rossini and his immediate successors.

GIACOMO PUCCINI (1858–1924)
Born Lucca; died Brussels

∾ Puccini was recognized early on as Verdi's successor. Choosing librettos that included moments of great poignancy and sometimes sadism – there are torture scenes in both *Tosca* (1900) and *Turandot* (1926) – Puccini evolved a vivid operatic style that combined his own ideas with techniques

evolved by Debussy, Wagner, and many others. Like Verdi, he was an inspired melodist which, with lush orchestration and tremendous surges of passion at climactic moments, makes his operas easy to identify. He generally preferred tragedy to comedy, and found the happy resolution of the icy princess's contest with Prince Calaf at the end of *Turandot* difficult to set to music. He died before he could accomplish this and *Turandot*, which should have been his greatest achievement, had to be completed by his pupil Alfano.

Spain

CRISTOBAL DE MORALES (c. 1500–53)
Born Seville; died ?Marchena

∞ Morales had the good fortune to be born in what was then one of the most richly endowed of Spain's musical centres, Seville. He was fiercely proud of his origins, adding 'Hyspalensis' (meaning born in Seville) to his name in his publication of 16 Masses in Rome. In Seville he was assured of an excellent musical education, which he put to good use, for along with Francisco Guerrero (see page 73) he became Spain's leading composer of church music before Victoria. After a spell at the ancient Gothic cathedral of Avila, he went to Rome where he joined the papal choir. He composed prolifically and his works received many performances in the enlightened musical atmosphere generated by Pope Paul III. Morales returned to Spain in 1545 where he became *maestro de capilla* at the all-important cathedral at Toledo; unhappy with his administrative duties and apparently unproductive there, he moved on to Malaga.

Although Morales followed the general 'rules' of polyphonic church music practised by his contemporaries in the Netherlands, his music has many personal features, including an inventive rhythmic style quite unlike Palestrina, some freedom with dissonance, and instances of harmonic daring.

TOMAS LUIS DE VICTORIA (1548–1611)
Born Avila; died Madrid

∞ Spain's greatest composer and one of the most significant church composers of the late Renaissance, Victoria was less prolific than his contemporaries Lassus and Palestrina. He has been represented in the 20th century by just a handful of works that tend to be the poignant, anguished ones, especially the extraordinary *Versa est in luctum* from the Office of the Dead. This is not the whole story, for many of his works are of an outgoing, optimistic character. His harmonic world is quite distinct from that of other composers of the period; for example, he favoured an ambiguous, chromatic type of progression which suggests the influence of the madrigalists on his exclusively liturgical output (all in Latin). Another misrepresentation of the original sound of his music is the modern preference for unaccompanied voices in Renaissance choral works, which flies in the face of historical evidence: John VI endorsed the liberal use of instruments to double the vocal parts, so supporting a common practice in 16th-century Spain.

ISAAC ALBENIZ (1860–1909)
Born Camprodón, Lérida; died Cambô-les-Bains, France

∞ At the tender age of four, when most of us cannot even read, Albéniz was astonishing audiences with his piano playing, inspiring charges of trickery. Later he took his astounding virtuosity to Paris where his compositions attracted the attention of Debussy and Ravel, both of whom were influenced by his strikingly innovative writing for the instrument and progressive harmony. Spanish traditional music undoubtedly helped to shape this dazzling piano style, and has done much to

Albéniz helped in the revitalization of Spanish music.

popularize his masterpiece, the *Suite Iberia* (1908), in which the piano imitates such distinctively Spanish instruments as the guitar and castanets.

Alongside his writing for the piano, Albéniz wrote enthusiastically for the opera house, and the fact that works such as *Pepita Jiménez* (1896) are currently neglected does not mean they will remain so, for his is an attractive style and Spanish operas are being widely revived now.

Falla married Spanish idioms to the harmonic language of Stravinsky.

ENRIQUE GRANADOS (1867–1916)
Born Lérida; died at sea

∞ Granados had much in common with his contemporary, Albéniz: both were outstanding pianists as well as composers, both composed music for the theatre with only limited success as far as posterity is concerned, and both are chiefly remembered for one piano work. *Goyescas* is Granados's masterpiece, and also the title of one of his operas, first performed at the

New York Met in 1916. Granados's Spanish heritage comes through strongly in his music, which is characterized by its wonderfully lively melodies and evocative colouring. Since the war his songs have been popularized by some great Spanish singers, including one of the most delightful of them all, Victoria de los Angeles.

Granados's end was a sad one. He and his wife were returning to Europe on the liner *Sussex* when it was torpedoed by a German submarine. Granados reached a lifeboat but jumped back into the water to save his wife and they were both drowned.

MANUEL DE FALLA (1876–1946)
Born Cádiz; died Alta Gracia, Argentina

∞ The revitalization of Spanish music in the latter part of the 19th century after many years of obscurity reached an interesting and indeed vital phase in the career of Falla. Thanks to a highly attractive fusion of Stravinsky's rhythmic innovations and traditional Spanish idioms, Falla became one of the most popular composers of his time. Like Granados he wrote in the profitable genre of the *zarzuela* (traditional Spanish operetta) in his apprentice years. Although Falla did not value highly what he wrote then, there is no doubt that the experience filtered through to his great dance works *El amor brujo* (Love, the Magician) (1915) and *El sombrero de tres*

picos ('The Three-cornered Hat') (1919).

More substantial projects came along later, notably the oratorio *Atlántida*, which a combination of ill health and the debilitating effects of the Spanish Civil War and fascism prevented Falla from completing; after years of work, this has now been done by a pupil of Falla. In this hugely ambitious work, which has little of the instant appeal of his earlier pieces, Falla attempted to capture the essence of Spanish music over the centuries, including sacred polyphony, and turn it into an all-encompassing contemporary idiom.

Germany & Austria

HEINRICH SCHUTZ (1585–1672)
Born Köstritz; died Dresden

∞ The first in the long line of great German composers, Schütz was a brilliant master of diverse musical styles. He seems to have been a pious man blessed with a sense of humour and mindful of the needy members of his Kapelle. Rather than risking isolation in Germany, he went to Italy to study the polychoral techniques of Giovanni Gabrieli. Having mastered these he produced a series of works, mainly psalm settings, in the late Renaissance style which

shows a mastery of counterpoint. He later went back to Italy to catch up on Monteverdi's advanced concerted style and other developments. He brought these techniques back to Germany and refined them in electrifying examples such as 'Saul, Saul, was verfolgst du mich' (*Symphoniae sacrae III*, 1650) which captures with stunning dramatic effects the very moment of Saul's conversion on the road to Damascus. Schütz's interest in opera resulted in just one work, *Dafne* (1627), which must be one of the most bitterly lamented of all lost compositions: the manuscript was destroyed in a Dresden fire in 1760. Schütz lived to a ripe old age, lost many of his friends and family, and expressed regret that he had not stayed in the legal profession!

JOHANN SEBASTIAN BACH (1685–1750)
Born Eisenach; died Leipzig

∞ It is remarkable that whereas Schütz, Handel and Haydn were well known throughout Europe in their lifetimes, the composer whom many would consider the greatest of all was better known as an organ virtuoso, and only a dozen or so volumes of his works were published before his death. Such was his lack of fame that he was only the runner-up for a post at St Thomas's, Leipzig. Happily for Bach, the favoured candidate, Graupner, withdrew, so leaving the way clear for him. Perhaps this low esteem can be attributed to his conservatism: he preferred to work with forms that were already well established and had little time for the new fads, which were eventually to lead to the glories of Haydn and Mozart. His music is dominated by counterpoint of all kinds; even his chorales (written for the cantatas and passions) have a liveliness in the inner voices that contrasts vividly with the works of others. He adopted Vivaldi's concerto form in many of his works, even transcribing works by the Italian and adding numerous ingenious counterpoints and enriching the harmony.

Works like the *St Matthew Passion* (1727 or 1729) and the *B minor*

Schütz: master of counterpoint and the first great German composer.

Mass (assembled c. 1749) attest to his religious devotion (he was a Protestant). He was by no means a passive man, for throughout his life he came into conflict with the authorities around him. In the early 19th century, Mendelssohn and many others fell under his spell, beginning many years of rediscovery; works were dug up (some literally) that scholars had thought lost forever.

GEORGE FRIDERIC HANDEL (1685–1759)
Born Halle; died London

∞Unlike Bach, who lived his life in the north and east of Germany, Handel was a cosmopolitan who travelled wherever his musical development took him. Exposure to Italian music offers one explanation why his music is often more harmonically based than Bach's. He exhibits a fondness for melodies in what were, for the Baroque, unusually clear and regular phrases. Indeed, his melodic writing is one reason why a famous singer could write in her score, 'I love Handel!', for few composers have written more noble or eloquent melodies than 'I know that my Redeemer liveth' (*Messiah*,1742), for example. The core of his output is the series of Italian operas he wrote for London, many of which are of superlative quality, and above all his invention of the oratorio, as we now know the genre (around 1732). This innovation was spurred by his declining fortunes as an opera composer, not through conviction. However, it led to a series of works that were immensely successful at the time, and a handful survived all the changes and vicissitudes of taste in the 19th and 20th centuries, especially the *Messiah*. Handel was the kiss of death to English music, which did not recover its own identity until late in the next century, but his instrumental, orchestral, and vocal music stand beside that of J S Bach as the most treasurable manifestation of the high Baroque style.

{ J S Bach was prolific in almost every area except opera.

CHRISTOPH WILLIBALD GLUCK (1714–87)
Born Erasbach; died Vienna

∞ Each century has seen one or more attempted operatic reforms when one composer or theorist takes exception to the elevated position of the singer and attempts to raise the dramatic profile of opera. This was Gluck's contribution in the 1750s, which resulted in his ballet *Don Juan* (1761), and the operas *Orfeo* (1762) and *Alceste* (1767). The most audible sign of change is the replacement of *recitativo secco* (dry, or un-accompanied, recitative) with accompanied recitative and the careful attention to the declamation of the text, producing works that are quintessentially dramatic. He wrote melodies of a deceptively simple hue that are often of a noble beauty. Berlioz was particularly attracted to the Classical qualities in Gluck's music. Gluck became the grand figure of European opera, living in luxurious (and somewhat alcoholic) style in Vienna.

JOSEF HAYDN (1732–1809)
Born Rohrau; died Vienna

∞Haydn's vast output is imbued with a deep strain of humour and humanism; his was an optimistic nature. For a few years (1770s) he was sucked into the emotional turmoil of the *Sturm und Drang* movement in the arts, writing disturbing minor-key symphonies, quartets and sonatas, but later he incorporated these features into a broader style. Often known as the 'Father of the Symphony', in later life he wrote works that are a triumph of the Classical style – a style he had brought to maturity – exhibiting a glorious equilibrium of harmony, melody and rhythm. He was a modest man, recognizing Mozart's genius as greater than his own (in range of achievement we must surely disagree with him now) and influencing Beethoven's. He spent much of his life working for the wealthy Esterházy family, though his fame spread far and wide, to such an extent that a London correspondent, shocked at the conditions of Haydn's employment advocated kidnapping the poor composer to bring him to London and civilization. Haydn was actually quite contented; in addition to a staggering array of musical duties on the princes' estates, he found time for fishing and shooting.

Weber: the most famous figure in the birth of German Romantic opera. }

composing by the age of five, and by 20 had produced a vast corpus of music; he soon extricated himself from the servitude experienced by most composers of the time, leaving Salzburg and becoming self-employed in Vienna. As a man he was not as refined as his music might suggest, exhibiting in his letters a fondness for scatological jokes, but he was not the adolescent buffoon portrayed in Milos Forman's film *Amadeus*.

LUDWIG VAN BEETHOVEN (1770–1827)
Born Bonn; died Vienna

∞ Beethoven was the end of the Classical line, extending the style of Haydn and Mozart in terms of duration, emotional power, dynamic, and almost every other imaginable parameter. Some writers regard the *Eroica* Symphony No. 3 (1803) as the first flowering of German musical Romanticism, but it is not a contradiction to view it as a triumph of Classicism at the same time. Curiously, works of a very dramatic nature, such as the Fifth Symphony (1808), often alternate in his oeuvre with such (relatively) abstract, conceptual projects as the lovely Fourth Symphony (1806); he commanded a huge battery of idioms and technical resources. His intensely idealistic nature is evident in his choice of topic for his only opera, *Fidelio* (1805/6–14), in which he turned a

conventional liberation theme into an uplifting paeon in praise of freedom and individual courage and loyalty. As a character he could be truculent and difficult, faults that were no doubt exacerbated by the deafness that certainly contributed to the suicidal Heiligenstadt Testament and his failure, not for want of trying, to secure a lasting relationship with a woman. Beethoven became a Romantic figurehead for the Victorians.

CARL MARIA VON WEBER (1786–1826)
Born Eutin, near Lübeck; died London

∞ Weber was a versatile musician who directed at the Prague and Dresden opera houses. His greatest achievement was securing the foundations of German Romantic opera in the Singspiel *Der Freischütz* (1821). In this work, which became a sort of German national anthem, he used German folk material as well as more traditional Italianate forms. *Euryanthe* (1823) succeeds in spite of a dreadful libretto; it anticipates Wagner's use of leitmotif and enlarges the role of the orchestra. Like a true Romantic, Weber died young of tuberculosis shortly after the premiere of *Oberon* (1826) in London, but generations of composers from Wagner to Debussy and beyond continued to benefit from his example.

FRANZ SCHUBERT (1797–1828)
Born Vienna; died Vienna

∞ Throughout his career Schubert cultivated the Classical forms of Beethoven in his piano sonatas and symphonies, quartets, and choral works. Late in life he succeeded overwhelmingly in works like the Ninth Symphony and String Quintet, but in so doing he set music firmly on course for Romanticism by raising the profile of melody and making the traditional balance between parameters struck by Haydn and Mozart hard to maintain. He also slowed down musical rhythm, anticipating Wagner. The central core of his achievement is some 600 Lieder, a genre that he brought to its first maturity. He was a lyricist of pure genius who had great influence in all musical forms, especially on

WOLFGANG AMADEUS MOZART (1756–91)
Born Salzburg; died Vienna

∞ Mozart's music is remarkable for its superb sense of balance and proportion. His pacing of events in a symphony or sonata has rarely been equalled, and one often encounters a depth of feeling, notably in the poignant minor-key works, that was rare in the 18th century. Even in his magnificent piano concertos one senses the opera house in a long clarinet cantilena, aria-style, over pulsating string accompaniment or the lively interchange between orchestra and piano. His greatest achievement is surely the sublime trio of operas to librettos by Da Ponte (*The Marriage of Figaro*, 1786, *Don Giovanni*, 1787, and *Così fan tutte*, 1790) which have rarely been out of the repertoire (much though the 19th century disapproved of the 'immorality' of *Così*). Considered the greatest natural genius in the history of Western culture, Mozart was

{ Haydn: with Mozart the chief representative of the high Classical style.

Beethoven: the last great figure of the Classical period. }

Schumann, Brahms, and Wolf. Sadly, one of the most promising careers of the 19th century was cut short by syphilis, from which he had suffered since 1822; Schubert shared the fate of so many of the poets whose verses he set.

FELIX MENDELSSOHN (1809–47)
Born Hamburg; died Leipzig

∞ Mendelssohn was born into an affluent and well-connected banking family, but even so his extraordinarily early development remains one of the great wonders of music. Whereas Mozart in his teens rarely succeeded in creating works that were truly inspired as well as skilfully crafted, Mendelssohn began to compose works of the most exquisite genius at the age of 16, the year of his comic opera *Die Hochzeit des Camacho*. It was followed by the magnificent overture *A Midsummer Night's Dream* (1826) and *Octet* (1825). Both works show many traits of early German Romanticism: the quest for the picturesque, the replacement of Beethoven's complex rhythmic forms with melodies often in regular four-bar phrases, and a general simplification of texture. Following Weber's example, Mendelssohn cultivated a typical 19th-century fascination with the supernatural, writing light fairy music that was seized upon by Berlioz and others. His Romanticism developed into the full-blooded lyricism of the Violin Concerto (1844) and jubilant Wedding March from the incidental music to *A Midsummer Night's Dream* (1842). Sometimes a Biedermeier cosiness creeps in, leading to charges of superficiality, but it cannot detract from the sheer inventiveness and poetry of his best works.

ROBERT SCHUMANN (1810–56)
Born Zwickau; died Endenich

∞ Schumann wrote music criticism in which he distinguished between the Florestan and Eusebius in his creative personality; the former was outgoing and ebullient, the latter withdrawn and

often melancholy. The interaction of the two states is immediately noticeable in the great series of solo piano works that he produced with such fluency up to around 1840. Many works of the period opt for small, interconnected forms quite unlike most of Beethoven's yet entirely characteristic of the early Romantics. He was a great experimenter in harmony, finding many progressions that shocked his conservative colleagues, and he was fond of unusual rhythmic patterns, often obscuring the beat altogether (for example in the last movement of the Piano Concerto, 1845). After his marriage to Clara Wieck he turned increasingly to Lieder, orchestral, chamber and choral music, but his passion for innovation did not let up: his Fourth Symphony (1841/51) in its final version is one of the first to be through-composed without breaks between movements.

{ **Mendelssohn: a composer who revealed his full, highly poetic genius very early in his career.**

RICHARD WAGNER (1813–83)
Born Leipzig; died Venice

∞ Portrayed by film director Ken Russell in *Lisztomania* as a vampire feeding off the blood of Liszt, Wagner wrote music that was in fact a remarkable synthesis of many threads in German, Italian and French Romanticism. He employed a species of Beethovenian motivic development in the leitmotivic thread of his mature operas from 1853, combining this with many attributes of grand opera (such as the trio of vengeance sung by Brünnhilde, Hagen and Gunther in Act II of *Götterdämmerung*, 1874). He developed harmony in *Tristan und Isolde* (1859) almost to the point of atonality, and had a vast influence on composers and other artists in every part of the Western world, obtaining cult status in late 19th-century Paris. As a man he was very demanding on the purses and minds of his friends and acquaintances: few composers have had so many views on so many subjects, ranging from vegetarianism to the future of the German race. A larger-than-life character with a strong instinct for survival, he was rescued when at his lowest ebb by a knight in shining armour – Ludwig II of Bavaria – who enabled him to build an opera house expressly for his operas (or music dramas as they are sometimes referred to) at Bayreuth in Bavaria.

ANTON BRUCKNER (1824–96)
Born Ansfelden; died Vienna

∞ Bruckner was a devout Catholic whose musical allegiance was with Wagner as well as Schubert. His mastery of counterpoint and form is at once evident in his startling First Symphony (1866/91), and as he developed so did the richness of his harmony and his debt to Wagner. Indeed, his Third Symphony (1877/89) was one of few symphonic works Wagner was content to see bearing his name in the dedication. Bruckner composed with huge blocks of material, generating massive climaxes, often for unison brass, after repeating short figures in ascending sequences in the *Tristan* 'Liebestod' manner. Brahms' charge that these monumental works were like "giant boa constrictors" only seems reasonable when applied to the very few

Wagner, perhaps the most influential of all composers.

HUGO WOLF (1860–1903)
Born Windischgraz; died Vienna

∞ Wolf devoted his life to the composition of Lieder. He developed the Lied to unparalleled eloquence through his devotion to the texts he set and the liberating effect of Wagner's harmony and motivic construction. Many of his songs have an ecstatic, uplifting quality, a radiance even. He also developed an acerbic, ironic style in the comic songs which had considerable influence on the 20th century. He wrote in short sharp bursts, whiling away his time in between with vitriolic music criticism directed at Brahms and sycophantic paeans to his hero, Wagner. He was always unstable, and syphilis led to his eventual madness and confinement.

GUSTAV MAHLER (1860–1911)
Born Kalischt, Bohemia; died Vienna

∞ For many years Mahler was valued first as a conductor and only secondly as a composer. In spite of the poison of the anti-Semitism then rife in Austria, he rose to one of the country's most prestigious positions – director of the Vienna Staatsoper – where he ruled with a will of iron. Often psychoanalyzed posthumously, Mahler himself went to Siegmund Freud, concerned over the crisis in his relations with his wife, Alma; the great man unremarkably diagnosed a 'mother-complex'. Deep emotions run through Mahler's symphonies, which constantly fluctuate between an innocent, naïve world conjured up so vividly in his Lieder settings of *Des Knaben Wunderhorn* (1892–98) and the corrupt, sensual world in which he lived. He drew inspiration from the instrumental and orchestral works of Schubert, often to the point of paraphrase in the Seventh Symphony (1905), and from Bruckner in the Fifth (1902). Mahler believed the symphony should reflect the world and he vastly enlarged the form, incorporating voices in the Second, Third, Fourth, and Eighth (1894, 1896, 1900,

1906). He did not live to complete his Tenth, his heart giving out before the surviving sketches could be filled out and orchestrated.

RICHARD STRAUSS (1864–1949)
Born Munich; died Garmisch-Partenkirchen, Bavaria

∞ The composer who disgusted Edgard Varèse by discussing financial matters to the exclusion of all else started life as a brilliant young radical who extended and intensified the language of Liszt and Wagner in a series of tone poems and his first mature operas. At one point he seemed destined to break ties with tonality altogether in *Elektra* (1909); yet much of his inspiration remained triadic, to such an extent that even in the most radical music he wrote there are patches that Mozart would have found familiar. The tone poems had a galvanizing effect on Bartók, Schoenberg, Syzmanowksi and others on account of their inspired orchestration and tremendous dynamism. As Strauss turned increasingly to opera he rejected the progressives, preferring instead to develop a rapprochement between the operatic styles of Mozart and Wagner in the conversational idiom of his later operas. He saw his world crumble to ashes in World War II, but even before the reconstruction of Salzburg, Vienna, Dresden and Munich in the early post-war years his works were revived and fêted.

ARNOLD SCHOENBERG (1874–1951)
Born Vienna; died Los Angeles

∞ Owner of one of the most extraordinary creative and pedagogic minds in the history of Western music, Schoenberg grew up in a working-class suburb of Vienna and had to wait patiently for the volume covering 'S' in an encyclopaedia to arrive before writing in sonata form. From around 1899 he started a series of works (with *Verklärte Nacht*), every one of which broke new ground in the organization of music. Finally he reached the conclusion that tonality had been exhausted, which led him to compose first in an atonal style (beginning with *Das Buch der hängenden Gärten,* 1909) and then to develop serialism. Although serial composition has not maintained a strong

movements that really fail to give a sense of overall form.

JOHANNES BRAHMS (1833–1897)
Born Hamburg; died Vienna

∞ Brahms began as a young firebrand producing fiery, Romantic sonatas and piano pieces that were, in their own way, Lisztian. However, within a few years he had become thoroughly absorbed into the Schumann circle and was well on his way to becoming the Romantic conservative so loathed by the Weimar School of Liszt, Wagner, and others. Sadly, this derogatory description still adheres to him, in spite of the great wealth of his musical vocabulary and expansion of musical forms. His chamber music, symphonies and concertos are astonishingly inventive redesigns of the forms of Beethoven and Schubert. He was passionately devoted to Clara Schumann – Robert having gone insane – but he never married. In his late works there is an autumnal sadness and wisdom that is the very essence of this great composer, whom Schoenberg preferred to call "Brahms the Progressive".

miniature, organic way without pouring it into the symphonic or operatic moulds favoured by Schoenberg and Berg. After the war Webern was idolized by the rising avant-garde, who considered him the most radical of the trio.

ALBAN BERG (1885–1935)
Born Vienna; died Vienna

∾ Berg was the sensualist of the New Viennese School; his legacy includes many partly solved riddles regarding his personal life. Much given to numeric puzzles and codes, he concealed programmes in his orchestral and instrumental music that reveal extra-marital affairs. Even the Violin Concerto (1935), ostensibly a requiem for Alma Mahler's daughter, seems to have just such a hidden agenda. Unlike Webern, who made a complete break with tonality in his serial works, Berg retained aspects of it; they help make his mature style rich harmonically and often intensely lyrical. Berg was a superb operatic composer, one of few in this century to have established an unchallenged hold over the world's operatic houses with *Wozzeck* (1922) and *Lulu* (unfinished, 1935).

KARLHEINZ STOCKHAUSEN (1928)
Born Burg Mödrath, near Cologne

∾ Stockhausen has been the pioneer *par excellence* in the post-war years. Many techniques that are now common coinage were first tried out by him, and even when others led the way, he invariably found interesting routes through electronic music, improvisation, total serialism, mixing acoustic and electronic media, and so on. His discoveries in the domain of time and rhythm were among his most startling, and are persuasively outlined in the essay '...wie die Zeit vergeht ...' (As time passes) (1956). Eccentric and complex, he is a consummate technician and has done more to shape the perception of avant-garde music than any other composer. He is now engaged on a gargantuan scheme to compose seven operas, which will make Wagner's *Ring* look like a mere trifle.

Scandinavia

FRANZ BERWALD (1796–1868)
Born Stockholm; died Stockholm

∾ In the 19th century Scandinavian music tended to be dominated by the 'mainstream' music cultures until Gade and Grieg came to the fore. Berwald, belonging to an older generation, still possesses a vein of individualism that shines through the obvious influence of early German Romanticism (mostly Mendelssohn and Schumann). Indeed, we find many hints of the way Scandinavian composers would soon be making the symphony very much their own, renewing it without breaking from traditional forms or harmony. There is something refreshingly individual in the way the bass instruments mark out their main figure at the opening of the aptly named Third Symphony, the *Singulière* (1845). Like many of his Scandinavian contemporaries, Berwald received his musical training in Germany and met with little recognition in his own country during his lifetime, critics finding his music too progressive. Some works had therefore to wait until the 20th century for their first performance, while others were sadly lost.

hold on the end of the 20th century, it was for many years the principal means of organizing musical ideas, and it was Schoenberg's New Viennese School (Berg and Webern) that led to the method's propagation. As well as composing, Schoenberg taught extensively, developing theories on harmony, counterpoint, form and musical logic that found their way into several publications both during his lifetime and posthumously; their influence continues to be felt.

ANTON WEBERN (1883–1945)
Born Vienna; died Mittersill

∾ During the war years Webern lived in Austria, where his compositions were banned and he was reduced to teaching and making vocal scores of operas. Just as the war was ending and his career could again begin to flourish, he was accidentally killed by an American solider, so ending the life of a meticulous musician whose posthumous influence was to be greater than that of his mentor, Schoenberg. Webern wholeheartedly embraced the serial method, but he chose to use it in a

EDVARD GRIEG (1843–1907)
Born Bergen; died Bergen

Grieg: Norway's greatest composer and an attractively idiosyncratic figure.

∞Grieg's rapid rise to prominence in Norway made him a crucial figure in his country's national revival. He studied extensively in Europe, where he came into contact with Liszt, who generously encouraged the young composer, but it was his return to Norway and a commission to write incidental music for Ibsen's verse-drama *Peer Gynt* (1876, the year Bayreuth opened with Wagner's *Ring*) that finally brought him to the fore. His natural talent for working in miniature forms is illustrated in the poetic movements he composed for the play, especially in the evocative mood picture 'Morning'. He cultivated large forms in the early years, perhaps most successfully in the Piano Concerto (1868), which was influenced by both Schumann and Liszt and remains one of the most popular of all Romantic concertos. However, his later songs and piano works, which are at the heart of his output, are all in the miniature forms pioneered by Beethoven and Schubert. Their sound-world could not be characterized as exclusively Norwegian, though there are modal passages and traces of folk song; but Grieg has certain melodic ideas that recur in different forms and instantly identify him as

Edv. Grieg.

the composer. Both his biography and his music suggest a warm but private individual whose initial desire to take the world by storm quickly turned to more modest aspirations.

CARL NIELSEN (1865–1931)
Born Nørre Lyndelse; died Copenhagen

∞ Like a breath of fresh air in the musty halls of the world's concert venues, Nielsen's theatrical and symphonic works radiate healthy optimism. Like his close contemporary Sibelius, he opted for the conservative option of working within 19th-century forms such as the symphony, and his grip on triadic tonality never slackened. Where he did take innovatory paths, giving his symphonies a quite unusual effect, is in the degree of through-composition: at the beginning one sets out on a journey with various resting points, obstructions, and triumphs on the way; because the musical circumstances keep changing, the amount of repetition is greatly reduced, especially in the epic Fourth and Fifth Symphonies (1916, 1922). Several of his works end in different keys to the starting ones (progressive tonality). He also tried out some unusual orchestral effects, not least in the Fifth Symphony, where the side-

Nielsen: one of the finest symphonists of the early 20th century.

drummer is called upon to improvise in such a way as to drown out the rest of the orchestra. While his symphonies are well known, the same cannot be said of much of his fine choral and chamber music; the lovely secular cantata *Fynsk foraar* ('Springtime in Fyn', 1921) deserves far greater renown for its fertile melodies and deft orchestration. Rare archive film of the composer confirms the sunny disposition and outgoing character demonstrated in so much of the music.

JEAN SIBELIUS (1865–1957)
Born Hämeenlinna; died Järvenpää

∞ Finland's greatest composer grew up with the legends and myths of his country, turning them into a musical tone poem *Kullervo* (1892) – in several movements with voices – worthy of the national epic the *Kalevala*. While Sibelius continued to show interest in the tone poem and theatre, his central achievement lies in creating a symphonic style that made a virtue of his conservatism in tonal matters. In their economy of means and variety these symphonies are among the highpoints of early 20th-century music. With its long, very beautiful melody, the finale of the First Symphony (1898) is typical of the young Sibelius and reminds us of his love for Tchaikovsky's music. This all-encompassing Romanticism had already been challenged in the first movement, and in his Second

Liszt: flamboyant virtuoso and prolific composer.

Symphony's (1901) first movement we find the essence of the Sibelius sound: short motifs initially presented in a fractured way, gradually gathering momentum and continuity as the movement brings disparate elements together and resolves them. The forms are often traditional, but the handling of them reinforces Sibelius's comment to Mahler that the symphony was about "profound logic creating a connection between all the motifs". With alcohol more appealing than composition, a projected Eighth Symphony (1929, destroyed) never materialized and for the last 30 years of his life his muse was silent.

Eastern Europe

FRYDERYK CHOPIN (1810–49)
Born Zelazowa Wola; died Paris

∞ Chopin was rare among Romantics in not being greatly influenced by Beethoven. His idols were Bach and Mozart, who inspired in him considerable fluency in the handling of form. Even in sonata movements he avoids mechanical reproductionin favour of his own distinctive procedures. Few composers have shown such total identi-fication with their instruments as Chopin for the piano, for although he wrote occasionally for orchestra, voice and chamber ensemble, most of his mature compositions are for piano solo. In the *Etudes* (1829–37) he seems to have entered into the very soul of the instrument. He tended to avoid the over-reliance on huge chordal textures found in other Romantics by imbuing his music with subtle contra-puntal textures; at the same time his adventurous chromatic harmony enriched the triadic basis of his music. Had Chopin produced more good pupils we might have been spared the extreme use of rubato in the performance of his music now, for Chopin himself was firmly against it in his lifetime, preferring a bassline securely on the beat.

FRANZ LISZT (1811–86)
Born Raiding, Hungary; died Bayreuth

∞ One of the most flamboyant 19th-century composers, Liszt made his mark as a pianist of astounding virtuosity, as a teacher, conductor and prolific composer. Among his triumphs as a conductor was the first performance of *Lohengrin* (1848), which he gave in Weimar in 1850. He was a radical thinker harmonically, developing many of the sonorities that were immediately taken up by Wagner, and almost parting company with tradition altogether in the mysterious (and only recently discovered) *Bagatelle sans tonalité*. His piano writing involves huge chords, rapidly repeated notes, double octaves, and sudden cadenzas that require deft finger technique. In addition to compositions for piano, Liszt invented the symphonic poem, thereby opening the floodgates to works by Balakirev, Tchaikovsky, Strauss and numerous others. He was a generous man, frequently helping out his future son-in-law Wagner, and he was not averse to the pleasures of the flesh, at least in his younger days. Later he became devout and officially took minor orders in Rome. He was once described as Mephisto disguised as an abbé, which vividly conveys his Romantic abstraction and worldliness as conflicting poles in a complex personality.

BEDRICH SMETANA (1824–84)
Born Litomyšl; died Prague

∞ Smetana manned barricades in the nationalist uprisings of 1848 and eventually became a focus of Czech nationalism; in World War II his great cycle of tone poems *Má Vlast* (1879) was played in defiance of the Nazi occupation of his country. He wrote one of the first and still one of the finest of all 19th-century folk operas, *The Bartered Bride* (1863–70), which is prized for its richly inventive dances and varied orchestration. His style is primitive in that he had only limited resources and beside Dvořák, for example, he can seem rather crude. At his best he used these resources to brilliant effect and even extended the harmonic palette he had borrowed from Liszt, one of his mentors. Deafness forced him to resign his directorship of the Provisional Theatre in 1874. One of the earliest signs of this deafness, a high-pitched whistling, was incorporated into his autobiographical string quartet *From my Life* (1876).

ANTONIN DVORAK (1841–1904)
Born Nelahozeves, Bohemia; died Prague

∞ Dvořák was introduced to the flowering of Czech nationalism early in his life when he played under Smetana at the Prague National Theatre. In common with many composers of his time, Dvořák had operatic ambitions that were often doomed to failure, and like the rest of Europe he was passionately affected by Wagner. His real

genius lay elsewhere, not least in the Slavonic Dances (1878, 1886), where

Lutoslawski (see page 62): noted for his use of aleatoric techniques.

his astounding melodic genius was allowed to flourish unfettered by the demands of traditional forms. Only late in his career, notably in the last two symphonies and Cello Concerto (1889, 1893, 1895), did he finally manage to shake off the influence of Brahms and Wagner to create an authentic symphonic style that was distinctively his own. Dvořák was a key figure in musical nationalism and one of a tiny handful of composers outside the charmed inner circle of Brahms and his fellow Germans or Viennese to make a major contribution to the symphony and other traditional forms. Unlike Brahms he crossed over to the progressive style of Liszt: his tone poems are fine examples of the genre. In his personal life he followed Mozart's precedent of marrying the sister of his first true love.

LEOS JANACEK (1854–1928)
Born Hukvaldy, East Moravia; died Ostrava

∞ There have been many late developers in the history of Western music, but few match Janáček's sudden emergence at the age of 50 when his opera *Jenufa* was finally performed in Brno (1904); he was 62 when it was successfully produced in Prague. Most of the works by which Janáček is best known, and which most effectively reflect his unique voice, date from his sixties and later, including the celebratory Sinfonietta (1926) and all the mature operas which are now staples of the opera repertoire (for example, *The Makropoulos Case, The Cunning Little Vixen, Katya Kabanova* and *From the House of the Dead*). The sound of Janáček's music reflects his study of the speech rhythms of the Czech people, which are reproduced in his strongly naturalistic operas and instrumental works. He relied heavily on persistently repeated rhythms or motifs (ostinato) to generate motor rhythms that drive his music on, and his harmonic style is a rare combination of traditional and progressive

Dvořák: one of the few to challenge the supremacy of German symphonists.

features; it is rarely as dissonant as that of Bartók. There is a passionate lyricism in his music, doubtless fuelled late in life by his love for Kamila Stosslova, who was some 40 years his junior.

BELA BARTOK (1881–1945)
Born Nagyszentmiklós (then Hungary, now Romania); died New York

∞ Bartók began his career strongly under the influence of Strauss's *Also sprach Zarathustra* (1896), which unlocked his creative impulses and resulted in the tone poem *Kossuth* (1903). Liszt's music was also an inspiration, especially the *Hungarian Rhapsodies*, which seemed in the 19th century to define Hungarian folk traditions. After much investigation of real Hungarian folk music and neighbouring cultures, Bartók began to integrate folksong at a deeper level, thereby freeing himself once and for all from Germanic styles. He became a new type of nationalist composer with major implications for many others living in central Europe. The musical style Bartók developed in the 1920s incorporated a freer, more flexible concept of tonality that often eschewed the triadic system altogether and made extensive use of clusters and other dissonant sonorities.

Rhythmically, too, his music was liberated by the use of strong, asymmetrical schemes with terrific dynamic energy. In one of his last works, the Concerto for Orchestra (1943), we hear his genius for orchestration, which often deployed the pure, unblended sounds of instruments, thus breaking the link with Strauss and Wagner. His forced emigration to America after the Nazis invaded his country meant heartbreak and hardship. There are many stories of his extraordinary hearing, which enabled him to locate sounds way beyond the normal sensitivity of people.

KAROL SZYMANOWSKI (1882–1937)
Born Tymoszówka, Ukraine; died Lausanne

∞ One of many composers unattracted to the atonal and serial innovations of Schoenberg, Szymanowksi nevertheless experimented with musical styles, finally reaching a synthesis of Strauss, Debussy and the Polish inheritance that meant so much to him. He was greatly attracted to the exotic: his opera *King Roger* (1924) is a *tour de force* in musical luxuriance with intoxicating melodies in the lushest imaginable orchestral garb. He cannot claim a central position in

{ Ligeti: his highly personal idiom found a vast audience in the film *2001*. }

is impossible to forget the sight of the film's obelisk accompanied by the busy micro-polyphony of Ligeti's *Requiem* (1965). (Micropolyphony involves multi-layered strands of chromatic material whose superimposition produces dramatically changing densities and dynamics.) Often Ligeti bases an entire piece on a single rhythmic idea whose shifting textures resemble the minimalists. His most familiar works are orchestral, but he has refined his style to work equally well in a chamber context: the Second String Quartet (1968) shows how an intricate intervallic style, derived ultimately from Webern, can be used to create structures of great sophistication. Ligeti has recently tended to favour a more melodic style (like Penderecki), perhaps in response to the theatrical demands of opera; this trend is evident in *Le grand macabre* (1978). Ligeti has occasioned some amusing scandals, not least the premiere of *Poème symphonique* (1962) for 100 metronomes set at different tempos: it was not what the audience or critics had come to hear!

the development of 20th-century musical language, but on his own terms he is a rewarding figure and the most prominent Polish composer of the pre-war years.

WITOLD LUTOSLAWSKI (1913–94)
Born Warsaw; died Warsaw

∞ After first trying out different styles, including Webernian serialism, Lutoslawski evolved a free style that incorporated aleatoric elements, in which players improvise within strict boundaries provided by the composer, often prescribing melodic contour but not rhythm. These alternate in works such as *Livre* with fully notated passages to produce works of considerable breadth and integration. His harmonic style is generally atonal, yet there are anchor points, and he allows a huge range of notes sounding together (vertical aggregations) from clusters to triadic sonorities. His music often has a symphonic sweep, and he likes to bring his works to a gripping central climax. In his later compositions he became more conservative; while aleatoric passages still appear in the Third Symphony, they no longer hold a central position and instead he seems more concerned with developing melodies in a traditional manner.

IANNIS XENAKIS (1922)
Born Braïla, Romania

∞ One of the great dilemmas of 20th-century music has been the rift between theory and practice. One sometimes gets the impression that a doctorate at the very least is required before one can read and understand programme notes by some post-war composers. Xenakis at first seems to pose this problem in an extreme form: he based his compositions on the laws of probability (he trained as an engineer at Athens Polytechnic). He uses, among other models, Markovian chains, game theory, group theory and set theory to generate the notes and rhythms of his music. In fact the music communicates with astonishing force and directness; in the solo-violin piece *Mikka* (1972) the impression is of a single process driving the music towards ever greater assertiveness and dynamic emphasis. It is very emotional music – the listener cannot be left unaffected – and the range of sounds he draws from largely conventional instruments is overwhelming. Perhaps the power of Xenakis' musical personality grew as a result of his suffering in the war; he fought for the Greek Resistance, lost an eye, and narrowly escaped execution in 1945. He settled in Paris in 1947 and became a French national.

GYORGY LIGETI (1923)
Born Discöszentmáron, near Kolzsvár, Hungary (now Tîrnăveni, Romania)

∞ Ligeti shot to unprecedented fame when, without consulting him, director Stanley Kubrick used some of his compositions in the film *2001: A Space Odyssey*. Even now it

KRZYSZTOF PENDERECKI (1933)
Born Debiça, Poland

∞ One could accuse Penderecki of plagiarizing one work of Stockhausen and constantly reworking it. There is no denying the seminal influence of *Carré* (1960) on the Polish composer's work, yet to dismiss him as merely derivative would be unjust. After a period trying out the different avant-garde techniques of the 1950s, mainly derived from Webern (total serialism), Penderecki renewed his music by concentrating on sound for sound's sake. Significantly, he followed Ligeti and others into the electronic-music studios, producing one work, entitled *Psalmus* (1961), and like them he soon grew frustrated by the early technological means available to him, preferring to use acoustic instruments in radical ways. He incorporated various 'extra-musical' sounds such as hissing by vocalists and rustling paper in

{ Rimsky-Korsakov: a father-figure in Russian nationalism. }

his numerous orchestral, choral and operatic works. His work for 52 multiply-divided strings, *Threnody for the Victims of Hiroshima* (1960), is one of the most potent examples of his style, and the opera *The Devils of Loudun* (1969) is a gripping dramatic experience.

Russia

MIKHAIL GLINKA (1804–57)
Born near Smolensk; died Berlin

∞ The senior figure in Russian music and forefather of musical nationalism received lessons from the Irish composer John Field. He was fortunate enough to have been born into a wealthy family, so he did not suffer the privations of others attempting to succeed in a country dominated by Italian and French musicians. It was eventually through the opera *A Life for the Czar* (1836) that Glinka began the process of cultivating a genuinely national idiom, though inevitably there are many cosmopolitan features in the work as well, usually derived from Italian opera. Just as influential as his

operas, the short orchestra piece *Kamarinskaya* (1848) demonstrated to the Russians the importance of virtuoso orchestration and how to avoid Germanic symphonic development by repeating a theme against a changing background. His was a lasting influence on Russian music.

ALEXANDER PORFIR'YEVICH BORODIN (1833–87)
Born St Petersburg; died St Petersburg

∞ Many musicians over the years have divided their time between composing and a separate career, but few have excelled to such an extent in both as Borodin; among his achievements in the medical profession was the foundation of a School of Medicine for Women. His musical output is modest in quantity, high on quality. A melodic luxuriance in his works, only partly drawn from folk song, was reflected in the crassest way when a bevy of his most attractive tunes were plundered in the musical *Kismet*. Melodies in works such as the Second String Quartet (1876) are brought together in a sort of patchwork construction that is a long way from the German models that Glinka wrestled with in his few chamber works. Sadly his scientific work kept him

from finishing his most ambitious project, the opera *Prince Igor*. Fortunately Rimsky-Korsakov and Glazunov were able to do this for him after his death.

MILY ALEXEYEVICH BALAKIREV (1837–1910)
Born Nizhny-Novgorod; died St Petersburg

∞ Balakirev figures prominently in the history of Russian music on account of his own works in the nationalist idiom – although these have not had quite the same hold on posterity as those of his fellow countrymen – and of his leadership from 1861 of the famous group of Five (Cui, Borodin, Mussorgsky, and Rimsky-Korsakov). In addition he was of great assistance to Tchaikovsky, especially in his constructive criticism of *Romeo and Juliet* (1869). In common with many others in the nationalist school, Balakirev's imagination was frequently caught by the exotic sounds of the East, not least in the piano fantasy *Islamey* (1869–1902), which surpasses even Liszt's feats of virtuosity.

MODEST PETROVICH MUSSORGSKY (1839–81)
Born Karevo; died St Petersburg

∞ Mussorgsky's was one of the most original musical minds of the 19th century. His thorough absorption of the folk music of his country and rejection of traditional harmonic practice led to some damning criticism of his music by musicians, if not audiences, while his use of natural speech rhythms in his operas, part of the new realism, produced a major shift away from the conventions of the day (especially the old division into recitative and aria). *Boris Godunov* (1869–73) alone would have ensured his survival, but there are also works of a more popular character in which unorthodox sonorities ravish the ears: chief among these is the piano work *Pictures at an Exhibition* (1874). A curiosity about the way Mussorgsky's music has come down to us is the strange but undeniable fact that barely a single work of his has been performed as he wrote it, at least until recently; *Boris* was usually performed in a complete recomposition and re-orchestration by

Rimsky-Korsakov, and *Pictures* is still best known in the ornate orchestral garb donated by Ravel. We are now far more willing to accept his rather austere orchestration and idiosyncratic harmony. A rather isolated figure in his lifetime,

Mussorgsky succumbed to alcoholism, which seriously eroded his output in later years.

PYOTR IL'YICH TCHAIKOVSKY (1840–93)
Born Votkinsk; died St Petersburg

∾Tchaikovsky stands somewhat apart from his nationalist compatriots: his music owes as much to Mozart, Schumann, and Liszt as to the cult of Russian folk song. In spite of that, many of his symphonies incorporate folk song, often with the rhythmic kinks ironed out, as in the finale of the Fourth Symphony (1878). The music is recognizable for its overwhelming use of passionate, stirring melodies, many of which sound operatically inspired. Following Glinka's example, Tchaikovsky often develops a melody by repeating it over and over with changing accompaniment, generating climaxes of awesome power. When he finally found his feet as a symphonic composer he produced a handful of works that hold their own with any in the repertoire – far more so than his

Russian contemporaries – and his achievement percolated through into the 20th century via composers as disparate as Stravinsky and Britten. He was not as varied a harmonist as Mussorgsky, but he compensated for this in his magnificent orchestration. He was a lonely, often melancholy man, thwarted in his emotional life by the homophobia of his period; it is thought that his suicide may have been forced upon him as a result of an earlier sexual relationship with a nobleman.

NIKOLAY ANDREYEVICH RIMSKY-KORSAKOV (1844–1908)
Born Tikhvin; died Lyubensk

∾Rimsky-Korsakov has the misfortune to be regarded as the least talented of the composers considered in this section. This may be so, but he left a handful of orchestral works that are among the most colourful and exciting of the period, especially the ravishing evocation of the exotic sea adventures of Sheherazade (1888; his first career was in the navy), which extended Liszt's genre of the symphonic poem to a truly symphonic scale. He was a master of orchestration, and his melodic invention reflected his publication in 1876–77 of *100 Russian Folk-Songs*. He completed almost as many works by other composers as he started himself, including Borodin's *Prince*

Borodin: his highly attractive output ran alongside important medical work.

Igor and Mussorgsky's *Khovanshchina;* that he performed these tasks with such mastery makes him a well-nigh unique figure in Western music.

Scriabin: an interest in mysticism became significant to this intriguing composer's music in later years.

ALEXANDER SCRIABIN (1872–1915)
Born Moscow; died Moscow

∾In a country that produced many strikingly individual voices Scriabin still stands out, though his individuality took a while to emerge. Many of the early works show how complete his absorption in Chopin and Liszt had been, but even in the relatively early Piano Concerto in F sharp minor (1896) there are many traces of the elevated melodic style of the later works, and every now and again an adumbration of later harmonic innovations. By the first decade of the 20th century he had largely given up triadic tonality in favour of chords based on fourths, culminating in a harmonic system based around one chord, the fascinating Mystic Chord. The chord's title reflects Scriabin's preoccupation with theosophy and mysticism: all his works from 1908 were a preparation for a 'supreme ecstatic mystery' which would precede the apocalypse. The work that would have crowned these aspirations was, unsurprisingly, left unfinished.

SERGEI RACHMANINOV (1873–1943)
Born Semyonovo, Starorussky; died Beverly Hills, California

∾Stravinsky conjured up the classic image of Rachmaninov as six feet of Russian gloom, at least hinting at his position as the last of the great Russian Romantics. For many years some musicians considered him more a pianist who had struck lucky in a few works, notably the Second Piano Concerto (1901), but now with the help of recordings his reputation has never been higher. His music is easily distinguished by its melodic style, which is derived from Chopin, Tchaikovsky, and others, yet certain traits make it unique; a good

Rachmaninov: a late Romantic Russian whose highly characterful music has enjoyed a huge resurgence of popularity in recent years.

Russian Ballet, his skilful deployment **Prokofiev: with Shostakovich the key figure in 20th-century Russian music.** of material and rhythmic inventiveness already go way beyond anything composed by The Five. Every subsequent work added a new ingredient to the nationalist mix, culminating in *The Rite of Spring* (1913), the single most famous score of the century. A new level of dissonance was reached and any sense of a triadic tonic relinquished. As time moved on so did Stravinsky: he turned his back on Russian nationalism after he left the country and cultivated his Neo-Classical style, adapting the forms of the 18th century. After Schoenberg's death he felt able to adopt serialism, though his music never lost its unmistakable voice. Stravinsky recorded much of his output for posterity.

SERGEY PROKOFIEV (1891–1953)
Born Sontsovka, Ukraine; died Moscow

∞ Prokofiev began his composing career as a brash, angry young man, producing some quite deafening orchestral effects in the early symphonies and music-theatre works. We hear a strikingly dissonant style, often close to Stravinsky's *The Rite of Spring*, with strongly syncopated rhythms. For many years he lived away from the Soviet Union, but by 1933 he was receiving commissions from the Soviet authorities, and in 1936 he was back for good. By then his style had mellowed considerably, replacing anger with irony, dissonance with piquant harmonies, and aggressive rhythms with an effortless melodic style that triumphed in the ballet *Romeo and Juliet* (1936).

DMITRY SHOSTAKOVICH (1906–1975)
Born St Petersburg; died Moscow

∞ With a characteristic passion for secrecy the Russians have buried much of Shostakovich's biography; numerous letters

example is the deeply poetic melody that opens the Third Piano Concerto (1909). He had a profound sense of beauty, creating the most ravishing effects out of apparently simple musical ideas in fleeting moments which linger long in the memory. The melancholy described by Stravinsky almost led to Rachmaninov's undoing after the disastrous first performance of the First Symphony (1895), but hypnosis restored his confidence and he produced the masterly Second Piano Concerto.

IGOR STRAVINSKY (1882–1971)
Born Oranienbaum; died New York

∞ Stravinsky stands alongside Schoenberg, Picasso, le Corbusier, Joyce and a select handful of others as one of the great trend-setters of the 20th century. At first his music reflected the influence of Rimsky-Korsakov, his principal teacher, but even in his first unequivocal masterpiece, *The Firebird* (1910), composed for Diaghilev's

by him were snapped up by his family, presumably to prevent the exposure of revelations about his love life, so we are left with numerous photographs of the lonely-looking, myopic figure who narrowly survived the worst excesses of the Soviet regime. Caution seems to have got the better of him at key moments, for after Stalin precipitated the hasty withdrawal of his opera *Lady Macbeth of the Mtsensk District* (1932), accusing the composer of 'bourgeois formalism' (which meant anything Stalin did not like), Shostakovich composed the conservative Fifth Symphony (1937) with an ironic, yet obviously table-thumping finale. After his earlier thirst for experimentation in orchestration, harmony, and form (so much a feature of the Fourth Symphony, 1936) had been drummed out of him, irony seemed the best answer to self-expression. One finds in the late chamber music a withdrawn, deeply personal idiom that frequently recalls the Beethoven of the late string quartets. Shostakovich's music is rooted in Tchaikovsky and Mahler, but gets its own signature by the use of percussion (especially snare drum) and spiky rhythms in the fast movements, despairing instrumental solos in the slow ones.

ALFRED SCHNITTKE (1934)
Born Engel's

∞ Even during the latter years of the Soviet regime, composers had begun to investigate avant-garde techniques; when the Berlin

Wall came down in late 1989 a mass of highly original music bubbled to the surface. Schnittke, Denisov, Gubaidulina, and others were working in styles far removed from the conservative Shostakovich. It is difficult to pinpoint any one feature as an abiding Schnittke characteristic other than his dazzling diversity: tonal passages sounding like Mozart alternate with vast clusters, and there is an unquenchable dynamism. His powerful *Requiem* with its exultant Credo is a good example of his disparate but compelling style.

New Worlds

United States

CHARLES IVES (1874–1954)
Born Danbury, Conn.; died New York

∞ Ives was one of the great original minds of the century, a real pioneer in the best traditions of his country. His father, a bandmaster, brought his son up in a most unconventional manner, insisting that he sing a melody in E flat while he accompanied in C, and he would encourage people at camp meetings to sing in their own idiosyncratic way, regardless of the end result. No wonder that Ives junior experimented with microtones and cultivated a harmonic language that embraced atonality and polytonality. Perhaps his most celebrated trait, however, is his use of citation through the use of numerous fragments of popular song, dance, and so on, which are often superimposed in a manner striking in its anticipation of post-war compositional techniques. Although he lived to a ripe old age, ill health forced him to stop composing in 1928 (the remarkable Fourth Symphony dates from 1916). Throughout his creative career he worked in an insurance agency entitled Ives & Co., which he co-founded in 1906.

GEORGE GERSHWIN (1898–1937)
Born Brooklyn; died Hollywood

∞ Gershwin was born of Russian émigrés who had settled in the USA in the 1890s. From an early stage in his career he worked for Tin Pan Alley, producing a succession of hit songs which gave him the confidence to write his own musicals. What singles Gershwin out as a special figure in the 20th century is his immense success in the concert hall with works like *Rhapsody in Blue* (1924) for piano and orchestra. It imitates many features of the classical concerto in the dialogue between soloist and orchestra, and yet it also imports the flattened thirds and rhythms of jazz, making it a seminal crossover work. Gershwin's invention is instantly recognizable, and his harmony combines a wide range of elements from Debussy-like parallelisms to blues chords. As well as composing for the concert hall, he produced a full-length Negro opera, *Porgy and Bess* (1935), considered the beginning of a folk-opera genre; whatever its classification, it has a superabundance of unforgettable ideas. Gershwin was also fond of sport: one of the composers he met in friendly games of tennis in Hollywood was Schoenberg, no less.

AARON COPLAND (1900–90)
Born Brooklyn; died New York

∞ Copland represents the American sound more vividly and more eloquently than any other composer. Listen to any one of a dozen film scores and his influence is inescapable in the syncopated rhythms, the distinctive solo trumpet and widely-spaced string chords. Copland arrived at this style as a result of a process of simplification from his earlier works, and although in later life he returned to serialism and other progressive techniques, his music never lost its native voice. His ideal was to unite industrial America with the creative arts, hence the deliberate signs of popularization in works such as *El sálon México* (1936) and *Rodeo* (1942). Both are typical in their absorption of folk or popular elements, though none dwell on them to the extent of the ballet *Appalachian Spring* (1944), which

Ives: a brilliantly original pioneer of bitonality.

uses a famous Shaker tune. Copland worked on behalf of the Co-ordinator of Inter-American Affairs and State Department in the 1940s.

ELLIOTT CARTER (1908)
Born New York

∞ One of many American individualists, Carter grew up in a richly experimental climate. He was first encouraged by Ives, who recommended he go to Harvard, where he studied with Piston and Holst. Along with many other American composers, he sought and found nourishment in Paris under the tutelage of Nadia Boulanger, the greatest composition teacher of the century. Slowly his compositional technique matured through working with Neo-Classicism after Stravinsky, serialism after Webern, and other contemporary techniques. His mature music makes use of a technique called 'metric modulation' in which a new metric scheme comes into being after first working against the old one in cross-rhythms; the First String Quartet (1951) includes excellent examples of this. Daunting technical descriptions should not prevent an appreciation of music that is brilliant in construction and often emotionally involving.

LEONARD BERNSTEIN (1918–90)
Born Lawrence, Mass.; died New York

∞ Early on Bernstein established himself as a conductor of enormous vitality. He was recognized by the veteran conductor of the Boston Symphony Orchestra, Serge Koussevitzky, and eventually succeeded Dmitri Mitropoulos at the New York Philharmonic in 1957, so embarking on his finest period at the podium. He also played piano in concertos and accompanied the likes of Dietrich Fischer-Dieskau and Christa Ludwig in Lieder recitals. He composed for both Broadway and the concert hall, prompting critics to claim that he tried to do too much. His phenomenal energy was not always as well focused as it might have been; it surely accounts for his own frustration with his failure to compose serious music of the quality to which he aspired. Nevertheless, he followed Gershwin in bridging the gap between popular and serious music, incorporating, for example, jazz into his symphonies. *West Side Story* (1957), his masterpiece, provides abundant evidence of his melodic gifts.

STEVE REICH (1936)
Born New York

∞ Reich is a key figure in the evolution of more accessible music styles in the post-war years. His solution is founded on gradual changes in musical time, often referred to as 'process music' or 'minimalism'. His music sounds remarkably simple in harmonic terms, and melodic features may be no more than a handful of notes; yet the subtly shifting rhythmic patterns and resultant transformations ensure that the surface of the music is never bland. His influence has been enormous and he has been much imitated.

Australia

PERCY GRAINGER (1882–1961)
Born Brighton, Melbourne; died White Plains, New York

∞ If some composers easily find their true métier in their music, there are many of near-genius who

> **Villa-Lobos infused Baroque counterpoint with Romantic melodies and folk styles.**

sometimes have to struggle. Grainger was an extraordinarily gifted writer, pianist, ethnomusicologist and composer, whose enduring legacy appears to be such delightful but rather slight pieces as the evergreen *Country Gardens* (folk song arrangement, 1918) and *Handel in the Strand* (1930). Their tunefulness and wit are obvious attractions, but there is much more to Grainger. His fascination with new sonorities and intensive research into folk song – he was the first to use wax cylinders to record it 'on the ground' – produced many serious works, including the haunting *The Lonely Desert-man Sees the Tents of the Happy Tribes* (1914–49). He was among the first 20th-century composers to specify 'elastic scoring', meaning works for which the instrumentation can be varied; *Harvest Hymn* (1906), scored for anything from two instruments (violin and piano) to orchestra, is a good example. He was a complex man: idealistic, energetic, generous, and possessed of a taste for sado-masochism.

Brazil

HEITOR VILLA-LOBOS (1887–1959)
Born Rio de Janeiro; died Rio de Janeiro

∞ Every so often a very accomplished composer achieves public acclaim, sometimes by chance, with a single composition. In Villa-Lobos' case this occurred in a series of works entitled *Bachianas Brasileiras*, especially in the Fifth (1938), which is ravishingly scored for soprano (who sings, hums, and vocalizes) and at least eight cellos, the composer's own instrument (he was in various symphony orchestras and played under Strauss in 1920). Villa-Lobos fuses Baroque counterpoint with a Romantic melodic line, the whole subtly infused with Brazilian folk song and dance. Later on his music became a vehicle for virtuoso display, as his Guitar Concerto (1951) vividly demonstrates. He was honoured in his country as the leading representative of Brazilian music and was fêted elsewhere as well, including France and the United States.

Japan

TORU TAKEMITSU (1930)
Born Tokyo

∞ Takemitsu freely explored various avant-garde techniques before arriving at his mature style, including musique concrète, electronic music, free improvisations, and experiments with visual presentation resembling today's 'installations'. The control of sound is central to Takemitsu's approach. Pieces evolve from the sonic material in ways that seem to have little to do with techniques related, for instance, to serialism. Takemitsu's interest in silence as a compositional tool is also important and, with his free experimentation in the way music is presented, points to kinship with John Cage, whom Takemitsu worked with in 1964 (they gave lectures together and staged joint events). Takemitsu later cultivated an interest in traditional Japanese instruments, so broadening still further the fascinating sound world of his superbly crafted music; his *November Steps* of 1967 uses the biwa, a lute-like instrument, and shakuhachi, an end-blown notched flute.

Women and the Creative Gift

Elizabeth Maconchy saw her music as "an impassioned argument".

IN 1880 THE AMERICAN MUSIC CRITIC George Upton claimed: "It does not seem that woman will ever originate music in its fullest and grandest harmonic forms. She will always be the recipient and interpreter but there is little hope that she will be the creator".

SUCH CATEGORICAL STATEMENTS WERE common in the 19th century. They are less likely to be heard today as more and more music by women composers, from the Middle Ages right up to the present, is being heard in concert halls or on the radio and becoming available on CD. The truth is that women have always composed music, in spite of the obstacles in their way.

For much of the history of Western classical music most women were denied the education and opportunities that enabled composers to develop their careers. Learning how to translate musical ideas on to paper and then gaining access to the musicians, promoters and venues needed to communicate the finished work to an audience is a complex process. Excluded from universities, conservatoires, apprenticeships and other avenues through which male composers learned their trade, some women obtained a musical education by living and working in a convent. Many of the earliest women composers, such as Hildegard of Bingen (1098–1179) or Isabella Leonarda (1620–1704), were nuns who, in the absence of men, wrote the music needed for worship. Other women, such as Francesca Caccini (1587– c. 1640), a composer at the Florentine court, learnt to write or play music from fathers or other members of their families who worked as musicians.

Even if they managed to acquire a basic musical education, women were barred from jobs in the music profession that would further their careers and give them valuable experience of the musical

Clara Schumann with her husband Robert in 1850.

world. Although the situation varied from country to country and from century to century, most women were excluded from playing in professional orchestras, from positions within the Church and from prestigious teaching posts at conservatoires or universities. Women were also kept out of many of the societies and informal networks that gave male composers important contacts and opportunities, though in many instances they set up their own organizations – in Britain, for example, the Royal Society of Female Musicians (founded in 1839 'for the relief of its distressed members') or the Society of Women Musicians (1911–72).

For centuries, a woman's place in Western society (especially if she came from a middle- or upper-class background) was supposed to be in the home. Although young women were encouraged to learn to play, sing or maybe even compose a little, such accomplishments were only to be displayed to family, friends or future husbands. Public exposure, including publication, was seen as shameful. Fanny Hensel, Felix Mendelssohn's sister, was dissuaded from publishing her music by her family, and some of her early works were even published under her brother's name. When Felix was invited to perform at Buckingham Palace in 1842, Queen Victoria asked him to play a particular song.

• SOME MAJOR MUSICAL TALENTS •

∞ **Hildegard of Bingen (1098–1179)** The abbess of a 12th-century convent, Hildegard was a mystic, writer, preacher, visionary and scientist as well as a composer. She wrote both words and music for her hauntingly ecstatic liturgical vocal music.

∞ **Barbara Strozzi (1619–64)** Strozzi lived and worked in Venice, where she frequently sang her own music for private musical gatherings of writers and intellectuals. Her output consists of vocal chamber music – arias and cantatas – with vivid word painting and strikingly dramatic moments.

∞ **Fanny Mendelssohn Hensel** (1805–47) Hensel had the same early musical training as her more famous brother, Felix Mendelssohn. Discouraged by her family from regarding herself as a composer, she nevertheless wrote over 400 works including songs, piano pieces, choral works and chamber music such as her gloriously lyrical Piano Trio.

∞ **Clara Wieck Schumann (1819–96)** Best known as one of the leading pianists of her day, Clara Schumann – who married Robert Schumann – was also a talented composer. She concentrated on writing songs and piano pieces, although an early piano concerto, written when she was a teenager, is often performed.

∞ **Ethel Smyth (1858–1944)** The daughter of a British Army general, Smyth channelled her energetic and passionate musical talents into writing a series of six operas that were performed all over Britain, Europe and the United States. Her other works include a commanding Mass in D and some compelling vocal and chamber music.

∞ **Rebecca Clarke (1886–1979)** Clarke worked for much of her life as a viola player. Her sensuous and fiery music includes a Viola Sonata, a Trio and some exquisite songs.

∞ **Lili Boulanger (1893–1918)** Younger sister of the renowned French musician and teacher Nadia Boulanger, Lili Boulanger composed powerfully beautiful works such as *Du fond de l'abîme* for soloists, chorus and orchestra and the song cycle *Clarières dans le ciel*.

∞ **Elizabeth Maconchy (1907–94)** Elizabeth Maconchy described her music as "an impassioned argument". Central to her output is an important series of tightly-constructed and expressively lyrical string quartets.

---

believed that women's work expressed a particular energy and directness.

The determination of women composers throughout the ages has left an important legacy of exciting music and paved the way for the many women composers working today. From the wide-ranging drama of Thea Musgrave (b.1928) and the mystical other-worldliness of Sofia Gubaidulina (b.1931) to the extraordinary sound worlds of Meredith Monk (b.1942) and the sparkling invention of Judith Weir (b.1954), contemporary women work in a huge variety of genres and styles and speak with many different but equally powerful voices. ♪

He later wrote in his diary: "I was obliged to confess that Fanny had written the song (which I found very hard, but pride must have a fall)."

Many women refused to accept the widespread belief that they were mentally incapable of the sustained logical and creative thought needed for composition. In 1566 the composer Maddalena Casulana became the first woman to have her music produced by the newfangled printing press. In one of her volumes of beautifully expressive madrigals she declared that her music was written "to show the world . . . the vain error of men, who so much believe themselves to be the masters of the highest gifts of the intellect, that they think those gifts cannot be shared by women".

Unfortunately, other women accepted what they were told about themselves. In 1839 Clara Schumann wrote in her diary: "I once thought that I possessed creative talent, but I have given up this idea; a woman must not desire to compose – not one has been able to do it, and why should I expect to? It would be arrogance . . ."

It was also commonly believed that, if they did write music, women were only capable of producing pretty, graceful and undemanding pieces. When they refused to conform to these expectations, listeners were often dumbfounded. George Bernard Shaw, while a music critic, wrote in 1892: "When E. M. Smyth's heroically brassy overture to *Anthony and Cleopatra* was finished, and the composer called to the platform, it was observed with stupefaction that all that tremendous noise had been made by a lady."

This belief that women's music would and should mirror qualities that were regarded as 'feminine' lasted well into the 20th century. In recent years there has been much discussion as to whether women's compositions reflect a distinct 'woman's voice'. For her part, Ethel Smyth

Ethel Smyth: an energetic and impassioned musical talent.

A-Z of Composers

ABEL, CARL FRIEDRICH (1723–87) Born Cöthen; died London. Subject of a Gainsborough portrait, this distinguished bass viol player collaborated with J C Bach, the London Bach, in a series of subscription concerts. Composed principally chamber music and symphonies.

ADAM, ADOLPHE CHARLES (1803–56) Born and died in Paris. Best known for his ballet *Giselle* (1841), this prolific composer for the stage also worked as a critic and professor of composition at the Conservatoire.

ADAMS, JOHN (1947) Born Worcester, Mass. Adopted minimalist methods of Reich with great success. Noted for operas, especially *Nixon in China* (1987), and orchestral pieces.

ADDINSELL, RICHARD (1904–77) born and died London. Although successful as a composer of film and theatre music, Addinsell's reputation rests on just one barn-storming Romantic work, the *Warsaw Concerto* from the film *Dangerous Moonlight* (1940).

AHO, KALEVI (1949) Born Forssa. Finnish composer whose extensive symphonic forms are influenced by Shostakovich and Mahler.

ALBINONI, TOMASO GIOVANNI (1671–1751) Born and died in Venice, where he produced nearly 50 operas. A pioneer in the composition of solo-violin concertos, his instrumental works, including trio sonatas and concertos, were admired by J S Bach.

ALBRECHTSBERGER, JOHANN GEORG (1736–1809) Born Klosterneuberg, near Vienna; died Vienna. Though a composer of religious and instrumental works, his espousal of counterpoint in theoretical writings is now better known, as is his teaching: Beethoven is his most famous pupil.

ALKAN, CHARLES-VALENTIN (1813–88) Born and died in Paris. A pianist of considerable virtuosity, his staggeringly difficult music for that instrument has lately been revived.

ALLEGRI, GREGORIO (1582–1652) Born and died in Rome. Served as priest, tenor, and composer mainly of church music. Allegri's famous *Miserere* for solo quartet and five-part chorus was once the sole preserve of the Sistine Chapel Choir. It is now one of the most popular pieces of *a cappella* church music in existence.

ANDRIESSEN, HENDRIK (1892–1981) Born Haarlem; died Heemstede. Dutch composer, organist, and teacher best known for his numerous sacred choral works, operas, and symphonic music, including the 12-tone Fourth Symphony. His son, Louis (b.1939), studied with him and is an important avant-garde composer of the younger generation.

ANTHEIL, GEORGE (1900–59) Born Trenton, New Jersey; died New York. He styled himself *Bad Boy of Music* in his autobiography, reflecting the mechanistic, industrial music of his early years, notably the *Ballet mécanique* (1923–25) for eight Pleyela pianos, percussion, propeller and siren. His later works are more traditional.

ARENSKY, ANTON STEPANOVICH (1861–1906) Born Novgorod; died Terioki, Finland. Arensky's operas, one ballet, symphonies, piano and chamber music are musically related to Tchaikvosky's in their tuneful, cosmopolitan style.

ARNE, THOMAS AUGUSTINE (1710–78) Born and died London. Composed operas and oratorios, the most ambitious being his opera seria *Artaxerxes* (1762). Composed 'Rule Britannia!'.

ARNOLD, MALCOLM HENRY (1921) Born Northampton. Early experience as a trumpeter in the London Philharmonic and BBC Symphony orchestras is reflected in the great brilliance of his orchestration in six symphonies, concertos and other works, many of an unabashedly popular nature.

AUBER, DANIEL-FRANCOIS-ESPRIT (1782–1871) Born Caen, died Paris. Remembered for around forty operas (mostly comic), of which *Fra Diavolo* (1830) is the most frequently performed. His works at times show the influence of Rossini.

AURIC, GEORGES (1899–1983) Born Lodeve; died Paris. After studying at the Paris Conservatoire and then with d'Indy at the Schola Cantorum, Auric joined 'Les six'. Like Poulenc he fell under Stravinsky's spell in his piano music, songs, orchestral works and highly successful film music, of which he composed a great deal.

BABBITT, MILTON (1916) Born Philadelphia. Pupil of Roger Sessions. Influenced by Webern and himself an influential part of American music's intellectual backbone. Composes in various genres, including opera and tape.

BACH, CARL PHILIPP EMANUEL (1714–88) Born Weimar, died Hamburg. Developed *Empfindsamer* (expressive) style in reaction to lightweight rococo style. Vital influence on early Classical period. Wrote symphonies, sonatas and diverse choral works.

BACH, JOHANN CHRISTIAN (1735–82) Born Leipzig; died London. The youngest son of J S Bach, he became the 'English Bach'. He wrote operas and instrumental music which were the main influence on the young Mozart.

BACH, WILHELM FRIEDEMANN (1710–84) Born Weimar; died Berlin. Bach's eldest son and recipient of the master's *Clavier-Büchlein* was a prolific and distinguished composer in a wide range of genres, including the symphony.

BADINGS, HENK (1907) Born Java. Dutch composer working in a wide range of traditional forms. Badings has also tried his hand at electronic composition, as in the radio opera *Orestes* (1954).

BALFE, MICHAEL WILLIAM (1800–70) Born Dublin; died Rownes Abbey, England. Leading composer of opera in 19th-century England. *The Bohemian Girl* (1843) is remarkable for the simple allure of its ballads.

BARBER, SAMUEL (1910–81) Born West Chester, Pennsylvania; died New York. Singer, pianist, conductor and composer who wrote mostly for the concert hall. The Adagio from his String Quartet (1936) is his best-known work and exhibits his warm, lyrical style.

BARBIERI, FRANCISCO ASENJO (1823–94). Born and died Madrid. Composer of some 60 *zarzuelas*, all of which are deeply permeated by Spanish folk idioms.

BARRAQUE, JEAN (1928–73) Born Puteaux, Seine; died Paris. A pupil of Jean Langlais and Messiaen, he worked with the ORTF Groupe de Musique Concrète. Barraqué's Piano Sonata is an impressively dense and exciting work.

BAX, SIR ARNOLD (1883–1953) Born Streatham, London; died Cork. Composer and poet. His music was influenced by Ireland and its folklore. Principal orchestral works include the haunting tone poem *Tintagel* (1919) and seven symphonies.

BEACH, AMY MARCY (1867–1944) Born Henniker, New Hampshire; died New York. Beach was one of several American symphonists who drew on the German Romantic traditions represented by Dvořák, Brahms. Later she was drawn to the impressionists.

BENDA, GEORG (1722–95) Born Staré Benátky; died Köstritz. Benda came from one of Bohemia's most accomplished musical families. He produced numerous works ranging from operettas to chamber music, Mozart and many others admired his pioneering trio of melodramas, notably *Ariadne auf Naxos* and *Medea* (1755).

BENJAMIN, ARTHUR (1893–1960) Born Sydney; died London. Benjamin is not alone in being best known for an occasional piece, namely his popular *Jamaican Rumba*, which has tended to conceal his symphonies, chamber music and plentiful film music. His sense of humour is evident in his several operas

BENNETT, SIR WILLIAM STERNDALE (1816–75) Born Sheffield; died London. Close in spirit and style to Mendelssohn, Bennett's music has been neglected in the 20th century in spite of its fresh invention and excellent craftsmanship. The piano concertos are representative.

BERIO, LUCIANO (1925) Born Oneglia, Imperia. Italian avant-garde composer who studied with Luigi Dallapiccola, sharing his preference for serialism. The impressive *Visage* (1961) combines electronic and vocally-produced human sounds.

BERKELEY, SIR LENNOX (1903–89) Born near Boars Hill, Oxford; died London. An English composer with a marked taste for French music (he studied with Nadia Boulanger) and Stravinsky. Among his works, those for the human voice stand out, including his oratorio *Jonah* (1935).

∞ **BERTINI, HENRI-JEROME (1798–1876)** Born London; died near Grenoble. A prolific composer, especially of piano and chamber music, his studies for piano continue to attract pianists on account of their musical qualities.

∞ **BIBER, HEINRICH IGNAZ FRANZ VON (1644–1704)** Born Liberec; died Salzburg. A violinist and composer who produced works of great difficulty for his instrument, developing many of its technical possibilities. He wrote some astonishingly graphic programme music.

∞ **BIRTWISTLE, SIR HARRISON (1934)** Born Accrington, Lancs. Member of Manchester School, has composed with great success for orchestra, voice and chamber ensembles. A serious figure with strong harmonic individuality and increasing mastery of music theatre, he is one of the most fertile English composers of his generation.

∞ **BLOCH, ERNEST (1880–1959)** Born Geneva; died Portland, Oregon. Much of his work reflects his Jewish faith. Best known work is *Schelomo* (Solomon) for cello and orchestra (1915–16).

∞ **BLOW, JOHN (1649–1708)** Born Newark, Notts.; died Westminster, London. Organist at Westminster Abbey. Composed much vocal music including a collection of songs entitled *Amphion Anglicus*. Also wrote for harpsichord.

∞ **BOCCHERINI, LUIGI (1743–1805)** Born Lucca; died Madrid. Composer and cellist. Prolific composer of string quintets, quartets, trios, and other chamber music.

∞ **BOIELDIEU, FRANCOIS ADRIEN (1775–1834)** Born Rouen; died Jarcy. In common with so many French composers of the 19th century, Boieldieu concentrated on the operatic stage in his compositions, scoring notable triumphs with works such as *La Dame blanche* (1825). His harmonically simple, melodious style continues to strike a sympathetic chord on the rare occasions his operas are revived.

∞ **BOISMORTIER, JOSEPH BODIN DE (1689–1755)** Born Thionville; died Roissy-en-Brie. Ridiculed in his day for his prolixity, Boismortier grew wealthy on the success of his published works and was the first Frenchman to name a work 'concerto'.

∞ **BOITO, ARRIGO (1842–1918)** Born Padua; died Milan. Boito's collaboration with Verdi is one of the most famous in the history of opera and produced the librettos of *Otello* and *Falstaff*. He was also a critic, and composer of *Mefistofele* (1868), an uneven but often compelling Romantic opera.

∞ **BORRIS, SIEGFRIED (1906)** Born Berlin. One of Hindemith's earliest pupils in composition, Borris shows the influence of his master, though he also incorporates more popular elements.

∞ **BOTTESINI, GIOVANNI (1821–89)** Born Crema; died Parma. A curious career divided Bottesini between the double bass, on which he was one of the most remarkable players of all time, and the opera houses of Paris, Barcelona, Cairo and London where he conducted and composed operas.

∞ **BOULANGER, NADIA (1887–1979)** Born and died Paris. Boulanger, sister of Lili (see page 69), was the greatest composition teacher of the 20th century. Evident in her handful of compositions (she stopped composing early on in her life) are the same veiled

harmony and eloquent melodies found in Fauré and Debussy. More progressive influences on harmony and rhythm are caught in her most famous work, the Three Pieces for Cello and Piano (1913).

∞ **BOURGEOIS, LOYS (1510/15–c. 1560)** Born Paris. Bourgeois is remembered for his contribution to the Calvinist *Psalter* for which he arranged existing tunes and wrote some of his own.

∞ **BOYCE, WILLIAM (1711–79)** Born and died London. Organist and composer. Compositions include church music, odes and cantatas, symphonies, chamber music and music for the stage.

∞ **BRIAN, HAVERGAL (1876–1972)** Born Dresden, Staffs.; died Shoreham. The 'English Mahler' – a prolific but rarely performed composer of no fewer than 32 symphonies, several of which require monumental forces. His distinctive style, conservative in nature, is beginning to attract greater interest now thanks to recordings and performances at festivals.

∞ **BRIDGE, FRANK (1879–1941)** Born Brighton; died Eastbourne. Composer, viola player and conductor. Began in Romantic tradition but drifted away from it after the First World War. Later works show the influence of Schoenberg and other progressive trends.

∞ **BRUCH, MAX (1838–1920)** Born Cologne; died Friedenau, near Berlin. Compositions include symphonies, violin concertos, operas, chamber music and choral works. His setting of the Hebrew melody *Kol nidrei* for cello and orchestra and First Violin Concerto are well known.

∞ **BRUMEL, ANTOINE (c. 1460–c. 1515)** A master of sacred music and considered the first great French Renaissance composer. His music reflects changing tastes in its orientation to text and harmony.

∞ **BRUNETTI, GAETANO (1744–98)** Born ?Fano; died Colmenar de Orejo, near Madrid. Prolific composer of symphonies and chamber music who is now little known. Recent research points to works with many progressive features such as intensive motivic development.

∞ **BUCCHI, VALENTINO (1916–76)** Born Florence; died Rome. Pupil of Frizzi and Dallapiccola, his music is largely diatonic with an enticing element of play.

∞ **BUCZEK, BARBARA (1940)** Born Kraków. Studied at the Kraków Conservatory with Schaffer and subsequently won the Fitelberg Competition with two improvisations for ensemble, the *Dwie impresje*.

∞ **BUSONI, FERRUCCIO (1866–1924)** Born Empoli, near Florence; died Berlin. Composer and pianist who embraced both German and Italian traditions. Wrote operas, symphonic music, and made many arrangements and transcriptions.

∞ **BUXTEHUDE, DIETRICH (1637–1707)** Born ?Oldesloe, Holstein; died Lübeck. Important composer of cantatas and organ music who is seen as an important precursor of J S Bach, as well as rewarding in his own right. Bach once tramped many miles to hear him playing in Lübeck.

∞ **CABANILLES, JUAN BAUTISTA JOSE (1644–1712)** Born Algemesi, near Valencia; died Valencia. Spanish composer of organ music who

worked at Valencia Cathedral in his later years. His complete organ works were reprinted in a critical edition edited by H. Angles (1927–52).

∞ **CAGE, JOHN (1912–92)** Born Los Angeles; died New York. Recognized as the pioneer of the prepared piano. An experimenter and philosopher, he is notorious for his silent work *4'33"* (1952) in four movements for any instrument or group of instruments.

∞ **CALDARA, ANTONIO (1670–1736)** Born Venice; died Vienna. A significant figure in oratorio and opera, composing over a 100 works in the genres as well as church music.

∞ **CANTELOUBE, JOSEPH (1879–1957)** Born Annonay; died Gridny. Although Canteloube composed many original works, his main claim to fame now is his wonderfully lush settings of folksongs entitled *Chants d'Auvergne* (1923-30).

∞ **CARISSIMI, GIACOMO (1605–74)** Born Marini, near Rome; died Rome. Organist, priest, and one of the first important composers of oratorios. His colossal output included Masses, cantatas, motets and oratorios.

∞ **CARVER, ROBERT (C. 1490–AFTER 1546)** Scottish composer and canon of Scone Abbey. His output was mainly liturgical. Among his many intriguing works, the 19-part motet 'O bone Jesu' is worthy of mention.

∞ **CASELLA, ALFREDO (1883–1947)** Born Turin; died Rome. After a brief dalliance with the avant garde, Casella turned to neo-classicism between the wars, and figured prominently in Italian music. He also organized concerts, conducted, and played the piano.

∞ **CAVALLI, PIETRO FRANCESCO (1602–76)** Born Crema; died Venice. Singer and organist at St. Mark's, Venice, he wrote over 40 operas, among them *L'Egisto* (1643) and *La Calisto* (1652). As in Monteverdi's works the growing importance of the aria can be heard.

∞ **CHABRIER, EMMANUEL (1841–94)** Born Ambert; died Paris. Well-connected French composer whose passion for Wagner – evident in the opera *Gwendoline* (1885) – did not stifle his talent for the witty and picturesque, most obvious in *España* (1883).

∞ **CHARPENTIER, MARC-ANTOINE (?1645/50–1704)** Born and died Paris. His compositions include two operas, other stage music, and several oratorios, a form not otherwise much cultivated in France at the time.

∞ **CHAUSSON, ERNEST (1855–99)** Born Paris; died Limay. Studied with Franck and Massenet. Compositions are Romantic in style and include the distinctly Wagnerian opera *Le roi Arthus*. Died in a bicycle accident.

∞ **CHERUBINI, LUIGI (1760–1842)** Born Florence; died Paris. Wrote numerous operas which had a great impact in the 1790s, and influenced Beethoven's *Fidelio*; also some highly successful Masses. He published *Cours de contrepoint et de fugue* in 1835.

∞ **CILEA, FRANCESCO (1866–1950)** Born Palmi; died Varazze. Italian opera composer and teacher whose music follows in the Romantic tradition. *Adriana Lecouvreur* (1902), his best known work, is typical of his attractive but limited melodic style.

∞ **CIMA, GIOVANNI PAOLO (c. 1570– AFTER 1622)** Early exponent of trio sonata and a major figure in Milanese musical life in the 17th century.

∞ **CIMAROSA, DOMENICO (1749–1801)** Born near Naples; died Venice. His greatest achievement was his opera *Il Matrimonio Segreto* (1792), a witty, attractive work that reflects the influence of Mozart's da Ponte operas. It is regularly revived.

∾ **CLARKE, JEREMIAH (c. 1674–1707)** Born ?; died London. A romantic fate befell this prolific composer and organist: after being refused in love, he shot himself in the house in St Paul's Churchyard (he was organist there). His current familiarity rests solidly on a keyboard piece entitled 'The Prince of Denmark's March', known as 'Trumpet Voluntary' and for many years mistakenly attributed to Purcell.

∾ **CLEMENTI, MUZIO (1752–1832)** Born Rome; died Evesham, England. A composer-pianist, the first in a line that led directly to Liszt and Chopin, Clementi later turned to publishing and piano manufacture. His piano sonatas influenced Beethoven and many of his works continue to be assiduously practised by students of the instrument.

∾ **COATES, ALBERT (1882–1953)** Born St Petersburg; died Cape Town. A Yorkshireman who made his name both as a conductor – he was one of the finest Wagner conductors of his day – and as a composer of opera, including *Samuel Pepys* (1929) and *Pickwick* (1936).

∾ **COATES, ERIC (1886–1957)** Born Hucknall; died Chichester. Coates preferred to write in a light style and encompassed many famous potboilers in his output, not least the stirring *The Dam Busters* march. His famous and exquisitely-finished *London* Suite (1933) is as quintessentially English in character as any work by his contemporary Vaughan Williams.

∾ **COUPERIN, LOUIS (c. 1626–61)** Born Chaumes; died Paris. Louis was uncle of François 'le grand' Couperin and a representative of one of the really great musical families of France, which played its part in the country's culture for almost two centuries. His keyboard works are of outstanding quality and had widespread influence.

∾ **COWELL, HENRY (1897–1965)** Born Menlo Park, Calif.; died Shady, New York. Experimental composer, developed tone-cluster technique, and incorporated new ideas in book *New Musical Resources* (1930). His works include 21 symphonies and a series of pieces entitled *Hymn and Fuguing Tunes*.

∾ **CRAMER, JOHANN BAPTIST (1771–1858)** Born Mannheim; died London. A major virtuoso pianist who studied with Clementi and composed piano studies that are still used by students. His other works involving the piano are largely neglected.

∾ **CRESTON, PAUL (1906–85)** Born New York; died San Diego. Organist, composer and theorist who began life as a bank clerk. His works include five symphonies in a fairly conservative harmonic idiom, and a Chthonic Ode for percussion, piano and strings which reflects his interest in unusual instrumental combinations.

∾ **CRUMB, GEORGE (1929)** Born Charleston, W. Virginia. Crumb has set only the verse of Lorca, using numerous vocal and instrumental effects. *Black Angels* (1970) is composed for the exotic combination of 'electric' string quartet.

∾ **CUI, CESAR (1835–1918)** Born Vilnius; died Petrograd. Cui's cosmopolitan musical bias did not prevent his being the fifth member of the famous Five 'nationalist' composers led by Balakirev. He was also a critic, a general and an authority on fortification.

∾ **CZERNY, CARL (1791–1857)** Born and died Vienna. Counting among his pupils Liszt, Czerny was a great virtuoso whose series of piano studies still form the backbone of many a budding pianist's technique.

His work list runs into four figures and encompasses virtually every genre of the time

∾ **DALAYRAC, NICOLAS-MARIE (1753–1809)** Born Muret, Haute Garonne; died Paris. Very popular and refined composer of nearly 60 comic operas.

∾ **DALLAPICCOLA, LUIGI (1904–75)** Born Pisino d'Istria (then in Austria); died Florence. Italian serialist. Much of his music is vocal, including two operas; he also wrote instrumental music.

∾ **DELIBES, LEO (1836–91)** Born St Germain-du-Val, died Paris. Held many organist appointments. Notable works are *Lakmé* (opera, 1883) and the hugely popular ballets *Sylvia (1876)* and *Coppelia* (1870).

∾ **DELIUS, FREDERICK (1862–1934)** Born Bradford; died Grez-sur-Loing. Romantic composer of mainly operatic, choral, and orchestral music. He was inspired by negro music. Rich chromatic harmonies and lush orchestration make his music unmistakeable.

∾ **DESSAU, PAUL (1894–1979)** Born Hamburg; died Berlin. German composer who worked with Bertolt Brecht in East Germany. He also wrote children's operas and film music.

∾ **DEVIENNE, FRANCOIS (1759–1803)** Born Joinville, Haute-Marne; died Paris. An important composer for the French Revolution, Devienne also contributed greatly to the literature of the flute, his principal instrument.

∾ **DITTERSDORF, CARL DITTERS VON (1739–99)** Born Vienna; died near Neuhof, Bohemia. Brilliantly successful composer of the Classical period and friend of Haydn. The opera *Doktor und Apotheker* (1786) is still revived from time to time.

∾ **DOHNANYI, ERNO (1877–1960)** Born Pozsony; died New York. The witty *Variations on a Nursery Song* (1913) clearly show his preference for German Romanticism over the Hungarian nationalism of his contemporary and compatriot Kodály. After a career as a concert pianist, he settled into teaching at Florida University.

∾ **DOTZAUER, FRIEDRICH (1783–1860)** Born Häselrieth, near Hildburghausen; died Dresden. Dotzauer contributed greatly to the evolution of the cello as a teacher, player, and composer, hence the 'Dresden School'; his music is largely forgotten now.

∾ **DOWLAND, JOHN (1563–1626)** Born and died London. His four books of 'Songes or Ayres' (1597–1603) were major contributions to the art of song.

∾ **DUKAS, PAUL (1865–1935)** Born and died Paris. Composer and critic. Notable works in the impressionist manner are the opera *Ariane et Barbe-bleue* (1907), tone poem *The Sorcerer's Apprentice* (1897) and ballet *La péri* (1912).

∾ **DUNI, EGIDIO ROMOALDO (1709–75)** Born near Naples; died Paris. Duni achieved international acclaim in the 18th century as a composer of French comic opera.

∾ **DUPARC, HENRI (1848–1933)** Born Paris; died Mont-de-Marsan. Pupil of Franck. Principally remembered for just sixteen wonderful songs, including *L'invitation au voyage* and *Phidylé*. Ceased composing after 1885 due to ill health.

∾ **DUPRE, MARCEL (1886–1971)** Born Rouen; died Meudon. Major French organist and organ composer who took on Widor's mantle (see page 79). His tonal idiom is enriched by bitonality and chromaticism.

∾ **DUREY, LOUIS EDMOND (1888–1979)** Born Paris; died St Tropez. Durey was a member of 'Les six', which he left in 1921. His best works, now rather neglected, are for chamber combinations.

∾ **DURUFLE, MAURICE (1902–86)** Born Louviers; died Paris. Duruflé's Requiem (1947) and several other sacred pieces continue to receive many performances, thanks to their distinctive modal melodies and harmony.

∾ **DUSSEK, JAN LADISLAV (1760–1812)** Born Caslav; died near Paris. An outstanding pianist at a time when the instrument was gaining hugely in popularity, Dussek wrote many concertos, trios, and sonatas for piano that are precursors of Romanticism.

∾ **EIMERT, HERBERT (1897–1972)** Born Bad Kreuznach; died Cologne. A major theorist who first systematically defined the twelve-tone system. Founder of the Cologne studio where so many avant-garde composers worked in the 1950s. His electronic compositions are among the earliest examples of sound synthesis.

∾ **EISLER, HANNS (1898–1962)** Born Leipzig; died Berlin. Eisler's works were proscribed by the Nazis and he was deported by the US government for his political views. He finally found a home in Vienna where he continued to compose film and theatre music.

∾ **ENESCU (ENESCO), GEORGE (1881–1955)** Born Botosani district (Romania); died Paris. Best known for his Lisztian Rumanian Rhapsodies, which represent only one side of his nationalism, Enescu was an accomplished composer in most standard forms as well as a violinist, conductor and teacher.

∾ **ERB, DONALD (1927)** Born Youngstown, Ohio. American composer whose works mix jazz, neo-classical, aleatory and other ingredients.

∾ **ERNST, HEINRICH WILHELM (1814–65)** Born Brno; died Nice. Virtuoso violinist in Paganini's wake – his works are still played occasionally.

∾ **FARKAS, FERENC (1905)** Born Nagykanizsa. Farkas has written extensively for the theatre in a cosmopolitan style that reveals his studies with Resphigi and his work collecting Hungarian folksongs.

∾ **FARNABY, GILES (c. 1563–1640)** Died London. A minor but vital figure from the golden age of English music whose canzonets and keyboard variations have many individual features.

∾ **FAURE, GABRIEL (1845–1924)** Born Pamiers; died Paris. Composer, organist, teacher. Fastidious French Romantic composer with sensuously lyrical style. Excelled in writing piano music and songs. His Requiem and chamber music also retain their appeal.

∞ **FELDMAN, MORTON (1926–87)** Born New York; died Buffalo. Feldman first came under the influence of Cage, who encouraged him to experiment with notation in the *Projection* (1951) series, but later he reverted to traditional means while retaining a strongly individual voice.

∞ **FERNEYHOUGH, BRIAN (1943)** Born Coventry. English composer who took his lead from Stockhausen and Boulez, producing serial works of breathtaking brilliance and complexity, especially for piano.

∞ **FIBICH, ZDENEK (1850–1900)** Born near Všebořice, Bohemia; died Prague. Czech composer trained largely in German tradition which he followed through his short but prolific compositional career.

∞ **FIELD, JOHN (1782–1837)** Born Dublin; died Moscow. Pianist and composer. Invented style and name 'nocturne' for a solo piano piece, and influenced Chopin. Wrote seven piano concertos which have been revived of late.

∞ **FILS, ANTONIN (1733–60)** Born Eichstätt, Bavaria; died Mannheim. Filtz was a leading cellist in the seminal Mannheim orchestra led by Johann Stamitz. He contributed to the vast output of symphonies by composers at the court.

∞ **FINNISSY, MICHAEL (1946)** Born London. Finnissy identifies in his music with the European avant-garde, employing many novel instrumental effects and dense textures.

∞ **FINZI, GERALD (1901–56)** Born London; died Oxford. English composer in pastoral tradition whose text setting is remarkable for its sensitivity and emotional range.

∞ **FIORILLO, FEDERIGO (1755–AFTER 1823)** Born Brunswick. Although his work-list is a long one, Fiorillo is remembered for one collection now, the 36 caprices for violin.

∞ **FISCHER, JOHANN CASPAR FERDINAND (c. 1623–1746)** Died Rastatt. German composer of Bohemian origin. He drew on French influences in his orchestral suites and anticipated Bach's '48' in his *Ariadne musica* (1702), a collection of 20 preludes and fugues in different keys for organ.

∞ **FLOTOW, FRIEDRICH (1812–83)** Born Teutendorf, near Neu-Santiz; Mecklenburg-Schwerin, died Darmstadt. Contemporary of Wagner whose operatic output leans towards France, especially in *Martha*, whose charming, *opéra-comique* character was once exceedingly popular.

∞ **FOSTER, STEPHEN COLLINS (1826–64)** Born Pittsburgh; died New York. Immensely popular composer of popular songs which are inseparable from American culture. *My Old Kentucky Home* (1853) and *Old Folks at Home* (1851) were adopted as official state songs for Kentucky and Florida respectively.

∞ **FRESCOBALDI, GIROLAMO (1583–1643)** Born Ferrara; died Rome. Italian organist and composer. His keyboard compositions, including ricercares, fugues, toccatas and capriccios, stand beside those of Sweelinck as the most important of the early 17th century.

∞ **FUX, JOHANN JOSEPH (1660–1741)** Born Hirtenfeld, Styria; died Vienna. Conservative composer in polyphonic style who marks the climax of the Austrian Baroque. He established a method for teaching Palestrina-style counterpoint in his *Gradus ad Parnassum* (1725) that is still taught.

∞ **GABRIELI, ANDREA (1533–85)** Born and died Venice. One of an influential succession of organists at St Mark's Cathedral, Venice, who contributed to the Venetian choral style that culminated in the work of Andrea's nephew, Giovanni.

∞ **GABRIELI, GIOVANNI (c. 1553/6–1612)** Born and died Venice. Giovanni composed motets for elaborate combinations of voices and instruments, often exploiting the spatial layout of St Mark's, Venice. He was extremely influential, even attracting the great German composer Schütz to study with him.

∞ **GADE, NIELS (1817–90)** Born and died Copenhagen. Important figure in nascent nationalism. Influenced by Mendelssohn and Schumann. Wrote piano solos and songs, chamber music, a concerto, symphonies, overtures and cantatas.

∞ **GALUPPI, BALDASSARE (1706–85)** Born Burano, near Venice; died Venice. Composed mainly for the opera house and vital in the development of *opera buffa*, he also became maestro di capella at St Marks in 1762. An imaginary toccata by Galuppi was the subject of a poem by Browning.

∞ **GEMINIANI, FRANCESCO (1687–1762)** Born Lucca; died Dublin. Geminiani was one of many continental composers to make his career – as a violinist and prolific composer – in England and later in Dublin. His long list of works includes a number of important treatises on performance.

∞ **GERHARD, ROBERTO (1896–1970)** Born Valls, Catalonia; died Cambridge. Spanish composer who settled in England. After studying with Schoenberg he pursued serialism, though he always placed great emphasis on tone colour and rhythm in his five symphonies and many works for stage and concert hall.

∞ **GESUALDO, CARLO, PRINCE OF VENOSA (c. 1561–1613)** Born ?Naples; died Gesualdo, Avellino. Renowned for the murder of his first wife and her lover. Composed madrigals, motets and a book of responsoria in advanced chromatic language that fascinated Stravinsky.

∞ **GINASTERA, ALBERTO (1916–83)** Born Buenos Aires; died Geneva. A key figure in Argentina's musical life, Ginastera drew on folk styles and legends for his music. The ballet *Panambí* (1940) is based on a South American Indian legend.

∞ **GIORDANO, UMBERTO (1867–1948)** Born Foggia, died Milan. Italian opera composer whose music took its cue from Leoncavallo's exciting new *verismo* style. *Andrea Chenier* (1896) and *Fedora* (1898) are his best-known works.

∞ **GLASS, PHILIP (1937)** Born Baltimore. Glass's minimalist style owes something to Reich, but his music is more extrovert in character. He has had several important successes in the opera house, including *Einstein on the Beach* (1976).

∞ **GLAZUNOV, ALEXANDER KONSTANTINOVICH (1865–1936)** Born St Petersburg; died Paris. Glazunov first found favour with the nationalists in Russia, but later his style became more typical of the European mainstream.

∞ **GLIER, REYNGOL'D MORITSEVICH (1875–1956)** Born Kiev; died Moscow. Glier was an establishment figure in Soviet musical life, writing in a conservative idiom considerably enlivened by virtuoso orchestration.

∞ **GODOWSKY, LEOPOLD (1870–1938)** Born near Soshly, Vilnius; died New York. Godowsky was an heir to the piano tradition of Liszt, producing compositions and transcriptions that still dazzle audiences.

∞ **GOEHR, ALEXANDER (1932)** Born Berlin. Member of Manchester School, he studied with Messiaen, though the New Viennese School shaped his musical language. Works include an opera, *Arden Must Die* (1967), and orchestral, chamber and vocal works.

∞ **GOLDMARK, CARL (1830–1915)** Born Keszthely; died Vienna. A composer in the Austrian Romantic tradition, Goldmark is chiefly remembered for his opera *The Queen of Sheba* (1875) and the delightful *Rustic Wedding* symphony.

∞ **GOLDSCHMIDT, BERTHOLD (1903)** Born Hamburg. Composer and conductor who settled in Britain during the Nazi period. His opera *Der gewaltige Hahnrei* (1930) is characteristic of his dark, brittle tonal style.

∞ **GORECKI, HENRYK (1933)** Born Czernica, Silesia. Górecki has, through the great expressive range of his choral and orchestral music, found a central place in contemporary Polish music. His Third Symphony is now one of the most popular 'classical' works of the century.

∞ **GOSSEC, FRANCOIS-JOSEPH (1734–1829)** Born Vergnies, Hainaut; died Paris. Gossec began life as a cowherd and was taken under the wing of Rameau to become one of Paris's most successful musical figures. He was France's first major symphonist.

∞ **GOTTSCHALK, LOUIS MOREAU (1829–69)** Born New Orleans; died Tijuca, Brazil. Gottschalk was a composer-pianist whose playing was compared with Chopin's. A handful of his works appear in recitals from time to time.

∞ **GOUNOD, CHARLES FRANCOIS (1818–93)** Born Paris; died St Cloud. Best known for *Faust* (1859), one of the most successful operas of all time. He also wrote church music and symphonies.

∞ **GRAUN, CARL HEINRICH (1703/4–59)** Born Wahrenbrück; died Berlin. Graun wrote a large number of operas, oratorios, Passions, cantatas and other choral music. His most famous opera is *Montezuma* (1755).

∞ **GRETRY, ANDRE-ERNEST-MODESTE (1741–1813)** Born Liège; died Paris. Brilliantly successful composer of comic opera who fused the best elements of Italian opera with French conventions.

∞ **GRIFFES, CHARLES T. (1884–1920)** Born Elmira, New York; died New York. Leant towards French impressionism. He wrote some striking music, including *The Pleasure Dome of Kubla Khan*.

∞ **GROFE, FERDE (1892–1972)** Born New York; died Santa Monica. Arranger for the Paul Whiteman Orchestra and orchestrator of Gershwin's *Rhapsody in Blue* (1924), Grofé wrote mainly light music. His *Symphony in Steel* uses, among other 'instruments', four pairs of shoes and pneumatic drill. His *Grand Canyon* Suite (1931) is still popular.

∞ **GRUTZMACHER, FRIEDRICH (1832–1903)** Born Dessau; died Dresden. Editor, performer and composer of music for the cello. A few of his works are still played occasionally, especially the studies.

∞ **GUERRERO, FRANCISCO (1528–99)** Born and died Seville. Stands alongside Victoria as the leading composer of sacred music in Spain in the 16th century. His numerous works display a sensuous, ecstatic vision that is typically Spanish.

∞ **GURNEY, IVOR (1890–1937)** Born Gloucester,;died Dartford. Although a poet too, Gurney's main achievement is his sensitive settings of English poetry in his songs.

∞ **GYROWETZ, ADALBERT (1763–1850)** Born Ceske Budějovice; died Vienna. Part of the European symphony industry, Gyrowetz contributed 60 symphonies in the Haydn manner and produced an opera on the subject of Hans Sachs half a century before Wagner.

∞ **HALEVY, FROMENTAL (1799–1862)** Born Paris; died Nice. Halévy taught an entire generation of French composers, including Gounod, Bizet and Saint-Saëns, and his numerous operas attracted praise from Berlioz and Wagner, not least for their orchestration.

∞ **HANSON, HOWARD (1896–1981)** Born Wahoo, Nebraska; died Rochester, New York. American symphonist who wrote in a conservative style. His opera *Merry Mount* was produced at the Metropolitan Opera, New York in 1934. He wrote five symphonies as well as songs, chamber, orchestral and piano music.

∞ **HARRIS, ROY (1898–1979)** Born Lincoln County, Oklahoma; died Santa Monica. Prolific composer. Rugged, characterful music in diatonic idiom draws on folksong and hymns. Composed in most forms.

∞ **HAUER, JOSEF MATTHIAS (1883–1959)** Born Wiener Neustadt; died Vienna. Hauer developed a system of composition in his works related to, but independent of, Schoenberg's. The animosity of the two men towards each other is renowned.

∞ **HAYDN, JOHANN MICHAEL (1737–1806)** Born Rohrau; died Salzburg. Sadly eclipsed by his famous brother Joseph, Michael was a wide-ranging composer whose music has periodically been mistaken for Joseph's. He served under the Archbishop of Salzburg at the same time as the Mozarts.

∞ **HEINICHEN, JOHANN DAVID (1683–1729)** Born Krössuln, near Weissenfels; died Dresden. German Baroque composer and theorist who spent much of his life in Dresden as Kapellmeister. His music is thoroughly international in style.

∞ **HELLER, STEPHEN (1813–88)** Born Pest; died Paris. A major composer of delightful short piano pieces in the Romantic salon style. Heller was admired by Schumann.

∞ **HENRY, PIERRE (1927)** Born Paris. Henry was a major exponent of *musique concrète* in the pioneering 1950s. His *Variations for a Door and a Sigh* are characteristic of his innovative, whimsical style.

∞ **HENSELT, ADOLF VON (1814–89)** Born Schwabach, Bavaria; died Cieplice. As a Romantic piano virtuoso and composer, Henselt contributed much to the development of his instrument.

∞ **HENZE, HANS WERNER (1926)** Born Gütersloh, Westphalia. Avant-garde composer dedicated to traditional forms. Influence of Schoenberg and Stravinsky in early work, but later open to

different styles. Enormously prolific, especially in ballet and opera.

∞ **HEROLD, FERDINAND (1791–1833)** Born and died Paris. French operatic composer in a country overwhelmingly disposed to opera. Herold scored one of his greatest successes with the opera *Zampa* (1831), which is representative of his straightforwardly tuneful music.

∞ **HERTEL, JOHANN WILHELM (1727–89)** Born Eisenach; died Schwerin. Composer of a symphony with eight obbligato timpani and much other orchestral music, Hertel was also highly praised for his rich and varied vocal music.

∞ **HEUBERGER, RICHARD (1850–1914)** Born Graz; died Vienna. In addition to his career as a choral director and music critic, Heuberger contributed one of the most enduring Viennese operettas, *The Opera Ball* (1898).

∞ **HINDEMITH, PAUL (1895–1963)** Born Hanau, near Frankfurt; died Frankfurt. Composer, theorist, performer, teacher and conductor. Composed in most forms and is associated with the idea of *Gebrauchsmusik* (utility music).

∞ **HODDINOTT, ALUN (1929)** Born Bargoed, Glamorgan. Welsh composer and teacher who has written in a wide variety of genres, including the symphony. His style is usually tonal, though chromatic and diverse harmonically.

∞ **HOFFMANN, ERNST THEODOR AMADEUS (1776–1822)** Born Königsberg; died Berlin. Hoffmann was one of the more colourful figures in burgeoning German Romanticism and played a major role in the growth of German opera, especially in *Undine* (1816).

∞ **HOLLOWAY, ROBIN (1943)** Born Leamington Spa. A refined sense of harmony and wide range of textures help make up Holloway's Romantic style which is spiritually related to Wagner.

∞ **HOLMBOE, VAGN (1909)** Born Horsens. Like that of many conservatives who have chosen to stay with tonal harmony, Holmboe's music relies on memorable melody to make its point. His 14 string quartets are at the heart of his œuvre.

∞ **HOLST, GUSTAV (1874–1934)** Born Cheltenham; died London. *The Planets* (1916), a cycle of pieces in a virtuoso orchestral idiom, is one of the most enduringly popular works of the 20th century. However, much of Holst's output is vocal and quite unlike *The Planets*.

∞ **HOLZBAUER, IGNAZ (1711–83)** Born Vienna; died Mannheim. As well as composing twelve operas (one in German), Holzbauer imitated the style of the Mannheim School in his 65 symphonies.

∞ **HONAUER, LEONTZI (c. 1730–c. 1790)** Born ?Strasbourg. Honauer's sonatas mix Italian and German styles to create a homophonic texture and movement order that is typical of the 1760s.

∞ **HONEGGER, ARTHUR (1892–1955)** Born Le Havre; died Paris. Helped formed 'Les six', though his serious temperament seems far removed from that of the other members in the group. A prolific composer, he is remembered for his portrayal of a railway engine in *Pacific 231* (1923), also symphonies and the operas *Le Roi David* (1921) and *Jeanne d'Arc au bûcher* (1938).

∞ **HOVHANNES ALAN (1911)** Born Somerville, Mass. A prodigiously productive composer by 20th-century standards, Hovhaness's music shows many Asiatic and Middle-Eastern influences.

∞ **HOWELLS, HERBERT (1892–1983)** Born Lydney, Gloucestershire; died Oxford. Howell's works are mainly in the conservative, pastoral tradition of English music. He wrote in a wide range of genres, but his liturgical settings are his most often performed works.

∞ **HUMMEL, JOHANN NEPOMUK (1778–1837)** Born Pressburg (Bratislava); died Weimar. Composer and pianist. Lived and studied with Mozart. Among his most important works are eight piano concertos and the popular trumpet concerto.

∞ **HUMPERDINCK, ENGELBERT (1854–1921)** Born Siegburg; died Neustrelitz. Humperdinck immersed himself thoroughly in Wagner's operas, even writing additional music for *Parsifal*. His most successful works are the two fairy-tale operas *Hänsel und Gretel* (1893) and *Königskinder* (1910).

∞ **IBERT, JACQUES (1890–1962)** Born and died Paris. Eclectic composer whose music ranges from the orchestral impressionism of *Escales* (1922) to the witty suite *Divertissement* (1930).

∞ **INDY, VINCENT D' (1851–1931)** Born and died Paris. Liszt and Wagner were important influences, though Franck was the figure most venerated by d'Indy. His compositions include the operas *Fervaal* (1895) and *La Légende de Saint-Christophe* (1915), symphonies and tone poems. He founded the Schola Cantorum, an academic institution, in Paris.

∞ **IRELAND, JOHN (1879–1962)** Born Bowdon, Cheshire; died Washington, Sussex. Ireland was an English Romantic with a personal style, especially harmonically, that cannot be mistaken for any other composer. In addition to symphonic music and songs, he wrote many sets of piano pieces.

∞ **JACCHINI, GIUSEPPE MARIA (c. 1663–1727)** Born and died Bologna. Cellist and composer who did much to liberate his instrument from accompanimental duties. He generally cultivated solo instrumental writing.

∞ **JANEQUIN, CLEMENT (c. 1485–1558)** Born Châtellerault; died Paris. Jannequin studied with Josquin and went on to display an unusual level of interest in programme music, composing works such as *The Capture of Boulogne*.

∞ **JOACHIM, JOSEPH (1831–1907)** Born Köpcsény; died Berlin. Joachim's current reputation rests on his association with Brahms and his violin playing, but his compositions were once popular, most notably the *Konzert in ungarischer Weise* so admired by Tovey.

∞ **JOPLIN, SCOTT (1868–1917)** Died New York. American composer and pianist known as the 'King of Ragtime' for his famous series of piano rags. They became very popular in the 1970s on account of their catchy melodies and rhythmic vitality.

∞ **KABALEVSKY, DMITRY BORISOVICH (1904–87)** Born St Petersburg; died Moscow. Worked well with the communist administration in the Soviet Union, producing patriotic works that reflect 'Socialist Realism'. Compositions include four symphonies, piano concertos, ballets and operas.

∞ **KALMAN, IMRE (1882–1953)** Born Siofok; died Paris. Although he was at one time a fellow student of Bartók and Kodály, Kálmán's main interest was light music. His operettas have a flavour comparable to Léhar's.

∞ **KANCHELI, GIYA ALEXANDROVICH (1935)** Born Tbilisi. Kancheli has composed jazz pieces, musicals and six symphonies (1967–81). Generating symphonic structures from folk melodies without necessarily quoting them, he is one of the most innovative of Georgian composers

∞ **KHACHATURIAN, ARAM IL'YICH (1903–78)** Born Tbilisi; died Moscow. His music, influenced by Armenian folk music, is mostly instrumental and written in the direct and comprehensible style favoured by Soviet authorities.

∞ **KNUSSEN, OLIVER (1952)** Born Glasgow. Knussen's symphonies and stage works are distinguished by their intricately imaginative scoring and subtle harmonic range.

∞ **KODALY, ZOLTAN (1882–1967)** Born Kecskemét; died Budapest. Key figure in 20th-century nationalism and music education. Active in collecting and publishing Hungarian folk melodies. His colourful works reflect Hungarian folk traditions and include the comic *Háry János* (1926).

∞ **KOECHLIN, CHARLES (1867–1950)** Born Paris; died Le Canadel. Output consists of symphonic works, stage and film music, choral works and songs, and chamber and instrumental works. His evocative orchestral and vocal pieces after Kipling's *Jungle Book* have recently been recorded to popular acclaim.

∞ **KORNGOLD, ERICH WOLFGANG (1897–1957)** Born Brno; died Hollywood. Composer, conductor, and critic. The opera *Die tote Stadt* (1920) was highly successful. His extensive work for Hollywood is seminal in the history of film music.

∞ **KOSMA, JOSEPH (1905–69)** Born Budapest; died Paris. Renowned for his songs, especially in France, Kosma studied with Eisler in Berlin and retained much of the German's directness of communication.

∞ **KRENEK, ERNST (1900–91)** Born Vienna, died Palm Springs. His first success was with the opera *Jonny spielt auf* (1926). He later adopted the twelve-note method of composition.

∞ **KUHNAU, JOHANN (1660–1722)** Born Geising, Erzgebirge; died Leipzig. Kuhnau is an interesting historical figure in his early attachment to the up-and-coming sonata (rather than suite) and in his colourful programme music, especially the *Biblical* Sonatas.

∞ **KURTAG, GYORGY (1926)** Born Lugoj; Romania. An heir to the miniaturism of Webern, Kurtág was also influenced by Hungarian music; both strands are represented in his vocal work *The Sayings of Péter Bornemisza* (1968).

∞ **LACHNER, FRANZ PAUL (1803–90)** Born Rain am Lech, Bavaria; died Munich. Although famous in his day as a composer of orchestral works, he is now better known for his early friendship with Schubert and the name of his family, so prominent in 19th-century Germany.

∞ **LALO, EDOUARD (1823–92)** Born Lille; died Paris. Colourful orchestration, exotic, lively melodies and vigorous rhythms made works such as the ballet *Namouna* (1882) and opera *Le roi d'Ys* (1888) a radical influence in 19th-century France. They appealed greatly to the young Debussy.

∞ **LAMBERT, CONSTANT (1905–51)** Born and died London. Composer, conductor and critic. His biggest success was the jazz-inspired choral piece *The Rio Grande* (1927). He published an entertaining book on contemporary music entitled *Music Ho!*.

∞ **LANDINI, FRANCESCO (c. 1325–97)** Born and died ?Florence. The composer who gave his name to a popular cadence figure of the day – the 'Landini cadence' – was probably the most celebrated musician of his time and a notable organist.

∞ **LANG, JOHANN GEORG (1722–98)** Born Svojšín; died Ehrenbreitstein. German composer whose keyboard concertos and symphonies were highly regarded and even attributed to Haydn and J C Bach.

∞ **LANNER, JOSEPH FRANZ KARL (1801–43)** Born Vienna; died Oberdöbling, near Vienna. Lanner was the director of the small orchestra in which Johann Strauss the elder played and was the first to produce light dance music for Vienna, mainly waltzes.

∞ **LAWES, HENRY (1596–1662)** Born Dinton, Wiltshire; died London. Lawes was one of the most valued English composers before Purcell, his praises being eloquently sung by Milton and Herrick. His surviving music is largely theatrical, notably the famous masque *Comus* (1634).

∞ **LEDUC, SIMON (BEFORE 1748–77)** Born and died Paris. Violinist, composer and publishe. Leduc had a compositional style that is sometimes referred to as the 'French Storm and Stress' – an allusion to the great German *Sturm und Drang* movement of which Haydn was such a remarkable part.

∞ **LEHAR, FRANZ (1870–1948)** Born Komarón; died Bad Ischl, Hungary. Famous as a composer of operettas; the best-known is *The Merry Widow* (1905).

∞ **LEIGH, WALTER (1905–42)** Born Wimbledon; died near Tobruk, Libya. Leigh composed a great deal for amateur performance and enjoyed a notable success with his comic opera *Jolly Roger* (1933).

∞ **LEONCAVALLO, RUGGIERO (1857–1919)** Born Naples; died Montecatini. Leoncavallo took advantage of *verismo*'s popularity to produce his one enduring masterpiece, *Pagliacci* (1892), a two-act opera often twinned with Mascagni's *Cavalleria rusticana*.

∞ **LEONIN (LEONINUS) (c. 1163–1201)**. On the evidence of Anonymous IV, a contemporary theorist, Léonin is a crucial figure in the early development of polyphonic church music, preceding Pérotin at Notre Dame, Paris.

∞ **LIEBERMANN, ROLF (1910)** Born Zurich. Although not a prolific composer, Liebermann's operas and his, for then, highly unusual Concerto for

Jazzband and Symphony Orchestra (1954) have attracted a great deal of attention.

∞ **LITOLFF, HENRY (1818–91)** Born London; died Bois-Colombes. Litolff devised a more orchestrally-based concerto form called 'concerto symphonique' which Liszt admired. The exquisite scherzo from the Fourth Concerto is often played alone.

∞ **LLOYD WEBBER, ANDREW (1948)** Born London. Although his musicals have taken the world by storm, Lloyd Webber has made forays into more traditional territory in his Variations (1978) and Requiem (1984) in which his popular approach has made a great impact.

∞ **LOCATELLI, PIETRO ANTONIO (1695–1764)** Born Bergamo; died Amsterdam. A pupil of Corelli, Locatelli did much to advance the violin as an instrument, introducing new devices for expressive effect in concerti grossi, violin concertos and 24 caprices (hence his title 'Paganini of the 18th century').

∞ **LOCKE, MATTHEW (c. 1621/2–77)** Born ?Devon; died London. Organist and innovative composer. He wrote incidental music and sacred and chamber works which had a marked impact on Purcell.

∞ **LOEWE, CARL (1796–1869)** Born Loebjuen; died Kiel. A fascinating but curiously neglected Romantic German composer whose fame rests mainly on his ballads, in spite of many other vocal and instrumental works.

∞ **LORTZING, ALBERT (1801–51)** Born and died Berlin. Lortzing is the main representative of *Singspiel* – opera with spoken dialogue – in 19th-century Germany. *Zar und Zimmermann* (1837) is among the most enduring of his operas.

∞ **LOTTI, ANTONIO (c. 1667–1740)** Born Venice or Hanover; died Venice. Another in the long line of musicians at St Mark's, Venice, Lotti composed music for the church and also formed his own opera company for which he wrote such enduring works as *Giove in Argo*.

∞ **LULLY, JEAN-BAPTISTE (1632–87)** Born Florence; died Paris. Did much to foster growth of the orchestra and a vital figure in history of French opera, which he dominated in his lifetime with works such as *Alceste* (1674). Died as a result of striking his foot while conducting.

∞ **LUTYENS, ELISABETH (1906–83)** Born and died London. A dedicated exponent of serialism in England, Lutyens composed numerous instrumental, orchestral, vocal and dramatic works in a refined, highly personal style.

∞ **LYADOV, ANATOL (1855–1914)** Born St Petersburg; died Polïnovka, Novgorod district. Studied with Rimsky-Korsakov. Notoriously idle, he produced only a modest output including the attractive symphonic poems *Baba Yaga* (1904) and *The Enchanted Lake* (1909).

∞ **MACDOWELL, EDWARD (1860–1908)** Born and died New York. Wrote in warm Romantic manner. His most characteristic works are for piano, including *Woodland Sketches* (1896) and *Fireside Tales* (1902).

∞ **MACMILLAN, JAMES (1959)** Born Kilwinning, Ayrshire. MacMillan has drawn on Scottish folk music for the inspiration of such dynamic and emotionally stirring scores as *Veni, Emmanuel* (1992), a percussion concerto for Evelyn Glennie.

MALIPIERO, GIAN FRANCESCO (1882–1973) Born Venice; died Treviso. His first work to gain recognition was the orchestral piece *Pause del Silenzio* (1917). He wrote numerous operas, though he campaigned against the operatic domination of Italian musical life.

MANFREDINI, FRANCESCO ONOFRIO (1684–1762) Born and died Pistoia. Manfredini studied with Torelli, whose influence is discernible in his pupil's slender (for the time) output.

MARENZIO, LUCA (1553/4–99) Born Coccaglio, near Brescia; died Rome. A major composer of madrigals whose works contributed to the popularity of the genre in England. He published 16 books of them and one of *madrigali spirituali*.

MARIN, MARIE-MARTIN MARCEL, VICOMTE DE (1769–AFTER 1861) Born St Jean-de-Luz; died Toulouse. Marin's main interest was in the harp, which he played and improvised on with rare genius. Most of his works, in a varied Classical style, are for harp.

MARINI, BIAGIO (c. 1587–1663) Born Brescia; died Venice. A violinist-composer who studied with Monteverdi. His extensive output includes the earliest known sonatas for solo violin and continuo.

MARSCHNER, HEINRICH AUGUST (1795–1861) Born Zittau; died Hanover. One of the most significant figures in the growth of German Romantic opera, Marschner was among the first to write a through-composed opera (*Lukretia*, 1821).

MARTIN, FRANÇOIS (1727–57) Died Paris. Composer and cellist whose symphonies of the 1750s are in the popular three-movement form of the period and show real sensitivity to orchestral colouring.

MARTIN, FRANK (1890–1974) Born Geneva; died Naarden. He used serialism very freely. His works include operas, incidental music, choral music, piano and orchestral music, all composed in a characterful, rhythmically energetic style.

MARTINU, BOHUSLAV (1890–1959) Born Policka, Bohemia; died Liestal, Switzerland. A prolific composer of operas (*Julietta*, 1938), ballets, instrumental, orchestral and choral music.

MASCAGNI, PIETRO (1863–1945) Born Livorno; died Rome. Remembered as the composer of the *verismo* masterpiece *Cavalleria rusticana* (1890). Although he wrote many other operas, he never experienced similar success again.

MASSENET, JULES (1842–1912) Born Montand, St Etienne; died Paris. Notable works are the operas *Manon, Werther* and *Thaïs* (1884, 1892, 1894), composed in a harmonious, pleasing style and well crafted.

MAW, NICHOLAS (1935) Born Grantham. Maw studied with Nadia Boulanger and Deutsch. He is considered conservative in his fondness for conventional forces, but his layering technique and the individuality of his harmony set him apart from mainstream European conservativism.

MEDTNER, NIKOLAI KARLOVICH (1880–1951) Born Moscow; died London. Although brought up in Russia, Medtner was of German descent and his music tends towards the warm radiance of German Romanticism. He was a fine pianist, which is reflected in the dominance of the piano in his music.

MEHUL, ETIENNE-NICOLAS (1763–1817) Born Givet; died Paris. Gluck exercised a considerable influence over Mehul, drawing him into operatic composition. Mehul reflected the events of the Revolution and Napoleonic period and was the finest French symphonist between Gossec and Berlioz.

MENOTTI, GIAN CARLO (1911) Born Cadegliano. An American composer of Italian birth. Menotti's operas are written in a deliberately popular style with real feeling for the human voice. He is a pluralist stylistically, adapting whatever seems suitable for works such as *Amahl and the Night Visitors* (1951).

MESSAGER, ANDRE (1853–1929) Born Montluçon, Allier; died Paris. The first conductor of Debussy's *Pelléas et Mélisande* was at his best as a composer of operettas, which are written in a tuneful, conversational style of considerable sophistication.

MESSIAEN, OLIVIER (1908–92) Born Avignon; died Paris. Founded the Jeune France group and developed a highly individual modal language. His passionate interest in the Catholic Church and in birdsong can be heard in numerous piano, organ and orchestral works.

MEYERBEER, GIACOMO (1791–1864) Born Berlin; died Paris. Produced commercially successful grand operas with librettist Scribe, notably in Paris, and influenced Wagner. Operas include *Robert le Diable* (1831) and *Les Huguenots* (1836).

MIASKOWSKY, NIKOLAI YAKOVLEVICH (1881–1950) Born Novogeorgiyevsk; died Moscow. Along with Prokofiev and Shostakovich, Miaskowsky fell foul of the Soviet authorities after the Second World War, yet his 27 symphonies are conservative works in which melody and tonal harmony dominate.

MILHAUD, DARIUS (1892–1974) Born Aix-en-Provence; died Geneva. Member of 'Les six'. Developed pointed harmonic style, often using bitonality in his operas, ballets, incidental music, and orchestral and chamber works. Taught for many years at Mills College, Oakland, California.

MOLTER, JOHANN MELCHIOR (1696–1765) Born Tiefenort, near Eisenach; died Karlsruhe. Minor German composer whose music reflects the changing tastes of his period. He was occasionally innovative in the way he linked movements, but his ideas failed to find general acceptance.

MONDONVILLE, JEAN-JOSEPH CASSANEA DE (1711–72) Born Narbonne; died near Paris. During the 'Guerre des Bouffons' – in which opinion was divided between support for traditional operas and the new, imported Italian *buffa* – Mondonville allied himself with the French, the Rameau faction. His national roots are apparent in his opera *Titon et l'Aurore* (1753). He introduced violin harmonics to the world in his sonatas.

MONN, MATTHIAS GEORG (1717–50) Born and died Vienna. Among several claims to fame, Monn is accredited with the first four-movement symphony (1740), though his 20 or so others follow the hitherto preferred three movements. In 1932–33 Schoenberg adapted a 1746 clavicembalo concerto by Monn as a cello concerto.

MONTECLAIR, MICHEL PIGNOLET DE (1667–1737) Born Andelot, Haute-Marne; died Aumont. Montéclair combined a career as a double-bass player in the Paris Opéra orchestra with teaching violin (for which he published manuals), and writing operas, cantatas, church and chamber music.

MORLEY, THOMAS (1557/8–1602) Born Norwich; died London. Morley was one of the prime composers of madrigals in England who lent the Italian form a distinctly English guise. He was also an editor, theorist and organist.

MOSCHELES, IGNAZ (1794–1870) Born Prague; died Leipzig. Moscheles' accomplishments as a pianist led Mendelssohn to invite him to head the piano department at the Leipzig Conservatoire. Of his piano compositions it is mainly the studies that have endured.

MOSZKOWSKI, MORITIZ (1854–1925) Born Breslau; died Paris. Moszkowski, like so many composers before and since, combined the jobs of playing piano and composition. His ambitions as a composer stretched to the composition of a symphony based on the life of Joan of Arc, but his lighter piano pieces have proved more attractive to posterity.

MOZART, LEOPOLD (1719–87) Born Augsburg; died Salzburg. Leopold's literary legacy – his letters to his son and the important Violinschule – are very familiar, but his music has not received the attention it possibly deserves. What we do hear shows flashes of genius, and there are some extraordinary instrumental combinations, including a Sinfonia 'da caccia' for a box of ammunition, dog yelps and human shouts.

MUSGRAVE, THEA (1928) Born Barnton, Midlothian. English serialist whose brilliant succession of choral and instrumental works have also embraced Lutoslawski's limited aleatoricism.

NICOLAI, OTTO (1810–49) Born Königsberg; died Berlin. Nicolai achieved comic perfection in *The Merry Wives of Windsor* (1849), the tuneful writing of which continues to commend it to opera houses. He also started the Vienna Philharmonic Concerts.

NONO, LUIGI (1924–90) Born and died Venice. Radical Italian composer on the militant Left, Nono made extensive use of electronic music and various avant-garde techniques.

NOVAK, VITEZSLAV (1870–1949) Born Kamenice nad Lipou; died Skuteč. Czech composer whose early music was mainly German in character; his later operas and symphonies had nationalist tendencies.

NYMAN, MICHAEL (1944) Born London. An English minimalist whose score, based on music by Purcell, for Greenaway's film *The Draughtsman's Contract* (1982) enjoyed considerable acclaim, as did that for Jane Campion's *The Piano* (1993).

OFFENBACH, JACQUES (1819–80) Born Cologne; died Paris. Composed brilliant series of operettas for Paris. Failed to complete his serious masterpiece, the grand opera *The Tales of Hoffmann*.

ORFF, CARL (1895–1982) Born and died Munich. A musical primitive in his use of harmony and repetitive rhythms, Orff was fascinated by medieval and Renaissance music. This resulted in the popular choral work *Carmina burana* (1936) which some regarded, perhaps mistakenly, as a deliberate simplification of music for the Nazis.

∞ **PACHELBEL, JOHANN (1653–1706)** Born and died Nuremberg. An important composer of Protestant church music before Bach, as well as a prolific composer of organ and other keyboard music.

∞ **PADEREWSKI, IGNACY JAN (1860–1941)** Born Kurytówka, Podolia; died New York. A leading piano virtuoso whose compositions for the instrument have remained in the repertoire, most notably his miniatures and concerto. They are written in the late Romantic manner of Liszt and early Rachmaninov. In later life Paderewski was appointed Prime Minister of Poland.

∞ **PAGANINI, NICOLO (1782–1840)** Born Genoa; died Nice. A charismatic violin virtuoso, many of whose compositions are display pieces for his own use, including the highly effective violin concertos.

∞ **PAISIELLO, GIOVANNI (1740–1816)** Born Roccaforzata, near Taranto; died Naples. Paisiello's comic operas left an imprint on Mozart's, and he also worked extensively in heroic and tragic operatic forms. He was fantastically prolific, composing over 80 operas and other vocal music.

∞ **PANUFNIK, ANDRZEJ (1914–91)** Born Warsaw; died London. Panufnik's works in the 1940s are brimming over with the new ideas of the Polish avant-garde, including quarter-tones, glissandos and so on. Later he developed an accessible tonal idiom in works such as *Sinfonia sacra* (1963).

∞ **PARROTT, IAN (1916)** Born London. English composer who has identified closely with the Welsh language and culture, not least in the folk opera *The Black Ram* (1966).

∞ **PARRY, HUBERT (1848–1918)** Born Bournemouth; died Rustington, Sussex. Respected Victorian composer who helped pave the way for an English musical renaissance, especially Elgar. His symphonies show the influence of Brahms.

∞ **PART, ARVO (1935)** Born Paide, Estonia. Up to 1968 Pärt composed in a progressive, serial idiom; since then his language has become simpler – his 'tintinnabuli' style – due partly to his study of medieval music.

∞ **PARTCH, HARRY (1901–74)** Born Oakland, Calif.; died San Diego, Calif. Independent-minded American who researched natural tuning systems of the past for his music and developed his own extraordinary instruments. He wrote a great deal for the stage and used few traditional instruments other than the human voice.

∞ **PEARCE, EDWARD (?1560–?1613)** Died ?London. Little is known about this composer and choirmaster who moved from Canterbury Cathedral to London. A tiny number of works survive, including three lute pieces.

∞ **PEDRELL, FELIPE (1841–1922)** Born Tortosa; died Barcelona. As the teacher of, among others, Albéniz, Granados, de Falla and Gerhard, Pedrell is regarded as the father of 20th-century Spanish nationalism. As a composer of many works in traditional forms, his reputation has proved less enduring.

∞ **PERGOLESI, GIOVANNI BATTISTA (1710–36)** Born Iesi, near Ancona; died Pozzuoli, near Naples.

Important figure in the development of Italian opera, especially for his short intermezzo *La serva padrona* (1733) which influenced Mozart's *buffa* style.

∞ **PERI, JACOPO (1561–1633)** Born Rome; died Florence. Member of the Florentine *camerata* and prominent musician serving the Medicis. To Peri goes the rare distinction of having written the first fully surviving opera, *Euridice* (1600).

∞ **PEROTIN (PEROTINUS MAGNUS) (c. 1160–1220)** Born ?; died ?. Composer working in France who followed and refined Léonin's work as a representative of *Ars Antiqua*. Among several impressive works attributed to him, *Viderunt omnes* is a highly developed example of the first flowering of polyphony.

∞ **PETTERSSON, GUSTAF ALLAN (1911–80)** Born Vastra Ryd, Uppsala; died Stockholm. Interest has centred around the symphonies of this intriguing Swedish composer. Large outbursts of dissonant sound alternate with gloomy, introspective music.

∞ **PFITZNER, HANS (1869–1949)** Born Moscow; died Salzburg. Conservative German composer whose earnest, exalted style reached its zenith in the opera *Palestrina* (1917).

∞ **PISTON, WALTER (1894–1976)** Born Rockland, Maine; died Belmont, Mass. Piston is another American composer who studied in Paris with Nadia Boulanger. He arrived at a style in his purely orchestral and instrumental output that is lively, traditional, and often highly contrapuntal.

∞ **PONCHIELLI, AMILCARE (1834–86)** Born Paderno Fasolaro, near Cremona; died Milan. Ponchielli's reputation lies with just one work, the grand opera *La Gioconda* (1876), whose libretto was written by Boito. Stylistically it looks ahead to *verismo* in its impassioned melodic writing.

∞ **POULENC, FRANCIS (1899–1963)** Born and died Paris. A member of 'Les six', Poulenc fell strongly under the spell of Stravinsky. His witty, tuneful works include chamber music for various instruments and superb songs.

∞ **PRAETORIUS, MICHAEL (?1571/73–1621)** born Creuzburg an der Werra, near Eisenach; died Wolfenbuttel. German composer who embraced the Venetian polychoral style of the Gabrielis. His *Syntagma musicum* (1614–20) is a vital treatise on Baroque instrumentation.

∞ **QUANTZ, JOHANN JOACHIM (1697–1773)** Born Oberscheden, Hanover; died Potsdam. Quantz was a major flautist-composer whose treatise *On Playing the Flute* (1752) ranks besides works by Leopold Mozart and C P E Bach as a major guide to practices of the time – it overshadows his music.

∞ **RAFF, JOSEPH JOACHIM (1822–82)** Born Lachen, near Zurich; died Frankfurt. One of Switzerland's most distinguished musicians of the 19th

century, Raff composed numerous works in every genre of the day, but his music suffers rather from a lack of individuality, for all its expert construction.

∞ **RAWSTHORNE, ALAN (1905–71)** Born Haslingden, Lancs; died Cambridge. A prolific and individual English composer who was greatly attracted to Classical forms such as the symphony and concerto. His music is often highly contrapuntal and dynamic.

∞ **REGER, MAX (1873–1916)** Born Upper Palatinate, Bavaria; died Leipzig. The most important Romantic German composer for organ, Reger also wrote many orchestral and chamber works in an unmistakeable chromatic idiom.

∞ **REIMANN, ARIBERT (1936)** Born Berlin. Composer, accompanist of Lieder and teacher. His operas – *Lear* (1978), in particular – and other works are widely performed.

∞ **RESPIGHI, OTTORINO (1879–1936)** Born Bologna; died Rome. Respighi composed nine operas and much else besides, but his reputation rests on a handful of brilliant orchestral fantasies for large orchestra and arrangements of early Italian compositions. Works such as *Fountains of Rome* (1916) have been great favourites of virtuoso conductors and orchestras.

∞ **RICHTER, FRANZ XAVER (1709–89)** Born ?Holleschau; died Strasbourg. One of many composers whose career reflects the changing nature (from Baroque to Classical) of German music in the 18th century. His works include both symphonies and trio sonatas.

∞ **RIETI, VITTORIO (1898–)** Born Alexandria. Of Italian parentage, Rieti composed ballets for Diaghilev as well as symphonies, concertos and other works in traditional forms. He writes elegantly in a neo-Classical idiom.

∞ **RIISAGER, KNUDAGE (1897–1974)** Born Port Kunda, Estonia; died Copenhagen. A Danish composer with a marked French bias whose neo-Classical music uses polytonality and often recalls Stravinsky.

∞ **RILEY, TERRY (1935)** Born Colfax, Calif. Riley is associated with the Fluxus group of composers in New York. *In C*, for piano, is among the most influential examples of process music (minimalism).

∞ **RODE, PIERRE (1774–1830)** Born Bordeaux; died Château de Bourbon, near Damazon. French violinist-composer and pupil of Viotti whom he succeeded. His violin concertos are the template for the French violin concerto.

∞ **RODRIGO, JOAQUIN (1901)** Born Sagunto, Spain. Enjoyed great public acclaim with his colourful Guitar Concerto (*Concierto de Aranjuez*) and *Fantasia para un gentilhombre*.

∞ **RODRIGUEZ, VICENTE (? –1760)** Born Onteniente, near Valencia; died Valencia. Spanish organist and composer whose *Libro de toccatas para cimbalo* are in the line of Scarlatti's sonatas in their wide range of harmonies and chromaticism.

∞ **ROUSSEL, ALBERT (1869–1937)** Born Tourcoing; died Royan. Composed symphonies, ballets, and chamber music in a neo-Classical style that reflected Stravinsky's innovations.

∞ **RUBINSTEIN, ANTON (1829–94)** Born Vikhvatinets; died Peterhof. Prolific Russian composer of operas, symphonies and much else besides who influenced, and was in his turn influenced by, Tchaikovsky and later the nationalists, though his music remained centred in the Germanic past.

∞ **RUGGLES, CARL (1876–1971)** Born East Marion, Mass.; died Bennington, Vermont. Original, pioneering composer of a tiny handful of works which are all of great quality, especially the orchestral *Sun-treader* (1931).

∞ **SAINT-SAENS, CAMILLE (1835–1921)** Born Paris; died Algiers. A composer of conservative temperament, Saint Saëns wrote very successful works such as the Third Symphony (1886) and *Carnival of the Animals* (1886).

∞ **SALLINEN, AULIS (1935)** Born Salmi. Sallinen is one of Finland's leading composers. Following Sibelius, he has opted for a free tonal idiom in his very varied vocal and instrumental works.

∞ **SAMMARTINI, GIOVANNI BATTISTA (1700/1–1775)** Born and died ?Milan. Sammartini was Milan's leading composer and a key figure in the evolution of the Classical style, though his music has many Baroque traits as well.

∞ **SARASATE, PABLO (1844–1908)** Born Pamplona; died Biarritz. Brilliantly talented violinist. His modest abilities as a composer are best sampled in the tricky *Carmen* Fantasy.

∞ **SATIE, ERIK (1866–1925)** Born Honfleur; died Paris. Eccentric and original composer who became the figurehead (though not a member) of 'Les six'. The ballet *Parade* (1917) is perhaps his most enduring achievement.

∞ **SCARLATTI, ALESSANDRO (1660–1725)** Born Palermo; died Naples. Major figure in mid-Baroque opera and oratorio. His works include the opera *La Griselda* (1721).

∞ **SCELSI, GIACINTO (1905–88)** Born La Spezia; died Rome. In his huge range of compositions, Scelsi embraced machine music, serialism, and neo-Romanticism. In later years his interest was in Eastern asceticism, resulting in visionary works based on the sparest of musical ideas.

∞ **SCHAEFFER, PIERRE (1910)** Born Nancy. A major figure in the *musique concrète* movement. Schaeffer's work draws heavily on technology and breaks down the distinction between 'noise' and 'music' in works such as *Symphonie pour un homme seul* (1950/66).

∞ **SCHARWENKA, XAVER (1850–1924)** Born Samter; died Berlin. A versatile musician famed for his piano playing (especially Chopin), conducting, concert organization and role as an educator. His piano concertos and other piano works, composed in a Romantic tuneful style, still attract performances.

∞ **SCHEIDT, SAMUEL (1587–1654)** Born and died Halle. An early German Baroque composer, one of the first to use the Italian concerto style. German traits such as a fondness for variation and the chorale are evident in his numerous religious choral works.

∞ **SCHEIN, JOHANN HERMANN (1586–1630)** Born Grünhain, near Annaberg; died Leipzig. Like Scheidt, Schein infused Lutheran church music with progressive strains of the Italian madrigal and concerto.

∞ **SCHMIDT, FRANZ (1874–1939)** Born Bratislava; died Perchtoldsdorf, near Vienna. Austrian composer in Viennese tradition who retained a strong hold on tonality in his symphonies and chamber works, several of which are often revived today.

∞ **SCHMITT, FLORENT (1870–1958)** Born Blamont, Meurthe-et-Moselle; died Neuilly-sur-Seine. A strong vein of exoticism runs through the intoxicatingly rich textures of Schmitt's most famous work, the ballet *La tragédie de Salome* (1907). He also composed much choral, chamber and piano music.

∞ **SCHREKER, FRANZ (1878–1934)** Born Monaco; died Berlin. Schreker's opera *Der ferne Klang* (1912) is influenced not by German opera so much as impressionism, and many aspects of it penetrated Berg's *Wozzeck*. His later operas, though composed in the same luxuriant manner, have failed to hold a place in the repertoire.

∞ **SCHULHOFF, ERVIN (1894–1942)** Born Prague; died Wülzbourg. Schulhoff's eclectic tastes led him through Romantic, impressionist, jazz and even Bartókian styles. Of Jewish descent, he died in a Nazi death camp.

∞ **SEARLE, HUMPHREY (1915–82)** Born Oxford; died London. Searle studied with Webern before the war. He became one of England's few serial composers, staying with this system in such substantial works as the Fifth Symphony.

∞ **SESSIONS, ROGER (1896–85)** Born Brooklyn; died Princeton. Sessions is a seminal figure in American music who beside adopting the serial method, which proved so successful in post-war America, also taught the likes of Babbitt and wrote extensively on contemporary music.

∞ **SHANKAR, RAVI (1920)** Born Varanasi, Uttar Pradesh. Indian sitar player who has incorporated his instrument into various ensembles and done much to popularize Indian music around the world.

∞ **SIMPSON, ROBERT (1921)** Born Leamington. Simpson's passionate faith in the power of the tonal symphony is evident in his often intensely dramatic orchestral and chamber works. He has also written extensively on Beethoven, Nielsen, and others.

∞ **SINDING, CHRISTIAN (1856–1941)** Born Kongsberg; died Oslo. One of Norway's most important composers after Grieg, Sinding drew heavily on German Romanticism and cultivated Liszt's cyclic form in his orchestral and instrumental works.

∞ **SOLER, ANTONIO (1729–83)** Born Olot, Gerona; died El Escorial. Like his teacher Domenico Scarlatti, Soler devoted himself to writing virtuoso keyboard sonatas. These are often in several movements, and make use of Spanish dance rhythms.

∞ **SOMERVELL, SIR ARTHUR (1863–1937)** Born Windermere; died London. Somervell's song cycles are his most enduring legacy, especially *Maud*, to poems by Tennyson.

∞ **SORABJI, KAIKHOSRU SHAPURJI (1892–88)** Born Chingford; died Winfrith. English composer, pianist and writer whose fiendishly complex scores often run to the length of a full programme.

∞ **SPOHR, LOUIS (1784–1859)** Born Brunswick; died Kassel. Popular and influential composer and violinist in early German Romanticism. His opera *Faust* (1813) was a major step in the evolution of German Romantic opera.

∞ **SPONTINI, GASPARE (1774–1851)** Born and died Maiolati, near Iesi. *La vestale* (1807) and other operas perfectly met the French desire for historical spectacle in Italian opera. Spontini's influence on the genre was extensive.

∞ **STAINER, SIR JOHN (1840–1901)** Born London; died Verona. Stainer's work as a musicologist has rather overshadowed his compositions, the majority of which were written for the church. *The Crucifixion* (1887) and several hymns still reverberate through the aisles.

∞ **STAMITZ, CARL (1745–1801)** Born Mannheim; died Jena. Like his father Johann, Stamitz contributed to the symphony craze sweeping Europe, but many of his most valued works are *symphonies concertantes*.

∞ **STAMITZ, JOHANN (1717–1757)** Born Nemecky Brod; died Mannheim. A key figure in the early evolution of the symphony. Stamitz's symphonies have great vitality and contributed much to the range of orchestral devices available.

∞ **STANFORD, SIR CHARLES VILLIERS (1852–1924)** Born Dublin; died London. Along with Parry, the Irish composer Stanford did much to bring Anglican church music out of the doldrums. He contributed major symphonic works, too, including the delightful Third Symphony (*Irish*, 1886).

∞ **STEIBELT, DANIEL (1765–1823)** Born Berlin; died St Petersburg. The vain Steibelt was not one of history's more likeable individuals. His music has almost disappeared, though a handful of works suggest a refined style rather like that of the early German Romantics best known to us.

∞ **STRADELLA, ALESSANDRO (1644–82)** Born Rome; died Genoa. A colourful figure in Italian music, Stradella was a prime mover in introducing a concertante mode of writing into instrumental music and differentiating aria and recitative in opera.

∞ **STRATICO, MICHELE (C. 1721– C. 1782)** Born ?Zara. An amateur violinist whose violin concertos and other works are close to those of his teacher and friend Tartini.

∞ **STRAUS, OSCAR (1870–1954)** Born Vienna; died Bad Ischl. Like Schoenberg, Straus was associated with Wolzogen's Uberbrettle in Berlin, a major cabaret venue. His highly successful operettas *A Waltz Dream* (1907), *The Chocolate Soldier* (1908) and *The Last Waltz* (1920) are still played.

∞ **STRAUSS, JOHANN (II) (1825–99)** Born and died Vienna. The 'Waltz King' composed a vast quantity of popular dance music, notably waltzes that include such masterpieces as *Tales from the Vienna Woods*. After meeting Offenbach he embarked upon an equally impressive series of operettas of which the finest is *Die Fledermaus* (1874).

∞ **SUBOTNICK, MORTON (1933)** Born Los Angeles. American composer who was among the first to use multi-media composition. *Sound Blocks* (1959) mixes musical, visual and verbal elements.

∞ **SUK, JOSEF (1874–1935)** Born Křečovice; died Benešov, near Prague. One of the generation of Czech composers who followed Dvořák. Suk's music is not strongly rooted in folklore, though like many others he set great store by memorable melody, as his otherwise complex *Asrael* Symphony (1906) suggests.

∞ **SULLIVAN, SIR ARTHUR (1842–1900)** Born and died London. Sullivan composed a number of 'serious' works for the stage, but it is his operettas to librettos by W S Gilbert and their humorous, often pastiche-based music that have made Sullivan one of the most popular English composers of all.

∞ **SUPPE, FRANZ (1819–95)** Born Spalato (Split); died Vienna. Suppé was the first Viennese composer of farces and subsequently also the first to adapt Offenbach's operettas to Austrian tastes.

∞ **SWEELINCK, JAN PIETERSZOON (1562–1621)** Born Deventer; died Amsterdam. Crucial composer in the evolution of keyboard music. Pioneered independent parts for organ pedals.

∞ **TAILLEFERRE, GERMAINE (1892–1983)** Born Parc-St-Maur, near Paris; died Paris. A member of 'Les six', Tailleferre is more closely related to Fauré and Ravel than Stravinsky, who was so much admired by Poulenc and others. Works such as *Six Chansons françaises* boast an eminently attractive melodic style.

∞ **TANSMAN, ALEXANDRE (1897–1986)** Born Lódz; died Paris. A great admirer of Stravinsky, Tansman ranged widely in his music, embracing both serialism and neo-Classicism.

∞ **TARTINI, GIUSEPPE (1692–1770)** Born Pirano, Istria; died Padua. Tartini wrote numerous virtuoso sonatas and concertos for violin, many of which reflect the emergence of the Classical style in Italy. His name is invariably associated with the sonata for violin, *The Devil's Trill* (c. 1747).

∞ **TAUSIG, CARL (1841–71)** Born Warsaw; died Leipzig. Outstandingly gifted Liszt pupil who left a small number of piano pieces in the flamboyant manner of his master and made many arrangements, including the vocal score of Wagner's *Die Meistersinger*.

∞ **TAVENER, JOHN (1944)** Born London. Since his early 'crossover' work *The Whale* (1966), released on the Beatles' Apple label in the 1960s, Tavener has written in a simplified style of great spiritual intensity. He enjoyed popular success with a recording of the cello-and-orchestra piece *The Protecting Veil* (1989).

∞ **TCHEREPNIN, ALEXANDER (1899–1977)** Born St Petersburg; died Paris. A restless spirit among Russian composers, Tcherepnin was constantly experimenting with musical language in many orchestral, dramatic and chamber works. Oriental influence appears in his Fourth Piano Concerto.

∞ **TELEMANN, GEORG PHILIPP (1681–1767)** Born Magdeburg; died Hamburg. Hugely prolific composer in various high-Baroque forms, including opera, concerto and suite.

∞ **THALBERG, SIGISMOND (1812–71)** Born Pâquis, near Geneva; died Posillipo, near Naples. A virtuoso to rival Liszt, in common with many others of his ilk he provided his own music, much of which is of the transcription/paraphrase variety.

∞ **THOMAS, AMBROISE (1811–96)** Born Metz; died Paris. Thomas enriched the forms of *opéra comique*. *Mignon* (1866) was one of the most successful operas of the time and continues to be revived.

∞ **THOMSON, VIRGIL (1896–1989)** Born Kansas City; died New York. American disciple of Satie's laconic style, Thomson was attracted to Baptist hymns in his numerous orchestral and vocal compositions. He was a trenchant commentator on the American musical scene.

∞ **TOMKINS, THOMAS (1572–1656)** Born St Davids; died Martin Hussingtree. Apparently taught by Byrd, Tomkins became a Gentleman in Ordinary of the Chapel Royal (c. 1620). He composed church music, keyboard works and madrigals of considerable expressive power.

∞ **TORELLI, GIUSEPPE (1658–1709)** Born Verona; died Bologna. Torelli is one of the main originators of the Baroque solo concerto and concerto grosso. His Op. 8 concertos follow the order fast-slow-fast and he maximizes contrasts between ritornellos and episodes (in the manner of Vivaldi).

∞ **TOSTI, PAOLO (1846–1916)** Born Ortano sul Mare; died Rome. Italian composer and singing teacher whose haunting songs continue to grace the repertoire of today's singers and have been extensively recorded since the inception of the gramophone.

∞ **TUBIN, EDUARD (1905–82)** Born Kallaste; died Stockholm. Estonian composer whose expressive symphonies are composed in a conservative style.

∞ **TUNDER, FRANZ (1614–67)** Born Bannesdorf, near Burg, Fehmarn; died Lübeck. The meagre surviving tally of Tunder's organ works points to an accomplished, inventive composer of chorale preludes and vocal works.

∞ **TURINA, JOAQUIN (1882–1949)** Born Seville; died Madrid. Turina left Seville when he was 20, yet the influence of the area permeates his music. Unlike his Spanish contemporaries, he broached larger North European forms, as in the *Sinfonia Sevillana* (1920).

∞ **VANHAL, JOHANN BAPTIST (1739–1813)** Born Nové Nechanice, Bohemia; died Vienna. Vanhal is accredited with over 100 symphonies, 100 quartets and much else. He is a major player in expanding sonata form and arriving at the mature form of the symphony.

∞ **VERACINI, FRANCESCO (1690–1768)** Born and died Florence. For several years the violinist-composer Veracini cultivated the popular monophonic style of his contemporaries. In later life regarding this as degenerate, he turned to increasingly intricate contrapuntal devices.

∞ **VIEUXTEMPS, HENRI (1820–81)** Born Verviers; died Mustapha, Algeria. Vieuxtemps was a great innovator as a violinist and composer, especially in his concertos which renewed the form in France in the 1840s.

∞ **VITRY, PHILIPPE DE (1291–1361)** Born and died Paris. Master of the isorhythmic motet and a major contributor to the development of new rhythmic modes, Vitry was responsible for coining the term 'Ars Nova', the title of a treatise by him (c. 1322–23).

∞ **WAGENSEIL, GEORG CHRISTOPH (1715–77)** Born and died Vienna. One of the most imaginative of the early symphonists, Wagenseil turned from the Baroque manner to the popular *galant* style that appealed so strongly to the young Mozart.

∞ **WALDTEUFEL, EMILE (1837–1915)** Born Strasbourg; died Paris. A French 'waltz king' who provided music for society functions. *The Skaters Waltz* (1882) is among his best-known waltzes.

∞ **WARLOCK, PETER (1894–1930)** Born and died London. As Philip Heseltine (his original name)

he wrote on, and edited, music. His compositions are mainly songs and have a striking sense of humour, also heard in the entertaining piano duet *The Old Codger*, an affectionate parody of Franck's symphony.

∞ **WEELKES, THOMAS (1576–1623)** Born ?Elsted, Sussex; died London. One of the finest English madrigalists and an inspired composer for the church, especially in his endlessly inventive counterpoint.

∞ **WEILL, KURT (1900–50)** Born Dessau; died New York. Founded popular opera in Berlin in the 1920s, drawing on cabaret and jazz. *Die Dreigroschenoper* ('The Threepenny Opera', 1928) brilliantly evokes the period. After the Nazis drove him out in 1933, he went finally to New York where he composed successfully for Broadway.

∞ **WEINBERGER, JAROMIR (1896–1967)** Born Prague; died St Petersburg, Florida. Weinberger reawakened the spirit of Smetana's nationalist opera *The Bartered Bride* in his *Schwanda the Bagpiper* (1927), whose polka and fugue are still very popular.

∞ **WEIR, JUDITH (1954)** Born Aberdeen. A student of Robin Holloway and Gunther Schuller, Weir has been strongly involved in music theatre, as in her opera *A Night at the Chinese Opera* (1987), where she has adapted a variety of techniques to communicate the drama effectively.

∞ **WIDOR, CHARLES-MARIE (1844–1937)** Born Lyons; died Paris. Although Widor's work-list embraces a wide range of orchestral, chamber and vocal works, his name is now associated with the great flowering of Romantic organ music in France. His Toccata from the Fifth Symphony is among the most popular organ works in the repertoire.

∞ **WIENIAWSKI, HENRYK (1835–80)** Born Lublin; died Moscow. Born into one of Poland's most celebrated musical families, Wieniawski was a fine violin virtuoso whose Second Concerto remains a great favourite for its Romantic colouring, Polish overtones and brilliant violin writing.

∞ **WILLIAMSON, MALCOLM (1931)** Born Sydney. Williamson settled in London and in 1975 was appointed to the position of Master of the Queen's Music, a distinction that partly reflected the overtly popular style of much of his music, which relies heavily on melody.

∞ **WOLF-FERRARI, ERMANNO 1876–1948)** Born and died Venice. Wolf-Ferrari's operas, especially the comic ones, are remembered rather more than his instrumental music. *Susanna's Secret* (1909), which draws on 18th-century conventions, is his masterpiece.

∞ **ZELENKA, JAN DISMAS (1679–1745)** Born Lounovice, Bohemia; died Dresden. Zelenka's reputation has risen considerably in recent years thanks to the rediscovery of six trio sonatas in a harmonically highly developed idiom that has led to comparisons with J S Bach, no less. He also wrote many sacred vocal works.

∞ **ZEMLINSKY, ALEXANDER VON (1871–1942)** Born Vienna; died Larchmont, New York. Conservative composer who followed in the style of Mahler. Developed a distinctive voice in his operas and *Lyric* Symphony.

FORMS AND STYLES

Diesen Tantz fängt man mit Coupes
piroles und pas=graues an in übrigen
kan ein jeder mit Curiosen Veränderun
gen selbst Schöne figuren machen die
Aria wird 2 mahl gespielt.

Dance

LIKE SOUND AND MUSIC, MOVEMENT AND
dance – 'body-music' – has always been a
part of human experience. Pre-historic dance
took many forms: ritualistic, erotic, medicinal,
propitious. Many non-European cultures – the
American Indians, for instance, with their
rhythmic, vocal, percussive drum/rattle dance-
songs, lasting for hours, even days – continue
to use dance in this way. The ancient Chinese
and Egyptians employed dance in symbolic
ceremonial rites. The Greeks turned it into an
honourable, Apollonian art – the art of priests,
gymnasts, actors, prostitutes – with the
Minoans of Crete even believing they invented
it. In Roman culture dancing was the preserve
of priests (public worship), peasants (feasts)
and professionals (social entertainment), the
upper echelons of society considering it beneath
their dignity. Nero, nevertheless, was a famous
patron. The Bible is rich in dance references.
Slow dance, generally, is associated with darkness and sorrow, fast dance with brightness
and hope.

THE CHURCH OPPOSED THE PHYSICAL, sexually suggestive nature of secular dancing as an obscene, corrupting, heathenish influence, but was powerless to stop it. Religious dance, on the other hand, was encouraged in France and Spain; ritual dance was also important, the convulsive displays of 11th–15th century flagellants "expressing the fright and despair of a population tortured by plague, fire, wars, and religious scruples".

Linked with the European bubonic plague epidemics of the 14th century, Holbein's 'Dance of Death' was a fanciful medieval/Renaissance conceit stressing the equality of all men before death. Liszt revived the spectre in his *Totentanz* (incorporating the plainchant 'Dies irae' sequence of the 13th century, a recurrent

Romantic symbol of death and damnation), while Mussorgsky's *Songs and Dances of Death* confirm the association.

The earliest notated instrumental dance repertoire dates from the beginning of the 14th century (estampie, saltarello). By the 15th century dance, not least the gliding, walking basse danse, had become an essential court entertainment, with the dancing master as important to the household as the court musician or chapel singer. The 16th century witnessed the popularity of many dances mentioned by Shakespeare, as well as the publication of Arbeau's *Orchesographie* (1589), a seminal book that included much of the music and dance steps of the day. The zenith of Baroque dance (traditional and new) was reached under Louis XIV, a ruler renowned as much for his extravagant patronage as enthusiastic participation.

"The people of Vienna," wrote Mozart's friend the Irish tenor Michael Kelly, "were in my time dancing mad; as the Carnival approached, gaiety began to display itself on

all sides; and when it really came, nothing could excel its brilliancy." Mozart, Haydn and Beethoven all wrote for the ballroom, refining the minuet and German dance into gracious expressions of art (just as the English virginalists had done for the 16th-century pavane and galliard, or Bach did for the allemande and sarabande a hundred years later). Vienna's princes of terpsichore (the Greek muse of dance) have been many, but it was the Strausses who were its undisputed kings, elevating social dance to new planes of artistic and emotional experience. In the eyes of his public, Johann the Younger, friend of Brahms and Bruckner, was like a veritable god. Romantic Europe was gripped by dance fever. It has been said that, following the Napoleonic wars, in the French capital alone there were over 1,800 dance salons reverberating nightly to quadrilles, polkas, galops and can-cans.

The 19th century universalized national dance. American dance was universalized in the 20th: ragtime, jazz, conga, rumba, tango and samba. ♪

"Dancing is practised to make manifest whether lovers are in good health and sound in all their limbs." (Arbeau)

Above: The Strauss waltzes were said to be to the Viennese what the Napoleonic victories were to the French.

Ballet

IF DRAMA IS A STORY ACTED AND OPERA A story sung, ballet is a story danced. Western ballet goes back to the 15th century, when it was associated with the costumed Renaissance festivities of the Italian, French and Burgundian courts. Early ballet ranged from simple dance sequences to elaborately choreographed representations involving mime, verse, song and ambitious staging. Originally it took place in the banqueting halls of palaces, danced by the nobility (up to and including kings, most notably Louis XIV). Only later, in the 17th century, was it transferred to the theatre, with virtuoso professionals replacing dilettante amateurs.

Poetry, music and dance in harmony developed out of masquerade, the allegorical/mythological *trionfi* of the Italians, equestrian ballet (*ballet de chevaux*) and social dance. The *ballet de cour* (or court ballet) was introduced to France in 1533 for the wedding of Catherine de' Medici and Henry II. The most celebrated example (and the earliest for which music survives) was the *Ballet Comique de la Royne*, given in October 1581 at the Hôtel de Bourbon in the Louvre. This extraordinary spectacular of dance, song, recitation and mechanicals, based on the Circe legend, lasted five-and-a-half hours and cost three-and-a-half million gold francs to stage. Its choreography was geometrical.

The Golden Age of ballet is associated with the height of the Bourbon dynasty and the Paris of Louis XIV. Molière and the Franco-Italian Lully created and perfected a new kind of terpsichorean entertainment, the *comèdie-ballet* (most illustriously in *Le Bourgeois gentilhomme*,1670). Lully went on to include ballet in opera, a precursor of Jean-Philippe Rameau's opera-ballets half a century later. Regional country dances achieved courtly status – the minuet, with its fanciful bows and curtseys; the gavotte, a favourite of Marie Antoinette; the passepied; the bourrée; the rigaudon; the pastoral, pipe-droned musette. The Academie Royale de Danse was established in 1661 and, according to Pierre Rameau (1725), Pierre Beauchamp (the king's superintendent of ballet) invented the five classic foot positions (though it is now thought he probably only codified them).

Ballet d'action raised the art of ballet in the latter half of the 18th century to the level of dramatic representation. Closely integrating (in the modern sense) scenario, music, choreography and design, its chief long-term significance was that it was wordless, telling a story through dance and mime only. Angiolini, Hilverding and John Weaver (the father of English pantomime) introduced the style, but it was left to a Frenchman, Jean-Georges Noverre – ballet master at the Paris Opéra – to define it (1758). Noverre wanted to do away with the clumsy leather masks, full skirts, panniers, periwigs, plumes and helmets of earlier practice, desiring instead a looser "dress more noble, accurate, and picturesque".

Vienna, the Hapsburg capital, was an important ballet centre rivalling Versailles and attracting the finest dancers and choreographers of 18th-century Europe. Here, during the reign of Maria Theresia, there could be as many as three new productions a month, with *divertissement* and dance a routine ingredient of opera. Taking his story-lines from the plays of Voltaire, Racine and others, Hilverding pioneered the dramatic pantomimic experience of *ballet d'action*. Vienna was a centre for equestrian dance – a 17th-century legacy that can still be seen in the modern Lipizzaner exhibitions of the Spanish Riding School.

Like Romantic instrumental music, Romantic ballet took technique and ornament to extremes. It was about freedom

Anna Pavlova rehearsing with the influential ballet-master and choreographer Marius Petipa.

A performance at the Théâtre Petit Bourbon, Paris, 1654. The golden age of ballet coincided with the height of the Bourbon dynasty.

• ROMANTIC & CLASSICAL BALLETS •

➤ *La fille mal gardée* This is one of the most popular ballets in the repertoire, famous from the 1960 Ashton/Lanchberry production for the Royal Ballet. An innocent country romance crossed with comedy, the original *Fille* appeared in 1789. The modern *Fille*, one of the great box-office successes of Romantic Europe, with additional tunes from Rossini operas plus extra music by Hérold, was created for the Paris Opéra in 1828. For a Berlin production in 1864, Peter Ludwig Hertel provided a completely fresh score, used by Petipa and Ivanov for their 1885 St Petersburg revival.

➤ *Giselle* A *ballet fantastique* in two acts, *Giselle* was first produced at the Paris Opera in 1841, to music by Adam. Inspired by Heine, it is about the love of a Rhineland peasant girl, Giselle, for a handsome count, Albert (Albrecht), whose station in life she is unaware of. Albert, betrothed to another, loves her in turn. Hilarion, a jealous gamekeeper whose feelings for Giselle are unrequited, reveals all. Giselle loses her mind and dies. Albert and Hilarion come to her grave. At midnight the Wilis, the ghosts of brides dead before their wedding day, drive Hilarion into the lake. Albert is saved from death only by the spirit of Giselle, who dances with him till sunrise. *Giselle* is the essence of Romantic ballet.

➤ *Coppélia* Another Paris Opéra success, first produced in 1870. Inspired by E T A Hoffmann, with music by Delibes, *Coppélia* combines the romance of Swanilda and Franz with the story of a doll-maker Coppelius who wants to make a doll with a soul, Coppélia – with whom Franz, of course, has to fall in love. It was an enormously popular ballet, coloured by some exotic Eastern European touches (a Hungarian *csárdás*, for example).

➤ *The Sleeping Beauty* Combining the best of French and Italian classical tradition, the legendary French dancer, choreographer and ballet master Marius Petipa (1818–1910) created Russian Romantic ballet and took it to its climax with this work. Based on a fairy story by Perrault, Tchaikovsky's *Sleeping Beauty* (St Petersburg, 1890) was his crowning achievement. The composer collaborated closely with Petipa, producing a score of mighty symphonic integration and powerful intuitive suggestion.

➤ *Les Sylphides* Fokine choreographed this one-act ballet for his wife and Pavlova, its first performance being in St Petersburg in 1907. Using piano music by Chopin, orchestrated originally by Glazunov, its cameos range variously from a Polish ballroom and wedding to a classically costumed set-piece and Neapolitan dance. An expanded version in 1909 – with Pavlova, Karsavina and Nijinsky among the principals – was produced in Paris by Diaghilev.

➤ *Nutcracker* The *Nutcracker* (illustrated) was Tchaikovsky's last ballet (1892). Petipa based it on a version of E T A Hoffmann's story *The Nutcracker and the Mouseking*. The child Klara is given a nutcracker for Christmas. In her dream she defends it against the Mouseking. The nutcracker turns into a handsome Prince, who takes her on a wondrous journey through a snowstorm to the Kingdom of Sweets, where she meets the Sugar Plum Fairy and encounters exotic dances from Spain to China. The *Nutcracker* is an eminently danceable entertainment, elegant, charming and tuneful, endorsing Tchaikovsky's belief that ballet in general was "a prettiment of life rather than an interpretation of life".

of physical movement made possible through the *tutu* (short skirt) and *maillot* (tights). The vigorous dancer Marie-Anne Camargo (1710–70) is credited with having shortened the skirt of traditional costume to allow for more flexibility. She also took over steps previously the prerogative of male dancers. The exquisite Swedish-Italian Marie Taglioni (1804–84) – taught by the vain, dazzling Auguste Vestris (1760–1842), the premier virtuoso *danseur étoil* of his day – was considered the most important ballerina of the Romantic age, transforming the dance on points which Amalia Brugnoli is said to have been the first to display during the 1820s.

Romantic ballet, with its phantoms and elemental beings, was the fantasy of early 19th-century Europe; classical ballet was the art of late 19th-century Russia. Ballet in Russia was reformed by Hilverding in the mid-18th century. It flourished during the 1800s, attracting the best dancers, ballet masters and choreographers from Europe. Under the despotic Marius Petipa it reached its zenith in 1862–1903 (with the Tchaikovsky ballets and Glazunov's *Raymonda*), at a time when ballet in the West was on the decline. From a *danse d'école* for children of the Tsar's court, founded in 1738, to the modern Kirov company, so named in 1935, St Petersburg (Leningrad) was the centre of a famous tradition that produced Pavlova, Karsavina, Nijinsky, Fokine, Diaghilev, Balanchine, Ulanova, Dudinskaya, Makarova, Nureyev and Baryshnikov. *Romeo and Juliet* (Prokofiev), *Gayaneh* and *Spartacus* (Khachaturian) were all Kirov productions. Moscow's eminence dates from 1773 and the founding of a ballet class attached to the Orphanage – the origin of the Russian national ballet movement of the 1820s and 1830s and today's Bolshoi. During the early 20th century Moscow was recognized as a stronghold of dramatic ballet. After 1945, with Prokofiev's *Cinderella*, Ulanova's transfer from Leningrad and the spellbinding presence and technical brilliance of Plisetskaya, it became the mecca of Soviet dance. "The Russian terpsichore's soul-inspired flight" was how Pushkin described Russian ballet.

Modern Dance

THE BALLETS RUSSES DE SERGE DIAGHILEV dominated ballet between 1909 and 1929. His dancers ranged from Pavlova, Karsavina, Fokine and Nijinsky to Balanchine, Dolin, Rambert and de Valois. Fokine, Nijinsky, Massine and Balanchine were among his choreographers and his stage designers included Benois, Bakst, Picasso, Matisse, Braque and Utrillo. The composers with whom he collaborated could not have been more illlustrious: Stravinsky, Ravel, Debussy, Richard Strauss, Satie, Falla, Prokofiev, Poulenc, Respighi, Milhaud. Diaghilev never choreographed a ballet but through his impresario flair and the imagination of his Ballets Russes he not only introduced the Russian tradition to

RITE OF SPRING

Stravinsky's two earlier Diaghilev ballets, *The Firebird* and *Petrushka*, told stories. *The Rite of Spring* – 'Pictures from Pagan Russia' in 14 interconnected tableaux divided into two parts ('The Adoration of the Earth' and 'The Sacrifice') – merely suggested one. After 120 rehearsals, Diaghilev staged the first performance at the Théâtre des Champs-Elysées, Paris, on Thursday 29 May 1913. Nijinsky was the choreographer, Pierre Monteux the conductor. The occasion was a riot. The *Rite* was like nothing else: it was new and disturbing, dispensing with all the usual methods of creating tension, climax and repose. It negated conventional tonality. It generated the power of a Russian spring through pounding rhythms and repetition, freed from metric restriction. It inhabited a world of cataclysmic unleashed forces offset by landscapes of the bleakest economy. To sensibilities brought up on the con-trivance and innocence of Romantic ballet, its morality was offensive. With the *Rite*, Stravinsky became the *enfant terrible* of the modern age.

Europe, he also gave early 20th-century ballet an entirely new weight and perspective, combining the classical with the nationalistic and stylization with naturalism.

Isadora Duncan and Ida Rubinstein introduced another dimension to dance. The American Duncan was of the anti-ballet, emotionally expressive, bare-foot, Greek antiquity revival school and Rubinstein, the Russian dancer, mime artist and actress who created Ravel's *Bolero* and *La Valse*, shared some of her ideas. In the United States George Balanchine, discovered by Diaghilev, revolutionized and modernized the art with examples like Stravinsky's *Jeu de cartes* and *Agon*. Others responsible for new directions in American ballet have included Antony Tudor, Martha Graham, the queen of modern dance, and the avant-gardist Merce Cunningham. At the Royal Ballet in Britain, de Valois, Ashton, Helpmann, Massine, Petit, Cranko, MacMillan and Rodrigues all helped develop 20th-century ballet into a dramatic, expressive art form, making London the ballet centre of modern times. Cranko later went to Germany,

in the process turning the Stuttgart Ballet into one of the world's great companies. At the Paris Opéra, the outspoken Serge Lifar, from the Diaghilev stable, remodelled contemporary French ballet.

Ballet in the 20th century has been about expansion, experiment and crossover.

Martha Graham in *Judith* (1950); music by William Schumann.

Karsavina in *The Firebird* at the time of its premiere in Paris in 1910.

• FIVE MODERN BALLETS •

➤ **The Firebird** Stravinsky's first ballet, choreographed by Fokine with costumes by Bakst, was produced by the Diaghilev company at the Paris Opéra in 1910. Drawing its inpiration from Russian folk tales and divided into set dances and mime (recalling the arias and recitatives of opera), it tells of Prince Ivan who captures the mysterious Firebird. She helps him kill the demon Kastchei who holds prisoner the beautiful Tsarevna with whom the Prince has fallen in love. If *The Sleeping Beauty* was the last great ballet of the 19th century, *The Firebird* was the first of the 20th. A work of vivid imagination and picturesque orchestration, its success (in both theatre and concert hall) was to change Stravinsky's life.

➤ **Daphnis and Chloë** Ravel called his *Daphnis and Chloë* (1912) a "choreographic symphony in three scenes". He based it on the well-known antique pastoral by Longus, telling of the love of the young shepherd Daphnis for the beautiful Chloë who is captured by pirates and is saved only through the intervention of the god Pan.

➤ **The Miraculous Mandarin** This lurid one-act pantomime by the Hungarian Béla Bartók, the finest of his dramatic works, was produced in Cologne in 1926. Banned on moral grounds by Konrad Adenauer and not revived until 1942, it is an expressionistic melodrama about three pimps who force a prostitute to steal from her clients. They try to kill a Chinese mandarin but he refuses to die until the girl gives in to his desires. The strongly defined gestures of the music, it has been suggested, virtually map out its choreography.

➤ **Romeo and Juliet** Central to the modern repertoire, Prokofiev's *Romeo and Juliet*, first seen in Brno in 1938 and then in Leningrad two years later, closely follows Shakespeare's tragedy, emphasizing in particular the social conflict of the feuding Montagues and Capulets. It is in the form of three acts and 13 scenes framed by a prologue and an epilogue, and has been called the most successful (symphonic) ballet since Tchaikovsky. It was not always so considered, however. The Bolshoi believed it was undanceable, and the Kirov claimed there was no duller narration in the world. Even Galina Ulanova, the first Soviet Juliet, disliked it: "It was better to turn to ourselves ... other melodies ... and create our dances to our own music".

➤ **Rodeo** Aaron Copland favoured scenarios with a strong American theme: *Billy the Kid* was a grand opera western, while *Appalachian Spring* for Martha Graham was concerned with puritanism and the pioneering spirit. According to its choreographer, Agnes de Mille, *Rodeo, The Courting at Burnt Ranch* (New York, 1942) dealt "with a problem that has confronted all American women from the earliest pioneering times and throughout the history of the building of our country – how to get a suitable man". A *divertissement*, its scenario is simple: the cowboys on a Texan ranch chase any woman in sight, unaware of a pretty cowgirl in their midst whose charms only become apparent at the Saturday night barn dance. With *Rodeo* Copland brought the square-dance into ballet, guaranteeing the 'storybook West' authenticity of his music through a brilliant adaptation of foot-tapping American folk tunes.

From classic to rock, theatre and social dance, from Dadaism to the choreography of great symphonies by Beethoven, Brahms, Mahler and Messiaen, modern ballet has flowered in many expressive and suggestive forms: Ballet-allegory; Ballet-film (Gene Kelly in *Invitation to the Dance*, 1952); Ballet-pantomime (especially popular in Denmark since Bournonville's 19th-century renaissance); Ballet with song (Stravinsky and Massine's *Pulcinella*, 1920); Ballet with words (Martha Graham's *American Document*, 1938, based on the Declaration of Independence, Walt Whitman and other texts); Burlesque (Stravinsky and Fokine's *Petrushka*, 1911; Stravinsky and Nijinska's *Le Renard* , 1922); Choreographic-comedy (Massine's *The Good-Humoured Ladies* after Scarlatti, 1917); Choreographic-fantasy (Henze's *Labyrinth*, 1951); Choreographic-legend (Hindemith and Massine's *Nobilissima Visione*, 1938); Choreographic-poem (Ravel and Nijinska's *La Valse*, 1929); Choreographic-tragedy (Auric and Lifar's *Phèdre*, 1950); Dance-poem (Debussy and Nijinsky's *Jeux*, 1913); Dance-solo (Fokine's *The Dying Swan* created for Anna Pavlova in 1907 to music by Saint-Saëns – the spirit of Romanticism incarnate);

Dramatic-ballet (Bernstein's *Age of Anxiety*, 1950); English pantomime (Berners and Balanchine's *The Triumph of Neptune*, 1926); Lyric-drama/opera-ballet (Henze's *Boulevard Solitude*, 1952); Madrigal-fable (Menotti's *The Unicorn, the Gorgon and the Manticore*, 1957); Masque, recollecting the Tudor/Jacobean equivalent of *ballet de cour* (Vaughan Williams and de Valois' *Job, A Masque for Dancing*, 1931); Melodrama (Stravinsky's *Persephone*, 1934); Narrative-ballet (Stravinsky's *L'Histoire du Soldat*, 1918); Realistic-ballet (Satie and Massine's *Parade*, with Cubist decor by Picasso, 1917). ♪

Bakst's costume for Nijinsky in *L'Après-midi d'un faune*.

Etude

THE FRENCH WORD ETUDE (TRANSLATED as 'Study' in English, 'Etüde' in German and 'Studio' in Italian) is most commonly used to describe a short instrumental piece. Other terms include 'Caprice' and 'Lesson'.

ETUDES ARE OF TWO BASIC TYPES. THE didactic study, specifically designed for the mastery of an instrument, usually finds technical considerations taking precedence over musical content, though the celebrated piano études of Clementi (especially *Gradus ad Parnassum*), Cramer, Czerny and Moscheles (in particular the *Characteris- ischen Studien*) are, for the most part, a congenial fusion of discipline and delight. (Brain-numbing, finger-aching tortures by the likes of Bertini, Kessler, Ravina, Schulhoff and Steibelt are now justly consigned to oblivion.) Rodolphe Kreutzer, Fiorillo and Rode wrote valuable pieces for the violin student, while cellists are well served by Dotzauer and Grützmacher. The second, more common, type of étude is a musical representation of some kind of dramatic situation or poetic imagery designed for the concert hall; in short, an instrumental piece which requires both technique and interpretation (which makes it a close relation of the symphonic poem).

It was Paganini, considered by his audiences to be the devil incarnate, who ushered in an era of unprecedented virtuosic wizardry. The manner in which he pushed violin technique to new horizons is typified

by his truly diabolical *Caprices* (1820). These études exerted a profound influence upon his contemporaries, in particular Liszt, whose *Grandes Etudes* (1839) are arguably the most difficult concert studies ever written for the piano. He later revised them – 'simplified' is not an appropriate word given their still awesome complexity – as *Etudes d'exécution transcendante* (1851). However, it was the more introspective Chopin who penned the most poetic yet

Niccolò Paganini (1782–1840), one of the most charismatic performers of all time. He hypnotized his audiences with a potent mix of stupefying technique and a bizarre appearance.

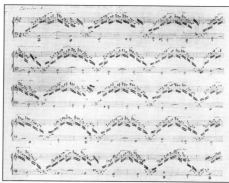

Autograph scores of Chopin's first étude, Op. 10 No. 1 in C major and (far left) Paganini's *Le Streghe* ('The Witches'). Paganini borrowed a theme from Sussmayr's *Il noce di Benevento*.

Chopin composing the C minor étude. He was 19 when he first heard Paganini, an experience which led to his 24 études for solo piano.

FIVE FAMILIAR ETUDES

➤ **Paganini: Caprice No. 24** Liszt, Schumann and Brahms as well as countless later figures, not least Blacher, Lutoslawski, Lloyd Webber, Rachmaninov and Schnittke, all wrote pieces inspired by the insidious little theme which provides the basis of Paganini's Caprice No. 24. The full extent of Paganini's technical vocabulary, not least left-hand *pizzicati*, harmonics and double-stopping, is displayed in 11 variations.

➤ **Chopin: *Revolutionary Etude*** The most famous of all Chopin's études, the last of the *12 Etudes*, Op. 10, was written at Stuttgart in April 1831 when the composer learned of the fall of Warsaw to the Russians. It is both an outburst of wild despair and a demanding essay in right-hand octaves set against rapid left-hand figuration.

➤ **Liszt: *Feux-follets*** ('Will-'o-the-Wisp') The feathery lightness of Will-'o-the-Wisp, the subject of Liszt's fifth *Etude d'exécution transcendante*, can only be achieved by a pianist with a truly transcendental technique – a rare ability to play at dare-devil speed yet with refined delicacy.

➤ **Alkan: *Le Festin d'Esope*** The final étude from Alkan's Studies in Minor Keys is a dazzling set of 25 variations on a theme which, in its quirkiness, comes close to rivalling Paganini's Caprice No. 24. Each variation depicts a different (and unspecified) creature in Aesop's fables.

➤ **Debussy: *Pour les Accords*** This concludes Debussy's études. It encapsulates the technical demands and the harmonic complexity of the composer's last great opus for piano and also signposts one direction for 20th-century music.

technically brilliant and emotionally varied études (two sets of 12: Opp. 10 and 25). Another notable contributor to the form was Chopin's next-door neighbour in Paris, Charles Morhange, better known as Alkan. His most testing contributions are the 12 Studies in Major Keys, Op. 35 (1847) and the 12 Studies in Minor Keys, Op. 39 (1857), the latter including both a concerto and a symphony for piano solo. Within a very short while the étude had become the ultimate display piece, with few among the great procession of virtuosi to appear in Liszt's wake able to resist the form. Henselt, Moszkowski, Anton Rubinstein, Xaver Scharwenka, Tausig and Thalberg are but a few of those who penned highly colourful, finger-twisting novelties.

When the torch passed to Schumann and Brahms they transformed and extended the scope of the concert étude via variation form, Schumann with his *Symphonic Variations* (1834) and Brahms with his *Handel Variations* (1861) and *Paganini Variations* (1862–63). Others, in particular the Russians, remained true to the traditional étude with its more modest proportions, though Liapounov emulated Liszt with his own set of 12 *Transcendental studies* (1900–5) and Rachmaninov personalized the form with two sets of *Etudes-tableaux* (1911 and 1916–17) which, for many, enshrine the soul of the Romantic piano. It was left to Claude Debussy to push forward musical frontiers with his *Douze Etudes* (1915). Written during his final creative surge, these pieces represent the very summit of the French keyboard tradition. ♪

LIFE AFTER THE SOLO ETUDE

The time eventually came when the étude reached such a degree of complexity that virtuosity became an end in itself. Godowsky's *Badinage*, for example, is nothing less than the simultaneous presentation of two Chopin études (Op. 10/5 and Op. 25/9). Godowsky also reworked Chopin études for the left hand alone. The challenge of writing for the left hand was also met by, among many, Brahms (including a transcription of nothing less than the famous Chaconne from J S Bach's Second Partita for solo violin) and Saint-Saëns (a set of six elegant études, Op. 136) as well as Bartók and Scriabin.

Individual virtuosity inevitably suffocated in its own web of tangled complexities. Only corporate virtuosity remained – hence a string of impressive 20th-century orchestral works requiring an unusual degree of facility. The list includes Stravinsky's *Quatre Etudes pour orchestre* (1929), Rawsthorne's *Symphonic Studies* (1939), Henze's *Symphonische Etüden* (1955) and Martin's *Etudes pour orchestre a cordes* (1956). Although Elgar described his *Falstaff* (1913) as a 'symphonic study' this is more closely related to the symphonic poem. Finally, mention must be made of Riisager's deft and witty arrangement of a selection of Czerny's piano studies for Lander's ballet *Etudes* (1948) – which is where we began.

Prelude

A S ITS NAME IMPLIES, THIS IS A PIECE OF music to be played as a preliminary: similarly, music which is played before an opera, play or ceremony.

IT IS COMMONLY AGREED THAT THE prelude evolved from brief improvisations made by instrumentalists checking the tuning of their instruments. From these beginnings there developed two types of preludes, the first an introduction to another piece (or group of pieces) in the same key or style, the second a composition which precedes a specific movement, for example a prelude and fugue. A third type of prelude, illogically named in that it has no sequel, is a short concert work usually for piano but occasionally for orchestra.

The earliest known preludes are of the first type and date back to the 15th century. It was not until the 17th century that the prelude with sequel came into its own. J S Bach's achievements, including many magnificent preludes and fugues for organ and the mighty *Das wohltemperierte Klavier* (*The Well-Tempered Clavier*) – two books of 24 preludes and fugues for keyboard known as 'The 48' – are unsurpassed for their mastery and logic. Bach, incidentally, also wrote many introductory preludes – for example, each of his six *Unaccompanied Cello Suites*, BWV1007–1012 and six *English Suites*, BWV 806–811 begin with a prelude before continuing with a sequence of dance movements.

Along with many other classical forms, the prelude was largely neglected during much of the 18th century and only enjoyed a revival thanks to the interest of Romantic composers. Mendelssohn's six *Preludes and Fugues for Piano*, Op. 35 (1837) are a happy reconciliation of the old with the new and Liszt's *Prelude and Fugue on B-A-C-H*, S260 (1853) for organ was written in homage to the great 'JSB'. Late in his life César Franck wrote two major works for piano – the *Prélude, choral et fugue*, M21 (1884) and the *Prélude, aria et final*, M23 (1888) – which, while being deeply personal, are steeped in Bach's influence.

The prelude as an independent concert piece appears to owe its existence to Hummel, whose 24 *Preludes*, Op. 67 were

Debussy's *La Cathédrale engloutie* was inspired by the legend of Ys.

(Painting: Rouen Cathedral, by Monet, 1894).

THREE CELEBRATED PRELUDES

J S BACH Prelude No.1 in C, BWV846 (*The Well-Tempered Clavier*)
The opening pages of one of the most familiar pieces in all music are nothing more than a succession of arpeggios. From that humbling simplicity rises one of the great landmarks in all music. Nothing can detract from its greatness – not even the cloying sentimentality of Gounod's addition of the implied melodic line and the title *Ave Maria*.

CHOPIN Prelude No. 15 in D flat, Op.28 (*The Raindrop*)
Chopin's preludes rank among his greatest achievements, masterpieces of a bewildering range of styles and moods. Most familiar is No. 15, known as *The Raindrop* on account of the story (attributed to Chopin's mistress, George Sand) in which Chopin (shown right in a drawing by Sand) is supposed to have been inspired by rain dripping from a roof. From monotony – the persistent repetition of a single note – Chopin creates poetry.

RACHMANINOV Prelude in C sharp minor, Op. 3/2
A work which the composer regretted having composed. Written in 1892 when Rachmaninov was in his late teens, and published as the second of five miscellaneous pieces Op. 3, it became one of the most popular works of its era and came to haunt the composer wherever he appeared. To add insult to injury, he earned no royalties from it, having sold the piece outright to his publisher. Rachmaninov later composed more characteristic preludes: a set of 10 (Op. 23 of 1901/3) and a set of 13 (Op. 32 of 1910).

published in about 1814. Chopin's 24 *Preludes*, Op. 28 did not appear in print until 1839. The flair and originality of Chopin's Op. 28 was not lost on his contemporaries and successors: Heller, Alkan, Cui and Busoni all wrote sets of preludes in the major and minor keys. Subsequent generations of pianist-composers, including such disparate figures as Szymanowski, Scriabin, Rachmaninov, Debussy, Gershwin, Messaien and Ginastera were, for the most part, content to pen preludes that were self-contained, non-programmatic concert pieces. Only Shostakovich returned to the prelude and

fugue format. His 24 *Preludes and Fugues*, Op. 87 (1950–51) encompass a unique emotional and intellectual diversity. Perhaps the most unorthodox 20th-century contribution to the form is Schoenberg's Prelude *Genesis*, Op. 44 (1945) for chorus and orchestra.

Finally, a mention of the orchestral prelude. Operatic composers occasionally replaced the formal overture with an atmospheric prelude, most familiarly Wagner (*Lohengrin* and *The Ring*) and Verdi (*La Traviata*). Liszt's *Les Préludes* has no connection with this musical form, being a symphonic poem. ♪

Nocturne

THE FRENCH FORM, NOCTURNE, COMMONLY defines a composition suggestive of night. By its very nature it is a slow, reflective piece and is invariably for piano.

The paternity of the romantic nocturne is attributed to the Irish composer John Field. His were trail-blazing compositions, being among the very first self-sufficient works for piano. Liszt publicly recognized the Irishman's achievements when he wrote (in an introduction to the first collected

DURING THE 18TH CENTURY THE ITALIAN word 'notturno' was used to describe a serenade-type composition of an undemonstrative nature which was usually scored for two or more solo instruments. Among the earliest known are those by Haydn for two lyre organizzate. (The lyra organizzata was a hybrid folk instrument resembling an uncomfortable marriage between a hurdy-gurdy and a small portable organ.) Haydn's admirer, Gyrowetz, wrote many notturni for various combinations of instruments though, as usual, it was Mozart who produced the most enchanting examples: his Serenata Notturna, K239 is scored for two orchestras (which results in some remarkable 'stereophonic' effects) while the Notturno, K286 (296a) is scored for no fewer than four orchestras.

• FAKE NOCTURNES •

➤ Debussy's choice of *Nocturnes* as a title for his three kaleidoscopic orchestral pictures was inspired by the American artist Rex Whistler, who had applied the term to his studies of the River Thames. Far from being 'of the night', Debussy's *Nocturnes* are concerned with the ever-changing qualities of light as depicted by Turner and the Impressionists.

➤ The title of Beethoven's *Moonlight Sonata* was none of the composer's doing but the brainchild of a misguided critic, Ludwig Rellstab (also remembered as a poet: Schubert set some of his texts to music). It does the work a distinct disservice as Beethoven was involved in some radical experimentation (see page 95) rather than portraying a night-time idyll. Similarly, the title *Notturno* for Schubert's single movement for piano trio was applied only by the composer's publisher and carries no significance.

publication of Field's nocturnes in 1859) "they have opened the way for all productions which have since appeared under such titles as Songs without words, Impromptus, Ballades etc.. To Field we may trace the origin of pieces designed to convey subjective and profound emotion". Today their charm seems rather modest and somewhat faded, particularly when compared with Chopin's work in the same genre. However, Chopin would have been the first to declare his indebtedness to Field – and there is no denying the fact that at times there are uncanny similarities: compare, for example, Field's Fifth Nocturne with Chopin's Tenth Nocturne. But nowhere in Field's output is there to be found Chopin's confidence, his unerring sense of direction or his remarkable construction.

The nocturne attracted the attention of many Romantic composers, in particular the French. Fauré's nocturnes are exceptional: the delicate sensuousness of his language was ideally suited to the medium and he produced 13 fabulously crafted master-pieces. German composers appeared less keen, with the obvious exception of Schumann who characteristically contrasted lyric and turbulent elements and thus produced fevered, hallucinatory 'night visions'. Such movements appear in *Phantasiestücke,* Op. 12 (1838) and *Bunteblätter,* Op. 99 (1852) though perhaps the finest examples are the four *Nachtstücke,* Op. 23 (1840). The Germans were also inclined to blend the night atmosphere of the nocturne with elements of the earlier *notturno,* a classic example being the Nocturne to Mendelssohn's *A Midsummer Night's Dream.* The Russians, including Balakirev, Glinka, Rimsky-Korsakov, Medtner, Scriabin and Tchaikovsky, were much taken with the nocturne, though these generally slight pieces are seldom heard.

The Dublin-born pianist and composer John Field, who wrote 18 nocturnes as well as seven piano concertos and a large body of chamber music.

In the 20th century the term nocturne has been freely applied to a wide range of compositions, though still with the intention of evoking some aspect of night. Most are confined to the quiet of night, though the third movement of Vaughan Williams's *A London Symphony,* titled 'Nocturne', is a striking exception. Here is a bustling miniature symphonic poem depicting the busy nightlife of the capital – even to the extent of simulating the sound of the mouth-organ. Among later composers, Britten was unusually preoccupied with the unease of night and the troubled world of dreams – evident in his early *Serenade,* Op. 31 (1943) and dominating the song-cycle *Nocturne,* Op. 60 (1958) and two works for solo guitar, *Night Piece* (1963) and *Nocturnal,* Op. 70. Bartók created some of the most exploratory 'night music' to grace the concert hall, not least the third movement of *Music for Strings, Percussion and Celesta* (1936), the central movement of the Third Piano Concerto (1945) and in the piano suite *Out of Doors* (1926). ♪

{ Many Romantic composers attempted to capture the atmosphere of night, as did many painters, including Casper-David Friedrich.

∙ CHOPIN'S NOCTURNES ∙
~

Chopin elevated the nocturne into an art form, transforming a simple, somewhat rudimentary idea into an exquisite miniature lyrical poem. Eighteen nocturnes were published during his brief life, initially in groups of three and later in pairs; three more (Nos 19–21) were published posthumously, No. 19 being written when he was only 17.

It seems that Chopin turned to the nocturne whenever he felt the need to confide his innermost thoughts to paper. They were written throughout his life and consequently provide a very clear indication of the manner in which his style blossomed and matured. The early pieces are already fine works and not the least unworthy of him, though the progression from Op. 9 to Opp. 48 and 55 reveals an extraordinary advance in the subtlety of his harmony, the expansiveness of his melodies and the way in which they are constructed. Somehow Chopin miraculously created a variety of moods within these pieces: No. 2, the most popular, has a sublime melodic directness, No. 13 resembles an eerie funeral march, No. 14 is unbearably sad and No. 17 strangely unearthly.

Convincing performances of these nocturnes usually tally with the composer's constant exhortation to his pupils that "everything must sing, nothing should sound forced".

Fantasia

The use of the Italian word for 'fancy' signifies almost any kind of musical composition in which style and form take second place to flights of the imagination. The number of variants in the spelling of the title are almost as numerous as the types of composition it defines, and include Fantasy, Fancy and Fantazie (English).

In the Renaissance and 17th century, 'fantasia' was a common musical term for an instrumental piece resulting from 'the play of musical invention'. The majority of these fantasias were for lute, keyboard and consort though, with such a free form, variants soon became commonplace. In France, Spain, Italy, Germany, Poland, the Netherlands and Britain fantasias became *de rigueur*. Within each country the form developed its own particular individuality.

In the 18th century the exhilarating freedom of the fantasy extended beyond form and concept to rhythm and tempo. J S Bach's second surviving son, Carl Philipp Emanuel, wrote fantasias which contain movements that are partly or wholly without barlines. Beethoven undertook some significant experiments under the guise of the fantasia. His two piano sonatas Op. 27 (1800–1) – the second of which is the familiar *Moonlight* Sonata – are marked 'quasi una fantasia' and find him wrestling with irregular movement form. (These two sonatas are possibly the first large-scale fantasias to be cast in separate movements.) Among Beethoven's later exploratory works two are specifically entitled fantasia, that for piano, Op. 77 (1809), and for piano, chorus and orchestra, Op. 80 (1808).

The Romantics became very much enamoured of the multi-movement fantasia. Schubert's contributions are among the most striking, none more so than his *Fantasia in C for Violin and Piano*, D934 (1827), which consists of seven contrasted movements linked thematically, and the *Wanderer Fantasy*, D760 for piano (1822).

The fantasia has enabled composers to experiment without fear of offending convention. Early it took a variety of forms and could be an improvised piece for one or many players.

Schumann's *Fantasia in C*, Op. 17 (1836), is the largest work in his output to bear the title 'fantasy', though he also fashioned what can only be called mini fantasias – sequences of small, highly contrasted movements which he called *Phantasiestücke*. (Many smaller pieces from the romantic keyboard repertoire, from Mendelssohn's *Songs without Words* and Grieg's *Lyric Pieces* to late works by Brahms, are, in effect, extensions of the *Phantasiestücke*.) Chopin's *Fantasie in F minor,* Op. 49 (1841), is another highly innovative score in that it resembles a small symphony for solo piano.

The term fantasy was also applied to a short-lived form which arose during the 19th century. This was the operatic fantasy, a pot-pourri of operatic melodies served up by the outstanding virtuosi of the day. Among pianists Tausig, Thalberg,

---

• FAMILIAR INSTRUMENTAL FANTASIAS •

➤ **Schubert: Fantasie in C, D760 (*The Wanderer Fantasy*)** This is a seminal work if ever there was one. Schubert's *Wanderer Fantasy* contains four easily recognized and self-contained sections which share thematic material and are played without a break. The principal inspiration for the melody is a quotation from Schubert's 1816 song *Der Wanderer*. Liszt was also very taken with this masterpiece and made a transcription for two pianos as well as a version for piano and orchestra.

➤ **Liszt: *Réminiscences de Don Juan (Mozart),* S418** This is surely the greatest of Liszt's operatic fantasias for solo piano and the only one to be devoted to Mozart. Composed in 1841, it is extremely ambitious in that its cruel technical demands exist not as a vehicle for display of skill but rather as a means of creating a synthesis of the complex character of the Don.

➤ **Chopin: Fantasie in F minor, Op. 49** The noblest of all Chopin's works. Completed in 1841, it contains an exceptional diversity of ideas, all of which have their origin in the opening march-like theme. At times their development becomes wild and near abandoned. A brilliant fusion of introspection and passion, darkness and light.

➤ **Sarasate: *Carmen* Fantasy, Op.25** To be frank, this is not great music *per se*: the emphasis is unashamedly on entertainment. Themes from Bizet's *Carmen* – an inspiration to so many composers – are presented with disarming directness by a fully spotlit violinist and an orchestra (or piano) in dutiful, respectful attendance. It is a superlative, foot-tapping show-stopper.

THE TALLIS FOUNDATION

The Fantasia on a Theme by Thomas Tallis is both Vaughan Williams's first major orchestral work and his first indisputable masterpiece. Written in 1910 when the interest in Elizabethan composers in general, and the fantasia in particular, was at its height, this is one of the composer's (shown right) most eloquent creations, a score which has become synonymous with contemplative wonder.

A theme which Tallis contributed to Archbishop Parker's *Psalter* of 1567 is Vaughan Williams's starting point. Scored for double string orchestra (one of the two being a double string quartet with double bass) and solo string quartet, the writing is hypnotically antiphonal.

Moszkowski, Pabst and Gottschalk all produced glittering and demanding concoctions, though the undisputed master was Liszt, with some 70 fantasias to his credit. Paganini, Wieniawski, Ernst and Sarasate did their utmost to ensure the violin held its own, while Bottesini produced operatic fantasias for the double-bass.

During the 20th century most composers were content to look back to earlier times, to dress fantasias in modern garb. In Britain there was an unusual resurgence of interest in the fantasia, due largely to an amateur violinist and musical patron, Walter Cobbett. Three of Bridge's most original chamber works – the *Phantasie* Quartet (1905), the *Phantasie* Piano Trio (c.1907) and the *Phantasie* Piano Quartet (1910) all owe their existence to Cobbett, as does a *Phantasy* Oboe Quartet, Op. 2 (1932), by Bridge's 18-year-old pupil Benjamin Britten. Other English composers turned to orchestral fantasias, notable examples being Vaughan Williams's *Fantasia on a Theme by Thomas Tallis* (1910) and Tippett's *Fantasia Concertante on a Theme by Corelli* (1953). The single, most demanding fantasia of the century is arguably Schoenberg's *Phantas,* Op. 47 (1949), his last instrumental work, written originally for solo violin, though a subservient piano accompaniment was added later. ♪

Solo Sonata

"*Sonata [from the Italian sonare, 'to sound'],*"Rousseau says in his Dictionary of Music *(1767), "is, for instruments, very much what Cantata [from cantare, 'to sing'] is for the voice." In the late 16th century, both represented a common formal type: a sacred or secular work in several sections, of contrasted speed, rhythm and character, the one motivated by abstract idea, the other by representational text.*

IN THE SENSE OF A 'SOUNDED PIECE', sonata as a literary label goes back 700 years. Its modern understanding, of a work divided into contrasted movements (linked or separated), is more recent. Growing out of the 16th-century instrumental *ricercari* of the Venetian Andrea Gabrieli and the *canzoni* of his nephew Giovanni, the baroque sonata, largely developed by the Italians and copied by the Germans and French, basically fell into four different types: the 'asymmetrical' (fast/fugal-dance-fast, or fast-dance-fast with frequently an adagio placed before or after the central dance); the five-movement 'symmetrical' (fast-slow-dance-slow-fast); the *sonata da chiesa* or church sonata (slow-fast-slow-fast); and the *sonata da camera* or chamber/court sonata (largely dance-based). It is often generalized that Corelli established the *chiesa* and *camera* forms. But, provocatively, he was also responsible for converging the two, thus blurring the distinction. Tradition has it that the suites and partitas of Bach and Handel developed from the mainly dance-like *sonata da camera*, the sonatas of the Viennese from the mainly abstract *sonata da chiesa*.

With Haydn, Mozart and Beethoven (plus the Italian Clementi and the Bohemian Dussek) the classical solo sonata came imposingly into its own, as a medium for profound argument, personal expression and philosophical aspiration on a par with the symphony, concerto and string quartet (themselves other, larger 'sonata' manifestations). Sonata form was expanded as a structural, tonal and dramatic principle, and the contrast of keys within and between movements, often instead of self-sufficient melody, was given an importance unknown to the Baroque. The acceleration and reconciliation of tonal tension became the mainspring of sonata action. In design the Viennese sonata was mainly confined to three movements (a fast-slow-fast pattern derived from the Italian overture type of Alessandro Scarlatti and from the North German examples of Bach's eldest son, Carl Philipp Emanuel). But (paralleling his symphonies and quartets) Beethoven in his canon of 32 piano sonatas broadened it to sometimes incorporate a minuet or scherzo (most famously in his early Op. 2 set and the *Hammerklavier,* Op. 106). Including his last, the transcendent C minor, Op. 111, he also wrote several in just two movements, as did Haydn. His younger contemporary, Schubert, generally composed sonatas in three and four movements, whose combination of dramatic intent with lyrically intense song and experiment with form and tonality is bold.

"The sonata style of 1790 is not that of 1840," commented Schumann. "The demands of form and content have increased above all." The post-Beethoven

Arcangelo Corelli, arguably the greatest of the Italian virtuoso violinist-composers, wrote a number of sonatas for the violin.

A 19th-century cover by Franz Stasser for the score of the *Moonlight Sonata.*

MONDSCHEINSONATE

• SOME IMPORTANT SOLO SONATAS •

Kuhnau: Biblical Sonatas for Keyboard Kuhnau (Bach's predecessor at St Thomas's, Leipzig) believed himself to have pioneered the keyboard sonata in its solo sense. His six multi-movement *Biblical Sonatas* on stories from the Old Testament (1700) are an early example of programme music post-Frescobaldi.

Bach: Sonata No 3 in C for Unaccompanied Violin, BWV1005 The massively conceived *Veni sancte spiritus* fugue and adagio of this sonata (as much an endurance test for the player as the celebrated chaconne of the D minor Partita) show why Bach's six sonatas and partitas for solo violin (1720), cross-fertilizing *da chiesa* and *da camera*, have for so long been admired.

Domenico Scarlatti: Harpsichord Sonata in E major, L23 (Kk380) In his old age in Spain Scarlatti, an exact contemporary of Bach and Handel, wrote over 550 single-movement keyboard sonatas (or 'Essercizi'), designed, so he tells us, not to display "any profound learning, but rather an ingenious Jesting with Art". Most of his sonatas are in two-part binary form, with embryonic suggestions of exposition, development and reprise.

Mozart: Keyboard Sonata in A major, K331 Made up of a set of variations, a minuet and the well-known *rondo alla Turca* (in the popular Ottoman or Turkish style of the 18th century), this work, written in the early 1780s, contains no movement in sonata form.

Haydn: Keyboard Sonata No 50 in C Haydn's successively imposing, pensive and humorous late C major Sonata dates from his second London visit (1794–95). Supporting the view of one 19th-century German critic that the sonata mould was a means for the Classicists "to show in the first movement what they could do, in the second what they could feel, and in the last how glad they were to have finished", it ranks among the finer expressions of Haydn's maturity.

Beethoven: Piano Sonata in C sharp minor, Op. 27 No 2 (Moonlight) The first edition of the *Moonlight* Sonata (1801) was described as a 'Sonata quasi una Fantasia', a sonata in the manner of a fantasy. Played without a break, it comprises an opening triplet-dominated adagio, a central *moment musical*-like dance that is neither minuet nor scherzo, and a closing sonata-form presto. It was a German critic, Ludwig Rellstab, who likened the music of the famous adagio to an image of Lake Lucerne seen by moonlight.

Beethoven: Piano Sonata in B flat, Op. 106 (Hammerklavier) Dedicated to the composer's patron the Archduke Rudolph of Austria, and written in 1817/18, this piece is a veritable symphony for piano, conceived on the grandest scale. Thematically and tonally integrated, it is a work epochal for its mix of sonata-form and large-scale fugal procedure, for the mercurial teasing and snarling temper of its scherzo (placed second), and for the celestial poetry of its adagio.

Schubert: Piano Sonata in B flat, D960 Posthumously published, Schubert's last piano sonata (1828) is a work of breadth, profundity and playful affection, constantly surprising in its melodic development and tonal digression. Over the past 50 years every leading pianist has performed it.

Mendelssohn: Organ Sonata in F minor, Op. 65 No 1 Sundry organ voluntaries, which bear little relation to classical sonata practice, make up Mendelssohn's six Sonatas Op. 65 (1845). Paying homage to Bach, the first movement of the F minor combines fugal texture with a chorale prelude (*Ich hab' in Gottes Herz und Sinn*). This is followed by a slow 'song without words', a recitative, and a finale written in the style of a brilliant toccata.

Liszt: Piano Sonata in B minor Dedicated to Schumann and modelled after Schubert's motto-cyclic *Wanderer* Fantasy (a favourite work of Liszt's) the B minor Sonata (1851-53) is an extraordinary hybrid: a linked work in four 'movements' (allegro, adagio, scherzo/fugato and finale, corresponding to the exposition, [double] development and recapitulation of a traditional sonata-form structure), flanked by a prologue and epilogue, and unified through variously transformed themes or motivic cells. Add an implicit Faustian programmatic tension and you have one of the most innovative, challenging sonata achievements of all time.

Scriabin: Piano Sonata No 9, Op. 68 (Black Mass) During the early years of the 20th century Scriabin turned the solo sonata into a spiritually electric fusion of melodic outpouring, tonal peculiarity and concentrated inter-relationship, climaxing his output in a series of single-movement works whose volatile, ecstatic complexity of organization and sub-division was not to be superseded even by Prokofiev or Medtner. He believed the so-called *Black Mass* Sonata (1911–14) to be not so much a ritual as a nightmarish vision of evil and imagined that whenever he played it he practised sorcery.

Bartók: Sonata for Unaccompanied Violin Bartók's last completed work (1944) is a four-movement epic courageously imagined. Dealing in the old forms and textures of sonata, chaconne, fugue and rondo, in inventive string techniques, in images of rustling 'night music', in brave new worlds of equal-tempered and quarter-toned sound, no finer 20th-century reply exists to Bach or the virtuoso violin schools of the Baroque. It was commissioned by Yehudi Menuhin.

---

sonatas of the 19th century are a mixed assemblage. In many, melody and literal repetition are more important than tonality or organic development. Chopin's three for piano all place the dance movement second. Brahms's Third is in five movements, recalling the 'symmetrical' model of the Baroque. Liszt's pioneering B minor plays continuously, its events recollecting historically the divisions and contrasts of an even earlier cantata/sonata/canzona genesis. During the Romantic age the solo sonata exchanged the privacy of the drawing-room soirée for the domain of the public recital. It lost its amateur status and became an occupation for professionals.

Many 20th-century composers have rejected the sonata tradition because they see it as old-fashioned and limiting. The sonata today is accordingly all things to all men: Post-Romantic extension (Berg's single-movement Op. 1); tone poem (Janáček's *I.X.*, 1905). Neo-Classical throwback (Stravinsky); Beethovenian rebirth (Boulez's Second, Tippett's Third); even 'sounded piece' (the serial cosmos, the black-hole silences, of Jean Barraqué).

Duo and Ensemble Sonatas

THE SONATA IN ALL ITS PRESENTATIONS from solo to orchestral, from Haydn, Mozart and Beethoven to Mahler, Sibelius and Shostakovich, has been the most important large-scale instrumental concept in Western music since the late Baroque. "The vehicle of the sublime", the pianist Charles Rosen calls it, playing "the same role in music as the epic in poetry, and the large historical fresco in painting. The proof of craftsmanship was the fugue, but the proof of greatness was the sonata". Writing a sonata gave a composer respectability.

For the Romantics and their heirs it was the supreme form of instrumental music, with Beethoven, bridging the eras, its universal godhead. To the Classicists sonata was a closed form. To the Romantics it was open. To the Classicists a sonata implied a work in three or four movements, each of a distinctive kind and in a specific order: typically, fast (sonata form), slow (variation, romance, abridged sonata form), dance (minuet, scherzo), and fast (rondo, variation, sonata form). To the Romantics it could mean (almost) anything – from traditionally derived experience (Chopin, Schumann, Brahms) to radical innovation (Liszt). In a sonata-structure movement the Classicists normally contrived the climax, the high point of tension, at the end of the development. The Romantics placed it at the end of the reprise, or even at the very end of a work. Classically, the emotional and intellectual gravity of a sonata was usually centred in its opening allegro. Romantically, a shift of climactic weight to the finale, followed by the progressive equality of other movements, mattered more, as Brahms reminds us.

For Baroque composers, and in particular the Italians (Corelli, Geminiani, Locatelli, Tartini, Vivaldi, Veracini), the accompanied virtuoso violin sonata was an important phenomenon. In this the violin was supported by a figured bass part for continuo, normally taken by two instruments (a harpsichord filling in the harmony, and a viola da gamba or cello doubling the bassline). Evolved from early 17th-century forerunners (notably, Marini's *Affetti musicali*), Corelli's 12 *Suonate a violino e violone o cembalo,* Op. 5 (Rome,

• NOTABLE DUO SONATAS •

➤ **Mozart: Sonata in E minor for Violin and Keyboard, K304** One of Mozart's sonatas (1778) in the French style, with two movements (the second a minuet). It is a work of Romantic prophecy, tellingly expressive in its use of the unison, its blend of violin and keyboard sympathetic. It has been queried whether it was the death of his mother or his loneliness in Paris that wrung from Mozart such a sudden, passionate lament.

➤ **Mozart: Sonata in E flat for Violin and Keyboard, K380** Among the first of Mozart's Viennese sonatas (1781), the E flat is a masterwork of genuine duo aspiration, with a central G minor slow movement of intense spiritual force. It is a sonata of vintage melody and sparkling layout, outwardly brilliant.

➤ **Beethoven: Sonata in A major for Violin and Piano, Op. 47** (*Kreutzer*) A sonata in the style of a concerto '*per il Pian[o]-forte ed un Violino obligato*' (1802–3). Opening with a phrase for unaccompanied violin (in the manner of the Fourth Piano Concerto) and including a set of slow variations, it brilliantly essays the tempestuous and lyrical sides of Beethoven's character. He dedicated it to the French violinist Rodolphe Kreutzer – who never played it.

➤ **Chopin: Sonata in G minor for Cello and Piano, Op. 65** A structurally diverse late sonata (1845-6) worth exploring for its unmistakeably Chopinesque qualities. The scherzo and tarantella-style finale are effective, the *largo* is a poem, but as a duo match it is awkward. Cellists feel overpowered by the instinctive complexity of the piano part, while pianists feel inadequate when confronted by the 'singing' *cantabile* of the cello line.

➤ **Franck: Sonata in A for Violin and Piano** An imposing sonata (1886) written for the Belgian violinist/composer Eugène Ysaÿe. In the Liszt tradition, it is a work of strong cyclic unity, its four movements bound together organically by common themes. The closing rondo is famous for its melodic interplay.

➤ **Brahms: Sonata in F minor for Clarinet (or Viola) and Piano, Op. 120 No 1** Indian summer music of mellow resignation, written for Richard Muhlfeld, principal clarinettist of Brahms's favourite Meiningen Orchestra. The F minor (1894) is a tightly organized, tersely constructed work, with two middle movements of intermezzo-like character and a powerfully intense finale.

➤ **Debussy: Sonata for Flute, Viola and Harp** Towards the end of his life Debussy planned to write a set of six sonatas for various instruments, serving, it has been said, the ideals of Rameau in preference to those of Beethoven. He only completed three, this one in 1916. In three movements – pastorale, interlude (minuet), finale – it is a work of captivating warmth and spontaneity, freely assembled to the point of self-indulgence. Of it the composer later remarked, "I don't know whether it should move us to laughter or tears. Perhaps both?"

➤ **Medtner: Sonate Vocalise for Voice and Piano, Op. 41 No 1** Medtner, a Russian of distant German descent, was considered by his contemporaries to have been the first real Beethoven in Russia: his teacher Taneyev used to say that he had been born with the knowledge of sonata-form within him. In the *Sonate Vocalise* (early 1920s), prefaced by a motto from Goethe, a vocalizing human voice becomes the instrument of the melody.

➤ **Hindemith: Sonata for Double Bass and Piano** The Hindemith sonatas for strings, woodwind and brass fill gaps in the repertoire other composers avoid. Ingeniously crafted, this cheerful post-war effort (1949) is as neat for the twist in the tail of its variation finale as for the way in which the prominent piano part is never at the expense of the principal protagonist.

➤ **Poulenc: Sonata for Flute and Piano** Dedicated to the memory of the American patroness Elizabeth Sprague Coolidge, this popular three-movement work (1956–57) is a throwback to the high Classical style of delicacy and wit.

1700) consolidated a model widely adopted by his students as well as by Bach and Handel (who broadened the medium to include flute and recorder).

The duo sonata proper – for any one instrument and piano – was a product of the Classical age. The modern understanding is of a work of equal partnership with neither player musically or technically subservient to the other. This wasn't always the case. Many early examples (Haydn's, Mozart's, Boccherini's) were effectively little more than 'accompanied' keyboard sonatas, with the obbligato instrument (in contrast to Baroque practice) confined to a supportive, decorative role. As the old-fashioned wording of the

{ The sonata has been said to play the same role in music as the large fresco does in art.

first editions of Beethoven's Op 102 Cello Sonatas ('for piano and violoncello', 1817) and Brahms's First ('for piano with violoncello', 1866) suggests, such distinction, if only as a convention, was to linger well into the Romantic period. The great duo landmarks of European tradition are principally associated with 19th-century Germany and Austria: between them Beethoven, Schubert, Mendelssohn, Schumann, Brahms and Reger left a legacy of violin, viola, cello and clarinet sonata – tangibly interactive duo music – that has never been bettered.

'Sonatas' for several players, variously (and often unpredictably) structured, are familiar from Giovanni Gabrieli's antiphonal *Sonata pian'e forte* (1597) and

{ César Franck. The Sonata for Violin and Piano is one his finest works. }

the many trio-sonatas of the Baroque. An interesting recent revival of the concept is found in the seven 'sonatas' for chamber ensemble (1975–87) by the British composer Sebastian Forbes. ♪

Quartet

Beginnings

IN THE MID-18TH CENTURY, AS THE Baroque era gave way to the Classical, there existed many different genres of music and many possible groupings of musicians. So-called 'chamber music' (to be played in small halls or 'chambers') might be for any available mixture of two, three or more instruments, but it was obviously unwise to have an unbalanced group. A flautist, a harpsichordist and two cellists would be unacceptably bottom-heavy, but substitute a viola for one of the cellos to fill the gap in the middle, then replace the flute with a violin, and a satisfying all-string group would result. Dispensing with the ubiquitous harpsichord was more difficult, for that instrument was the stand-by voice which underpinned the ensemble, provided

inner harmonies in all chamber and orchestral music at the time, and was the instrument from which a performance was directed. But dispensed with it was, most likely by accident, when a second violin

became available. This occurred, probably about 1757, at Baron Carl Joseph Fürnberg's estate at Weinzierl, Lower Austria, when Joseph Haydn was asked to provide music for a priest, the estate manager, Haydn himself, and Antonius Albrechtsberger (brother of Beethoven's later teacher): that is, two violins, viola, and cello.

However, this hardly pinpoints the invention of the string quartet. Works by F X Richter (his Op. 5) may be earlier, G B Sammartini and Vivaldi composed *sinfonie à quattro* (symphonies for four [string] instruments) much earlier still, consort music for four viols dates back to the 16th

---

• THE QUARTET'S RISE TO MATURITY •

➤ **Giovanni Gabrieli:** *Due canzoni per sonar a quattro* **(Two Songs for Four Players, 1608)** This is written for 'unbroken consort' (that is, all strings), and playable by a standard string quartet, though viols were used originally.

➤ **Alessandro Scarlatti:** *Sonata à quattro in D minor, per due violini, violetta e violoncello senza cembalo* **(by 1725)** The title is important: '. . . without harpsichord'. Exclusion of the harpsichord is remarkable since it allows that both the viola and the cello, which were previously subservient in their harmonic roles, might be permitted independence, and not only in the fugue.

➤ **Vivaldi: Sonata in B minor,** *Al Santo Sepolcro,* **RV169 (c. 1730?)** This work is for

four strings without continuo, thus again dispensing with harpsichord and entrusting the bassline to cello.

➤ **G B Sammartini: Symphony in G, JC39 (before 1744)** This delightful symphony is for two violins, viola and bass but is equally effective on the standard string quartet.

➤ **Mozart: Quartet in G, K80 (1770)** This first quartet, the first of 23 by Mozart, is a link with the past.

➤ **Haydn: Quartet in F, Op. 77/2 (1799).** Haydn's last complete quartet looks strongly to the future. Highly developed themes, a scherzo-minuet with cross-rhythms, variations and a symphonic finale all relate to Beethoven's first quartets of the same period.

century, and the concept of four (vocal) voices forming a balance between upper, middle and lower ranges, when the upper part may be duplicated for strength, was known in the Middle Ages. Like all other musical genres, then, the string quartet was not invented; it evolved. Many of the *sinfonie à quattro* by Sammartini, Locatelli, Stratico and other Italians are scored for two violins, viola and bass. The 'bass' part was playable on cello or double bass alone, or on cello, double bass, harpsichord and other continuo instruments if upper parts were multiplied for orchestral performance. As the string quartet developed, the bass (cello) part became increasingly elaborate until it proved unplayable on a double bass. Such is the feature of Haydn's early quartets: it is one of the factors that marks the watershed between 'orchestral quartets' and the pure string quartet about 1760. Incidentally, Haydn was still referring to the cello as 'basso' as late as 1772.

Formally, Haydn used his ready-made five-movement *divertimento/cassatio* layout which had already served him for his outdoor music: fast-minuet-slow-minuet-fast. One of the minuets was later excluded

as the quartet form developed, though Haydn retained the terms *divertimento* and *cassatio* until his Op. 33 set in 1781, when he changed to *quartetto*. Four movements for four instruments, then, but other composers favoured three (Vaňhal, Boccherini, Dittersdorf), and half of Cambini's 200-plus quartets are in two.

In 1770 Mozart wrote the first of his 23 string quartets, K80. All four movements are in G major and the first is an adagio, both features reflecting the old church-sonata style. Originally planned in three movements, slow-fast-minuet, it recalls Sammartini's symphony in the same key with its final minuet, but Mozart allows the lower strings a considerable degree of freedom.

Little over a decade later, in 1782, Mozart composed his first string quartet masterpiece, K387, the first of six dedicated to Haydn. It is clear from Mozart's manuscripts that he was swimming in unfamiliar waters. His composing facility was so fluent, his manuscripts usually so clear and free of corrections, that when one encounters the messy, heavily crossed-out pages of these quartets one understands the anxiety he must have felt to get things right. Haydn's influence from the Opp. 20 and 33 quartets loomed over Mozart, and it was with great humility that he submitted his work for approval to his friend. True, they echo some of Haydn's techniques, but they also possess the mark of Mozart's genius, hard-won though it was. After Mozart's death it was left to Haydn single-handedly to bring the genre, through his last 14 complete quartets, Opp. 71, 74, 76 and 77, to the dawn of the new century.

Beethoven and After

HAVING GROWN TO ITS SYMPHONIC maturity in about half a century in the hands of many composers led by Haydn, it took Beethoven only 25 years to transform the quartet into something unrecognizable. His Op. 18 set of six (1800) advanced the Haydn model only slightly, but the Op. 59 set of three (1806) and the *Harp* Quartet, Op. 74 (1809) open up new, deeply personal worlds while the 'Late Quartets' (1823–26) take the genre into uncharted philosophical realms. When Beethoven remarked of them "My music will be understood in 50 years' time", he was overestimating public perception, for these incredible works surely have yet to reveal all their secrets. As with his symphonies, subsequent composers stood back amazed and cowed, then took different paths, for Beethoven's line of development had pro-duced a temporary cul-de-sac. Composers such as Schubert (15 quartets between 1812 and 1826, ten of them in the first three years), Mendelssohn (seven between 1823 and 1847) and Schumann (three, 1842), added their own personalities to the quartet but took it hardly any distance beyond late Mozart, whose line of development they followed. The middle of the 19th century saw a quartet recession. A few peripheral figures wrote in the genre, among them Franz Berwald, whose quartets (two in 1849, plus two early works, one of which is lost) are interesting and enjoyable but hardly important, Louis Spohr (no fewer than 36 quartets between 1807 and 1857) and Joachim Raff (eight, between 1855 and 1874), who both offer pleasant listening but no progress. Three of Beethoven's late quartets had shunned the four-movement convention in favour of five, six, and even seven, but a return to four movements came with Brahms, Dvořák and a number of their contemporaries. With Beethoven, looking over his shoulder, (Brahms's phrase), it was to him that Brahms turned in his first two quartets (1873), but in the third he looked further back to his great love, Haydn, thus trying to avoid the inevitable Beethoven-Brahms comparison that so bedevilled him.

Antonín Dvořák's profuse outpouring of quartets (14 between 1862 and 1895) began with diffuse, overlong works – the first six average three-quarters of an hour each – but, while these expansionist tendencies continued, later works gained in substance and, of course, the folk element is

---

• BEETHOVEN'S LEGACY •

➤ **Beethoven: Quartet No. 13 in B flat, Op. 130 (1825)** This is the most approachable of the 'Late Quartets' and with its new finale the easiest way to enter the secret world of Beethoven's last period.

➤ **Brahms: Quartet No. 3 in B flat, Op. 67 (1876)** The spirit, if not the language, of Haydn is apparent in this quartet. It is almost as if Brahms were attempting to advance the Haydn style by a century.

➤ **Dvořák: Quartet No. 12 in F, *American* (1893)** While in America Dvořák spent much time in Bohemian settlements, and it is their folk idioms, rather than American, that give this quartet its attractive melodies.

➤ **Bartók: Quartet No. 3 (1927)** This, the most concise of Bartók's quartets, takes dissonance and violence to extreme lengths.

➤ **Shostakovich: Quartet No. 8 in C minor, Op. 110 (1960)** The composer's visit to the war-ravaged city of Dresden drove him almost to despair and inspired this work, which makes extensive use of his musical signature, DSCH.

➤ **Crumb: *Black Angels* (1970)** Inspired by the Vietnam war (the 'Black Angels' of the title are helicopter gunships), this is a compendium of extraordinarily sinister effects: vocal mouthings, whistling, nail scratching, ghostly harmonics, percussion instruments, etc. It uses the titles of the movements of Beethoven's Piano Sonata No. 26, *Les Adieux*, and divides into 'Thirteen Images from the Dark Land'.

Antonín Dvořák (right) and his family arrive in the United States in 1892, the year of the quartercentennial celebrations of the discovery of the continent by Columbus.

Helicopter gunships of the US Air Cavalry over South Vietnam in 1966. Such scenes inspired many works of art, literature and music during the 20th century as artists expressed their response to the horror of modern warfare.

than entertaining and, like Bartók's, they have been compared in importance to Beethoven's. If, as is hoped, Shostakovich's example indicates the way forward, it is tempting to overlook the excesses of Schoenberg and Crumb which introduce voices as well as extending even further the instrumental experiments of Bartók, but therein may well lie useful techniques and ideas for the future. ♪

strong. This is Dvořák's role in quartet history: to confirm the genre's continuing viability and to reintroduce (as Brahms had failed to do) the eastern European elements that Haydn had so entertainingly drawn on a century earlier.

With the new century came an enormous change, though folk music still played a prominent part. After three attempts, Béla Bartók entrusted his First Quartet to the world, or at least to the small part of it that could play it, in 1909. Five more appeared, the last in the final months of 1939, a few days before he left his beloved Hungary for America, never to return. Together, these quartets changed the course of the genre, as Beethoven's had done early in the previous century. Instruments are tested to their utmost, as are listeners' ears, by the barbarous rhythms, novel timbres and original instrumental techniques. Multiple stopping (the sounding of more than one string simultaneously) sometimes extends to all four strings of an instrument, and the 'Bartók pizzicato', whereby a string is plucked so violently that it rebounds off the fingerboard, is used to give a sharp, percussive effect. However, not all is done for effect. Bartók's quartets have a profound

Béla Bartók, photographed in 1927 at the time he was writing his Third String Quartet.

message and are regarded as the true successors to Beethoven's, even though they occupy different sound worlds.

Shostakovich came late to the quartet, producing his first in 1938 (about the time of Symphony No. 5) and writing 14 more between 1944 and 1974. With their vivid contrasting ideas, from severe drama to sheer slapstick comedy, they are rarely less

Variations

VARIATION FORM MAY HAVE ARISEN IN *early strophic song, where the tune in successive verses was varied by imaginative singers. Accompanying instrumentalists would have contributed their own spontaneous variants, and different aspects of the melody, rhythm and, later, harmony, would have been examined, to the surprise and delight of the listeners. An enduring feature of variations is the unchanging or only slightly altered bassline; this serves as an anchor for the performers, discouraging them from drifting too far from the shape and rhythm of the melody.*

A COMPOSER TAKES MUSICAL IDEAS FROM A basic stock, selects those that fit with his preconceived notion of what he wants to write, and arranges these ideas into a logical order. In so doing, he analyses them and will find alternative possibilities arising. If it happens that a melody suggests many new ideas that relate one to another and to the melody itself, the composer may decide to write a set of variations to reveal the subtleties of the melody in all its aspects. This illustrates his skill in discovering surprising facets of a tune and exercises the listener's mind in following his thought processes.

Variations have been popular for many centuries. In the 16th and 17th, keyboard variations in several guises entertained both gathered nobility and the solitary performer, and this extended through Antonio Soler (a

C.A.E: C.Alice Elgar. H.D.S.P: H.D.Steuart Powell. R.B.T: R.B Townshend. W.M.B: W.M.Baker.
R.P.A: R.P.Arnold. Ysobel: Isabel Fitton. Troyte: Troyte Griffith. W.N: Winifred Norbury.
Nimrod: A.J.Jaeger. Dorabella: Dora Penny (Powell). G.R.S: G.R Sinclair. B.G.N: Basil Nevinson.
✲✲✲ Lady Mary Lygon. E.D.U: Edward Elgar.

remarkable fandango for harpsichord) and Mozart in the 18th century, Beethoven, Schumann and Brahms in the 19th, and Schoenberg (notable among many) in the 20th. Earlier, Vivaldi and Handel had introduced variations as independent movements within longer works, and orchestral sets became frequent. Mozart concentrated on variations for the keyboard, while Haydn used them in divertimenti and symphonies (twice in the *Schoolmaster* Symphony No. 55) and invented the double variations. In this form, two related themes are varied alternately, giving added interest to the textures. A good example is the slow movement of the *Drumroll* Symphony No. 103.

Beethoven's love of verbal puns is reflected in his many sets of variations, where obscure meanings are revealed. His variations for harp on a Swiss folk tune are a typical, if slight, example of his art; the

• ELGAR'S ENIGMA • VARIATIONS

Elgar was 42 when his *Enigma* Variations put him on the musical map in 1899. He dedicated the work to his 'friends pictured within'; each variation is a musical portrait, and an enigma lay in the fact that he identified them merely by initials, only later revealing their names. Many have musical connections with the composer. After his wife (Variation I), Elgar pictures an amateur pianist (II), a lady viola-player (VI) whose string-crossing exercise is featured, and a cellist (XII). The final variation (XIV) is Elgar himself. Elsewhere he represents his friends' characteristics – their manners, their demeanour, their laughs – but the most memorable variation, 'Nimrod'

(IX) recalls his friend A J Jaeger and their discussion of Beethoven's slow movements. Also notable is XI, in which a friend's dog (G R Sinclair's bulldog) plunges into the River Wye, paddles about, retrieves a stick, comes ashore and barks excitedly. Elgar's friend challenged him to set the scene to music, which he did.

The larger enigma lies within the theme itself. Elgar stated that it was merely a counterpoint to a famous tune, but he never said which. Various theories have been put forward, among them 'Auld Lang Syne' (which is appropriate in this context), but the mystery remains to this day. Perhaps there never was a 'famous tune'.

In the 18th century keyboard instruments were the foundation of opera, choral and orchestral performances, while in domestic surroundings a harpsichordist, often with other instrumentalists, would play popular sonatas and variations to delight the assembly of family and friends.

{ One evening when Elgar was relaxing after dinner, idly playing the piano, his wife ('CAE') remarked "That's a good tune." Surprised, Elgar said, "Is it? Well, Powell ['HDSP'] would have done this ... and Nevinson ['BGN'] this ..." Thus, after a tiring day teaching the violin, a great work was born. Each of the composer's 'friends pictured within' is identified in the portrait gallery shown left.

• SIX FAMOUS SETS OF VARIATIONS •

➤ **Pachelbel** The first part of his Canon and Gigue, originally written for organ and arranged frequently since, is a set of variations which gradually create tension over 28 repetitions of an eight-note bass theme.

➤ **Bach** reputedly composed his *Goldberg Variations* for his pupil J G Goldberg to play to lull Count Keyserlingk to sleep. The Aria and 30 Variations constitute a magnificent display of Bach's imagination, technical prowess and wit.

➤ **Diabelli** In 1819 the publisher Anton Diabelli invited 50 Austrian composers to contribute a variation each to his waltz. These were published, the composers being presented in alphabetical order. Beethoven at first declined, then produced 33 of his own which form a virtual farewell to the piano.

➤ **Schubert** The fourth movement of his *Trout* Quintet varies the melody of his song *Die Forelle* ('The Trout')

➤ **Brahms** worked a miracle of compression in the finale (a passacaglia) of his Fourth Symphony by contriving 30 variations on an eight-bar theme. In so doing he created a work of amazing tension.

➤ **Rachmaninov** varied a Paganini caprice in his *Paganini Rhapsody*, at one point transforming it completely by the simple means of inverting it.

---

finale of the *Eroica* Symphony No. 3 is a much more substantial piece. It is based on a country dance he used also in the ballet *Prometheus*. Several other of his major works include variations. At much the same time, Paganini composed his violin caprices. The 24th has been chosen again and again as a theme to be varied, Brahms, Rachmaninov and Andrew Lloyd Webber being among those who have tackled it.

Particularly fine sets of variations are Brahms's on the *St Anthony Chorale* (a theme attributed falsely to Haydn), Mahler's on 'Frère Jacques' in Symphony No 1, Nielsen's anarchic finale to Symphony No 6, and Britten's on a theme of Frank Bridge. Related to the form is Hindemith's *Symphonic Metamorphoses on Themes of Weber*, which takes Weber's original melodies and radically transforms them. Such works prove that the variation form itself may be subject to variations.

Not all variations go under that name; a canon, a passacaglia and a rhapsody are nonetheless squarely in the variation tradition. ♪

Overture

IN THEIR INFANCY OVERTURES SERVED A *practical purpose. They were not for listening to; they signalled that a stage performance was about to commence: time for the audience to settle down, take their seats and stop chattering. Consequently, a blast of trumpets lasting a few seconds comprised the overtures to Monteverdi's operas. At that time the term was 'toccata', 'intrada' or 'sonata' ('call' [to attention], 'introduction' or 'instrumental sounding'). Apparently these* proved insufficient to quell audience uproar, so composers extended them, still retaining 'intrada' but sometimes using the term 'sinfonia' (an instrumental 'sounding together'). Gradually a format evolved: the noisy first part yielded to a quieter section – another ploy to gain audience compliance, since the sudden cessation of orchestral sound often has the effect of awakening interest – and then, to whip up expectation for the drama to come, a short, fast piece.

ITALY, HOME OF OPERA AND OF SINFONIA, exported the idea. In France the word was 'ouverture', in Portugal 'averture' (cf: 'ouvert', open; 'louvre', opening; aperture, etc); the first 'u' was lost in Germanic languages. But while the Italians kept to short, bright sinfonias, the French made several courses of it: a slow beginning in jerky, dotted rhythm (which reflected the actors' rapid arm movements to seize audience attention before an important line) followed by a fugal section and then often a string of dances accompanying a stage spectacle before the main event. These long 'ouvertures', or 'suites', eventually assumed separate identity: Bach's four Orchestral Suites are still called Ouvertüren in Germany.

The three-movement sinfonia grew in importance and popularity by the early 18th

{ To opera audiences at the end of the 19th century the overture was regarded as a mood-setter, and an opportunity to hear the 'hits' of the day. Shrewd composers would insert a potential 'hit' in the overture in the hope of increasing the popularity of the opera.

Johann Strauss in *The Gipsy Baron* (1885) shows a little more care, but modern Broadway composers find that the medley technique works extremely well now that most of the show tunes have already received intensive media exposure. There is nothing like a popular sing-along melody to put an audience in a receptive mood.

One aspect of the operatic overture remains to be discussed. Early in the 18th century an overture often had no connection with the opera it preceded: it could be, and often was, switched from opera to opera. Cimarosa and others were so popular, and therefore so busy, that the chore of writing an overture for an imminent opera production was left until the last moment. Either little thought was given to its quality, or an old overture was borrowed from another production. Gluck decided that this wasted a good opportunity. In his overtures to *Alceste* (1767) and *Iphigenia in Aulis* (1774) he heralds the mood of the dramas to come with suitably sombre music to prepare the audience for tragic happenings on stage. Cherubini, Méhul and Weber were among those who followed his example. ♪

century and began to feature in concert performances. Thus, the concert symphony came into existence and for many years it shared with the operatic overture the three movement fast-slow-fast format before it sprouted a minuet. One need only examine Mozart's symphonies to discover that many began life as operatic overtures. His Symphony No. 32 (1779) is actually titled *Overture in the Italian Style* and consists of a quick first movement leading to an andante and thence to an abbreviated repeat of the first movement.

It was at about this time that a new idea appeared in the overture. Some operas received many performances and the draw was often the heroine. Her singing of favourite arias might be the talk of the opera-going set, and the sheet music was available for home performance. Composers were aware of which arias were likely to be 'hits', so would preview one in the slow

section of the overture. Seasoned opera-goers would recognize it, nudge one another, then expectantly await the soprano's version. Interest would be increased and the popularity of the opera enhanced. In his *Leonora* overtures Nos 1–3 Beethoven introduces instead the hero Florestan's aria, and in Nos 2 and 3 he goes further and includes the trumpet calls that herald Don Fernando's arrival. It was only a matter of time before composers were compiling their entire overtures from tunes in the opera. In England the hurriedly assembled Medley Overtures were popular.

{ This illustration depicts an audience enjoying a performance of Gluck's opera *Parnaso confuso* (1765). For this work Gluck composed an overture in C major which consists of a jog-trotting allegro and a soothing slow movement. The final statement of the allegro is interrupted almost immediately by the opening scene of the drama.

• **OVERTURES FOR THE STAGE** •

➤ **Mozart:** *The Marriage of Figaro* **(1786)** At an average tempo this superb little overture lasts four minutes. This fact has attracted to it the name 'the egg-timer'.

➤ **Rossini:** *The Barber of Seville* **(1813)** First used for the opera *Aureliano in Palmira* (1813), then for *Elisabetta, Regina d'Inghilterra* (1815), this overture found its final resting place with *The Barber* in 1816. Of all Rossini's overtures it is the most popular, but it would be unwise to describe it as his best.

➤ **Schubert:** *Rosamunde* **(1820)** Another example of a migrating overture. Although written for the play *The Magic Harp*, the overture eventually became attached to the play *Rosamunde, Princess of Cyprus* in 1823.

➤ **Weber:** *Oberon* **(1826)** An overture that draws elements from the opera into a most convincing piece. The evocation of fairyland at the start is extremely effective.

➤ **Wagner:** *The Mastersingers* **(1868)** This picture of 16th-century Nuremberg in mid-19th century musical language presents many strands and moods of the opera and combines them most skilfully.

➤ **Vaughan Williams:** *The Wasps* **(1909)** The overture and incidental music to Aristophanes's play finds Vaughan Williams at his liveliest and happiest. The eponymous insects are very evident at the start.

The Concert Overture

THE MOOD-SETTING OVERTURES OF THE late 18th century gradually acquired descriptive ingredients. And just as the early sinfonias had migrated to the concert hall to enjoy a separate existence, so the overture grew a new scion which led a life detached from opera but often related to stage drama or a literary theme. Beethoven's overtures to *Coriolan* (1807) and *Egmont* (1810) introduced plays by, respectively, Collin and Goethe. They owe no debt to the three-movement overture, nor yet are they symphonic movements, adrift, as it were, from parent works. They point towards a new genre which, as yet, had no name apart from the convenient tag 'overture'.

Among the first overtures to be dissociated from stage works (for convenience they are termed 'concert overtures') was Weber's *Ruler of the Spirits* (1811), though even this had its origin in the unfinished opera *Rübezahl*. Schubert's two *Overtures in the Italian Style*, borrowing a title chosen for Mozart's Symphony No. 32 but for a different reason, are purely for concert performance. Mendelssohn's *Calm Sea and Prosperous Voyage* (1828) is based on Goethe but is not intended to preface stage action. It is a clever essay depicting a becalmed ship and its desolate crew; then, with a breeze blowing up on, appropriately, woodwind, the sails billow out and there is a triumphant return to harbour with a rich cargo. Similarly descriptive is *The Hebrides* (1832); also called *Fingal's Cave*, this is a sound impression of the composer's sea trip to the Isle of Staffa and its imposing natural cave.

Other composers contributed descriptive concert overtures of varying success;

Mendelssohn was awed by Fingal's Cave when he viewed it from a boat during his Scottish holiday. He subsequently expressed his response to it in a fine descriptive overture.

then, in 1863, Bruckner wrote his Overture in G minor for which he divulged no programme (it is highly unlikely he envisaged one) and which appears to have no purpose other than that which we associate with his symphonies: that they are 'absolute' music.

To some composers the term 'overture' seemed a ludicrous description for a pictorial work not associated with the stage. How could a work that failed to 'open' anything be called an overture? César Franck invented

In 1812 the Russians defeated Napoleon at Moscow. The subsequent retreat was celebrated 68 years later in Tchaikovsky's *1812* Overture, which originally required chorus, orchestra, Moscow's church bells, and cannon shots at specific points in the score.

• FAMOUS CONCERT OVERTURES •

➤ **Schubert:** *Overture in the Italian Style* in **D, D590 (1817)** This is a pure joke. Schubert, envious of the success of Rossini's overtures, wrote his own to show just how easy it was to copy the style.

➤ **Beethoven:** *Consecration of the House,* **Op. 124 (1822)** This multi-sectioned work ending with a whirlwind fugue marks the opening of the Josefstadt Theatre in Vienna on 3 October 1822.

➤ **Mendelssohn:** *The Hebrides,* **Op. 26 (1832)** A convincing sound portrait commemorating Mendelssohn's Scottish holiday. His voyage to the Hebridean tourist attraction is described in what the composer called *The Lonely Isle: Overture in B minor.*

➤ **Brahms:** *Academic Festival Overture,* **Op. 80 (1880)** Written for Breslau University on the occasion of Brahms' doctorate of philosophy, this overture is a medley of student songs, worked out symphonically.

➤ **Tchaikovsky:** *1812 Overture* **(1880)** The Russian victory over Napoleon is commemorated in one of Tchaikovsky's most resplendent works. It includes French and Russian anthems and features an optional choral opening.

➤ **Elgar:** *Cockaigne* **(1901)** Subtitle: *In London Town.* The word 'Cockaigne' (land of luxury) is also the (disputed) origin of 'Cockney', a true Londoner. An early critic, misunderstanding both title and robust music, thought it represented a drug trip.

the term the world was waiting for, 'symphonic poem', for his *Ce qu'on entend sur la montagne* (1846). The concert overture had spawned its own offspring. Franck, Liszt and others used the newly created phrase for a kind of fantasia based on Romantic texts. Less ambitious composers used the alternative term 'tone poem' (see page 108), but when Richard Strauss adopted the idea it grew out of control. One finds it difficult to distinguish semantically between his descriptive *Alpine* Symphony (1916) and the tone poem after Nietzsche, *Also sprach Zarathustra* (1896), both ultimately descendants of the concert overture.

Earlier, lines of demarcation were becoming increasingly blurred. In 1891–92 Dvořák wrote a 'suite' or 'cycle' of three 'overtures' depicting nature, life and love:

Amid Nature, Carnival and *Othello*, which are in fact tone poems. The three works are united by a single theme but are otherwise independent and are frequently performed separately; *Carnival* more frequently than the others, it being the most popular. Since the music has little to do with symphonic form the cycle cannot qualify as a symphony; on the other hand they are overtures in name only.

Earlier still, in 1880, Brahms had composed two overtures of contrasting character. The *Academic Festival* Overture is a rare example of Brahms in cheerful mood, the festivities even extending to the flippant sound of a triangle. Living up grimly to its title, the *Tragic* Overture is remarkably vehement and baleful: a study in blind anger. Interestingly, its form shows traces of the old

fast-slow-fast sinfonia/overture. In the same year, Tchaikovsky wrote his famous *1812*, far surpassing Brahms's festivities by including cannon detonations and, if the composer's intentions are followed, "all the bells of Moscow". Tchaikovsky wrote the piece "without affection and enthusiasm", and thought there would be no merit in it as a result. As an introduction to celebrations of a great victory, 1812 might just qualify for the title 'overture', but there is little justification for its French subtitle *Ouverture solennelle*.

The concert overture survived into the 20th century. Elgar's *Cockaigne* (1901) and *In the South* (1904) are pictorial, while Arnold's *A Grand, Grand Overture*, written for the first Hoffnung Festival in London in 1956, includes parts for three rifles, three vacuum cleaners and a floor polisher. ♪

Symphonic Poem

A 16th-century representation of sorcery at a witches' sabbath.

PURISTS INSIST THERE ARE DIFFERENCES between a symphonic poem and a tone poem, the latter being less dependent upon the rigours of symphonic argument. Others are inclined to use both terms synonymously. Whatever the terminology, the symphonic or tone poem is an orchestral composition, nearly always a single movement, which portrays a narrative story or a visual image. A more satisfactory label would be 'sound poem'.

THE SYMPHONIC POEM WAS A CHILD OF THE Romantic era, its father being that arch-Romantic, Liszt. Though much of his enormous output is shot through with literary, dramatic and pictorial elements it was not until 1848–49 that he first applied the term 'Sinfonische Dichtung' to one of his works – *Ce qu'on entend sur la montagne*, a self-contained orchestral movement constructed solely by 'thematic metamorphosis'. Inspired by the writings of the likes of Goethe, Hugo and Schiller or by familiar paintings, Liszt went on to compose a further 12 works in similar vein.

European composers of the second half of the 19th century used the form as a means of portraying powerful emotions and vivid dramatic situations. In Germany, Richard Strauss painted orchestral pictures of astonishing detail and clarity. Early works – *Don Juan* (1888–89) and *Till Eulenspiegel* (1894–95), for example – were a natural extension of Liszt's blueprint but later pieces became hugely ambitious, from the philosophical musings of *Also sprach Zarathustra* (1895–96) to the riotous humour and touching pathos of *Don Quixote* (1896–97) via the autobiographical meanderings of *Ein Heldenleben* (1897–98) and *Symphonia domestica* (1902–3).

In central Europe the symphonic poem became an expression of nationalistic fervour. Smetana's cycle of six symphonic poems *Má vlast* ('My Country') (1872–79) – including the popular 'Vltava' – is perhaps the ultimate in musical patriotism. It inspired many younger composers, not least Fibich, Novák, Janáček and, most significantly, Dvořák and Suk.

{ Shakespeare's *Romeo and Juliet* has inspired many scores. Among operatic versions, Sutermeister's is forgotten while Gounod's keeps a tenuous place in the repertoire. Tchaikovsky's 'overture-fantasy' is the most popular depiction, though Berlioz's 'dramatic symphony' and Prokofiev's ballet are close seconds.

attractive yet neglected pieces (all inspired by Russian legends) by Balakirev, Mussorgsky, Borodin and Rimsky-Korsakov. Tchaikovsky was more inclined to literature: *Romeo and Juliet* (1880), *Hamlet* (1888) and *Francesca da Rimini* (1876) are highly organized symphonic poems, although none are described as such. Sibelius's brooding and desolate *Tapiola* (1926) would appear to be the last masterpiece in the genre, the final blossom of a brief but glorious flowering. ♪

French composers championed the symphonic form with characteristic brio. Saint-Saëns produced four in the space of six years, the most popular being *Danse macabre* (1874). In contrast to Saint-Saëns's atmospheric portrayal of his subjects, Dukas's *L'apprenti-Sorcier* (1897) is dazzling in its detailed imagery. These works, along with Debussy's *Prélude à l'après-midi d'un faune* (1892–94) have overshadowed other highly individual creations by Duparc, Franck, Ravel, Chausson, Roussel and Koechlin.

British composers came late to the form.

Though William Wallace's *Villon* and *The Passing of Beatrice* (both 1892) are often cited as the first examples of the British symphonic poem, Henry Nixon's *Palamon and Arcite* was completed ten years earlier. However, few made any lasting mark with the exception of Bax, Bridge, Delius and Elgar, the latter's *Falstaff* (1913), though described by the composer as a 'symphonic study', being the most explicit musical representation of a literary subject. Russian composers, though, eagerly took up the symphonic poem. Glinka's *Kamarinskya* (1848) was the prototype for a long line of

SAINT SAENS'S DANSE MACABRE

~

*M*idnight chimes (harp). In the shivering cold (strings) of a winter night Death (solo violin with its E string tuned down a semitone thus creating an eerie dissonance) plays his fiddle in a churchyard. Skeletons emerge from their graves and begin to dance (a xylophone suggests clattering bones). At first their movements are cumbersome but as Death continues to play proceedings become increasingly frenzied (the orchestra here given full rein). Eventually a cock crow (oboe) announces the arrival of dawn. Death plays a melancholic farewell and the skeletons scatter back to their graves.

FIVE OF THE FINEST

> **Liszt:** *Les Préludes* This is a classic example of the composer's concern for philosophical concept – in this instance life being nothing but a series of preludes – rather than graphic pictorial illustration. The ingenious transformations of a single theme creates many contrasted moods.

> **Smetana:** '**Vltava**' The second of the six symphonic poems which comprise Smetana's *Má vlast*. This is a graphic yet lyrical description of the course of the river Vltava from its source to its majestic arrival at Prague and eventual disappearance into the Elbe.

> **Tchaikovsky:** *Romeo and Juliet* This is not a blow-by-blow reconstruction of Shakespeare's drama but an imaginatively conceived synthesis. All the elements of the tragedy, notably the feuding families and the love of Romeo and Juliet (expressed by one of Tchaikovsky's most inspired melodies), are readily apparent.

> **Mussorgsky:** *Night on Bare Mountain* Few works have endured such a chequered history as Mussorgsky's solitary extended work for orchestra – even to the correct translation of its title. The composer's choice was *St John's Night* [that is, Midsummer Eve] *on Bare Mountain*. (Bare or Bald Mountain, depending on how you translate the Russian, is a mountain near Kiev.) The work, depicting a witches' sabbath, entered circulation via Rimsky-Korsakov's well-intentioned but sanitized version. The original, written in only 12 days in 1866, contains far more startling orchestrations and daring harmonies.

> **Dukas:** *The Sorcerer's Apprentice* The composer's most popular work, which he described as a "symphonic scherzo". It is a faultlessly constructed comment on Goethe's ballad, employing vivid imagery and graphic orchestration.

Incidental Music

INCIDENTAL MUSIC NORMALLY ACCOMPANIES *a play or theatrical production, and is usually subordinate to the action. It can prepare and round off scenes, be a background for set pieces, link acts, provide cover for scene changes and suggest mood and atmosphere. Incidental music was integral to pre-Christian Greco-Roman theatre and to the secular stage of the Middle Ages (the earliest surviving play with music, based on popular tunes, being Adam de la Halle's late 13th-century* Le jeu de Robin et Marion*).*

SYMBOLICALLY AND PRACTICALLY, IT WAS A key element of the Miracles, Mysteries and Moralities of medieval France and England. In the comedies and fables of formerly Renaissance Italy and latterly the Catholic and Protestant empires of western and central Europe, its modern usage was established.

In the playhouses of Elizabethan and Jacobean England incidental music, both vocal and instrumental, was staple fare. The dramas of Shakespeare contain numerous musical references, stage directions and song lyrics; like Fletcher, Beaumont and Jonson, he recognized that for his audiences the sound of music (harsh, sweet, squealing, 'divine', loud, soft, fast, slow) could tangibly reinforce emotions and mysteries, trigger senses and intensify and underline the action in ways words could not. Shakespeare's and Fletcher's reliance on music, it has been said, was largely responsible for capturing the imagination of the Restoration playwrights and composers. Most of Purcell's music for stage (overtures, entr'actes, dances, songs) was incidental to plays by, among others, Dryden, Southerne, Fletcher, Congreve, Shadwell and D'Urfey.

For nearly 400 years, providing incidental music for revivals of Shakespeare has been a necessary, obsessive preoccupation. In France, Molière's *comédies-ballets*, written in collaboration with Lully, were daily entertainment in the Paris of the Sun King, Louis XIV, while in late 18th/early 19th-century Germany Goethe and

{ Mendelssohn's *A Midsummer Night's Dream* was inspired by Shakespeare's play, depicted here by Fuseli.

• FIVE ROMANTIC GREATS •

> **Beethoven:** *Egmont* Beethoven wrote his music to Goethe's historically distorted five-act play on the life and martyrdom of the 16th-century Flemish general and statesman Lamoral, Count of Egmont, in response to a commission from Vienna's Imperial Theatre (1809–10). The incidental music is variously fragmentary and substantial, and for this reason, perhaps, only ever comes fully into its own in a stage setting. The overture, on the other hand, concentrating the drama, is a self-contained tone-poem, powerfully imagined in its mix of fateful gesture and victorious apotheosis – a model for many later composers.

> **Schubert:** *Rosamunde* Forgotten playwright, forgotten play, great composer, great music sums up the score Schubert provided in 1823 for two performances in Vienna of *Rosamunde, Princess of Cyprus*, a romance by Helmine von Chezy, the hapless librettist of Weber's *Euryanthe*. The charm of Schubert's entr'actes, ballet sequences, contralto aria and choruses makes for a timeless masterwork, unlike the far-fetched plot.

> **Mendelssohn:** *A Midsummer Night's Dream* The precocious 17-year-old Mendelssohn wrote his astonishing overture to Shakespeare's lyric comedy in 1826. Refreshingly imagined, the incidental music – including the celebrated 'Wedding March' – followed for a Potsdam revival in 1843. Ingeniously underwriting the play's scenes or characters – for example, an interval of a ninth imitating an ass's bray to depict Bottom – the majority of the 13 movements, because of their musical sufficiency, work well in either playhouse or concert room.

> **Bizet:** *L'Arlésienne* (1869) This tale of disastrous love in exotic Provence, with a heroine (the girl from Arles) who never once appears on stage, was a collaboration between Bizet and the gifted playwright Alphonse Daudet. "Only those who have heard the score in relation to the dramatic action", says Bizet's biographer Mina Curtiss, "can know the delicacy and subtlety of its psychological characterization, the power and beauty of the choruses, the skill and ingenuity with which Bizet orchestrated [for a band of just 26 musicians]." However, the

first production of *L'Arlésienne* was a flop, playing to near-empty houses.

> **Grieg:** *Peer Gynt* The semi-autobiographical verse drama *Peer Gynt* has been called the richest and the most imaginative and fantastic of Ibsen's plays. Picturing scenes and characters from the troll lands ('The Hall of the Mountain King') to Arabia ('Anitra's Dance'), Grieg, portrayed here in 1900 by the German painter Franz von Lenbach, wrote his music (1874–75) at the express wish of the dramatist, who knew exactly what he wanted and had no qualms about saying so (however unpractical the request may have been). The two popular orchestral suites (1888, 1891) draw on eight of the 23 numbers.

Schiller specifically called for incidental music in their plays, a challenge met by both Beethoven and Weber.

The Romantic Age was an era celebrated for its Byronic fervour (exemplified by Schumann's incidental music to the dramatic poem *Manfred*) no less than its revivals of receding and ancient pasts (Mendelssohn's Shakespeare and Sophocles scores, Humperdinck's *Lysistrata*). In Victorian and Edwardian England, the Oxbridge performances of the Greek classics in their original language were supported with incidental music by Parry, Stanford and Vaughan Williams. Among the Scandinavians, Ibsen stimulated Grieg to write *Peer Gynt*. The Belgian Maeterlinck's dream-like *Pelléas et Mélisande* generated not only an opera (Debussy) and a symphonic poem (Schoenberg), but also incidental music from Fauré and Sibelius, while the London

success of Flecker's *Hassan* was largely due to Delius.

Incidental music as a 20th-century art form is found in Debussy's 'mystery' *Le martyre de St Sebastien*, and Elgar's 'imperial masque' *The Crown of India* – resplendent pre-Great War examples of dance, mime, solo, chorus and writing for large orchestra. Economic rather than lavish, Stravinsky's *L'Histoire du Soldat*, a

story told, acted and danced for eight instruments, and Boulez's music for Claudel's French translation of Aeschylus's *Oresteia*, stand in complete contrast. In their audience-aware currency of popular/satirical song and dance, the political plays of Brecht with incidental music by Weill, Eisler and Dessau parallel medieval practice. Yesterday's incidental stage music is today's soundtrack. ♪

Incidental music owes its existence to plays and theatrical productions. In Elizabethan and Jacobean playhouses music was used to fire the imagination and the emotion of the audience, while never up-staging the dramatic action.

Programme Music

PROGRAMME MUSIC ATTEMPTS TO CONVEY a story, picture, landscape (or any other form of extra-musical idea) without words. Before defining it in more detail, however, an important question has first to be answered. Should the term 'programme music' be confined only to works which are precisely descriptive or do we include music that is evocative, atmospheric and suggestive? Few authorities appear to be of one mind on this

matter, which no doubt explains why definitions of programme music vary so widely. Some insist that programme music can only be the opposite of 'absolute music' – abstract works such as a prelude and fugue by J S Bach, a piano sonata by Beethoven or a symphony by Brahms, all of which are composed in accordance with some kind of established musical principle. Others are of the opinion that programme music is any composition

which succeeds in portraying some extra-musical subject, regardless of whether it has been composed strictly by the book or not – in which case it can safely be stated that programme music has been in existence just about as long as music itself.

A winter's day in the Piazzetta, Venice. The seasons were depicted famously by Vivaldi – who was born in Venice and spent much of his working life there – in the first four of the Opus 8 set of concertos.

PROGRAMME MUSIC THROUGH THE AGES

➤ **Cabanilles:** *Batalla Imperial* (date not known) One of the most endearing pieces of battle music. Cabanilles wrote many such works, most for organ, though this piece is occasionally played on the harpsichord to equal effect. It encompasses drumbeats, pounding horses' hooves and the whole hubbub of battle as heard through 17th-century ears.

➤ **Vivaldi: Violin Concerto No. 4 in F minor, RV297** *(Winter) (c. 1725)* The last of the *Four Seasons*, this opens with icy blasts, stamping feet and chattering teeth – in marked contrast to the central movement, which reflects the satisfaction of those who stay indoors by the fireside. The finale takes us outdoors again. The aim is to stay upright on the ice, even to avoid drowning if the ice gives way.

➤ **Beethoven: Symphony No. 6 in F, Op. 68** *(Pastoral)* **(1808)** Beethoven went to a great deal of trouble to set down in print what he was striving to achieve in this score. This is "not a picture but a work in which are expressed the emotions aroused in us by the pleasures of the countryside". The few realistic representations – the bird calls of the second movement – were, apparently, intended to be a joke.

➤ **Honegger:** *Pacific 231* **(1923)** Another dazzling example of music being simultaneously programmatic and abstract, in this instance a series of highly inventive variations. Honegger stated that he was not attempting to imitate the sound of a locomotive but to convey "the visual impression and lyrical satisfaction" of a heavy locomotive from its straining start to its magnificent full head of steam.

MUCH OF THE EARLIEST SURVIVING programme music is concerned with war, typically Janequin's chanson 'La Bataille' (*La Guerre*), which is thought to refer to the Battle of Marignan of 1515, and Byrd's keyboard suite *The Battle* (c.1570–80) which contains movements entitled 'The Soldiers' Summons', 'The March to the Fight' and 'The Retreat'. But composers did not shrink from infinitely greater challenges. Of Kuhnau's six *Biblical* Sonatas (1700) for keyboard the first is entitled 'The Fight Between David and Goliath', the last 'Jacob's Death and Burial'. French keyboard works of the 17th and 18th centuries offer a rich source of descriptive pieces, such as François Couperin's *The Frightened Linnet* and *Les Tricoteuses* ('The knitters') which even includes an episode in the minor depicting *mailles lâchées* (dropped stitches)!

Perhaps the most popular descriptive subject of the 17th and 18th centuries was nature, Vivaldi's *Four Seasons* being one of the prime examples of the genre. These concertos are the first four of his 12 concertos Opus 8 (c.1725) entitled *The Trial Between Harmony and Invention* – proof that music is sometimes intended to be both illustrative and 'abstract'. Beethoven's *Pastoral Symphony* (1808) is another example of 'abstract' music which is also highly atmospheric programmatic music. In many respects Berlioz's *Symphonie fantastique* (1830) is even more remarkable: not only is it 'symphonic' and descriptive but also strongly autobiographical.

Hector Berlioz was one of the most innovative orchestrators of the 19th century.

SYMPHONIE FANTASTIQUE

Berlioz's memoirs and biographical writings tell us a great deal about his infatuation with the Irish actress Harriet Smithson and the trials of their protracted courtship. Subtitled *Episode in the Life of an Artist*, the symphony was written to demonstrate the intensity of the composer's feelings for her – perhaps even to warn her of what might result if she rejected him.

The whole premise of the symphony's narrative is that of an over-sensitive artist who, disappointed in love, overdoses on opium. Dreams and nightmares ensue, in which the beloved is represented throughout by an *idée fixe* – a theme which first appears as the long, sinuous melody after the extended slow introduction and recurs throughout the work in various guises.

MISS. H. SMITHSON,
In the Character of Ophelia.

I Rêveries; Passions The young hero dreams of his beloved with passionate yearning. But the beloved remains unattainable.

II Un Bal A ball where the beloved is only fleetingly glimpsed among the bustling crowd.

III Scène aux champs The hero wanders aimlessly in the fields on a summer evening. Two shepherds call to each other with their pipes. The beloved appears – only to disappear again. Despair and loneliness ensue as one shepherd continues to call, this time ominously answered by thunder.

IV Marche au supplice The hero has a nightmare in which he kills the object of his love and undergoes a terrifying journey to the scaffold accompanied by jeering crowds. The ultimate price for his passion is paid as the guillotine drops.

V Songe d'une nuit du Sabbat The full horrors of the Witches' Sabbath. The *idée fixe* appears grotesquely distorted. The hero's soul is delivered into Satan's hands.

Liszt was the first to define 'programme music', though he applied the term in a somewhat narrow way. For him programme music could only be termed thus when it was prefaced by some literary or pictorial subject (providing emotional and illustrative signposts for the listener) and constructed in a free, non-symphonic way. Most, however, will probably agree that the pictorial qualities of Berlioz's 'abstract' *Symphonie fantastique* are far more potent than the 'atmospheric' qualities of Liszt's programme music. With the expansion and development of the orchestra in the 19th century, few composers resisted the opportunity to create orchestral pictures: in short, programme music came into its own.

Concerto

J S Bach plays the harpsichord solo in one of the first keyboard concertos ever written.

A CONCERTO IS A WORK FOR ONE OR MORE *solo instruments and orchestra. Its primary purpose for the last three centuries has been to display the skill of the soloist(s), but before that the word 'concerto' covered various possibilities, and there have been divergences from this course since 1700. The origin of the word (first recorded in 1519) and its meaning are obscure but the most likely seems to be the Italian* concertare, *to gather together, which is what early concerto performers did. They were singers who, in late 16th-century Italy, gathered with perhaps some instrumentalists to perform concertos by Andrea Gabrieli and his nephew Giovanni. This sacred music was widely copied throughout Italy. Concertos for instruments alone followed but works recognizable today as concertos did not emerge until late in the 17th century when Alessandro Stradella produced a number of works with the title 'sinfonia' that set three or four string soloists against a larger string group.*

TERMINOLOGY WAS STILL SETTLING DOWN. 'Sinfonia', 'serenata', 'sonata', and 'concerto' were used indiscriminately, and the terms might apply to a piece of music or to the group playing it. Popular at the time were chamber sonatas for a few string instruments. The violin had been invented relatively recently and enthusiastic amateurs all over Italy enjoyed testing their fiddling skills against one another. In large establishments, of which there were hundreds able to afford embryonic orchestras, some groups would divide into two to give a stereo effect and to vary the dynamic range. Echo effects would be introduced, and if an echoing group interjected virtuoso flourishes, an element of competition crept in. Gradually from these sonatas and sinfonias there evolved a satisfying grouping of two violins and cello, playing against a larger string band.

The most far-reaching event of this kind occurred in Rome. Arcangelo Corelli had written trio sonatas (two violins, cello and continuo) but extended them into *concerti grossi* ('great concertos') which employed this larger grouping. This was probably

{ A painting of four musicians by Jacob Toorenvliet, 1678.

and three trombones with string orchestra. Around mid-century the ensemble concerto tended to die out (except in England where *concerti grossi* still ruled): its progeny, the *symphonie concertante*, lay in the future.

Other developments occurred in Italy during Corelli's time, leading to a radically different kind of concerto. Corelli's *concerti grossi* consist of anything from five to 12 sections comprising largos, fugues, arias and dances in alternating tempi. Composers such as Torelli and Albinoni chose a more clear-cut design borrowed from the emerging operatic sinfonia: fast-slow-fast, and the virtuoso element was usually focused upon one player rather than a group. This was the result of two parallel forces: the desire of players to draw increasing versatility from their instruments in order better to display their own virtuosity; and the progress of instrumental makers in improving their wares.

The very first solo concerto was written about 1690 by Torelli for his Bolognese chief trumpeter G P Brandi. It started a craze for solo concertos that, over the next 40 years, expanded to include virtually every court instrument of the time (and even rural instruments such as the hurdy-gurdy), and spread outwards from Italy to France, Germany, England, Russia and out-lying areas such as the Iberian peninsula. ♪

in the final decade of the 17th century but the works were not published, as Op. 6, until 1714, a year after his death. So-called concerti were popular also in Russia around 1700: these were sacred vocal pieces for two or three choirs without instruments. They feature polyphonic exchanges but otherwise there is no connection with the *concerti grossi* that evolved in Italy at this period.

Meanwhile, Corelli's *concerti grossi* had been copied and sold elsewhere in Europe, and so influential were they that wherever they were played local composers imitated them. One ramification of this occurred in England. In his early days Handel had studied Corelli's work and when he composed his own *concerti grossi*, Op. 6, in London in 1739 they, too, were widely admired and English composers continued to be influenced by them for at least two decades. This served to put back the development of English music. It lagged behind the rest of Europe until the influential Bach-Abel concerts brought newer Continental styles to public notice in the 1760s. Even after that, Handel's oratorios and concertos retained much popularity.

So-called 'ensemble concerti', for two or more soloists, developed from the *concerto grosso* style and as 1750 approached their coverage became wider. Bach's *Brandenburg Concertos* show a dazzling variety of instruments: violino piccolo, violin, hunting horns, high trumpet, oboes, recorder, flute and harpsichord, and in Nos. 3 and 6 large groups of string soloists, recollecting the old consort style. Telemann also produced multiple concertos, such as an ambitious grouping of recorder, gamba, oboe, cornetti

---

• THE FIRST SOLO CONCERTOS •

➤ **Trumpet:** Torelli wrote the first trumpet concerto in Bologna in about 1690.

➤ **Violin:** Torelli, in his *Concerti musicali* published in 1698, wrote the first concertos for solo violin, and the first for two violins appeared in the same set.

➤ **Cello:** Giuseppe Maria Jaccini composed the first cello concerto as part of his *Concerti per Camera*, Op. 4, in 1701. He was a cellist himself, working in Bologna.

➤ **Oboe:** Domenico Marcheselli composed the first oboe concerto in 1708. Apart from his Arcadian name, 'Academico Formato', nothing else is known about him.

➤ **Viola:** Telemann's Viola Concerto in G dates probably from before 1721 but it may be an arrangement of a now lost concerto for another instrument.

➤ **Flute:** Alessandro Scarlatti's seven 'sonatas' of 1725 are actually concertos for flute and strings.

➤ **Bassoon:** The first datable bassoon concerto (1729) was written by Joseph Bodin de Boismortier. There are two caveats, however: Boismortier's work is playable equally on cello or viol; and some of Vivaldi's undated bassoon concertos may be earlier.

➤ **Harpsichord:** J S Bach arranged one of his own concertos (probably for violin) for a new harpsichord installed in 1737 at the Leipzig court. His son C P E Bach wrote a concerto in A minor for the same occasion.

The Birth of the Virtuoso

IN 1711 ANTONIO VIVALDI'S FIRST concertos were published as Op. 3 in Amsterdam. Titled *L'Estro Armonico* (Harmonic whim), this set of 12 works divides into three: Nos. 3, 6, 9 and 12 are for solo violin, Nos. 2, 5, 8 and 11 are for two violins (Nos. 2 and 11 including cello) and the rest are for four violins (Nos. 7 and 10 including cello). In instrumental line-up they mix the old Corelli style with the new, but in seven the three-movement plan of fast-slow-fast adopts Albinoni's preferred scheme. It set the trend for the next century and more.

Vivaldi's fast movements are in simple rondo form. The ripieno (string band) states a melody, the solo, accompanied, takes over, then the ripieno returns, and so on, the pattern repeated several times: A-B-A-C-A-D-A. When other themes or keys occur in the 'A' sections, one senses the beginnings of sonata form. But it was the solo sections that were the purpose of the concerto. Within these episodes the soloist was given the opportunity to display such virtuosity as the composer could invent, and if the soloist's prowess exceeded the composer's imagination an impromptu (or perhaps well-rehearsed) solo episode might take place before the final ripieno. In this way the cadenza came about. With his *Art of the Violin*, published in 1733, Locatelli took this to extremes: to each of the 24 fast movements in the set is appended a capriccio of breathtaking virtuosity.

Like Vivaldi, Locatelli was a virtuoso violinist; both knew the limits of their instrument and set about

Riva degli Schiavoni, Venice, with the Ospedale della Pietà at the left.

Antonio Vivaldi, pictured in 1723. He was called the 'Red Priest' because of his auburn hair.

extending them. Tartini, in his 140-plus violin concertos and 194-plus violin sonatas, also helped to extend the violin's possibilities. He moved closer than his colleagues to achieving sonata form and he anticipated the Romantic era by attaching emotional poetic texts appropriate to their mood to many of his movements.

Such excesses – for emotional excesses they often were – together with the desire to turn the concerto increasingly into a vapid showpiece, brought about the cult of the virtuoso. Audiences became interested only in the fiddler (or the keyboardist, flautist, whoever); the composer was merely a means to an end. The soloist became the hero, and this, too, as with the three-movement form, stayed with the concerto for many years and stays with it still. However, some concertos eschewed the use of soloists altogether. Vivaldi probably began this genre but others, among them Zani and Telemann, continued the line.

If one group of concertos stands out in popularity among the many hundreds written in the first half of the 18th century it must be Vivaldi's *Four Seasons*. They employ a richly programmatic style that also appeared in other concertos of the period, though rarely so vividly. Descriptive music goes back to the dawn of the art, but after Vivaldi it is rarely present in the concerto. ♪

Pietro Antonio Locatelli, one of the finest violin virtuosos of his day.

P. LOCATELLI

Né en 1690, Mort en 1764.

Gravé par Lambert d'après le Dessin Original appartenant à M.r Cartier.

Mozart and the Concerto

HANDEL, IN THE ORGAN CONCERTOS HE inserted into oratorios, and J S Bach, with the concertos he arranged for his new harpsichord, may have invented the keyboard concerto inadvertently, but it took Bach's son Carl Philipp Emanuel to carry it forward. His 50 harpsichord concertos are emotional, well-developed works which advance the Vivaldian rondo pattern well into sonata form, and into the era of the piano. His last concerto, written in 1788, pits the brilliance of the harpsichord against the fuller tone of the still imperfect fortepiano, and unless there is some obscure musical enclave still to be explored that refused to bow to progress, C P E Bach's is

• MOZART'S CONCERTOS •

➤ By the 1770s the violin concerto was yielding to the keyboard concerto, as is reflected in the attention Mozart gave to each genre. However, he wrote five violin concertos (1773–75) plus several concerto movements within serenades. The Violin Concerto No. 1, K207, is his earliest original concerto. Neither did he neglect wind instruments. The lone Bassoon Concerto (1774) is the earliest; three more apparently are lost. An oboe concerto (1777) was written for Giuseppe Ferlendis, himself a composer, then rewritten for flute for a Dutch amateur, Dejean. Flute Concerto No. 2 dates from 1778. The four horn concertos, written for Joseph Leutgeb, are numbered against their chronology. Their order is: No. 2, K417 (1783); No. 4, K495 (1786); No. 3, K447 (?1787); No. 1, K412 (1791). The different-coloured inks Mozart used, supposedly to twit Leutgeb, are probably coded messages indicating dynamic shading, and so on. Mozart's last concerto (1791) was for a clarinet that became obsolete. It has

recently been rebuilt, the reconstruction being called 'basset clarinet'.

➤ A number of multiple concertos exist, the earliest being the Concertone ('large concerto') for two violins (1774). For Countess Lodron and her daughters Mozart supplied a concerto for three keyboards (1776), and, for himself and his sister, one for two (1779). That year saw the great *Sinfonia Concertante* for violin and viola, one of his greatest concertos.

➤ To select the finest keyboard concertos is an onerous task: all, after K450 (1784), have strong claims. Few listeners, however, would contest the greatness of the two minor-keyed works, K466 in D minor (1785) and K491 in C minor (1786), the latter giving an opening gambit to Beethoven for his Third Piano Concerto. Köchel 467 (1785) and K488 (1786) are possibly the most perfect, K482 (1785) the most noble, and K503 (1786), with its trumpets, drums and grand gestures, the most imperious.

the last 18th-century concerto for which harpsichord was specifically required.

For all the emotion and fire of his concertos, C P E Bach created only a chronological link with the future. It was, ironically, the much milder, friendlier art of Johann Christian Bach, whose first harpsichord concertos were published in 1763, that forged the artistic connection. The following year the eight-year-old Mozart met J C Bach in London. During amiable discussions, Mozart learnt so much from Bach that it deeply influenced his development. The boy later made concertos out of Bach's keyboard sonatas and arranged works by Raupach, Honauer and others as his first four harpsichord concertos in 1767, but it took six more years before he embarked upon his first original keyboard concerto, K175 in D.

The harpsichord was fighting a vain

This portrait of Mozart, painted about 1789 by Joseph Lange, hangs today in the Mozart Museum in Salzburg. Lange left it unfinished, but out of the many portraits of Mozart that have survived it is in this one that the representation of the composer's features is said to be the most faithful.

Faustine Parmantié paris 1784.

Theresia von Paradis, blind god-daughter of Empress Maria Theresia, who were graced with fine works, and a Mlle Jeunehomme from France, for whom Mozart wrote K271 when she visited Salzburg in 1777.

The Vivaldi-style rondo had been honed by now into a symphonic structure heavily reliant upon sonata form and with the orchestral and solo sections well integrated. One Vivaldi rule survived, however: the long opening statement had to be made by the full orchestra. For Mlle Jeunehomme Mozart broke this rule for his first and only time. The piano enters at the second bar. Furthermore, the final movement is spelt in French: rondeau.

Mozart's innate grasp of keyboard style brought the piano prominence and favour as a concert instrument. Up to K503 in 1786 he continued to perfect his concertos, but the last two, K537 (1788) and K595 (1791), show something of a loss of interest. Nonetheless, Mozart alone brought the piano concerto to a state in which the torch could be taken up by Beethoven. ♪

Maria Theresia von Paradis, though blind from childhood, composed three operas and played the keyboard. She founded a music academy in Vienna, and at the time that this portrait was executed Mozart wrote a piano concerto for her.

rearguard action against the piano during the 1770s, and it was J C Bach's *Sei Concerti per il Cembalo o Piano e Forte*, Op. 7 that first admitted the piano as a possible concerto performer in 1776. Thereafter piano concertos proliferated, as did pianists to play them. Mozart was himself an expert keyboardist and he wrote many of his concertos for his own appearances, but before 1782 they appeared only fitfully. The piano concerto was still in the making; indeed, K175 itself may have been intended for organ. Occasionally Mozart wrote for certain performers. Among the recipients were the pianists Barbara Ployer and Maria

PIANO CONCERTO NO.22 IN E FLAT, K482
~

The opening march is a rhythm popular with Mozart. Wind instruments contribute prominently through several melodies. The piano enters with its own material, soon integrated with the orchestral themes and leading to ideas rather daring for their period. Halfway through, the march heralds the recapitulation. Wind is again important in the romantic C minor andante, as in the hunting rhythm of the finale. The sylvan scene is interrupted by a slow and graceful minuet but returns to end the work robustly. The cadenza would have been spontaneously improvised.

The 19th - Century Concerto

• TOP CONCERTOS OF THE ROMANTIC ERA •

➤ **Beethoven: Piano Concerto No. 5 in E flat, Op. 73, *Emperor* (1809)** A concerto of surpassing grandeur, consisting of a first movement of imperious gestures, a beautiful central section, and a finale of teasing key changes. Note the timid theme of the finale, encroaching upon the adagio as if seeking permission to enter.

➤ **Chopin: Piano Concerto No. 1 in E minor, Op. 11 (1830)** For their time Chopin's concertos were the ultimate in 'hero' display pieces. Apart from setting the scene and providing harmonic support, the orchestra is totally subservient to a piano part which is among the most difficult in the repertoire.

➤ **Mendelssohn: Violin Concerto in E minor, Op. 64 (1844)** With applause-proof linking of its three movements, this continuous outpouring of lovely melody is extremely effective for the soloist without being too self-congratulatory. A perfect combination of 'hero' music and sincere composition.

➤ **Tchaikovsky: Piano Concerto No. 1 in B flat minor, Op. 23 (1875)** Described irreverently as 'The Tadpole' because its enormous starting paragraph never returns and is not balanced by later events, this is nonetheless the most popular piano concerto of its time. It was, however, not well received at first.

➤ **Brahms: Concerto in A minor for Violin and Cello, Op. 102 (1887)** More a symphony than a concerto, Brahms's Double has a compact, almost curt, first movement, a meltingly lovely andante and a 'Hungarian' finale. This was Brahms's last concerto, full of the wisdom and regret of an arduous life as one who never really escaped from the shadow of Beethoven's greatness.

➤ **Dvořák: Cello Concerto in B minor, Op. 104 (1895)** One of Dvořák's last works, this is a deeply introspective concerto, composed with great insight into the unique character of the cello, one of the most difficult concerto instruments of them all.

WITH THE SIMULTANEOUS COMING OF THE age of Romanticism and the virtuoso display concerto, plus dramatic advances towards perfecting the piano, the early 19th century produced a composer ideally placed to exploit all three. As pianist-composer, Beethoven created miraculous extemporizations and wrote solos and concertos for his own performances. He took the more masculine works of Mozart, applied his own symphonic instinct

The violinist and composer Joseph Joachim in 1890. When Brahms wrote his Violin Concerto in 1878 he turned to his friend Joachim for advice on the solo part.

and originality and produced five piano concertos, one for violin and another for piano trio (the Triple Concerto, an underrated work). The first two piano concertos skilfully follow conventional lines, although with typical Beethoven humour, and the Third, in C minor, is a deeply serious work (echoing the mood adopted by Mozart's in the same key) until the brilliantly witty finale. In No. 4 Beethoven broke a sacred rule even more violently than had Mozart in K271 by opening a piano concerto with the soloist rather than the orchestra, and in No. 5, *Emperor*, only a commanding chord precedes the pianist's opening flourishes.

Whereas Beethoven's concertos might be termed 'heroic-symphonic', Chopin's appeal to the hero-worshipping listener by following Mozart's feminine musical characteristics. With Chopin, the orchestra is relegated to an accompanying role; his numerous solo works suggest he would have preferred it absent altogether. Mendelssohn, Schumann and Grieg took a similar line but allowed the orchestra considerably more responsibility. The importance of the orchestra's contribution is at last fully realized in Brahms's two piano concertos. His First (1858) was criticized as "a

symphony with piano" (it was conceived originally as a symphony), and the second, with four demanding movements, is also symphonic but with a more rewarding piano part. Tchaikovsky's, while being concertos for the virtuoso pianist worshipper, do at least share the musical argument with the orchestra.

The start of the century saw renewed interest in the violin, with violinist-composers such as Pierre Rode, who wrote 13 much-admired concertos. Like Beethoven's of 1806, they display the skill of the soloist while still recognizing the need for musical value. Less fussy was Nicolò Paganini, who devoted his life and health (and, some said, his soul, forfeited to the Devil) to proving that he could fiddle more spectacularly than anyone. His concertos impressed Liszt, who then created equally virtuosic piano concertos, and Berlioz, who wrote *Harold in Italy* for Paganini's viola,

but the Italian refused to play it because, he said, it lacked virtuosity. It is, after all, a symphony. Paganini wrote his last concerto in 1830; in 1844 Mendelssohn produced his in E minor, in which virtuosity and musicality are perfectly wedded. Max Bruch followed this trend, though less successfully, with his No. 1 (1868), and ten years later with No. 2. And it was in that same year, 1878, that two radically different violin concertos appeared. Tchaikovsky's took Mendelssohn's as a model but increased the virtuoso input (to the discomfort of some critics), while Brahms followed Beethoven's intensely lyrical line and made the soloist serve the music rather than vice versa.

Many other composers contributed to a greater or lesser degree of importance to the romantic piano concerto, including Ignaz Moscheles (seven concertos, 1819–38); Anton Rubinstein (seven, 1847–74) and Xaver Scharwenka (four, 1876–1908),

while the violinist's repertoire was enriched by Louis Spohr (12 concertos, 1802–27) and Joseph Joachim (three, somewhat in the style of Brahms, 1855–99). Piano and violin, then, ruled the concerto circuits; the cello came third with only Schumann's (1850) and Dvořák's (1895) making a decisive impact. Other instruments were neglected, perhaps because the visual aspect lacked excitement but also because their limited ranges were unsuited to virtuoso display. Flute, oboe, clarinet and horn were awarded concertos, but not one has survived in the mainstream.

The multiple concerto also received contributions. A notable exponent was Louis Spohr, who wrote two for two violins, two for violin and harp, and one for string quartet and orchestra. However, only one multiple concerto stands out in this period: Brahms's difficult, severe but surpassingly beautiful 'Double Concerto' for violin and cello, his final orchestral composition. ♪

The Romantic Legacy

AS THE 19TH CENTURY DIED, AN ELEMENT of giganticism entered music. Works had to be bigger than before, more splendid, more exotic, more colourful, more fulsome – more everything. At the same time Romanticism appeared to have run its course and become tired and over-indulgent, yet it still attracted large audiences. There were, indeed, large halls now to accommodate increased audience sizes and crowds of musicians, and instruments had improved sufficiently to fill large spaces crammed with sound-absorbing people. Notably, the piano had evolved. The rather weak-toned and unreliable instrument of Beethoven's day had, with the mid-century invention of the iron frame, acquired increased power with its higher string tensions. The soloist-as-hero was still very active, though most of the virtuoso mountains had been climbed by phenomenal 19th-century showmen. Audiences now preferred the solo concerto, being unwilling to divide attention between heroes; this trend had developed despite the appearance of Brahms's Double Concerto.

The post-romantic period produced a mere handful of memorable string concertos. Elgar's for violin (1910) stands out as an essentially 'English' work by a composer whose musical background was in fact strongly Germanic. Walton's (1939) uses more modern language but lies in the same rhapsodic line; similarly, the style of Elgar's Cello Concerto (1919) is to some extent reflected in Walton's Viola Concerto of ten years later. Together with, for example, Samuel Barber's concertos for violin (1940) and cello (1945), they are lyrical works distinct from contemporary developments in continental Europe.

As chief concerto protagonist the piano remained supreme. Concertos by Scriabin (1896), and Dohnányi (1899) maintained a line which was given an enormous boost by Rachmaninov's post-Tchaikovskian Second Concerto (1901), while Delius in 1906 blurred the edges of form by reworking his early three-movement concerto into a one-movement fantasia-like work, thus reinforcing the trend towards formal integration. Busoni's massive concerto of 1904, a stirring work in grand Romantic style, includes a choral finale (as had Mondonville's Violin Concerto in 1752 and Steibelt's Piano Concerto No. 8 of 1820, so the idea was hardly new).

Rachmaninoff

77

The Russian composer Sergei Rachmaninov may be regarded as the spiritual heir of Tchaikovsky and the Romantic tradition, although in his later works he began to follow a more 'modern' path stylistically.

• PROMINENT POST-ROMANTIC CONCERTOS •

➤ **Richard Strauss: Horn Concerto No. 1 (1883)** Although in one movement, there are three distinct parts. Written for his horn-playing father, it evokes the spirit, if not the style, of Mozart, the composer Strauss most revered.

➤ **Rachmaninov: Piano Concerto No. 2 in C minor (1901)** With a portentous crescendo opening on to a broad and ardent theme, this is the epitome of everything Romantic. The composer had been close to breakdown when the dedicatee, Dr Dahl, encouraged him to continue to compose.

➤ **Sibelius: Violin Concerto in D minor, Op. 47 (1903)** None of Sibelius's distress, faced as he was with alcohol and money problems,

is reflected in this concerto. It is one of the most concise and satisfying in the violin repertory. Even so, two years later, Sibelius substantially revised it, tightening the argument still further.

➤ **Dohnányi: *Variations on a Nursery Theme*, Op. 25 (1913)** Not a concerto, but a work which employs concerto techniques in a neat accumulation of romantic qualities. The severe introduction to the trite nursery tune is a deft touch of humour.

➤ **Elgar: Cello Concerto in E minor, Op. 85 (1919)** This understated, introspective work presents the essence of late Elgar: a twilit world of regret and resignation. It was his last major orchestral work.

The main driving force, however, came from Russia, where concertos by Liapounov (1909), Rachmaninov (No. 3 in 1909) and Glazunov (No. 1, in two movements, 1911) adhered strongly to the Romantic ethic, and only Alexander Tcherepnin, who fled Russia in 1921, explored ways of escaping from Romanticism too, in his six concertos between 1920 and 1965. The Ukrainian-born Szymanowski's Symphonie Concertante (1932, also known as Symphony No. 4) has a fearsomely difficult piano part which is closely integrated with the orchestra and introduces Polish and Slavic folk songs and dances. It combines the Brahmsian wish to give orchestra and soloist equal responsibility, folk influences, virtuosity and Romanticism, all in a work that revives an ancient generic title.

Elsewhere the piano concerto flourished as a Romantic, rhapsodic showpiece. Max Reger's (1910), Max Bruch's (for two pianos, 1912), William Walton's (1928, another Sinfonia Concertante, though using the Italian term and treating the piano as part of the orchestra) and John Ireland's (1930) may still be regarded as Romantic in style, and in China the notorious *Yellow River* Concerto, written by a committee in about 1965, sounds, according

to one commentator, "like a mixture of Liszt, Mahler and Rachmaninov". Much the same was said about Richard Addinsell's *Warsaw* Concerto, a film score from 1942. Shostakovich's Concerto No. 2 (1957) combines modernism and Romanticism: its slow movement is almost pure Rachmaninov.

While 'symphonie concertante' and such-like titles identified the 'symphonic' concerto, other titles were employed for concerto-like works. One encounters Burleske (Richard Strauss), Rhapsody (Dohnányi), Concertino (many examples, denoting a 'small' or 'short' concerto), Diversions (Britten), Fantasy or Fantasia, Capriccio and others. They might be in any format, from one to many movements, or in variation form; for any soloist; and the orchestra might be small or large. Nevertheless, these offspring still demand virtuosity. Falla's *Nights in the Gardens of Spain* is in the same sub-category.

Mention should be made of two unusual works lying firmly in the Romantic tradition: Rodrigo's *Concierto de Aranjuez* for guitar and orchestra (1939), an evocative and beautiful impression of Spain, and Glière's wordless Concerto for Coloratura Soprano (1943). ♪

Celia Johnson and Trevor Howard in David Lean's film *Brief Encounter* (1945). Its romantic mood was heightened by Rachmaninov's Piano Concerto No. 2.

The Modernists

INEVITABLY THERE WAS A REACTION TO Romanticism. It had exceeded its brief, become too self-indulgent, and music needed new directions. They were not lacking. In 1911 Prokofiev stunned his tutors and the world with the originality of his one-movement First Piano Concerto. While acknowledging the piano's lyrical possibilities, he saw it (rightly) as a percussion instrument, and this work did more than any other to establish a trend of modernism in the 1920s and 1930s. Sorabji, always one to take a radical course, issued his incredibly complex one-movement

Concerto in 1920. Its formidable piano part requires almost superhuman intellect and endurance, needing up to five staves for clarity. Tighter and better organized is Bloch's Concerto Grosso No. 1 (1925) for piano and strings, while Bartók's First Concerto of the following year is a gritty, impenetrable work. The physical and mental requirements of these, Bartók's No. 2 (1931), Ravel's Concerto in G (1930), and the concertos of Honegger, Martinu and Janáček, put extra strain upon performers – as well as upon listeners, who were expected to absorb new forms and radical alterations to old ones, with cadenzas cropping up here, there or nowhere; ruthless motor rhythms; widened harmonic language that regarded dissonance as normal; unfamiliar folk elements and shock tactics – and still applaud at the end.

Instruments other than the piano were

similarly treated: violin (Bartók, No. 1, 1908, and No. 2, 1938; Stravinsky, 1931), flute (Nielsen, 1926, with a trombone as co-soloist), clarinet (Nielsen again, 1928, with side-drum obbligato) and harpsichord (Falla, 1926, a work with just six accompanists somewhat in the chamber tradition).

Other new factors also invaded concerto form. Atonalism and serialism abolished key and key relationships in works by Schoenberg, Berg and Webern, as well as those of their followers. Neo-Classicism, a reverse trend looking back to 18th-century language, forms and proportions, is heard in Stravinsky's *Dumbarton Oaks* Concerto for chamber orchestra (1938), literally a 20th-century *Brandenburg*, and in Walter Leigh's Concertino for harpsichord or piano and strings (1936). The spare and restrained purity of Webern's Concerto for violin, clarinet, horn, piano and strings (1928)

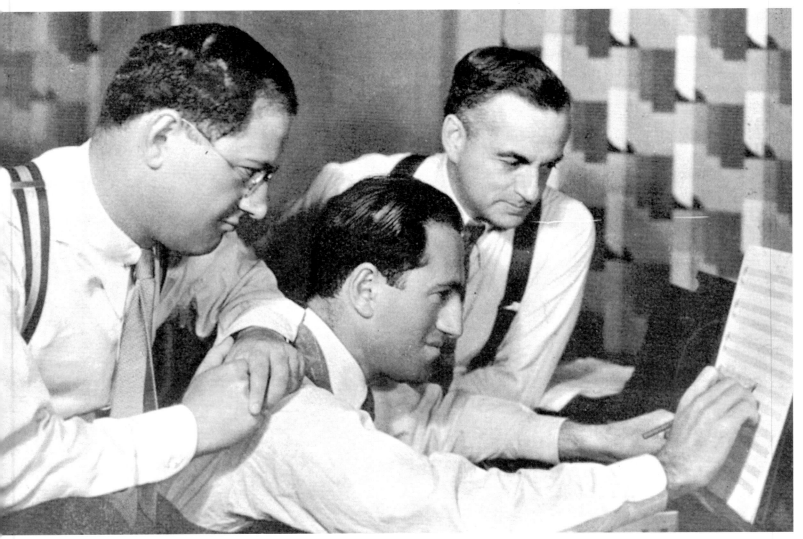

Béla Bartók, pictured
c. 1930 with his second
wife Ditta Pásztory, an
ex-pupil, and their son
Péter, born in 1924.
Fascism in Hungary was
soon to affect their lives.

George Gershwin (seated at the piano), with his brother Ira (left), a prolific lyricist, and Guy Bolton, with whom he collaborated on the film score of *Delicious* (1931).

combines the new serialism with the restraint of the classical period.

Another powerful influence was jazz. First heard in Gershwin's *Rhapsody in Blue* (1923), his Piano Concerto (1925), and Aaron Copland's Piano Concerto (1926, an example of orchestral forces applied to the jazz idiom), this influence continues. Stravinsky was also fascinated by jazz and jazz musicians. For the Woody Herman Orchestra he composed his *Ebony* Concerto for clarinet (which was made of black wood) and jazz band in 1945. The Austrian composer Fritz Pauer was influenced by Bud Powell, Bill Evans and the classical/jazz pianist Friedrich Gulda when he wrote his Concerto for Big Band and Symphony Orchestra. Concerted works by Morton Gould take in blues and modern dance rhythms.

Pianist Paul Wittgenstein (brother of the philosopher Ludwig Wittgenstein) lost his right arm early in World War I while serving in the Austrian Army but refused to give up playing. He commissioned many concertos and other pieces for left hand, some of which have become popular. Perhaps Hindemith's and Franz Schmidt's (both 1923) and Richard Strauss's *Parergon on Symphonia Domestica* (1924) do not hold audiences today, but Ravel's Concerto for the Left Hand (1930), Prokofiev's Fourth Concerto (1931) and Britten's *Diversions* (1940) are well loved. But to Wittgenstein Prokofiev's Concerto was "aggressively modern", so he checked that Alexander Tansman's style would be acceptable before commissioning the Concert Piece from him in 1943.

Grave international events diverted attention from musical progress during the 1940s. Only Bartók's Piano Concerto No. 3, Viola Concerto and Concerto for Orchestra, Strauss's Horn Concerto No. 2, and Stravinsky's Concerto for Strings are notable contributions from this period. ♪

• THE MODERNISTS •

➤ **Stravinsky: Concerto for Piano, Wind and Timpani (1924)** Three of Stravinsky's preoccupations are combined here: the fascinating effects of wind sonorities, Neo-Classical use of form and Neo-Baroque contrapuntal textures (the first movement, like many of Corelli's, is in several sections), and jazz.

➤ **Nielsen: Clarinet Concerto (1928)** In this one-movement work the clarinet is in almost constant conflict with the orchestra, and an elaborate side-drum part acts as a third combatant. The solo part is extremely difficult, the music severe.

➤ **Shostakovich: Piano Concerto No. 1 in C minor, Op. 35 (1933)** A light-hearted work in the composer's most witty vein, with a trumpet taking an important but subsidiary part. The impudence of the music upset Communist Party officials who took themselves too seriously and expected all Russia to do likewise.

➤ **Bartók: Violin Concerto No. 2 (1938)** Although dated 31 December 1938, Bartók made alterations until shortly before the first performance on 23 March 1939. The work is formally Classical, with sonata form outer movements (which employ similar thematic ideas), and variations in the andante. There is even a first movement cadenza in the expected place. Hungarian influence is apparent everywhere in this lyrical work.

➤ **Martinu: Concerto for Two String Orchestras, Piano and Percussion (1938)** Complete integration of the piano within the double orchestral context links this concerto with the baroque *concerto grosso*. The musical vocabulary is modern, terse but approachable. Criticism is often made that Martinu was uncritical of his own music, but this concerto is well thought out, effective, and among his finest works.

➤ **Bartók: Piano Concerto No. 3 (1945)** Written for his wife, Ditta Pásztory, but not quite complete at his death, Bartók's Third Concerto is among his least enigmatic works and is in three well-proportioned movements. Hungarian national rhythms are satisfyingly absorbed within the textures.

Today's Concerto

SINCE WORLD WAR II THE 'EXCESSES' OF the inter-war years have been far surpassed. For one thing, no instrument is safe from the attention of the concerto composer. A few of the less-likely concerto instruments, with their composers, are: piccolo (Bucchi, 1973); trombone (Parrott, 1967); alphorn (Farkas, *Concertino Rustico*, 1977), sitar (Shankar, 1971; 1976), panpipes (Zamfir, c. 1982), cor anglais (Borris, *Concertino*, 1949); 12 unaccompanied voices (Barbara Buczek, 1969); xylophone (Lang, 1961); kettledrum (Cresswell, c. 1974); bassoon and double bassoon (Badings, 1964); double bassoon alone (Erb, 1986?), military snare drum (*Geigy Festival* Concerto, Liebermann, 1958), and typewriters, cash registers and calculating machines (Liebermann, c. 1963). For another thing, concertos, with a few exceptions, have become shorter, which may not be to their detriment; and modern concertos put conventional instrumentalists to more stress and excess than ever before.

It is not enough to make a piano concerto. In 1951 John Cage wrote one for 'prepared piano' and chamber orchestra. Cage first 'prepared' a piano in 1938 by interfering with its workings. Drawing pins adorned the felt hammers to give a twanging effect, and rubber and metal objects were placed on and between the strings. This altered the character of the tone somewhat, and the alterations were not always predictable. Rubber bounces. Henze found that it was not enough to have a soloist and orchestra in his Violin Concerto No. 2 (1971) so he threw in taped effects and poetry readings. The ploy of introducing prominent subsidiary instruments has an honourable history. Nielsen had done so in the 1920s, Brahms and Tchaikovsky had focused attention on solo cello in their piano concertos, and Beethoven had included a cadenza in the piano arrangement of his Violin Concerto that featured an accompanying timpanist.

The purpose of a concerto is to provide a vehicle for artistic display, but to do so while creating an intellectually satisfying work is more of a challenge. Shostakovich's concertos for string soloists (two for violin, two for cello) display symphonic characteristics – in fact they are hardly less symphonic than his symphonies, though this is not true of his two piano concertos. This earnest symphonism does not neglect virtuosity – indeed, technical and musical accomplishment of the highest order is always vital – but it takes second place to purely musical argument.

This line of development is found in Penderecki's one-movement Violin Concerto (1976) which, though dedicated to a supreme artist, Isaac Stern, concentrates upon introspective symphonism. The Viola Concerto of 1983 is similarly earnest, in one concentrated movement lasting barely 20 minutes. The less inward-looking Panufnik offers greater brilliance, as in the Piano Concerto (1962) and the *Festive*

John Cage was an advanced musical thinker and also a mycologist – an expert on fungi. This photograph, taken in 1977, shows him occupied in his kitchen in New York.

Malcolm Arnold, composer of some of the 20th century's most approachable music, pictured in 1951.

Ravi Shankar, sitar virtuoso, who introduced Indian music to the West.

Concerto (1979), a dazzling display piece for the London Symphony Orchestra. Even the Bassoon Concerto (1985) is less introspective than much of Penderecki's work despite being written in memory of the murdered Polish priest Father Popieluszko. There is little doubt that the concerto's future is secure with works as diverse as Lloyd's Piano Concerti, tonal, virtuosic and listener-friendly, and Panufnik's exploratory concerto for timpani, percussion and strings (1980).

Such works are important, but composers have also written less intense concertos intended more for display. Jan Seidl's Oboe Concerto No. 2 (1955) and

Jíri Pauer's Bassoon Concerto (final version 1960) were written for artists who play instruments out of the traditional concerto ambit, or just to see whether it still could be done. Vaughan Williams's Bass Tuba Concerto (1954) and his Romance for

harmonica written for Larry Adler (1951), and Vittorio Rieti's Harpsichord Concerto for Sylvia Marlow (1955) are further examples. All these were designed to display the talents of specific artists, just as were Vivaldi's nearly three centuries ago. ♪

• RECENT CONCERTOS •

➤ **Britten: Cello Symphony, Op. 68 (1963)** Called 'Cello Symphony' because of the close integration between soloist and orchestra, this work adheres to traditional frameworks such as sonata form and passacaglia.

➤ **Shostakovich: Cello Concerto No. 2, Op. 126 (1966)** Despite its imaginative use of percussion and, like the First Cello Concerto, arresting horn parts, this work puts the emphasis squarely on the solo while simultaneously integrating it with the orchestra. It is even more of a 'cello symphony' than Britten's.

➤ **Arnold: Concerto for Phyllis and Cyril, Op. 104 (1969)** The husband-and-wife piano duo Phyllis Sellick and Cyril Smith were faced with disaster when Smith suffered a stroke in 1956, paralysing his left arm. They played three-handed thereafter, and this approachable concerto in popular style is among the works specially written for them in, as Sir Malcolm Arnold says, "affection and admiration" for their courage.

➤ **Bourgeois: Concerto Grosso for brass (1979)** A virtuoso work for all the members of the brass orchestra. As in the old *concerto grosso* style an element of competition results in effective spatial and antiphonal effects within an easy, sometimes joky, context, with samba rhythms and much display.

➤ **Adams: *Grand Pianola Music* (1982)** Minimalism with a difference. John Adams manages to combine repetitive, economical melodies with a heroic style reminiscent of the grand gestures of Beethoven and Brahms. The two pianists imitate a mechanical pianola effect at times and three sopranos sing wordlessly almost throughout.

➤ **Schnittke: Cello Concerto No. 1 (1986)** The advanced tonal style of Schnittke's language puts great strain upon the soloist, not only to be heard against the heavy orchestration but also to conquer the demanding technical writing. Schnittke's message is one of pain, despair and cynicism, but his intense treatment of the material puts the work into line for future widespread acceptance.

Suite

A *SUITE IS COMMONLY A SET OF instrumental or orchestral pieces, often dances, which are designed to be performed as a collection. There are a number of alternative titles, including Ordre (Old French) and Partie or Partita (Old German).*

THE SUITE WAS THE COMMONEST FORM OF instrumental music until around the middle of the 18th century, when it went into a sharp decline. Because the form eventually made a spirited comeback, the genre during its first, most lively, period of existence is commonly referred to as the 'classical' suite (though it will be referred to here as 'suite').

The first known examples of the suite date back to the 14th century. They are nearly all for lute and almost always comprise a collection of contrasting dance movements, often with thematic connections. Suites for keyboard appeared in the early 17th century. From surviving publications which date from this time, the basic format of the suite can be summarized as two or more contrasting movements which share the same key or some kind of thematic link. Gradually the suite expanded, frequently assuming a four-movement format of contrasting slow and fast dances, these initially being allemande-courante-sarabande-gigue.

The four-movement form prevailed between 1650 and 1725, though the dances varied considerably, much depending on fashion. French composers proved an exception; they were more inclined to lengthier suites, with movements carrying highly descriptive titles – Couperin's First Ordre for harpsichord (1713), for example, has no fewer than 18 movements.

The freedom surrounding both the number and nature of movements also applied to such basic 'unifying' factors as themes and key; Handel, for example, favoured thematic connections in his suites though the majority of his contemporaries did not. The question of tonality was also very personal; some, including Purcell, Couperin and J S Bach, kept for the most part to one basic key, while Corelli and Handel occasionally slipped into a relative minor or major. Perhaps the only common factor linking the diverse and complex

François Couperin was known as 'Couperin le Grand', partly in order to distinguish him from the other nine or so members of his musical family who were active from the 17th to the 19th centuries, but also in recognition of his stature as a composer.

The opening page of
Handel's *Water Music*,
written c. 1715.

variety of compositions termed 'suites' is that each movement was of a single, basic character. (It was the introduction of contrasts, be it of key or dramatic elements, which heralded the start of sonata form – and the ultimate demise of the suite.) Although the suite was for long an instrumental vehicle, the orchestra, as it grew in number and capability, inevitably began to participate. By the end of the suite's heyday – the first half of the 18th century – orchestral suites were as popular as instrumental suites.

Two of the greatest composers of the era made significant contributions to the form. With the obvious exception of the familiar *Water Music* and *Fireworks Music*, Handel's suites are principally for keyboard. The 20 or so that survive reveal a large variety of ideas (and a varied level of inspiration). It was J S Bach who mastered the form as no other composer before or since. Some 45 suites for various combinations (mostly instrumental) have survived, among which is an unprecedented emotional range.

Then, just as it reached its full, magnificent flowering the suite unceremoniously slipped into obscurity, pushed to the sidelines by the emergence of the sonata, concerto and symphony. ♪

• THREE POPULAR BACH SUITES •

The fact that all three suites listed here date from Bach's time at Cöthen (1717–23) is no coincidence. During this period he was court conductor to the Calvinist Prince Leopold, who was strongly opposed to the idea of music in church: instrumental and orchestral music consequently dominated Bach's output.

➤ **Cello Suite No. 5 in C minor, BWV1011**
The six cello suites are a remarkable contrast to the six solo violin works. While the latter tend to strive more towards the heavens the cello suites are largely content to entertain, as is evident from the fact that all six, after an opening prelude, comprise a succession of dance movements, many of a decidedly light and direct nature.

The Fifth Suite is perhaps the most individual of the set. It employs *scordatura* (mistuning) – in this instance the top A string is tuned down a whole tone – which gives the entire suite a much darker character compared with its companions. The prelude is unusually formal, the allemande more powerful than amiable, the courante edgy rather than courtly and the sarabande unassuming. After a pair of gavottes there follows a surprisingly melancholic gigue.

➤ **Partita No.2 in D minor, BWV1004** This is a suite in every respect save the name. Bach's own title for his unaccompanied violin works was (in Italian) Six Solos for Violin without Accompanying Bass, though they have been subsequently divided into three partitas and three sonatas. The sonatas follow the four-movement pattern of the *sonata da chiesa* (church sonata), with rarely an appearance of the dance, while the partitas comprise a sequence of dances.

The most unusual feature of the Second Partita is the concluding ciaconna (chaconne), one of Bach's most monumental creations (longer in fact than the duration of the preceding movements). It comes after a flowing yet unusually positive allemanda, an equally assertive corrente, a near-sensuous sarabande and a carefree, skipping giga. Its appearance is breathtaking in its unexpectedness and awesome in its cumulative effect. Once the theme of the chaconne has been stated there begins a series of 29 variations of infinite variety and extraordinary invention.

➤ **Orchestral Suite No. 3 in D, BWV1068**
Bach's four orchestral suites were not conceived as a set, though they adhere to the French pattern of placing a sequence of contrasting dance movements after an overture. The Third Suite, written about 1730, is scored for strings, trumpets and timpani. The substantial overture is in French style (slow introduction with a faster fugal middle section and a slow conclusion) and dominates the entire work. Another unique feature of this suite is that Bach inserts a non-dance movement – the celebrated air which he scores only for strings – before proceeding with a pair of gavottes, a bourrée and a gigue.

Vue des Feux d'Artifice et des Illuminations données par Monseigneur le Duc de Richmond de Lenox et d'Aubigny,

When the Peace of Aix-la-Chapelle was signed in 1748 it brought an end to the war of the Austrian Succession. Preparations for a celebratory firework display in London began, King George II requesting accompanying music from Handel in which only martial instruments were used. After the first performance on 27 April 1749, Handel added string parts.

The Post-classical Suite

THE SUITE MADE A REMARKABLE COMEBACK in the middle of the 19th century. In its resurrected form it is commonly referred to as the 'post-classical' suite.

The British composer William Sterndale Bennett was among the very first to re-employ the word 'suite' – in his *Suite de pièces*, Op. 24 for piano (1841) – although

Schumann, who much admired Bennett's composition, had already penned notable suites of dances for piano, his choice of title being a descriptive generic – *Papillons*, Op. 2 (1831), *Davidsbündlertänze*, Op. 6 (1837) and *Carnaval,* Op. 9 (1837). In the 30 or so years from the middle of the 19th century, several composers, the majority of them German, did their utmost to restore the suite to an equal footing with the symphony and the sonata. Raff wrote two orchestral suites as well as one for piano and orchestra and another for violin and orchestra; Lachner produced eight extended orchestral suites. In France, Saint-Saëns was one of the

first to return to the ancient form, though his Suite for Cello and Piano, Op.16 (1866) contains no antique dance forms. Massenet wrote nine orchestral suites, most of the colourful movements being highly pictorial rather than a deliberate look-back to earlier forms. Like the symphonic poem the suite also became bound-up in nationalistic feelings, as is evident in the works of Grieg, Sibelius, Nielsen, Tchaikovsky, Rimsky-Korsakov and Glazunov.

'Concert suites' – extracts from stage works – also became very numerous during the 19th and 20th centuries. Bizet's *Carmen* Suite (opera), Grieg's *Peer Gynt* Suite

• 20TH-CENTURY SUITES •

➤ **Bartók: Dance Suite** Written for the 50th anniversary of the merging of Buda and Pesth as the Hungarian capital in 1923, Bartók's Dance Suite is, as its title implies, entirely rooted in the dance, in this particular instance folk music of a somewhat diabolical quality (although all the material is original). Five dances and a finale are played without a break, each linked by a touching little refrain. Full of gleaming colours and pounding rhythms, this is one of the composer's most instantly accessible works.

➤ **Grofé: *Grand Canyon* Suite** Grofé first came to fame as pianist and orchestrator to the band leader Paul Whiteman who premiered the original version of *Grand Canyon* Suite in 1931. However, it is the later technicolor full orchestral version by which Grofé is best known. The majesty and power of the Grand Canyon, portrayed at sunrise and sunset, as well as a thrilling depiction of a cloudburst, is achieved by a virtuoso use of the modern symphony orchestra.

➤ **Richard Strauss: *Le bourgeois Gentilhomme*, Op. 60** We can only be thankful that Richard Strauss rescued his incidental music to Molière's *Le bourgeois Gentilhomme* and fashioned it into an orchestral suite, for this is one of the wittiest yet most tenderly touching scores in all 20th-century music.

➤ **Holst's *The Planets*** It was Clifford Bax, brother of the composer Arnold Bax, who was responsible for introducing Holst to astrology in 1913. The subject strongly appealed to Holst, who had a life-long fascination for all things mystic, though he later emphasized that it was the astrological character of each planet rather than the mystical associations which he was attempting to express in his music. Written between 1914 and 1916, *The Planets* brought him unaccustomed fame, which he intensely disliked: "Every artist ought to pray that he may not be 'a success'," he said. Holst's largest orchestral score is a seven-movement suite scored for vast forces (numbering such exotic instruments as bass flute, bass oboe, tenor and bass tubas as well as a large battery of percussion instruments, xylophone, celesta, organ and women's chorus).

➤ **Mars, the Bringer of War** Written before the outbreak of World War I, this was a prophecy of the cruelty and stupidity of war. It contains menacing rhythms – the movement is in 5/4 time – and thunderous sounds.

➤ **Venus, the Bringer of Peace** This movement is of a profound serenity.

➤ **Mercury, the Winged Messenger** Holst's scherzo moves with swift, effortless ease, changing direction like quicksilver.

➤ **Jupiter, the Bringer of Jollity** The full orchestra reassembles to portray the enjoyment of life. This movement is full of rollicking good humour and, at the appearance of a majestic melody (which Holst later set as the patriotic hymn *I Vow to Thee My Country*), positively exuding contentment and geniality.

➤ **Saturn, the Bringer of Old Age** Holst's favourite movement. Desolation and despair at the inexorability of old age are expressed. Feelings reach panic level at the terrifying central climax, full of the clangour of bells. Acceptance of the inevitable is, however, quickly evident and the movement ends in calm resignation.

➤ **Uranus, the Magician** A grotesque dance not far removed from Dukas's Apprentice (which was unknown to Holst when he composed this movement). There are screams and shouts of riotous glee and many magical goings-on which abruptly end very softly.

➤ **Neptune, the Mystic** Mysterious, disembodied sonorities are emphasized by wordless female voices. Sounds stretch further and further into limitless space. It is as if the work never ends but simply passes from our hearing.

(incidental music) and Tchaikovsky's *Nutcracker* Suite (ballet) are classic and hugely popular examples of the genre.

Some 20th-century composers continued to favour the suite. The majority are pastiche in style and it is no coincidence that these are frequently from the pens of the master orchestrators – to cite two examples from 1920, *Le bourgeois Gentilhomme* by Richard Strauss and *Pulcinella* by Stravinsky. Others have created genuinely original suites, none more so than Bartók (Dance Suite) (1923),

Schoenberg (Suite for strings) (1935), Berg (Lyric Suite for String Quartet (1925–26), three movements of which were later transcribed for string orchestra, and Holst (*The Planets*). ♪

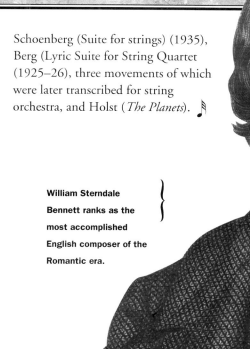

William Sterndale Bennett ranks as the most accomplished English composer of the Romantic era.

The development and expansion of the orchestra in the mid 19th century led composers to reassess the suite as a musical form. The wider palette of sound available enabled composers such as Grofé in his *Grand Canyon* suite to depict the full majesty and power of nature. (Painting: *The Miracles of Nature* by Thomas Moran)

Symphony

OLD REFERENCE BOOKS IDENTIFY HAYDN as the father of the symphony, but studies over the last century have shown this to be a myth. Researchers have dramatically revised our knowledge of the symphony's roots: we know now that when Franz Joseph Haydn was born in 1732 the symphony was already in its late infancy.

THE WORD 'SYMPHONY', TAKEN FROM THE Greek and meaning 'a sounding together', had been used for an early instrument, a kind of hurdy-gurdy in which the melody string 'sounded together' with one or more drone strings. By extension, the word could be applied to any group of two or more instrumentalists 'sounding together', but eventually it came to specify one type of form which, for the sake of clarity, we might describe as a sonata for orchestra.

The earliest symphonies appeared before 1700 and had their origins in a number of different styles, evolving slowly and haltingly from the suite, sonata and overture and developing alongside the concerto. A suite is a succession of dance movements sometimes prefaced by a non-dancing prelude during which the players, often an ad hoc group brought together by chance or circumstance, would accustom themselves to each other's playing while the dancers prepared to enjoy the evening. Movements of a suite might be played in any order, omitted, repeated, perhaps even played faster or slower according to requests from the floor, so there was nothing fixed about a composer's work; it was all very informal. A sonata was more formal. It might be designed for church use, in which case it had to be solemn and in keeping with religious occasions, or for the chamber, when dance movements were required. There were also mixtures of both types. The emerging symphony drew elements from both church and chamber sonata, from the suite, and from the operatic overture.

Likewise, the early symphony itself might be intended for church or chamber. Giuseppe Torelli, writing grand music for the

• EARLY SYMPHONIES •

➤ **Torelli's** symphonies/concerti/sonatas (he was inconsistent over terminology) include possibly the first truly symphonic piece, the *Sinfonia à 4* (Symphony of Fours), G33, for two orchestras totalling four oboes and four trumpets, with bassoon, trombone, timpani, strings and two organs. Such splendour was rare before 1700.

➤ **Vivaldi's** *Concerto ripieno* (literally 'full concerto') in B flat, RV163, titled *La Conca* (The cave, possibly an allusion to a stage work) is an eccentric piece based on a falling B flat octave, teased out and distorted throughout all three movements. Such 'thematic transformation' predates the experiments of Schumann, Franck and Brahms by well over a century. Another forward-looking

Concerto ripieno, RV127 in D minor, presages the *Sturm und Drang* movement of the 1760s and 1770s, being a veritable fireball of furious string writing. Its three movements run for a total of about three and a half minutes.

➤ **William Boyce's** little three-movement overture to *Peleus and Thetis* (?1734) is probably the earliest English example of a symphony.

➤ **Locatelli** composed six *Introduzzioni teatrale* for strings in 1735. The term equates with 'overture' but they were designed for either the theatre as overtures or concert use as symphonies.

➤ **W F Bach's** strange Symphony in F, F67 (c. 1740) is a four-movement suite in all but name.

ceremonies in St Petronio, Bologna, composed many stirring pieces for one or more trumpets with an orchestra of strings and organ, often supported in the lower notes by a trombone or two. Meanwhile, the chamber symphony was undergoing a far more modest birth. Gradually, the dance movements of the old suite were improving in quality, so why dance to them when good music was worth sitting down to listen to? Encouraged by this, composers put more and more art into their music for dancing and people were content to just listen. In time the diffuse form of the suite was condensed to three movements, fast-slow-fast, thus paralleling the operatic overture, which in Italy was called *sinfonia* (symphony). The second and third movements were still based on dances, the second possibly a gavotte or an air, the finale a minuet or jig, but there were many exceptions and variations. In first place was a bustling movement full of energy.

Torelli was again among the first to compose this type of symphony; others included Albinoni, Manfredini and Sammartini – all Italians, for it was in Italy that the symphony was born. Among these and a host of lesser-known figures, one

name stands out: Antonio Vivaldi. As a leader of a girls' orchestra in Venice and the bearer of an extremely heavy workload, he

yet managed to keep up with current trends and invent new ones. He produced concertos for many different solo instruments, and some with no soloists at all. These last he called *concerti ripieni*, reserving the word *sinfonia* for his operatic overtures. With the new *concerto ripieno*, Vivaldi experimented with form and style, bending and hammering the symphony this way and that and producing stimulating, and sometimes weird, sounds. Another aspect heard in Vivaldi's symphonies is that of contrast within movements. In his solo concertos he would move from the basic key of a piece to related keys for the solo sections, giving tonal contrast. At the same time, naturally, the soloist would introduce new ideas which contrasted with the main theme. Later composers adopted this dual contrast and it developed into sonata-form, in which a first theme would be followed by a contrasting second theme in a different key. ♪

William Boyce, Master of the King's Musick, wrote possibly the earliest English symphonies but is remembered for a set of eight written between 1739 and 1756 and published in 1760.

The 'Pre-Classical' Symphony

WITH A FEW EXCEPTIONS, THE GRAND occasional symphony such as Torelli's trumpet-bedecked work was to lapse temporarily in favour of the chamber symphony. These intimate works were almost without exception for string band only. Woodwind and brass were to make a concentrated entrance about 1740, and one may pinpoint the main location: Mannheim.

Vivaldi and his compatriots were becoming known outside Italy. Johann Sebastian Bach admired their music, Dresden was the recipient of many Vivaldi concertos, and Italian composers were looking to north European publishers, notably in Amsterdam, to print their music because the quality was better than that produced at home. In Mannheim the Elector Karl Theodor was busy recruiting young composers to write for his orchestra. As its leader he chose a Bohemian named Jan Václav Antonín Stamic (Germanicized to Johann Wenzel Anton Stamitz) who set about creating a well-disciplined orchestra including woodwind and brass. It was the Mannheim orchestra which impressed Dr Burney when he visited there in 1772: "An army of generals", he called it, "as fit to plan a battle as to fight it." Indeed, Stamitz and his colleagues, among them Holzbauer, Richter and Filtz, produced some of the most exciting symphonies to be heard anywhere before Haydn and Mozart. Stamitz breathed fire into his orchestra, and his music held audiences spellbound. He dramatically advanced ensemble and virtuosity in symphonic writing. Flutes, oboes and bassoons were the Mannheim complement of woodwind; brass was represented by trumpets (there were no fewer than 12 of them in 1756) and horns. Stamitz wrote testing parts for horns, including the highest note written for it in the 18th century (c''' for a horn pitched G). Drums were also sometimes used.

Another Mannheim symphony feature was the contrast between a bold opening melody and a contrasting second theme. The origin of this contrast lies with Vivaldi and his Italian contemporaries, but the Stamitz circle greatly developed it. There is also the matter of key contrast; again, this had been a feature of Vivaldi's works, but at Mannheim it became an important focal point and led to the enormous expansion of sonata form.

The dozen or more composers at Mannheim left a body of symphonies

The Mozart family: father Leopold, son Wolfgang, and daughter Nannerl. Between them, father and son wrote about 120 symphonies.

amounting to over 500 in number. Most are unknown and unplayed today but in the middle of the 18th century they were enormously influential. Mozart benefited from them, they were all the rage in Paris and London, and they established an excellence of orchestral playing that was a proud example to the rest of Europe.

Four movements were the norm at Mannheim: fast-slow-minuet-fast. This was the layout favoured also in Austria, where Wagenseil was busy composing many chamber symphonies, and in Salzburg, home of Leopold Mozart. Perhaps the music of Wolfgang Amadeus's father cannot equal the quality of his son's, but it is imaginative and attractive and deserves to be better known.

In north Germany, King Friedrich II (Frederick the Great) ran a tight military regime in Potsdam but spent his evenings playing the flute. His composer-servant Quantz faithfully produced over 300 concertos for his master and, while the royal personage played, a squat figure crouched quietly over the harpsichord playing a humdrum continuo. This was Carl Philipp Emanuel Bach, Johann Sebastian's second musical son, who was a seething volcano under his bewigged exterior. When released

Frederick the Great of Prussia playing one of Quantz's flute concertos.

Seated at the harpsichord is Carl Philipp Emanuel Bach.

• 'PRE-CLASSICAL' SYMPHONIES •

➤ **Boyce: Symphony No. 5 in D of 1739** After a splendid fugal movement, two dances, gavotte and minuet complete this embryonic symphony, which is Handelian in style.

➤ **François Martin: Symphony in G minor, Op. 4/2** Of the six symphonies Martin published in Paris in 1746, this one uses strings with great imagination, but the first movement resembles the early Scarlatti-type two-part form, lacking contrast. The pretty pizzicato andante precedes a finale whose earnestness approaches Vivaldi at his most severe.

➤ **Leopold Mozart: *Hunting* Symphony in G, Eisen G9** A symphony which includes a shotgun to be discharged at specified moments. Four hunting horns are thrillingly displayed in this work.

➤ **Johann Stamitz: The Symphony Wolf E flat 1** Composed before 1755 and typical of the Mannheim style, this symphony has a spiky, aggressive first movement and prominent wind in the marching second theme, followed by a crescendo.

➤ **Anton Filtz: The Symphony in A (c.1755)** This introduces every Mannheim fingerprint: crescendo, sighing phrases, exciting wind and vibrant string writing, plus a melodic charm that is comparable to Mozart's of 20 years later.

➤ **C P E Bach: Symphony in F, W175/H650 (1755)** Bach's exhilarating art is heard in the vivid string writing complemented by flutes and high horns. Bach introduces less contrast between themes but his energetic ideas exert a powerful fascination.

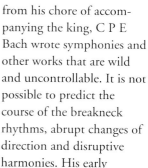

Sanssouci, Frederick the Great's palace at Potsdam.

from his chore of accompanying the king, C P E Bach wrote symphonies and other works that are wild and uncontrollable. It is not possible to predict the course of the breakneck rhythms, abrupt changes of direction and disruptive harmonies. His early symphonies display a furiously hyperactive imagination but strongly attract by virtue of their sheer oddity. It seems he was determined to make people really listen. Bach's colleagues at Potsdam, Graun and the brothers Benda (the latter a family imported from Bohemia), copied his style with limited success. North German symphonies are invariably in the fast-slow-fast format; such a superheated environment was no place for placid minuets.

In France, the Mannheim style influenced composers such as Gossec, a Belgian who worked in Paris. In England the symphonies of Boyce and, at first, Arne, were still recovering from the overwhelming influence of Handel. Only gradually did England catch up with the rest of Europe.

Haydn & Mozart

THE CIRCUMSTANCES OF HAYDN'S LIFE HAD far-reaching consequences upon his symphonic output. He produced his first symphony in 1757 (the year of Johann Stamitz's death), plus several more before his employment with Prince Eszterházy in 1761. Haydn's style is based on Austrian conventions but even the earliest symphonies display an imagination several degrees above that of his contemporaries. The numbering of the early symphonies is confused: there are some 20 pre-Eszterházy works, yet the first he wrote there are numbered 6-8. These are the famous 'Morning-Noon-Evening' trilogy, probably emulating Vivaldi's *Four Seasons* of 36 years earlier but without copying them.

While in the employment of Prince Eszterházy Haydn wrote over 70 symphonies. The composer later explained that because he was removed from contemporary musical influences (the Prince's reluctance to leave Eszterháza meant that his musicians were required to stay on the estate for long periods), he was forced to be original. This originality reveals itself in progressively adventurous music. The four-movement plan was basic but not unviolable, instruments are treated imaginatively, and rare keys often introduce disturbing effects.

By the late 1770s Haydn's music was being heard beyond Eszterházy. His six 'Paris' symphonies (Nos 82–87), commissioned by that city, meet Parisian taste in their brashness and colour; the next five, also for Paris, show further advances. Then, in 1790, Salomon, an impresario-composer from London, visited Haydn. "I've come to fetch you," he said, and the 58-year-old composer embarked on his greatest adventure: to face London's audiences. His 12 new symphonies won their hearts. The music charts new directions of charm, vigour, humour, drama and tunefulness, but with a new depth. This

· HAYDN'S SYMPHONIES ·

To Haydn's 104 numbered symphonies, written between 1757 and 1795, should be added two earlier works (one originally thought to be a string quartet, the other a partita) and substantially different versions of two more. No. 88 (1787) is among the finest examples of Haydn's joy in life, a joy which extends in the slow movement to contemplation of spacious beauty. No. 92, *Oxford* (1789), continues this line. By now, Haydn's blending of orchestral mastery and good humour is complete. The *Surprise* Symphony, No. 94 (1791), with its sudden loud chord in the quiet second movement, is one of the first of the London series: Haydn wanted to ensure that his symphony would be talked about. Number 101, *Clock* (1794) again derives its nickname from the slow movement, an insistent tick-tock that stops halfway for rewinding. The last two symphonies, No. 103, *Drumroll*, and No. 104, *London* (1795), are the acme of Haydn's symphonic achievement. Of the earlier works, two series stand out: the 'Storm and Stress' (*Sturm und Drang*, see page 23) works of 1768-72 and the symphonies written for Paris in 1785-86. In the earlier series Haydn experiments far more radically than any contemporary composer, and in the Paris symphonies he consolidates the advances he has made.

· MOZART'S SYMPHONIES ·

M ozart's last symphony bears the number 41; this is misleading and diminishes his achievement. First, once the spurious Nos. 2, 3 and 37 are removed, a further unnumbered 19 symphonies have to be added (of which five are lost and one doubtful), making a total of 57. Another dozen three-movement overtures which Mozart used as concert symphonies, and seven serenades which he adapted for concert use, all have to be taken into account. The grand total is 76, composed between 1764 and 1788. The greatest are the last six. Number 35, *Haffner* (originally a serenade), and No. 36, *Linz*, show amazing skill, but No. 38, *Prague*, is greater still, revealing a hitherto unsuspected depth. The last three, Nos 39-41, were all composed within six weeks, and the character of each is totally distinct from the others: tuneful and friendly; tragic; imperious and monumental respectively. Of earlier symphonies, Nos. 32 and 33 (both 1779) are notable for their strong Mannheim influences, while earlier still come No. 25 (1773), a dark and brooding G minor work in which may be found the seeds of the later G minor Symphony, No. 40; and the astonishingly accomplished No. 29 (1774), tuneful and sunny throughout.

was Haydn's high maturity, and during it music entered a new realm, preparatory for the new century. Haydn spent most of his life in congenial employment and died old and rich; Mozart had a sketchy freelance career and died young and poor. He early displayed amazing precocity and started composing at the age of five. His father, a

first-class opportunist, saw money in his son and daughter (a fine keyboard player) and whisked them off on a Europe-wide tour during which Mozart wrote his first symphony, in London in 1764. There he was befriended by Johann Christian Bach, youngest son of Johann Sebastian and a charming, civilized man from whom Mozart

learnt a great deal. More symphonies followed during later tours until, by the time he was 20, Mozart had written about 65. Each is a gem in itself: skilful, tuneful, but often lacking individuality. In 1778 came the first of Mozart's truly great symphonies: No. 31, *Paris*. Further advances came with the next six, but the great miracle occurred in summer 1788, when his last three masterpieces appeared, Nos 39-41. Each takes the development of the 18th-century symphony to its peak.

Haydn and Mozart are often lumped together, as if their music is indistinguishable. The truth is that Mozart could no more have written a Haydn symphony than vice versa. One might say that Haydn laid the path, Mozart perfected it. ♪

Built at enormous expense in marshlands at Süttör, Esterháza Castle was modelled on Versailles. Through the gates, the visitor enters a huge courtyard and encounters a double staircase at the front of the horseshoe-shaped 126-room castle. Behind the castle are gardens (now greatly reduced in size) with avenues radiating to the south. Substantially completed by 1770, the site eventually included a Chinese pavilion, temples, a marionette theatre and an opera house.

Beethoven

BEFORE BEETHOVEN ENTERED THE symphonic scene in 1800 countless composers had perfected the symphony. In addition to Haydn and Mozart, there were Vanhal, Kozeluh, Albrechtsberger (one of Beethoven's teachers) and Gyrowetz in Vienna; Dittersdorf in Vienna and Bohemia; Michael Haydn in Salzburg; Abel and J C Bach in London; Gossec and Leduc in Paris; Brunetti and Boccherini in Spain, as well as Italians, Bohemians, Scandinavians and a large group of Mannheimers – and that is the tip of a vast iceberg comprising hundreds of composers.

Four movements were now standard: fast-slow-minuet-fast, and slow introductions were commonplace, but changes were afoot. The most obvious affected the minuet. Haydn's quartets had greatly increased its tempo, and Beethoven's First Symphony adopted this new style. Altogether, the gradual process that had formulated the classical symphony was about to be accelerated rapidly by Beethoven. "These are the rules," he seemed to say; "now I shall break them."

Symphony No. 1 starts in the wrong key, and the finale begins with a slow introduction. To similar formal innovations, No. 2 adds a challenging musical language. One critic likened the finale to a wounded animal lashing its tail. Number 3, *Eroica*, broke most of the surviving rules: melody, harmony, rhythm, proportions, emotional depth, all were enriched, but its length gave listeners the greatest problems. Only slightly shorter, but much less formidable, No. 4 restored humour and good nature, but this was a feint: the mighty Fifth literally brought

symphonic form to its knees by using it as a vehicle with which to fight a titanic battle with Fate. After that, the *Pastoral* Symphony, No. 6, brought relaxation and reflection. Both Nos. 5 and 6 link their respective final movements, an innovation Beethoven was not to maintain.

Symphony No. 7 takes rhythm as its basis. Massiveness and rhythm feature in the introduction, a mighty portal to the driving first movement whose excitement is intensified by the use of horns in their high register. Rhythm pervades the pulsating second movement and the scherzo, but its full violence is unleashed in the finale, which Weber dismissed as a madman's ravings. Smaller in proportions but containing much substance, No. 8

Friedrich Schiller, whose 'Ode to Joy' appears in the Ninth Symphony.

A stylized, romantic view of Beethoven. The flowing locks, piercing eyes and untidy clothing faithfully reflect contemporary reports, but he did not deliberately project a fashionable image. Work on his *Missa Solemnis*, the score of which he is holding here, began in 1819, the year of this painting.

Schiller

opens without introduction and creates great tension which is dissipated in the final remarkable throw-away phrase. A teasing scherzando and a minuet lead to a finale of fearsome difficulty and breathless impetus.

The *Choral* Symphony, No. 9, sums up Beethoven's symphonic philosophy in three grand movements, then introduces voices to invite humanity to join with one another in joy, having rejected the earlier movements. This variation finale passes through a fugue, a march and other events before joining forces to implore mankind to seek God.

Beethoven's achievement, apart from his technical experiments, was to appeal directly to the listener's emotions through the strength of his message. His intimidating greatness has ensured continued popularity but at first it prevented many composers from attempting to follow his symphonic thought. ♪

The title page of the *Eroica* Symphony, which originally bore a dedication to Napoleon. When Napoleon showed self-interest rather than true democratic spirit, Beethoven scratched out the tribute so violently that he tore the paper.

• BEETHOVEN'S SYMPHONIES •

➤ **No. 1 in C, Op. 21 (1800)** is reliant upon Haydn models but Beethoven's radical tendencies are already showing.

➤ **No. 2 in D, Op. 36 (1802)** extends the scope and language of the symphony.

➤ **No. 3 in E flat, Op. 55, *Eroica* (1803)** was originally intended as a tribute to the great liberator Napoleon, but the dedication was savagely rubbed off the title page when the Frenchman proclaimed himself emperor. "He is no better than all the rest," grumbled Beethoven. The 'hero' of the title may be taken to refer to the great liberator of music, Beethoven himself. He said that the symphony is dedicated 'to the memory of a great man', presumably the man whom he once perceived Napoleon to be.

➤ **No. 4 in B flat, Op. 60 (1805)** is a remarkable example of sustained good humour. This is the first symphony to extend the standard minuet/scherzo and trio form into a scherzo-trio-scherzo-trio-scherzo plan.

➤ **No. 5 in C minor, Op. 67 (1808)** is sometimes erroneously called Fate because Beethoven is said to have described the opening as "Fate knocking at the door". He also suggested that it represented the song of the yellowhammer, so perhaps Beethoven's own explanations might sometimes be taken as unreliable fancy.

➤ **No. 6 in F, Op. 68, *Pastoral* (1808)** is Beethoven's descriptive impressions of a country holiday, though he protested that it was feelings rather than pictures he was conveying. The bird-calls in the slow movement and the vivid thunderstorm in the fourth (the only appearance of drums in the symphony) are certainly graphic representations of country life.

➤ **No. 7 in A, Op. 92 (1812)** was described by Wagner as "the apotheosis of the dance" – but just try to dance to it! Its four movements are a study in sustained rhythmic excitement and original sonorities.

➤ **No. 8 in F, Op. 93 (1812)** includes a gentle dig at the inventor of the metronome, Johann Maelzel. The second movement ticks incessantly to the irritation of the strings, who try to scrub it out.

➤ ***Battle* Symphony, Op. 91 (1813)**, also called *Wellington's Victory*. This vulgarly descriptive work commemorates Napoleon's defeat in Spain at the hands of Wellington's troops.

➤ **No. 9 in D minor, Op. 125, *Choral* (1823)** The choir and four vocal soloists appear only in the last movement, but since this is the largest of Beethoven's symphonic movements it dominates the work. The words are based upon Schiller's 'Ode to Joy', with additions by the composer.

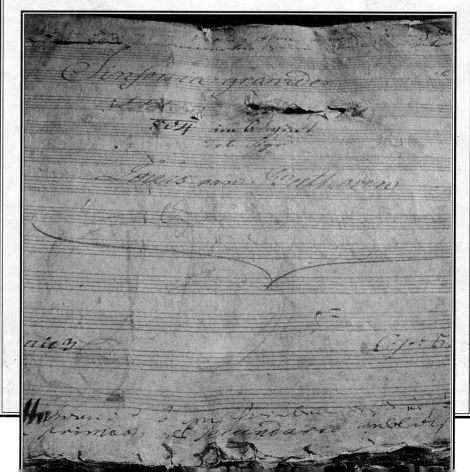

Beethoven's Legacy

BEETHOVEN'S SHADOW LOOMED OVER 19th-century composers. Who could write symphonies worthy to follow his? One way was to side-step the issue by continuing the Haydn/Mozart line, as did Schubert in his first six symphonies (1813-18). Only with maturity did Schubert produce works great enough to stand comparison with Beethoven's: in the *Unfinished* (No. 8, 1822) and the *Great C Major* (No. 9, 1825–28). Emphasis continued to be upon sonata form (even Beethoven had not

• THE SYMPHONY AFTER BEETHOVEN •

➤ **Schubert Symphony No. 9 in C, D944, *Great*** Begun in 1825, Schubert's last complete symphony reached its final form only three years later. Cast unadventurously in four movements, it has other noteworthy features. Each movement is spun out expansively (Schumann called it "the symphony of heavenly length"), but even more remarkable is its inexhaustible fund of melody. It is an outpouring of glorious tunes, all totally Schubertian in style except for the touching reference to Beethoven's 'Ode to Joy' theme in the finale.

➤ **Berlioz *Symphonie fantastique* in C, Op. 14** When this fantasy appeared in 1830 it confused audiences. What was this? Passion, a waltz, a mountain walk, an execution, a witches' sabbath? Was a symphony the place for such things? Since it is Berlioz's most popular work the answer would appear to be yes, for what one critic called the composer's "baffling originality" served to widen symphonic scope for figures such as Mahler.

➤ **Mendelssohn Symphony No. 4 in A, Op. 90, *Italian*** This was the last of Mendelssohn's symphonies to be published. He planned to rewrite the finale, but died before he could accomplish this. It is an exhilarating picture-postcard work recalling a Mediterranean holiday. Although given the number four, it was in fact the third of his mature symphonies, completed in 1833.

➤ **Schumann Symphony No. 4 in D minor, Op. 120** It took Schumann a decade (1841, rev. 1851) to complete this symphony. During those years he perfected his technique of thematic transformation. The whole work is built on one theme and its derivatives, transformed to suit the different contexts of a continuous four-movement work.

➤ **Bizet Symphony in C** Bizet was 16 when he wrote this symphony in 1854. Not for Bizet the torture of agonizing over the 'worthiness' of a post-Beethoven symphony; just high spirits and *joie-de-vivre*. This brilliant work waited 80 years for its first performance.

managed to invent anything better), but the content of Schubert's later works is emotionally charged and inhabits a world quite different from Beethoven's. Had Schubert lived beyond the age of 31, how different might have been subsequent symphonic development.

Mendelssohn also adhered to earlier concepts. His dozen string symphonies of 1821–23 tend to look back half a century

Franz Schubert worshipped Beethoven from afar, apparently unaware that his own genius approached that of his hero.

or more for inspiration, but the official No. 1 (ie, the first to be published) is purely classical in style. Next came No. 5 (1830; the numbering is chaotic), called *Reformation* and commemorating the 300th anniversary of the Lutheran Augsburg Confession, with references to Luther's hymn *Ein' feste Burg* and the *Dresden Amen*. No. 3, *Scottish*, No. 4, *Italian*, (recalling the composer's travels) and No. 5 break no new symphonic ground, and No. 2 (1840) follows Beethoven's *Choral* by introducing soloists and choir in the finale. Mendelssohn wrote it to commemorate 400 years of printing and the famous Gutenberg Bible, and called it Hymn of Praise – a Symphony-Cantata.

To Schumann's four symphonies (1841–51) should be added a G minor symphony (1831, two sketched movements). They show a development of 'thematic transformation' which had begun with Vivaldi but reached a climax in the final version of No. 4. Formally, Nos 1 and 4 follow traditional principles; No. 2 reverses the middle movements, putting the slow movement third, and No. 3 follows the same course and adds an extra movement: a solemn evocation of Cologne Cathedral. For all their charm and skill, Mendelssohn's and Schumann's symphonies failed to advance symphonic thought, merely adding modest new dimensions.

Berlioz, however, forged new concepts. His *Symphonie fantastique* (1830) is a garish semi-autobiographical outpouring of torrid emotion, and *Harold in Italy* (1834) defies tradition by including a solo viola part written for Paganini, who shunned it as not being virtuosic enough. *Romeo and Juliet* (1839) is a dramatic vocal piece rather than a symphony, and the *Symphonie funèbre et triomphale* (1840) includes military band, solo trombone and choir. It is only convention that prevents these works being classed as true symphonies. They opened the way for even wider influences, via the *Dante* (1856) and *Faust* Symphonies (1857) of Liszt and eventually to the dramatic introspective symphonies of Mahler. Another development was the linking of movements of Beethoven and Mendelssohn and thematic transformations of Schumann which led to the one-movement symphonies of, for example, Sibelius and Roy Harris. Meanwhile, composers of less imagination were writing symphonies of solid workmanship but scant originality, Louis Spohr (from 1811 to 1857) and Niels Gade (from 1840 to 1871) among them. ♪

SCHUBERT'S SYMPHONY
◆ NO. 8 IN B MINOR, D759 ◆
UNFINISHED

~

Why was this magnificent work left incomplete? No one knows for sure, but Schubert's early death (at 31) was not the reason. Did other work take precedence? Did he feel that three movements in three-time (for he began a scherzo) did not offer sufficient contrast? The symphony was discovered in Vienna by Sir George Grove in 1867, 45 years after it was composed, and August Ludwig and Frank Merrick are among those to have written two concluding movements. The best solution is probably Brian Newbould's completion of the scherzo and the addition of the *Rosamunde* Entr'acte in B minor, this being of the right date and key, and possibly the original finale.

In his *Rhenish* Symphony, No. 3, an evocation of Rhineland life and scenery, Robert Schumann included a movement that reflects his impression of Cologne Cathedral. It is an awesome, slow-moving piece, religious in feeling and conveying the wonder he felt upn entering the massive echoing edifice on the east bank of the Rhine.

Nationalism

SO-CALLED SERIOUS MUSIC IS ROOTED IN folk art. It could not be otherwise, for the earliest composers, with their innate musical awareness, would have absorbed folk tunes in their youth. As 'art music' developed it moved away from its roots and became increasingly highly sophisticated until any suggestion of folk influence was regarded as quaint. Haydn's Symphony No. 28 (1765) was dismissed by a critic because of its Hungarian folk influence. When Mozart jeered at inept musicians in *A Musical Joke* (1787), when Beethoven portrayed peasants in his *Pastoral* Symphony (1808), or when Mendelssohn evoked Italian dancing in his Symphony No. 4 (1833), they imitated folk music.

By the 1840s the symphony was spreading outwards from south, central and western Europe, and as it did so it gained new dimensions: national elements. Suddenly, composers were proud rather than ashamed of their musical heritages and wished to distribute them for appreciation, if not always admiration, to other countries. The Dane Niels Gade achieved this ambition by accident. His Symphony No. 1 of 1841,

NATIONALIST SYMPHONIES

➤ **Gade Symphony No. 1 in C minor, Op. 5 (1841)** Danish folk music reveals a gentle, wistful nature, often best conveyed by wind instruments. In the third movement the oboe melody resembles a folk song, and another appears on oboes and cellos in unison as the second subject of the finale. There are many typical Scandinavian touches elsewhere, and in view of the close links in the past between Scandinavia and Scotland it is not surprising that some Mendelssohn-Scottish feeling is detectable in the theme that opens the work and returns in the finale.

➤ **Sullivan Symphony in E minor, *Irish* (1866)** The Englishman Sir Arthur Sullivan certainly gained knowledge of folk music from his Irish father. The most obvious Irish connection in this symphony occurs in the third movement, where song and jig combine with more sophisticated matters. A certain Irishness may be detected in other parts, too. This was Sullivan's only symphony.

➤ **Borodin Symphony No. 2 in B minor (1869)** Melodically, rhythmically and harmonically this symphony could be none other than Russian. Furthermore, every note proclaims its nationality. There are gloomy chords, undulating melodies on solo woodwind or brass, galloping and syncopated rhythms, a mysterious, even threatening, mood in some quieter passages – all wholly typical of Russian nationalism.

➤ **Tchaikovsky Symphony No. 2 in C minor, *Little Russian* (1872, revised 1880)** Little Russia is the old name for the Ukraine. In the symphony several Ukrainian folk songs are used as thematic starting-points: 'Down by Mother Volga' in the first movement, a spinning song in the andantino and 'The Crane' in the finale, as well as folk-inspired ideas elsewhere.

➤ **Dvořák Symphony No. 8 in G, Op. 88 (1889)** Bohemian folk music is full-blooded, rhythmic and usually joyous. This symphony represents an ideal wedding of folk and art elements. The 'symphonic' opening soon yields to folk-like phrases, mainly on woodwind, and in the adagio there is an unashamed imitation of a folk band. One variation in the finale is a boisterous dance with horns literally going over the top.

Antonín Dvořák, who honed Bohemian nationalism into a keen and effective edge in his symphonic music and chamber works.

On Sjaeland's Fair Plains (Sjaeland, or Zealand, being the part of Denmark closest to Sweden) introduces Danish folk music but it could not get a hearing at home. Gade sent it to Mendelssohn who gave its premiere in Leipzig. Thereafter, Gade lost interest in nationalism in his other seven symphonies.

In Slavic lands nationalism took a firmer hold. Russians had long relied upon imported foreign composers for their music and now wished to regain lost ground. Glinka was the power behind Russian nationalism and Borodin benefited from Glinka's experience. It is perhaps easier for western listeners to 'feel' the Russian-ness of a melody or harmony than to define it,

The songs of slaves, heard on Kentucky plantations such as the one depicted in this painting of 1859, fascinated Dvořák during his trips to America.

The flamboyant colours of Russian attire such as these wedding costumes are often reflected in Russian music of the 19th century, a vivid art that captures the spirit of the Slavic people.

but there are interesting parallels with American symphonies of the 20th century. Slow music, with broad, melodic lines and rich harmonies, seems to reflect the vast expanses of their respective countries, while faster sections convey the spirited nature of the people at dance and play after the day's work. In typical Russian music there are other elements, too: regret and sadness at the harsh history of the land and battles being refought in stern, proud music.

In Bohemia, Smetana and Dvořák stand out as the foremost nationalist composers. In his earliest symphony, *The Bells of Zlonice* (1865), Dvořák introduced local elements into the music. He lived in Zlonice for four years and the village bells are clearly heard shortly after the start of the symphony. As his experience widened, Dvořák succumbed to other influences – especially that of Wagner – but in Symphony No. 6 (1880) the Bohemian

element strongly resurfaces in the scherzo, an exhilarating Czech furiant with alternating 3/4-2/4 rhythm. By now, critics welcomed such folk influences. It is in his last symphony – No. 9, *From the New World* (1893) – that we hear an interesting mixture of Czech and American folk tunes. If we did not know that Dvořák worked in America we might regard No. 9 as a wholly Bohemian symphony, but hindsight, and the composer's own comments, draw our attention forcefully to the influences he gained from meeting African-Americans. Their music fascinated him: their work songs and spirituals undoubtedly suggested ideas to him, but the very ambiguity of the influences shows the pitfalls in trying to identify a folk source from the music alone. Is a given phrase derived from Bohemia's plainsfolk or African-American slaves?

It is unfortunate that the most powerful nationalist composers either regarded the symphony as too exalted to include folk music, or failed to write one. Grieg, Liszt, Smetana, Mussorgsky, Glinka, Chopin and Brahms (with his Hungarian fascinations) must perforce be excluded here. ♪

{ **Johannes Brahms (1833–97) as a young man. His early career was as a pianist, but he possessed a logical and analytical mind that little by little led him to become a great symphonist. However, he continued to return to the piano throughout his life.**

The Late Romantics

BRAHMS'S FUTURE AS A SYMPHONIST WAS inevitable, for his early works already show his logical approach to composition. He tried to avoid the lyrical symphonic line which ran from J C Bach through Mozart and Mendelssohn, had no sympathy with Wagner's work, and favoured instead the highly organized techniques of the Haydn-Beethoven progression. But as the self-appointed heir to this progression he found a formidable obstruction in his way: Beethoven's symphonies themselves. To Brahms, they were almost unsurpassable. It would take strenuous work and enormous courage to become a worthy successor.

His first symphonic attempt, unwisely choosing the key of Beethoven's *Choral* (D minor), ran aground and eventually became the first piano concerto. Two serenades and the *St Anthoni Variations* served Brahms as superior preparatory exercises, and only then did he permit his First Symphony to proceed. That was in 1876; he was 43 years old. It was greeted as Brahms had hoped: as a successor to Beethoven's. Some called it 'Beethoven's Tenth', pointing unkindly to the similarity of the finale's theme to that of Beethoven's 'Ode to Joy'. "Any fool can see that," snapped Brahms, though he had not foreseen the criticism. As a journey from strife to victory the work does echo Beethoven, but Brahms had been influenced by the 'lyrical' elements he despised and they interfere with his logical processes.

One must take Brahms's symphonies not as successors to Beethoven's but on their own merits, which are high. Each takes a different line of development and advances it. After the drama of No. 1, the Second (1877) is frankly lyrical but also extremely tightly organized: analysts argue that the entire work stems from the three opening notes. As in No. 1, the third movement eschews the scherzo style favoured by Beethoven, preferring a gentle pastoral interlude before the excitement of the finale. Number 3 (1883) is intensely emotional in the outer movements and ends

---

• TCHAIKOVSKY'S LATE SYMPHONIES •

➢ **No. 4 in F minor, Op. 36 (1878)** According to the composer's letters, this symphony represents man's struggle against fate; and the man is evidently Tchaikovsky himself. He had been drawn against his nature into a marriage and the ensuing trauma brought him almost to suicide. His anguish is heard in the tortured fanfare that opens, and dominates, the first movement, returning more confidently in the last. The most original movement is the pizzicato ostinato (literally, 'obstinate plucking') of the scherzo with its contrasted middle section for winds. A folk song, 'The Birch Tree' occurs in the finale.

➢ **No. 5 in E minor, Op. 64 (1888)** Again, Tchaikovsky's letters yield background. He admitted to fearful doubts about the quality of the work but was reassured when audiences were enthusiastic. And again, a motto pervades the work, a gloomy march that, movement by movement, finds a positive tone and

concludes the work in triumph. In the third movement is a vintage Tchaikovsky waltz.

➢ **No. 6 in B minor, Op. 74, *Pathétique* (1893)** Tchaikovsky departed rarely from formal convention, but in his last symphony he does so tellingly by ending with a long slow movement. Recent research suggests the reason. An early homosexual indiscretion with a fellow student, now a prominent lawyer, had come to light. An illegal court tried Tchaikovsky and condemned him to die by his own hand. At the time this symphony was partly completed. It seems that the composer amended it so that the finale should be a despairing farewell to life. What is evidently an autobiographical work then took on a meaning of utmost poignancy. The central movements are remarkable: a 'waltz' which is an aural illusion, being in the wrong-footing rhythm of 5/4, and a march that, in other circumstances, might have served as a roof-lifting finale.

---

unexpectedly quietly, while the two middle movements offer insufficient contrast. The second virtually ceases to move on several occasions, and the third is a slow song, but the finale has compensating passion. Number 4 (1884) harnesses the severe logic of Bach to deliver, for all its slowish first two movements, one of the most irresistible of all symphonic arguments, and that without resorting to the device of connected movements which Schumann and Beethoven had employed. Brahms's finale is an intensely concentrated set of variations on an eight-note theme. Its cumulative power is overwhelming.

Tchaikovsky admitted that his symphonies were far from perfect. They derive from a Russian strain of introspective melody and have no time for the rigour of Brahms. All the better for it, some say, though they cannot wholly escape the charge that they are disguised ballet music. For all that, they produced healthy progeny: even the severely logical symphonic mind of Sibelius was infatuated by them at first.

Brahms and Tchaikovsky occupied the symphonic high ground in the late 19th century, but other figures were also active. In Russia, Rimsky-Korsakov lent his vivid gifts as an orchestrator to three between 1861 and 1886, and Glazunov produced eight symphonies between 1882 and 1906 (a ninth is incomplete). In France, Camille Saint-Saëns wrote four conventional symphonies (1850–59), then the unconventional and masterly Organ Symphony (1886), called 'No. 3' because two earlier symphonies were unnumbered at the time. Its four movements are cast as two pairs, and in the second half of each pair (that is, apparently, movements two and four) an organ appears, providing deep harmonic support here, weight and drama there. The work shares with César Franck's lone symphony and Schumann's Fourth an economy of thematic material that gives it a strong, if subliminal, cohesion.

Sadly, we hear little of the thousands of symphonies by hundreds of composers working then. Occasional performances of works by Bruch, Klughardt, Lachner and Rott allow us to glimpse the symphonic climate that laid the path to the future. ♪

New Spirits for a New Century

AS THE END OF THE 19TH CENTURY approached the symphony seemed to have reached its summit. What was left to do? Brahms had surely raised it to its intellectual height. Tchaikovsky had poured heart and soul into it, Dvořák had explored the rich mine of folk music, Berlioz had crammed it with programmatic material and original orchestration, and sonata form, the stand-by formula, was collapsing under the strain. One figure strode a separate path, virtually ignoring all current developments.

Anton Bruckner was a provincial organist who wrote symphonies. Other musicians became interested in them and suggested 'improvements'. Bruckner accepted these specialists' amendments, some of which were sound, others not. The result is one of the most confused episodes in music, for anyone expecting to hear a Bruckner symphony must first discover who edited it.

The description 'cathedrals in sound' is apt for Bruckner's symphonies. Though they generally adhere to traditional forms they extend them into great and magnificent edifices that can stagger the imagination. Bruckner was a strongly religious Catholic: Symphony No. 9, which is unfinished, is actually dedicated to God. There are 11 (the first two bearing the numbers '0' and '00') spanning the years

---

MAHLER'S SYMPHONY No. 6 IN A MINOR (1904)

➤ Few works better convey the spirit of the new century than Mahler's Sixth. At the time of its composition his personal and professional life were happy, yet the symphony is bitter, sarcastic, negative. The trudging first movement is a march through life towards a fateful end. At times fate marches with the hero, while in a subsidiary idea the music is a joyful portrait of Mahler's wife, Alma. When the hero ascends a mountain in search of respite, cowbells create an image of peace amid nature.

➤ In the scherzo the march acquires an acid bite, but the Trios apparently represent the play of his two children. If this movement seems episodic, the andante is an unbroken chain of sublime melody, its lines intertwining serenely as mountain sounds return.

➤ Ideas from the first two movements are drawn into the enormous finale. Fate's ominous presence is felt: there can be no escape. Mahler graphically suggests impending catastrophe and attempts to evade it, but a deadening stroke ("like the blow of an axe", said Mahler) signals a bitter crisis. Increasing grotesquerie enters the music until a second hammer blow brings a return to earlier ideas, now less vigorous. Fate has not yet done with Mahler: a third stroke fells him like a tree. Oblivion.

1863–94; together they contributed to the impression that the symphony could go no further, for Bruckner's musical language remains much the same over these three decades, grand gestures merely becoming grander, long-breathed melodies ever more expansive, climaxes increasing in power and packing harder punches, while the four-movement layout and basic sonata form are essentially untouched.

Outside Germanic countries the symphony was acquiring new life, though fitfully, as if awaiting the freedom the new century promised. In Russia, Rachmaninov produced his First Symphony (1895), then attempted to destroy it because of its unfavourable reception. He had already aborted an attempt at a symphony four years earlier. In Finland, a new voice was emerging with Sibelius. After the impressive but diffuse symphony *Kullervo* (1892), based on Finnish folk legends, he turned for musical inspiration to Russian composers for his First Symphony (1900), which carries some of the individuality he put to such telling use later. Another Scandinavian was also beginning a fiercely individual symphonic career. As early as 1894 Carl Nielsen's First Symphony had dared to begin in one key and end in another, against all textbook advice. Nielsen, with justification, believed that the symphony as a genre had become over-inflated and too

Mahler rehearsing his 'Symphony of a Thousand' (No. 8) in Munich, 1910.

Anton Bruckner liked nothing better than to improvise at the organ for hours on end.

self-regarding; he set about rectifying these trends by writing leaner music, omitting over-sentimental feelings and making statements without elaboration or hyperbole. His concentration upon the 'identities' of keys, as if they possessed lives of their own, was to become the driving force behind his later symphonies.

In Austria, Gustav Mahler was working along similar lines tonally, but in every other respect the two composers inhabited different universes. The name *Titan* was appended to Mahler's First Symphony (1888), then dropped as later works proved to be progressively more titanic. Today, No. 1 seems a normal-sized, almost conventional, symphony; after it, Mahler succumbed to his own philosophy that "the symphony should

Mahler in 1909, the year of the composition of *Das Lied von der Erde*, a symphony in all but name.

contain everything". So blurred became his concept of what a symphony should or should not be that there is constant cross-fertilization with song (symphonies No. 2, 3, 4 and 8 all include vocal parts), and only convention excludes *Das Lied von der Erde* ('The song of the earth') (1909) and perhaps even *Das klagende Lied* ('Sorrowful song', 1880) from being classed as symphonies. Instrumentally, Mahler threw everything into the symphony, and, in No. 8 (1906), so much that it became the largest symphonic score in history. ♪

20th-Century Masterworks

FAR FROM BECOMING EXTINCT, THE symphony was rejuvenated early in the new century by new ideas. Suk's *Asrael* Symphony (1906), Rachmaninov's Second (1907), and Elgar's two (1908; 1910) illustrated that there was still life in Romanticism, but the mood favoured fresh voices. In 1901 Sibelius's Second Symphony was an amalgam of new and old, and while No. 3 (1907) followed a similar but less opulent line, the Fourth (1911) shook the establishment with its austerity of scoring and severity of mood. Mahler, in his gigantic Eighth (1906) and deeply searching Ninth (1909) had displayed size, length, emotion and warmth, even though his ultimate message had been despair; Sibelius eschewed all these things: "I offer only cold water," he said. His Fifth (1915) functions in a warmer climate, recalling the Second, and later works show compression and concision of thought, culminating in the one-movement Seventh (1924).

In Denmark, Nielsen also favoured concision, never using two notes when one would adequately convey his meaning. No. 2, *The Four Temperaments* (1902) is a study of human characteristics, a subject which fascinated him, and No. 3, *Espansiva* (1911) is a warm-hearted symphony with two wordless vocalists in the second movement. Written in 1916, the Fourth, *Inextinguishable*, finds a man deeply concerned for the fate of humanity in war, yet, with a hard-won battle between timpani

---

• EARLY 20TH-CENTURY SYMPHONIES •

> **Sibelius: Symphony No. 5 in E flat, Op. 83 (1915)** By making the first movement and scherzo continuous, Sibelius moved towards the complete integration he achieved in Symphony No. 7. The wistful second movement, with its rhythmic 'hook', ends with unexpected abruptness and the finale builds with a swinging theme to a stunning and still unsurpassed conclusion.

> **Prokofiev: Symphony No. 1 in D, Op. 25, *Classical* (1917)** Prokofiev chose Haydn models, though each of this symphony's four movements could have been written only by a 20th-century composer. In place of a minuet, he put a gavotte which he used again in the *Romeo and Juliet* ballet.

> **Nielsen: Symphony No. 5, Op. 50 (1922)** Against a featureless backdrop evil shapes emerge, to be challenged by a noble theme. A battle ensues, the side-drum attempting to disrupt the music. The second, final movement pulls the battle through two fugues before snatching victory in the final seconds. Sonata form is abandoned in this work; Nielsen invents his own deeply satisfying constructions.

> **Vaughan Williams: Symphony No. 4 in F minor (1934)** "I don't like it, but it's what I meant," said Vaughan Williams. This is exceptionally violent and uncompromising music. Modelled on Beethoven's Fifth, it uses modern language to head towards victory. At the last moment the ugly opening chords return to thwart the promised triumphant ending.

> **Roy Harris: Symphony No. 3 (1937)** This one-movement essay is essentially American, with its expansive melodies, spicy rhythms, exciting orchestration and decisive conclusion. It is a concise, moving work.

> **Shostakovich: Symphony No. 10 in E minor, Op. 93 (1953)** Starting where Tchaikovsky's *Pathétique* finishes, the gloomy first movement climbs to ecstasy via an impressively sustained climax. The scherzo, a study in fury, is a portrait of Stalin, while the allegretto possibly represents a struggle between small-minded bureaucracy (a march parody) and noble man (imperious horn calls). The ever-present sequence D-E flat-C-B, Shostakovich's musical signature, emerges forcefully to close the work.

Jean Sibelius

The Great Ice Barrier, 1903. Scott's tragic Antarctic Expedition of 1912 was brought to the cinema in 1948;

Vaughan Williams's score for the film subsequently became his Seventh Symphony in 1953.

and orchestra in the finale, it wins through to prove that life is inextinguishable. This led, six years later, to arguably the greatest 20th-century symphony: the Fifth. After that, No. 6 (1925) seems to offer pessimism but eventually enjoys a riotous outcome.

That very year Dmitri Shostakovich amazed his professors with a highly accomplished First Symphony. Thereafter, living under Communism, he wrongly assumed that 'modern' sounds were required and wrote accordingly, but a vicious attack in the newspaper *Pravda* impelled him to withdraw his Fourth Symphony in 1936; with typical irony, he wrote an ending in which the symphony takes its own life. The next year came the Fifth, *A Soviet Artist's Reply to Just Criticism.* In reality it is a rude gesture, though authority was too musically illiterate to hear it as anything but an apology. For the rest of his life Shostakovich fought a private battle with the state, including in many works a four-note phrase (D-E flat-C-B, or, in German, DSCH, his monogram) with which he asserts his right to be himself.

Prokofiev's seven symphonies (1917–52) are more balletic than symphonic, Stravinsky's three (1907–45), though superb music, add nothing to the story of the symphony, and William Walton's First (1935) leans too heavily on Sibelius, so for fresh features we must turn to America. Samuel Barber, Roger Sessions, Walter Piston and others are important symphonists, while Roy Harris's Symphony No. 3 epitomizes the American style. In England, Vaughan Williams's uneven output stretches from the *Sea* (1912), *London* (1913) and *Pastoral* (1921) symphonies, through three masterpieces, Nos 4–6 (1934–47), to the movie-inspired *Antarctica* (1953) and the lighter, highly entertaining Nos 8 and 9 (1955–58). ♪

A SYMPHONY FACING BOTH WAYS?

*S*hostakovich was trapped in Leningrad in 1941 during the German Army's siege of the city and wrote the first two movements of his Symphony No. 7 in C, Op. 70, *Leningrad,* as shells fell nearby. He also worked as a fire-fighter at this time, having been rejected for military service because of his poor eyesight. When evacuation became possible he and the others moved to Kuybyshev (1600 miles/2575 km east of Moscow) and completed the work there in comparative safety. Nonetheless, the constant threat is evident in all four movements and there is a notorious march sequence in the first. The slow crescendo is said to represent the relentless approach of the German army, but it seems unlikely that even so intrepid a composer would dare risk the retribution of an enemy he has portrayed as mindless, inhuman automata. Could the march (hardly a threatening melody) suggest that any change from Communism would be welcome?

An early performance of Shostakovich *Leningrad* Symphony in Novosibirsk. The composer sits facing the camera with conductor Mravinsky to his left. Shostakovich had wanted Mravinsky to conduct the premiere but circumstances of war prevented it.

Jan Sibelius, photographed in 1915, the year of his Fifth Symphony.

Exploration and Consolidation

SINCE WORLD WAR II THE SYMPHONY'S history has been one of exploration and consolidation. Shostakovich's last five (1957–71) have shown both sides, Nos 11–13 being political in nature (No. 11 is grossly undervalued because of its perceived 'message'), No. 14 a song cycle about death, and No. 15 an enigmatic divertimento. The Englishman George Lloyd composed his first in 1932 and has released 12 so far. His is a determinedly melodic muse, immediately appealing and boasting catchy tunes. So is Malcolm Arnold's some of the

time, but there are disturbing works among his (to date) eight symphonies (from 1951). Robert Simpson is far more challenging. Taking Nielsen as a starting point, his 11 symphonies (1951–94) are intellectual exercises characterized by irresistible momentum and often relying for inspiration upon Simpson's other interests, science and astronomy. Also active in the British Isles are Sir Michael Tippett with four symphonies (1945–77) and Sir Peter Maxwell Davies with five (1962–94); both of these composers have enthusiastic followings despite, in the latter case especially, producing music that is sometimes obscure.

In Germany, Hans Werner Henze's seven symphonies (1947–84) are exploratory, exciting, inventive and excellently scored, giving up their qualities gradually. The symphonies of the Estonian Eduard Tubin have been recorded recently.

He composed ten between 1934 and 1973 in a hard-hitting, intensely personal style that appeals strongly on repeated hearings. In contrast, the Swede Allan Pettersson, who wrote 17 symphonies between 1952 and 1980, has only a small following because of his unrelieved gloom and the great length of the majority of his symphonies. Moisei Vainberg in Russia, although somewhat dependent stylistically upon his friend Shostakovich, has produced 23 symphonies since 1942 which keep to tonal models and are intriguing in their original scoring. Giya Kancheli in Georgia favours slow tempos in most of his seven symphonies (1967–86) and his spare, evocative, atmospheric scoring is often relieved by heavy passages involving hammered rhythms.

It is instructive to note that the serial and atonal experiments of the early 20th century, strictly developed by Schoenberg,

Sir Adrian Boult, with Michael Tippett attending to a performance under Boult's sympathetic direction.

• THE SYMPHONY SINCE WORLD WAR II •

Tubin: Symphony No. 10 (1973) The four movements become a single unit, necessitating taut compression in a work of great dramatic power. Tubin's language remains strongly tonal and his use of orchestral resources is original without being anarchic.

Vainberg: Symphony No. 12, Op. 114 (1976) Dedicated to Shostakovich, this is among Vainberg's largest symphonies. Grief associated with the loss of his dear friend colours the language, and the violence may also show frustration at the plight of an imaginative composer working under an oppressive regime.

Górecki: Symphony No. 3, *Sorrowful Songs* (1976) Minimalism is naturally anti-symphonic, since development is either curtailed or non-existent. Górecki's brand of minimalism gives an impression of archaic time-lessness to a soprano's laments based on folk sources.

Simpson: Symphony No. 7 (1977) Simpson's intellectual approach is typified by his use of the fifth. However, his remark that listeners need not know a fifth from a rissole frees them to appreciate instead the powerful drive of the music towards a curiously negative ending – and to contemplate the meaning of it.

Hovhaness: Symphony No. 50, Op. 360, *Mount St Helens* (1983) In May 1980, Mount St Helens in Washington state erupted, losing some 1,500 feet (457 m) of its previous height of 9,671 feet (2948 m), covering an enormous area in a thick layer of volcanic dust and destroying nearby Spirit Lake. Hovhaness evokes the grandeur of the mountain and the placid beauty of the lake, but ominous sounds open the finale. The eruption then occurs with devastating realism, timpani beating a grotesque dance of death for the mountain. The symphony ends with a hymn to the rejuvenating power of nature.

Lloyd: Symphony No. 12 (1990) An introduction, four variations, an adagio and a finale, played continuously, comprise the unusual form of this work. The music is friendly and uncomplicated throughout.

have been largely discredited now. The British composer Humphrey Searle espoused them but his five symphonies (1953–64) are rarely played today. Less strict but hardly tonal in feeling, Havergal Brian's symphonies are gaining in popularity. When he died aged 96 in 1972 he left 32 symphonies (1922–68), all using elliptical and forthright language. His full value may not yet be recognized, but the impression given is of a composer writing for his own benefit rather than listener satisfaction. An even more prolific symphonist is Alan Hovhaness, an American composer of Scottish-Armenian descent. His is music of enormous beauty, timeless, strongly tonal, and evincing great space. Among his many hundreds of works, he numbers at least 75 symphonies (since 1936) which have attained, and deserve, cult following. He often chooses Eastern religious subjects but just as frequently finds inspiration in natural features and phenomena. He lives in Seattle "to be near mountains".

Finland continues to produce symphonists, among them Kalevi Aho (seven since 1969) and Aulis Sallinen (six since 1971). Their original and attractive music may lead the way to the future.

It seems that the symphony may

yet have a healthy future, although formally anything may happen. After much diversification earlier, it has somewhat settled down. A modern work might be expected to be about 25-45 minutes in duration, orchestral (occasionally with voices), basically tonal, and 'listener friendly'. What remains unpredictable is the musical language it will adopt.

A recent survey shows that some 25,000 symphonies are, or were, in existence (many have been lost), of which about 16,000 date from before 1800. ♪

Hans Werner Henze's obsession with socialism has undermined the value of his works, but he remains a powerful voice in modern music.

ENSEMBLES

Chamber

WHAT IS CHAMBER MUSIC? THE TERM IS difficult to categorize exactly. Some authorities define it simply as music for small ensembles; but that would mean including vocal music (madrigals, glees, Lieder and so on) which has developed according to its own needs and pressures, not least the demands of word-setting. A better definition might be music with one player to each part; but that would not rule out Schoenberg's First Chamber Symphony (for ten wind instruments and five strings) nor Richard Strauss's Metamorphosen for 23 solo strings, neither of which would be performable in anything resembling a 'chamber', and both of which require conductors. If music for small instrumental groups is accepted as the definition, a large amount of virtuoso display music would then have to be included, such as Sarasate's Zigeunerweisen and Carmen Fantasy (both for violin and piano), which is plainly written for the large concert hall. For many, intimacy is a prime characteristic of chamber music, plus the idea of pleasure in making music with others, professional or amateur. Both these notions are older than is sometimes realized, and they have strongly influenced the manner in which many composers have written for small groups of instruments, whether they be woodwind, brass or strings, with or without keyboard, in any combination from two to ten players.

THE RISE OF INSTRUMENTAL MUSIC IN Europe began in earnest in the Renaissance. Instrumental contributions in the accompanied madrigal and lute-song became increasingly important. As interest in cultivated music-making spread beyond the courts, a new kind of domestic musical activity began, aided by instruction books in which gentlemen were encouraged to develop playing skills; Baldassare Castiglione's *Il libro del cortegiano* (The Book of the Courtier) of 1528 is a famous example. Instrumental music gradually began to develop a life of its own through arrangements of popular vocal pieces, followed by works specifically written for such forces: the instrumental canzona for instance, or the viol consort. The latter reached the height of sophistication in 16th- and 17th-century England with the fantasias and *In nomines* of Byrd, Gibbons, Purcell and William Lawes.

The Baroque era saw the rise of the virtuoso instrumentalist and of a new instrument, the violin. The style of non-vocal music changed accordingly. The emergent form was the sonata, usually for one or two violins and continuo (providing the harmonic 'filling-in'), though since the continuo could consist of harpsichord, organ or lute plus cello or bass viol, a 'trio sonata' (a popular form until the middle of the 18th century) would often feature four performers. Corelli was the most celebrated and influential master of the latter form. The beginnings of division of function in instrumental music were marked by the appearance of two new terms: *da chiesa* (for the church) and *da camera* (literally 'for the chamber', and thus, supposedly, more intimate in style), though the edges could still be blurred. The violin held sway in Italy, but in the early 18th century German and, later, French composers began to include wind instruments: small ensemble works by Telemann, Couperin, Rameau and Bach are outstanding.

The beginning of what is termed the Classical period was marked in chamber music by the rise of another new instrument – the fortepiano, ancestor of the modern piano, with a greater potential for brilliant and expressive playing than the harpsichord. Keyboard writing moved rapidly away from the continuo style of the Baroque era, though relics of the continuo remain, for instance the cello's support of the piano's bassline in the trios of Haydn and Mozart. The piano now took centre stage from the violin; what we now call the violin sonatas of Mozart were, like many others of the period, initially published as sonatas for keyboard with violin accompaniment. But the emancipation of the keyboard was to

lead to greater freedom for the strings. The string quartet (two violins, viola and cello) allowed both independence of voices and the maintenance of four-part harmony, once secured by the continuo. Haydn's six Op. 33 quartets (1781), composed, according to Haydn, "in a new and special way", consolidated the medium as a form in its own right, the simple melody-accompaniment texture of early Classical music replaced by a dynamic interaction of the four instruments. This was the form that Beethoven was to raise to unequalled heights in his last five quartets (1823–26): these still remain a model and a challenge to composers, though it was quite a while before the musical public accepted them.

By the time Beethoven and Schubert died, in 1827 and 1828 respectively, chamber music was pre-eminently a German form. The outstanding post-Beethovenian chamber works are the quintets, quartets and trios of Mendelssohn, Schumann and Brahms, but not all

chamber music was on such a level of high seriousness. Echoes of the court entertainment ensemble pieces of Mozart's day survived via Beethoven's septet (three winds and four strings) in the octets of Schubert and Mendelssohn and the octet and nonet of Spohr, and music for enjoyment at home by the rising bourgeoisie appeared in reams. Many of the Romantics did not consider chamber music a suitable vehicle for their deeper utterances (Wagner, Mahler and Richard Strauss wrote virtually none, while Bruckner left a solitary mature quintet), and it was not until the latter half of the 19th century that composers outside the Austro-German world began to respond to its special challenges. Dvořák, Smetana, Franck, Fauré, Tchaikovsky and Borodin wrote fine works for various kinds of ensemble, though there is often a lingering tendency to think in orchestral terms.

In the 20th century the reaction against Romantic excess brought a revival of interest in chamber music, or at least in small instrumental forces. The string quartet remained central for many composers (notably Schoenberg, Bartók and Shostakovich), but the impact of Schoenberg's revolutionary *Pierrot lunaire* (1912), for reciter plus two winds, two strings and piano, brought the mixed ensemble back with a vengeance. Works as diverse as Ravel's *Chansons madédcasses* (1927), Messiaen's *Quatuor pour la fin du temps* (1941), Stravinsky's *Septet* (1953) and Boulez's *Le Marteau sans maître* (1955) could all be seen as being in some way indebted to *Pierrot*. Among those affected by Neo-Classicism, Martinu included a series of 'madrigal' pieces in his long list of chamber works, while Hindemith's equally extensive catalogue contains sonatas for cor anglais, tuba and double bass, as well as more conventional groupings. Recent years have seen the rise of professional chamber groups specializing in new or recent music and providing all kinds of exotic combinations, with or without conductor. The extent to which the music they have inspired represents an engagement with the chamber music tradition or a reaction against it varies enormously from composer to composer. ♪

The image of the three women (left) shows chamber music as an increasingly acceptable form of domestic entertainment. The picture above depicts chamber music at its height, before the age of commercial recording.

Duos

THE ORIGINS OF ACCOMPANIED SONG (voice plus instrument or instruments) are undatable, but the voice, the bearer of the words, has remained prominent. In instrumental music the question of who is the accompanist and who the accompanied is much more complicated. The rise of the violin virtuoso in the 17th century, and the development of keyboard instruments, led to the emergence of a new medium for instrumental display: the solo sonata, for violin and continuo. In many ways this is the precursor of the two-instrument form we now call the 'violin sonata', though as the continuo could feature two instruments (lute or keyboard and string bass), it cannot be simply classified as a duo.

With the appearance of the fortepiano, ancestor of the modern piano, the keyboard part took prominence. The violin sonatas of Mozart, Beethoven and their contemporaries were commonly printed as sonatas for piano with violin obligato accompaniment, which was, at first, a fair description, though in the sonatas of Mozart and Beethoven the relationship between the violin and the piano develops into something closer to an equal partnership. In Romantic violin sonatas, for instance those of Brahms, Fauré and Franck, the violin regains something of its former leading role, though it is its melodic, singing qualities that tend to be most richly exploited, and the piano contribution can be just as demanding, technically and expressively. Sonatas for cello and piano are rarer in the 18th and 19th centuries, not surprisingly, since virtuoso cello soloists were a much rarer breed. There are fine examples, however, by Beethoven and Brahms, and in the 20th century by Debussy, Shostakovich, Prokofiev and Britten. Bach's three sonatas for harpsichord and viola da gamba (a bass viol held between the knees like the modern cello) could also be seen as ancestors.

Although duos on one instrument were not unheard of before the Classical period, it was in the late 18th to early 19th century that the piano duet emerged as a form of private music-making (demanding a degree of physical as well as musical intimacy), for which it was to remain widely popular until well into the 20th century. Mozart left some enjoyable duet sonatas, and some of Schubert's finest piano music is found in this form. In the 19th century the piano duet became increasingly popular as a form

• UNUSUAL DUOS •

➤ **Rossini:** Five Duets for two horns (c. 1806); *Duetto* in D major for cello and double bass (1824).

➤ **Hindemith:** *Konzertstück* for two alto saxophones (1933); Duet for viola and cello (1934): Sonata for English horn and piano (1941); Sonata for double bass and piano (1949); Sonata for bass tuba and piano (1955).

➤ **Martinu:** Three Madrigals for violin and viola (1947); *Divertimento* for two recorders (1957).

The Duet (1633) by Cornelis Saftleven shows the basic early Baroque form: melody instrument (here, typically, a violin) and continuo.

for amateur music-making, often of a lighter character. Brahms's *Hungarian Dances* and Dvořák's *Slavonic Dances* are famous examples, as are Bizet's *Jeux d'enfants*, Fauré's *Dolly* Suite, Debussy's *Petite* Suite and Ravel's *Ma mère l'oye* (Mother Goose), though these are all better-known now in their later orchestral versions. In the days before commercial recordings, arrangements for piano duet were the means by which many ordinary music-lovers got to know the orchestral classics. Unfortunately, with the arrival of the long-playing record, and still more the compact disc, this very enjoyable form of amateur music-making has gone into eclipse. Works for two pianos are, for obvious practical reasons, rarer, though there is a splendid example by Mozart (K448), two suites by Rachmaninov, and a powerful late sonata by Debussy, *En blanc et noir*.

While keyboard or keyboard-string instrument duos have been the most popular forms, keyboard-wind partnerships are not uncommon. Weber and Brahms left important works for clarinet and piano, Bach wrote four flute sonatas, and in the 20th century the wind-piano duo repertory

has burgeoned, with contributions for all manner of woodwind and brass instruments by Poulenc, Prokofiev, Martinu, Hindemith and many others. Duos without keyboard have been much rarer, as the results tend to sound harmonically thin, but there are striking sonatas for violin and cello by Ravel and Kodály, and two astonishingly resourceful duos for violin and viola by Mozart. ♪

Family Portrait (c. 1780/81), by Johann della Croce, shows the Mozart family, with Maria Anna and Wolfgang Amadeus seated at the piano, Leopold with violin.

• FAMOUS DUO PIECES •

VIOLIN AND PIANO

➤ **Beethoven: Sonata in A major/minor Op. 47,** *Kreutzer* **(1803)** Stormy, passionate, brilliant, this was *the* Romantic violin sonata for succeeding generations. Tolstoy's story of adulterous passion, *The Kreutzer Sonata*, centres on an amateur performance of this.

➤ **Franck: Sonata in A major (1886)** This is gentler, more wistful than the Beethoven, but with moments of impassioned instrumental song.

CELLO AND PIANO

➤ **Beethoven: Sonata in D major, Op. 102 (1815)** One of the first foretastes of Beethoven's 'late' manner: a dark, contemplative slow movement and an exhilarating fugal finale.

➤ **Shostakovich: Sonata in D minor, Op. 40 (1934)** Lyrical and savagely satirical by turns, this is rapidly becoming the most popular 20th-century cello sonata.

FLUTE AND PIANO

➤ **Poulenc: Sonata (1956)** Cool Gallic lyricism, exquisitely conceived for the flute.

CLARINET AND PIANO

➤ **Weber:** *Grand Duo Concertant* **(1816)** A first-rate virtuoso display piece.

➤ **Brahms: Sonatas Op. 120, No. 1 in F minor, No. 2 in E flat (1894)** The clarinet shows its mellow, more lyrical side.

PIANO DUET (FOUR HANDS)

➤ **Schubert: Fantasie in F minor, D940 (1828)** One of Schubert's most haunting tunes forms the basis of a richly contrasted one-movement fantasy.

➤ **Ravel:** *Ma mère l'oye* **(1908)** A fairy-tale world, poignantly evoked in piano music ideal for the competent amateur. Ravel's later orchestral version offers more colour, but something of the duet intimacy is lost.

TWO PIANOS

➤ **Mozart: Sonata in D major, K448 (1781)** Perfect piano chamber music – two instruments in sparkling or intimate conversation.

➤ **Debussy:** *En blanc et noir* **(1915)** Colourful, brilliantly pianistic fast movements frame an unusually sombre, war-haunted slow movement.

Trios

THE ANCESTRY OF THE MODERN PIANO TRIO (violin, cello and piano) is somewhat complicated. One of the most popular small genres of the Baroque era was the so-called trio sonata. The composition was usually two violins and continuo (though German composers showed a penchant for introducing wind instruments, particularly flutes or oboes), but since the continuo would normally comprise a keyboard instrument or lute plus a string bass, such a 'trio' could often be a foursome. In this form the violins or winds tended to dominate, the fundamental role of the continuo being to provide a bass and fill in the harmony. Something like the modern piano trio began to emerge in the latter half of the 18th century, the new expressive freedom and virtuosity of the keyboard writing plainly inspired by the possibilities of a new instrument, the fortepiano. But in the trios of Mozart and Haydn and their contemporaries the cello often shadows the piano bassline, in the manner of the old continuo, and violin parts could be no more than embellishments of the piano's right hand figurations. Some of these early 'trios' were in fact published as 'sonatas for keyboard with violin and bass accompaniment'.

In the midst of this, however, something new was stirring. Some of Haydn's later trios, and especially Mozart's E major Trio K542, give the cello more than a supporting contribution, and with Beethoven the democratic tendency gathered momentum. In his two Op. 70 trios and the famous *Archduke* Trio, Op. 97, the cello competes on something like equal terms. The huge time-scale of the last work, closer to that of a Beethovenian symphony than any previous trio, also characterizes the two piano trios of Schubert, in which the melodic potential of the two strings is exploited as never before.

In the 19th century the piano trio continued to grow in popularity. Mendelssohn, Schumann, Brahms, Dvořák and Franck made important contributions to the repertory, and arrangements of larger works for piano trio were much in demand for performance in the home (Beethoven arranged his Second Symphony for this purpose). In Russia, where at first composers tended to regard chamber music as unsuitable for serious thoughts, Tchaikovsky's A minor Trio, written in memory of his friend Nikolai Rubinstein, inspired a series of fine, elegaic piano trios in memory of friends and colleagues by Arensky, Rachmaninov and Shostakovich.

Though outstanding piano trios in the 20th

> While string quartets and piano trios grow in number the string trio remains a rarity, tackled only by the adventurous.

> Woodwind and/or brass were preferred for outdoor 'chamber' music.

century are somewhat rarer, as well as the Shostakovich (known as 'Piano Trio No 2' since the re-emergence of youthful work) those by Fauré, Ives and especially Ravel stand out, and in recent years there have been some signs of a revival of interest in the medium.

The question of whether other trio combinations with piano should be termed 'piano trios' has no easy answer – in fact the whole question of classification is problematic. Mozart's Trio K498, for clarinet, viola and piano, is usually referred to a 'clarinet trio', as are Beethoven's Op. 11 and Brahms's Op. 114, both for clarinet, cello and piano. Brahms's Trio, Op. 40, for horn, violin, and piano, is a 'horn trio', though an ensemble of four horns (as used by Tippett and Hindemith) would most likely be described as a 'horn quartet'. Trios without piano are harder to pigeonhole, though significant examples are rarer, due to the difficulty of sustaining a full harmonic texture. There are a handful of major 'string trios' (violin, viola and cello) – Mozart's magnificent, inappropriately entitled *Divertimento*, K563, Beethoven's single Op. 3 and Op. 9 Nos 1–3, and

Schoenberg's uncompromising, but in the end eerily beautiful, Op. 45. Combinations with one or more wind instrument tend to be much less ambitious, and few have survived long in the repertoire, though Poulenc's witty Trio (1926) for oboe, bassoon and piano is still to be heard occasionally. ♪

• SOME FAMOUS TRIOS •

TRIO SONATA
(TWO SOLOISTS AND CONTINUO)
➤ **Corelli: Sonatas 'a tre', Op. 1–4 (1681–94)** Baroque instrumental music at its most elegant and brilliant, enormously influential in its own time.

PIANO TRIO
(VIOLIN, CELLO AND PIANO)
➤ **Mozart: Trio in E major, K542 (1788)** Probably Mozart's greatest piano trio, like the 'London' trios of Haydn, full of striking intimations of things to come.
➤ **Beethoven: Trio in B flat major, Op. 97 (*Archduke*) (1811)** The piano trio acquires new symphonic scale and breadth of expression. This is also one of Beethoven's most generously tuneful chamber works.
➤ **Shostakovich: Piano Trio (No 2) in E minor, Op 67 (1944)** One of Shostakovich's most intense and dramatic chamber works, written in memory of a close friend, and of a Russia shattered by war and Stalinism.

CLARINET TRIO
➤ **Mozart: Trio in E flat major, K498 (1786)** (clarinet, viola and piano) Lighter in character than the great Clarinet Quintet, but abundantly tuneful, with the three instruments very much on equal terms.
➤ **Brahms: Trio in A minor, Op. 114 (1891)** (clarinet, cello and piano) A dark, enigmatic product of Brahms's last years, still somewhat undervalued.

HORN TRIO
(HORN, VIOLIN AND PIANO)
➤ **Brahms: Trio in E flat major, Op. 40 (1865)** Brahms achieves miracles with this near-impossible acoustical balancing-act. The mood is mellow and exuberant by turns, with a uniquely powerful slow movement.
➤ **Ligeti: Trio (1982)** A noted modernist pays tribute to the Brahms Trio in one of his own most directly appealing works. Its success has inspired a revival of interest in the horn trio among younger composers.

Quartets and Quintets

THE TERM 'QUARTET' IS OFTEN USED TO imply a special combination: the string quartet (two violins, viola and cello). Haydn and Beethoven's unparalleled quartet-cycles established this as the supreme genre of chamber music, one in which a composer could express his or her most original thoughts in their most concentrated form. Mozart's quartets – especially his six *Haydn* Quartets – should also be mentioned, though for many chamber music

connoisseurs his three great string quintets, K515, K516 and K593 (not everyone is agreed about the final K614), represent something even more personal and finely wrought.

There are, of course, other combinations of four instruments around which smaller but still significant bodies of work have grown. In the 17th-century English consort repertory there are some beautiful polyphonic essays in four parts (including nine of Purcell's 'fantazias' of 1680). But in the Classical period and afterwards, the only medium that came remotely close to rivalling the string quartet was the piano quartet (violin, viola, cello and piano). Mozart, Dvořák and Fauré wrote two piano quartets each, Mendelssohn and Brahms

three, and Schumann produced a solitary mature example (there is also an early 'Schubertian' piano quartet, originally Op. 5). In the 20th century composers generally seem to have lost interest in the medium, though there were signs of a lingering affection in Britain: Bridge's *Phantasie* Piano Quartet (1910) and Howells's Piano Quartet (1916) deserve to be better known, and there is an immature but very appealing Piano Quartet by the teenage William Walton (1919, revised 1921).

Other quartet combinations, with or without piano, are rarer still, though the saxophone quartet (soprano, alto, tenor and baritone/bass) seems to be gaining interest among younger composers. Messiaen's outstanding chamber work, *Quatuor pour la fin du temps* ('Quartet for the end of time', 1941) uses clarinet, violin, cello and piano in different combinations in its eight movements. Webern's Quartet of 1930 is scored for clarinet, tenor saxophone, violin and piano. Anton Arensky's String Quartet No. 2 (1894), written in memory of Tchaikovsky, calls for violin, viola and two cellos, a strange, bottom-heavy ensemble, but used with great skill and imagination.

The established quintet repertoire is much more diverse. The piano quintet

(piano plus string quartet) has obvious practical advantages: the string quartet can compete with the modern piano on something closer to equal terms,

A fascinatingly mixed ensemble that would pose major problems of balance in the modern concert hall. Note the seating of the players round a single music table.

and its four-voice texture allows it complete harmonic independence in conventional tonal music; also the bringing together of a piano soloist and a full-time string quartet for a concert or part of a concert is relatively easy to arrange. Yet there are surprisingly few great piano quintets: Schumann's Quintet in E flat, Op. 44 (1842), Brahms's F minor Quintet, Op. 34 (1864), Dvořák's mature Piano Quintet (1887), the F minor Quintet of Franck (1880) and Shostakovich's G minor Quintet (1940) stand out, and there are two by Fauré (1905 and 1921), the latter especially typical of his introverted 'late' manner. Schubert's irresistible *Trout* Quintet (1819), for piano, violin, viola, cello and double bass, is a uniquely successful variation.

Mozart and Beethoven's most famous quintets with piano, however, are with wind quartet (oboe, clarinet, bassoon and horn), and both were drawn rather more by the string quintet, as comprising two violins, two violas and cello. For Mozart, the

A company of musicians as portrayed by Louis le Nain (1635).

addition of a second viola gave a potential richness to the inner part-writing which he exploited superbly. Beethoven's single original String Quintet, Op. 29 (1801) sounds leaner in comparison, though he returned to the medium in his last years (a fragment of a second quintet remained at

his death). Brahms too relished the greater richness this so-called 'viola quintet' offered: his two String Quintets (1882 and 1890) are especially admired. Dvořák's mature quintet of 1893 is more uneven, but there is also, surprisingly, an interesting mature quintet by Bruckner (1879), with a fine slow movement. String quintets for other combinations are much rarer, though Dvořák's Quintet (1875) for string quartet and double bass is an entertaining one-off, and the work many consider the greatest quintet of all, Schubert's Quintet in C (1828), follows the example of the majority of Boccherini's 100-plus string quintets in calling for one viola and two cellos.

The one other successful fivesome is the wind quintet (flute, oboe, clarinet, horn and bassoon), a modern descendant of the 18th-century wind divertimento, though some works written for it have been much more ambitious. Schoenberg (1924), Nielsen (1922) and Ligeti (1968) have provided substantial examples, and there is a delightful *divertissement* by Barber, *Summer Music* (1956). Schoenberg's most influential quintet, however, has been the instrumental ensemble (flute/piccolo, clarinet/bass clarinet, violin/viola, cello and piano) supporting the reciter in his revolutionary *Pierrot Lunaire* (1912), ancestor of many modern mixed ensembles, Messiaen's *Quatuor pour la fin du temps* included. ♪

• SOME FAMOUS QUARTETS AND QUINTETS •

PIANO QUARTET

➤ **Mozart: Piano Quartet in G minor, K478 (1785)** A dark-hued, dramatic first movement (in G minor, the key which so often brought out the best in Mozart) is counterbalanced by a wonderfully light-hearted finale.

➤ **Fauré: Piano Quartet No 1 in C minor, Op. 15 (1879, revised 1883)** The intimate, lyrical world of Fauré's chamber music is most accessible here.

OTHER QUARTETS

➤ **Messiaen: *Quatuor pour la fin du temps* (1941)** (clarinet, violin, cello and piano) Written while Messiaen was a prisoner-of-war in Silesia, this is a haunting Christian meditation on the nature of time, and on the final, redemptive moment when there will be 'time no longer'.

PIANO QUINTET

➤ **Brahms: Piano Quintet in F minor, Op. 34 (1864)** The young Brahms at the peak of his powers – stormy, impassioned, mysterious, majestic.

➤ **Dvořák: Piano Quintet in A major, Op. 81 (1887)** As sunny and relaxed as the Brahms is dark and intense, with a delicious flavouring of Dvořák's native Czech folk music.

STRING QUINTET

➤ **Mozart: String Quintet in G minor, K516 (1787)** (quartet plus second viola) In few of Mozart's works is there such a sense of private unburdening; the slow movement surpassing even that of the great G minor symphony in expressive power.

➤ **Schubert: String Quintet in C major, D 956 (1828)** (quartet plus second cello) Liberated from the need to sustain the bass, the first cello sings rapturously in this marvellous autumnal work.

WIND QUINTET

➤ **Nielsen: Wind Quintet (1922)** The great Danish symphonist at his most intimate and charming – a work in the classical tradition of chamber music as shared music-making. Nielsen said that writing it deepened his ability to "think through the instruments themselves".

Sextets, Septets, Octets and Nonets

THE FORERUNNERS OF THE LARGER chamber ensembles can be found in the entertainment music – the serenades, divertimentos, cassations and so on – of the 18th century. The quantity and general quality of Mozart's 'diversions' is staggering, all the more so when one considers that many of the noble patrons who commissioned this kind of thing would have seen it as little more than tasteful musical wallpaper. But although some of these works have endured and been performed as chamber music – notably the Divertimento for string trio K563, and the Serenade for 13 wind instruments K361 – most of this music falls outside the chamber category. Performance in large halls or outdoors, as background to grand social functions, tended to rule out the classic chamber music quality of intimacy, whether between players and listeners or among the players themselves.

There are, however, works that seem to straddle both worlds. Beethoven's lightweight but very appealing Septet, Op. 20, for clarinet, bassoon, horn, violin, viola, cello and double bass, was hugely influential (Beethoven came to resent its enduring popularity). Schubert's Octet, D803, for Beethoven's forces plus second violin, Spohr's Octet (clarinet, two horns, double bass and string quartet) and Nonet (flute, oboe, clarinet, bassoon, horn string trio and double bass) and Hummel's Septett

Militaire (flute, clarinet, trumpet, violin, cello, double bass and piano) are all clear descendents of the Beethoven. Alongside these stand Spohr's four 'double string quartets' (two string quartets placed antiphonally) and Mendelssohn's superb, youthful string octet – somewhere between a large chamber work and a practice run for full-scale symphonic music.

On the whole, music for larger ensembles, especially mixed wind and strings groupings, has tended to be lighter in character, a long way from the high seriousness demanded by the string quartet and string quintet repertoire. However, there are some substantial string sextets (two violins, two violas, two cellos): the young

Brahms wrote two warmly romantic sextets (1862 and 1866), there is a delightful example by Dvořák (1878), and Schoenberg's ardently expressive early tone poem *Verklärte Nacht* ('Transfigured Night', 1899), now popular in Schoenberg's own arrangement for string orchestra, was originally written for string sextet. The more intimate, confidential manner of the chamber version is a powerful plus in a work dealing with intensely private erotic feeling. One other sextet should be mentioned, even if it is not quite chamber music technically: Richard Strauss begins his opera *Capriccio* (1942) with a gorgeous prelude for off-stage string sextet, representing the art of his composer-hero Flammand.

In the 20th century the large chamber ensemble underwent a revival, partly in reaction to the orchestral extravagances of late Romanticism. The mixed quintet accompanying the reciter in Schoenberg's *Pierrot Lunaire* (see Quartets and Quintets) was a major catalyst. Schoenberg also wrote a suite for piccolo clarinet, clarinet, bass clarinet, piano and string trio (1926) and a serenade (1923) for the colourful mixture of

clarinet, bass clarinet, mandolin, guitar and string trio (plus baritone solo in the fourth movement). Stravinsky's thorny, serial septet (1953) for clarinet, bassoon, horn, piano and string trio is clearly indebted to Schoenberg's example, but his more popular octet (1923, revised 1952), for flute, clarinet, two bassoons, two trumpets and two trombones, looks back further to 18th-

century entertainment music, mixed with hints of jazz and baroque styles. Janáček's *Mladi* ('Youth', 1924), for wind quintet plus bass clarinet, is another work with echoes of the classical divertimento, as is Poulenc's sextet (1939) for wind quintet and piano. While Poulenc, Janáček, Stravinsky and Schoenberg glanced backwards, the avant-garde visionary Edgard Varèse left a short but volcanically powerful octet, *Octandre* (1923), for flute/piccolo, clarinet/piccolo clarinet, oboe, bassoon, horn, trumpet, trombone and double bass, which seems to point only forwards. It had many imitators among the modernists of the 1960s and 1970s. Over the last three decades the emergence of large mixed chamber groups of high quality has led to a huge growth in this kind of repertoire, giving rise to works as widely contrasted as Harrison Birtwistle's angular, atonal *Tragoedia* (1965) for wind quintet, harp, string quartet and double bass, and Steve Reich's modal, repetition-based octet (1979) for flute, clarinet, two pianos and string quartet – works in which something of the spirit of intimate, communal music-making survives, though radically transformed. ♪

Procession of Notre Dame de Sablon (1616) by Alsloot – ensemble music in the service of the church and possibly one of the canzonas of Giovanni Gabrieli or a composition in similar polyphonic style.

• SOME FAMOUS WORKS •

STRING SEXTETS
(TWO VIOLINS, TWO VIOLAS, TWO CELLOS)
➤ **Brahms: Sextets No 1 in B flat major, Op. 18 (1862), No 2 in G major, Op. 36 (1866)** The sextet is a natural medium for a composer with such a fondness for rich, sonorous textures. The melodic spontaneity of both works, but especially No. 1, recalls Schubert.
➤ **Schoenberg: *Verklärte Nacht* (1899)** Night: a married woman and the man she truly loves open their hearts to each other against a dream-like forestscape. Richard Dehmel's poem inspires a sumptuous chamber fantasy in Schoenberg's early, post-Wagnerian manner.

SEPTET
➤ **Beethoven: Septet in E flat, Op. 20 (1800)** (clarinet, bassoon, horn, string trio and double bass) Apart from *Wellington's Victory*, this was the biggest hit of Beethoven's career in his own day, and a work with countless imitators. It is not perhaps Beethoven's most profound utterance, but it is certainly witty and delightfully tuneful.

OCTET
➤ **Schubert: Octet in F, D803 (1824)** (clarinet, bassoon, horn, string quartet and double bass) Inspired by the Beethoven, but with a gentle 'out of doors' atmosphere all of its own: melodically generous, cheerful, but with passing shadows.
➤ **Stravinsky: Octet (1923, revised 1952)** (flute, clarinet, two bassoons, two trumpets and two trombones) The instrumentation, the idea for which came to Stravinsky in a dream, is brilliantly handled in one of the most attractive of the composer's Neo-Classical works. Stravinsky found in smaller mixed combinations such as this the perfect antidote to the inflated soundscapes of the Late-Romantic orchestral repertoire.

NONET
➤ **Spohr: Nonet in F, Op. 31 (1813)** (wind quintet, string trio and double bass) Deservedly one of Spohr's best-known works today, this represents the spirit of communal music-making at its most relaxed and enjoyable.

String Ensembles

THE PERMANENT ORCHESTRAL STRING ensemble as such is a relatively recent invention. A milestone in its development as a separate entity was the foundation, by the English musician Boyd Neel, of the Boyd Neel Orchestra in 1932. This was a group of outstanding young string players with a core membership of around 18; later string ensembles have tended to be of similar size. Benjamin Britten wrote his *Variations on a Theme of Frank Bridge* for

• SIX FAMOUS PIECES •

➤ **Bach:** *Brandenburg* Concerto No. 3 in G, BWV1048 (1713?) The ultimate Baroque display piece for string ensemble, the 10 strings (three each of violins, violas and cellos plus continuo) creating uniquely rich sonorities.

➤ **Mozart:** Serenade in G, K525, *Eine kleine Nachtmusik* (1787) The most enduringly popular of all Mozart's serenades and divertimentos, tuneful and finely wrought. However perfect it may seem, it is in fact incomplete: originally there was an extra movement, between the first and the slow movements.

➤ **Tchaikovsky:** Serenade in C major, Op. 48 (1881) One of Tchaikovsky's few predominantly joyous masterpieces, also one

of the very few successful Russian marriages between German Classicism and Slavonic nationalism.

➤ **Vaughan Williams:** *Fantasia on a Theme by Thomas Tallis* (1910, revised 1919) Tallis's modal hymn tune forms the basis of an impassioned, powerfully original 'fantasy', uniquely English in flavour, in which the sound of antiphonal string ensembles is exploited as never before.

➤ **Britten:** *Variations on a Theme of Frank Bridge,* Op. 10 (1937) The 23-year-old Britten's brilliant homage to his teacher Bridge established itself immediately as one of the masterpieces of the string orchestral repertoire and one of its composer's most enduringly popular pieces.

Boyd Neel, British pioneer of the modern string ensemble.

Neel's orchestra in 1937, and several other important 20th-century string works were to enter its repertoire, but it was in its pioneering work on behalf of Baroque music that the Boyd Neel Orchestra was particularly influential. It may be difficult to believe now, but in the orchestra's early days, even such major works as the Handel's 12 *Concerti Grossi*, Op. 6, were very much a minority, connoisseur interest.

The pioneering figure in contemporary music for string orchestra was the Swiss conductor and philanthropist Paul Sacher. His Basle Chamber Orchestra, founded in 1926, was not purely a string ensemble, but many of the works written for it were for strings alone: these include Stravinsky's Concerto in D and Bartok's *Divertimento*. Alongside these are Sacher commissions which are strings-based, but with contributions from other instrumental families, for example Bartok's *Music for Strings, Percussion and Celesta*, Martin's *Petite symphonie concertante* (two string orchestras, harp, celeste and piano) and Honegger's Second Symphony (string orchestra, with optional solo trumpet in the coda of the finale).

Sacher too had a keen interest in pre-Classical music. Along with Neel, and important later advocates like Sir Neville Marriner, whose Academy of

Paul Sacher conducting his Basle Chamber Orchestra in the Conservatoire Hall in Basle. A list of those who wrote for him reads like a Who's Who of 20th-century composers.

St Martin-in-the-Fields was founded in 1959, he was a major force in the mass rediscovery of the Baroque string repertoire: Handel, Corelli, Vivaldi, and lesser, but still important, figures such as Torelli and Geminiani. A typical feature of the string (plus keyboard continuo) Concerto Grosso was the division of the players into solo (or 'concertato') and orchestral (or 'ripenio') groupings. This was to have a marked influence on some 20th-century composers. Tippett's *Fantasia Concertante on a Theme of Corelli*, for instance, divides the string players into three groups, seated separately: three soloists (two violins and cello as in the concertato sections of Corelli and Handel), here labelled 'Concertino', and two full string ensembles, marked 'Concerto Grosso' and 'Concerto Terzo'. Elgar's division of his forces in the *Introduction and Allegro for Strings* into solo quartet and string orchestra also has a partly Baroque inspiration. In Vaughan Williams' *Fantasia on a Theme by Thomas Tallis* the string forces are divided into solo quartet and two string orchestras, the second comprising just nine players. As in the rather later Tippett work, Vaughan Williams seems to have had the string 'fantasies' or 'fancies' of Tallis's own age in mind, as well as the obvious Baroque models.

The rediscovery in this century of the richness of the Elizabethan string repertory may explain why the string ensemble seems to have had particular appeal for English composers. Apart from the Elgar, Vaughan Williams, Britten and Tippett works mentioned above, there are highly distinctive contributions from Bridge, Holst, Peter Warlock, Lennox Berkeley, Alan Rawsthorne and Nicholas Maw.

Between the pre-Classical and modern eras, significant works written specifically for string orchestra are much rarer, these tending to be played by the string sections of full symphony orchestras or by ad hoc groups. Mozart's serenade *Eine kleine Nachtmusik* is normally played by string orchestra today (though it is not clear if it was intended for multiple or solo strings), and in the latter half of the 19th century one finds Tchaikovsky's Serenade in C, Dvořák's Serenade in E and Grieg's Holberg Suite. However, quite a few of the works now popular in the string orchestral repertoire were not originally conceived for multiple strings. Schoenberg's *Verklärte Nacht* was first written for string sextet, Barber's Adagio was adapted from the slow movement of his String Quartet, and the work now widely known as Shostakovich's Chamber Symphony, Op. 110a, is an arrangement by Rudolph Barshai of his Eighth String Quartet.

While the Boyd Neel orchestra core of around 18 players has remained typical, it is not unusual for string ensemble works to be played by something closer to the full modern orchestral complement of strings. And some composers are very specific about the number of strings required: Bach's *Brandenburg* Concerto No. 3 calls for three violins, three violas, three cellos and continuo (string bass and harpsichord), while Strauss's *Metamorphosen* is scored for 23 solo strings. Penderecki's *Threnody for the Victims of Hiroshima* specifies 52 strings, while Ligeti's *Ramifications* can be played by an ensemble of 12 solo strings or a larger string orchestra. ♪

◆ BARBER'S ADAGIO ◆

This piece entered the world as the slow movement of Barber's String Quartet (1936), but its emotional power and noble simplicity completely eclipses the two framing fast movements. Perhaps realizing this, Barber made the famous arrangement for string orchestra within a year. This was not the end of the story, though: 33 years later, in 1967, he adapted it for chorus to the text of the Agnus Dei from the Roman Catholic Mass. However, it is the string version that has made this one of the most popular classical compositions of the 20th century. Its mood of heartfelt sadness is given a special solemnity by the chant-like theme, with its easily recognizable (but non-specific) religious overtones. These qualities made the Adagio a particularly suitable accompaniment for the state funerals of two American presidents, Franklin D. Roosevelt and John F Kennedy. It has also been used to great effect in film – to suggest the desolation of war at the end of *Platoon* and to express the inner desolation of the piteously deformed John Merryck in *The Elephant Man*.

The Orchestra

Early forms to the Beethovenian revolution

As so often with musical terms, the word 'orchestra' originally meant something rather different from what it means now. The Ancient Greek *orkhestra* was the area in front of the theatre stage where the chorus sang and danced. The idea of reviving the conditions of Greek drama was one of the inspirations behind the first operas, created in the late 16th century, and the word 'orchestra' came back into use. It was not long before the meaning shifted from the place the musicians played in to the musicians, collectively, themselves. These early orchestras could be rich and colourful affairs – with strings, woodwind, brass, keyboards and plucked instruments all present – but it was only later that they began to assume a life of their own, away from the stage. The decisive influence was probably the rise of the violin: much more brilliant and assertive than its predecessor, the viol, and capable of holding its own before a large audience. The growing popularity of the new breed of violin virtuosos in the latter part of the 17th century led to a huge demand for new musical forms, hence the emergence of the concerto, in which instrumental soloist or soloists contrasted with a group of instruments centred on the continuo.

At first, distinctions between orchestral and chamber music were blurred: how many and what kind of instruments one used depended on the size of the performance venue. However, numbers and instrumental colours could be extensive. At the court of Louis XIV of France, Lully had a magnficent ensemble at his disposal, the Grande Bande – essentially a string orchestra (the 24 Violons du Roi), but with the possibility of adding the 12 Grands Hautbois (10 oboes, or members of the oboe family, and two bassoons), and on occasions trumpets and drums.

Such opulence was rare when Lully took up his post in 1653, but by the early years of the next century it had spread wider. An account of the 1717 performances of Handel's orchestral *Water Music* suites mentions "50 instruments of all sorts" accompanying George I's boat party on a special barge; another specifies trumpets, horns, oboes, bassoons, German flutes, recorders and strings (probably with harpsichord continuo).

Use of the term 'strings' today suggests,

musical form, the symphony, rose rapidly as the means of showing off an orchestra's brilliance and expressive power.

This was the collective instrument that Beethoven inherited. Three of his first four symphonies call for the standard late-18th-century orchestra: one or two flutes, pairs of oboes, clarinets, bassoons, horns, trumpets and drums, plus strings (the Third Symphony, the *Eroica*, adds a third horn). Use of the continuo was in decline, though a brief, fully written-out keyboard part in the finale of Haydn's Symphony No. 98 suggests that it was still common as late as 1792. Instruments were becoming more sophisticated as composers' writing for them grew more demanding (which was the cause and which the effect is not always easy to gauge). Horns and trumpets still lacked valves, which meant that notes outside the natural 'harmonic series' were not easily obtained. The orchestra's layout could still vary enormously (with individual sections

sometimes mixed), but composers were increasingly specific about which instrumental colours they required.

It is with Beethoven's Fifth Symphony – revolutionary in so many senses – that the orchestra takes a big step nearer to its modern form. At the point where the finale's C major main theme enters, *fortissimo* dispelling the C minor gloom of the scherzo, the effect is underlined powerfully by the use of instruments never before employed in a symphony: piccolo, contrabassoon and three trombones (before this the trombones tended to be used only in church compositions or to suggest the supernatural in opera, for instance the statue's appearances in Mozart's *Don Giovanni*). Two trombones appear in the 'Storm' movement of the Sixth Symphony, the *Pastoral*, and all three return, along with the piccolo and contrabassoon, in the Ninth, where the orchestra is further amplified by two extra horns and the so-called 'Turkish' percussion (cymbals, bass drum and triangle). The effect of Beethoven's orchestral innovations on succeeding generations of composers was enormous.

if not a standard size, at least standard proportion: first violins, second violins, violas, cellos and double basses in a ratio of something like 4, 4, 3, 3, 2 (multiply this by four and you have a standard modern complement of symphonic strings). In the first part of the 18th century that ratio could vary enormously, but by the end of the century it had stabilized into something like the modern grouping, though viola and cello sections tended to be smaller. The rest of the orchestra was consolidating too: the earlier orchestral works of Haydn, Mozart and their contemporaries usually call for pairs of oboes and horns, with perhaps a flute (or two), two bassoons, and on occasions pairs of trumpets and drums. In the later 18th century the new clarinets began to appear (again in pairs): the Duke of Saxony's virtuoso Mannheim orchestra (led by the composer Johann Stamitz), which so impressed the young Mozart, included clarinets. A new, dramatic kind of

---

• ORCHESTRAL FORCES •

➤ **Handel:** Suite in D, from the *Water Music* (performed 1717) Two oboes, 1 bassoon, two horns, two trumpets, strings (including continuo). Wind parts may have been doubled, or even further amplified.

➤ **Haydn:** Symphony No 104 in D major (*London*, 1795) Two flutes, two oboes, two clarinets, two bassoons, two horns, two trumpets, timpani, strings.

➤ **Beethoven:** Symphony No 5 in C minor, op. 67 (1808) Piccolo, two flutes, two oboes, two clarinets, two bassoons, contrabassoon, two horns, two trumpets, three trombones, timpani, strings.

➤ **Berlioz:** *Symphonie fantastique* (1830) Two flutes (the second doubling piccolo), two oboes (the second doubling cor anglais), two clarinets (the second doubling E flat clarinet), four bassoons, four horns, two cornets, two trumpets, three trombones, two ophicleides, timpani (four players), bass drum, snare drum, cymbals, bells, two harps, strings.

➤ **Mahler:** Symphony No 8 in E flat major (*Symphony of a Thousand*, 1906) Piccolo*,

four flutes, four oboes, cor anglais, E flat clarinet*, three clarinets, bass clarinet, four bassoons, contrabassoon, eight horns, four trumpets, four trombones, tuba, timpani (two players), bass drum, cymbals, tam-tam, triangle, deep bells, glockenspiel, celeste, piano, harmonium, organ, two harps*, mandoline*, strings. Plus offstage brass: four trumpets, three trombones. Vocal resources: two soprano soloists, two altos, tenor, baritone and bass, boys' choir and two mixed choirs (soprano, alto, tenor, bass)

➤ **Bartók:** Concerto for orchestra (1943, revised 1945) Three flutes (the third doubling Piccolo), three oboes (the third doubling cor anglais), three clarinets (the third doubling bass clarinet), three bassoons (the third doubling contrabassoon), four horns, three trumpets, three trombones, tuba, timpani, triangle, side drum, bass drum, cymbals, tam-tam, two harps, strings (this is more or less the standard line-up for a modern symphony orchestra).

*Indicates parts may be doubled, or further amplified

Big is Beautiful

THE COMPLETE ORCHESTRAL LINE-UP for Beethoven's Ninth Symphony looks very close to that of the standard modern symphony orchestra: two each of woodwind plus piccolo and contrabassoon, four horns, two trumpets, three trombones, timpani, percussion and strings – compare that with the orchestration of Bartók's Concerto for Orchestra (see page 165). But Beethoven uses his full forces only in the late stages of the finale, after the chorus have entered: the three trombones, for instance, are used only in the trio section of the scherzo, and from bar 265 onwards in the finale. For most of the work the orchestration is much closer to the familiar 18th-century band.

It was Berlioz who took the decisive step into new territory. In his own time he was known as the 'Virtuoso of the Orchestra', just as his contemporaries Paganini and Chopin were the virtuosos of the violin and the piano. His treatise on orchestration, the *Grand trait d'instrumentation et d'orchestration modernes*, has remained a classic study. The range of colour, size and proportions in the orchestration of his *Symphonie fantastique* (see page 165) heralds many developments in the late 19th-century orchestra – Mahler is just one later orchestral master who was hugely indebted to this work, Strauss was another. Another of Berlioz's innovations was his use of space for dramatic effect: the cor anglais calling to an offstage oboe in the *Symphonie's* slow movement for instance, or the offstage bells in the finale. In this, as in several other respects, Berlioz was influenced by his early experiences in the opera house – the orchestra showed a new, theatrical potential.

Some of his later works call for huge forces, famously the Requiem, with its 8 bassoons, 12 horns, 16 timpani and 4 offstage brass bands. Berlioz was responding partly to his own inclinations, but there was a social influence too. The audience for orchestral concerts, and hence the size of concert halls, was growing, and bigger spaces call out for bigger forces.

As composers grew more adventurous, instrument-making became more sophisticated. In Beethoven's time, orchestral horn and particularly trumpet parts were largely limited to the notes of the natural harmonic series, but the invention of valves in the second decade of the 19th century, allowing players to alter the effective length of the tubing, brought gradual change. By the time of Bruckner and Tchaikovsky, all brass instruments were completely chromatic (as trombones, with their slides, had always been). Theodor Boehm's developments to the flute, especially the use of levers to extend the compass of the players' fingers, began to influence the construction of the other woodwind instruments. New instruments appeared, including Adolphe Sax's saxhorns and saxophones, but the one which found a permanent home in the symphony orchestra was the tuba, which was increasingly used to provide an extended bass to the trombone section, or sometimes (as in Wagner's *Siegfried* and Mahler's Sixth Symphony) as an important colour in its own right. Harps began to appear more frequently in orchestral scores, and the colour of the woodwind section was often enhanced by the use of cor anglais or bass clarinet.

In the 18th century, the beat – and to some degree artistic direction – was provided by the continuo player or the orchestral leader, but as orchestras grew in size it became obvious that a special, prominently placed director was needed. By the middle of the 19th century this new 'conductor' had become an accepted figure,

Satyrisches Bild.

Berlioz is portrayed here as the general of a vast instrumental army as he conducts one of his works. This is a recurring image in caricatures of conductors up to the present day.

and his function became more and more interventionist: not only giving the beat, but conveying subtleties of interpretation which, it was felt, could no longer be entrusted to collective intuition, or conveyed by a few hints from the leader. At this stage however, the most influential conductors were themselves composers: Spohr, Mendelssohn, Berlioz and Wagner.

The phenomenon of the specialist 'star' conductor, first and foremost a virtuoso performer, treating the orchestra as his (or, today, her) instrument, was still to come. ♪

A performance at the Concertgebouw in Amsterdam, with the resident orchestra's current music director, Riccardo Chailly.

• SOME FAMOUS CONCERT HALLS •

AMSTERDAM: CONCERTGEBOUW
➤ Home of the Concertgebouw Orchestra, this hall was opened in 1888. It has one of the world's best-loved acoustics, atmospheric but refreshingly clear. Sighs of relief were heard when recent work on the foundations was found not to have damaged the sound. Willem Mengelberg gave important festivals of music by Mahler and Strauss here in the 1920s.

BIRMINGHAM: SYMPHONY HALL
➤ Home of the City of Birmingham Symphony Orchestra, this magnificent hall, specially designed to be acoustically adaptable, is a triumph of engineering. By means of the movement of a raised canopy above the stage and the opening of doors into acoustic chambers, the character of the acoustic can be changed. Since its inauguration in 1991, orchestras and conductors have been lining up eagerly to try it out.

LONDON: ROYAL ALBERT HALL
➤ The Royal Albert Hall was opened in 1871 as a memorial to Prince Albert. This vast hall, with a total audience capacity of 6,500, comes close to acoustic disaster (the dome has had to be filled with flying saucer-like discs to prevent excessive reverberation), but it remains hugely popular, especially as the venue for the annual summer Henry Wood Promenade Concerts. Gounod conducted the first concert, and Brucker was one of the first to play the splendid Wills organ. Among the many premieres given here was the first professional performance of Havergal Brian's immense *Gothic* Symphony (No. 1) – few other spaces would have been adequate for the number of orchestral players and chorus required.

NEW YORK: CARNEGIE HALL
➤ Opened in 1891, the hall seats over 2,780, and yet even solo recitals have come over well in this enormous but surprisingly adaptable space. The list of famous musicians who have performed here is impressive. Tchaikovsky was guest of honour at the inaugural concert. Later visitors included Rachmaninov, Mahler and Prokofiev.

VIENNA: GROSSER MUSIKVEREINSAAL
➤ Opened in 1870, the Grosser Musikvereinsaal was designed by Theophil Hansen to stand proudly among the imposing architecture of the Vienna Ring. It is the home of the Vienna Philharmonic Orchestra and has over 1,650 seats and 300 standing places. It is sometimes called the 'Goldener Saal' ('Golden Hall') on account of its magnificent acoustic and elaborate decoration. Important first performances given here were Brahms's Second and Third symphonies; Bruckner's Third (which was disastrous) and Eighth; and orchestral extracts from Wagner's operas.

Challenges amid Standardization

THE TENDENCY TOWARDS EXPANSION AND colour enrichment of the symphony orchestra continued in the late 19th and early 20th centuries. Some composers remained faithful to the relatively modest band one finds in, say, Tchaikovsky's symphonies: double woodwind plus piccolo, four horns, two trumpets, three trombones and tuba, timpani, percussion and strings. In many cases there were good practical reasons for doing so, but the enlarged forces that were used by Wagner in

• SOME NATIONAL ORCHESTRAS •

CHICAGO SYMPHONY
➤ A typical five-star modern American orchestra, superbly balanced, but with the brass especially inclined to be forceful. The sound can be sumptuous, the ensemble superbly synchronized, but for some it can be disturbingly lacking in character and expressive intimacy.

KIROV
➤ The conductor of the orchestra of St Petersburg's Maryinsky Theatre, Valery Gergiev, is a passionate advocate of Russian national sound and style. The famous 'Slavic wobble' of older times has been toned down, but the sound remains grainier, the strings huskier, and the solo playing style intensely expressive.

MONTREAL SYMPHONY
➤ Widely dubbed 'the finest French orchestra', this is a superbly disciplined band, again rich in tone, but capable of great delicacy and transparency, particularly appropriate in French repertoire – all characteristics encouraged by conductor Charles Dutoit.

VIENNA PHILHARMONIC
➤ The epitome of the plush, warm-toned Austro-German orchestra at its modern best, with a highly characteristic way of playing certain national rhythms, for example the lilting 3/4 of the Viennese Waltz. The great works of the Viennese Classical and Romantic ages remain the orchestra's core repertoire.

{ The renowned Vienna Philharmonic Orchestra in its 'home', the Great Hall of the Musikverein in Vienna, where it has premiered some of the greatest works of the Viennese concert repertoire.

his operatic *Ring* cycle (including 15 woodwind, 17 brass and 6 harps) set a trend which culminated in such mammoth forces as those of Mahler's Eighth Symphony, Stravinsky's *Rite of Spring*, Schoenberg's *Gurrelieder* and the biggest of them all, Havergal Brian's *Gothic* Symphony.

However, in the post-World War I world there was a reaction against what one composer described as 'elephantitis'. The large chamber ensemble (which was inspired partly by Schoenberg's 15-strong First Chamber Symphony and the mixed quintet in

{ Elgar conducting an early recording of one of his works. The primitive technology of the day demanded many compromises, including a drastic scaling down of the orchestral forces, yet these early recordings can sound surprisingly authoritative and are preferred by many to the technically perfect recordings of today.

his *Pierrot lunaire*) grew in popularity, especially among composers on the modernist wing. Others, like Sibelius, stuck to much more modest forces, on mid-19th-century lines, in their orchestral works. There were prophecies that the symphony orchestra was doomed to extinction, but what followed was a period of consolidation. Orchestras all over the world began to conform broadly to a standard large-orchestral line-up: the forces given for Bartók's Concerto for Orchestra on page 165 are typical.

The layout of the orchestra also began to standardize, even though some conductors, for instance Leopold Stokowski, continued to experiment. The loudest instruments, the percussion and 'heavy' brass (trumpets, trombones and tuba) were placed at the back, on raised platforms. Strings, still the core of the orchestral sound, were placed at the front. A standard positioning of the strings has emerged: first violins to the left of the conductor, with second violins, violas and cellos placed in that order, in roughly semi-circular pattern. However, variations have persisted: some orchestras prefer the left-to-right order of first and second violins, cellos and violas, while Sir Adrian Boult and his pupil Vernon Handley preferred a once-popular pattern with first and second violins placed left and right respectively. The

interweaving of violin lines in, for example, the Ninth and Tenth symphonies of Mahler can be heard with far greater clarity when the firsts and seconds are separated in this manner. The recent growth of interest in period instruments has resulted in attempts to revive older seating arrangements, some with the instrumental sections mixed; see the diagrams of authentic and traditional layouts on page 175.

As recordings – especially older ones – will confirm, standardization of forces did not immediately lead to standardization of orchestral sound. Different national traditions of instrument-making were partly responsible, but playing styles varied too. Russian brass, for instance, have tended to produce a distinctive, wide vibrato, which immediately sets them apart from the much purer English sound. Until recent times French bassoons and oboes were easily identifiable by their more reedy, nasal tone quality. In the age of digital recording and mass migration, however, there has been an increasing internationalization of orchestral styles. Instrumental design has continued to develop, if more slowly than in the 19th century, with the brass for instance capable of producing more volume of sound for larger concert halls. There are also signs that orchestral sound as a whole is becoming more homogenous – less like a huge chamber ensemble and more like a kind of

human synthesizer. This, argue some of the period instrumentalists, has made the modern orchestra less suitable for performing the orchestral works of the pre-late-Romantic era, and performances and recordings of symphonies of Beethoven, and even Schumann and Brahms, on older instruments (or copies of older instruments) have been rising in popularity. The difference in the tone colour of, say, a late-18th-century oboe and its modern descendant can be startling at first.

In the modernist 1960s and 1970s the symphony orchestra was challenged from other directions: by those who found its sound superannuated and inappropriate to their more experimental way of thinking, and by those who found it politically suspect – the epitome of the bourgeois 'luxury product'. Hans Werner Henze's Sixth Symphony divides the players into two 'chamber orchestras', including banjo and electric guitar, depicting a conflict between 'bourgeois' and 'revolutionary' music. Despite this, and more recent economic threats, prophecies of imminent end have not so far been fulfilled. Composers seem once again to find in the symphony orchestra the ultimate instrumental challenge, while some film scores (for instance those of Hollywood's John Williams) have brought back the huge forces and colour-resources of Mahler and Strauss. Commercial recordings have allowed listeners to raise themselves out of the concert hall auditorium and place themselves in a kind of idealized conductor's position (though most of them would be surprised if they were to discover what a conductor actually hears). The idea of the orchestra as a super-sophisticated instrument, with the all-powerful conductor as its master, has never been more popular. ♪

The Conductor

TODAY, THE STAR CONDUCTOR IS ONE of the most glamorous figures in musical life. He – or she – is variously described as a general at the head of an army of musicians, a virtuoso performer on the ultimate musical instrument, a tyrant, the composer's mouthpiece or (as some musicians would have it) an imposter, taking the credit due to others. All of these images imply power, and it is often for this that the conductor is most admired – or envied.

HOWEVER, THE SPECIALIST CONDUCTOR, BY profession a conductor and nothing else, with ultimate responsibility for the quality and character of the performance, is a relatively recent innovation. In music of any complexity it has often been necessary for someone to give the beat: there are illustrations of choral polyphonic performance in Renaissance times which show someone beating time, and even medieval plainchant would sometimes need a director to indicate the rise and fall of the melodic line. Evidence suggests that this role was normally taken by leading performers, and this seems to have remained the preferred practice even when choirs or groups of instruments were distributed in antiphonal groups around large buildings.

In the Baroque era, the continuo player took on the role of director, indicating the basic beat and changes of tempo. Other artistic decisions could be involved too, especially when it was the composer who was doing the directing. In opera houses the director/conductor would often be expected to coach the singers, who were – and are – not always as musically literate as their instrumental colleagues. The rise of the violinist, and the dominance of strings in the orchestral personnel, led to directorship sometimes being passed to the first violinist – to this day he or she is referred to as 'leader' or 'concert-master'. The beat would be indicated by the violinist waving his bow, or even

Jean-Baptiste Lully, a key figure in the history of the conductor. He used a large cane to beat time.

his instrument, though there were other solutions: Lully, for instance, banged the floor with a large stick. Unfortunately he struck himself in the foot one day, giving himself an injury which eventually proved fatal. Surprisingly, other French directors adopted this dangerous and noisy practice after Lully, and it seems to have survived into the early 19th century.

It was around Beethoven's time that conductors began to take up positions in front of the orchestra. Descriptions of Beethoven's colourful ways of indicating crescendos, diminuendos and other expression markings make entertaining reading. The artistic importance of this non-playing musician, standing with his back to the audience and indicating complicated instructions with hands, stick or rolled-up paper, was gradually accepted, but the idea that this could be a career in itself took longer to assimilate. The first significant conductors were primarily known as composers: Spohr, Mendelssohn, Weber, Berlioz and Wagner. Wagner was a hugely influential figure. Among his voluminous writings is a treatise called *On Conducting*, which shows how understanding of the conductor's role had developed. Not only must he find the right tempo, he must indicate the inflections of that tempo – rubato, larger accelerando and ritardanos – which prevent it from being merely exact and therefore lifeless. When the melodic line is passed from instrument to instrument, he must ensure that it is heard as a continuous line. A new idea was emerging: the conductor was not merely a disciplinarian or artistic first among equals; he was the interpreter. Artistic success depended upon his imagination and the ability to convey his ideas.

{ The American pianist Murray Perahia conducting a performance from the piano.

In Wagner's wake there emerged figures who were to become internationally famous as conductors per se. Artur Nikisch and Hans Richter are prominent examples, though like many conductors of that age they were also outstanding instrumentalists. In this century, two hugely important figures – sometimes seen as musical antitheses – were Arturo Toscanini and Wilhelm Furtwängler. Toscanini is often characterized as a classicist, concentrating

---

• TEST PIECES FOR CONDUCTORS •

STRAVINSKY:
THE RITE OF SPRING
➤ Notorious for its rhythmic complexities, this linked series of dances, scored for huge orchestra, can still catch out the unwary conductor. The final 'Sacrificial Dance' begins with the metrical sequence 3/16 (pause) 2/16 3/16 3/16 2/8 2/16 – and that is fairly typical of the movement as a whole.

MAHLER:
SYMPHONY NO 6 IN A MINOR
➤ As with the Stravinsky, immense orchestral forces need careful balancing, but the extra test here is to sustain an intense, impassioned musical argument for around 80 minutes – and to keep something in reserve for the cataclysmic finale.

BRUCKNER:
SYMPHONY NO 8 IN C MINOR
➤ By no means as spectacular as the Mahler or the Stravinsky, this slow-moving, approximately 75-minute work nevertheless demands thorough understanding of its composer's unique architectural processes if it is to succeed. At the same time, it is not all architecture – balance between the elemental and the human is vital.

DEBUSSY: *LA MER*
➤ Debussy's tone poem about the sea is subtitled 'Three Symphonic Sketches', and again balance is crucial: sensitivity to Debussy's orchestral colours, to his grand and subtle mood-painting must be balanced by feeling for the ebb and flow of the symphonic undercurrents. This balance is by no means always achieved in performance.

IVES:
SYMPHONY NO 4
➤ Ives's teeming orchestral textures can easily sound confused or opaque. A conductor should be able to spotlight the important details – but not so as to rob the swirling mixture of its vitality. The finale, with its contrasted strands of tempo, has been done with three conductors, but some brave souls have attempted it solo.

---

on precision and rhythmic muscularity, while Furtwängler continued the Wagnerian emphasis on the longer melodic line and fluidity of tempo. For many, Toscanini is also the great podium dictator, famous for his tantrums and blistering criticism of players. At the same time conductors were now singled out not only for their particular interpretative style and ideals, but also for their specific orchestral sound, and it was often argued that the same orchestra could sound quite different under two different master conductors.

When does veneration of conductors become over-veneration? Audiences and orchestral musicians tend to have widely divergent answers to that question, but when a conductor becomes more important even

{ The conductor as performer – Bochle's silhouettes capture Mahler's famously flamboyant gestures.

than the composer – when great works are merely the means for a monster-egoist to display his personal genius – surely that is a sad comment on the artistic priorities of audiences. There have been signs of a reaction against this in recent years. The composer-conductor Pierre Boulez, for instance, has rejected emphasis on sound in favour of concentration on levels of musical meaning, and in the early days of the period instrument movement one of the dominant aims (especially in music of pre-Beethovenian times) was to bring back more collective artistic responsibilty. The rise of such figures as Nikolaus Harnoncourt, Roger Norrington and John Eliot Gardiner, however, shows how important the charismatic director has remained. At the same time, a general complaint has arisen that the phenomenon of the great, inspired and inspiring conductor is in terminal decline. The nightmare schedules of some modern orchestras and the economic problems of getting adequate rehearsal time are often blamed. Whether this trend is real, and if so, whether it can be reversed, remains to be seen. ♪

INSTRUMENTS

Sounds Authentic

POPULAR CLASSICS RECEIVE SO MANY hearings that promoters and artists seek new ways to present them in order to avoid staleness. One way of doing this is to look afresh at how the music would have sounded originally. It has been discovered that numerous bad habits have developed over the years, particularly during the Victorian era of grand and grandiloquent crazes.

{ Stringed-instrument makers in a manufactory in 1767. Prominent on the wall is a serpent.

viola and cello, though there were numerous local variations.

The string family evolved from viols, but the only member to have retained the sloping viol-type shoulders is the double bass. There were many varieties, with from three to five strings, and tuning varied enormously. To play a period work, today's double bassist must discover the original tuning envisaged by the composer.

Flutes and oboes had fewer keys. Their sounds were more differentiated than today's, the flute softer, the oboe richer and with stronger lower tones. Clarinets were sharper in tone (the name means 'little clarion'), while bassoons were more mellow, with a rather woolly sound.

Horns, no more sophisticated than hunting instruments, were difficult and unpredictable, and would play in only one key. Consequently, horn players carried 'crooks', lengths of metal to fit between instrument and mouthpiece to change the key. A concerto calling for notes outside a key's harmonic series needed unusual skill from the performer. He had to plunge his hand into the bell to make a note sound lower; this would change its character to either a muffled or a piercing sound but at least it would approximate to the required pitch. Composers took such varied tones into consideration, thus giving more light and shade to phrases than is possible on the 'perfected' modern double horn with its ability to produce any key by means of valves to direct the air into selected channels.

Trumpets were also limited until the invention of keys, then valves, enabled the playing of chromatic parts. Timpani bowls were shallower and the animal-skin heads gave a drier, sharper impact compared to today's sonorous tunable instruments.

Until about 1770 (much later in places) a harpsichord would have been a permanent orchestral fixture. From its keyboard the director, in association with the lead violinist, would control the performance, giving audible cues to keep the ensemble together. ♪

AN ORCHESTRA OF 1750 WOULD BE ALMOST unrecognizable to a time-traveller from today. Generalities are impossible because orchestras differed from country to country, city to city, court to court. Furthermore, individual instruments differed substantially even from player to player. Violin necks and fingerboards were shorter and bridges less arched than today's. Strings were mainly of catgut (made from sheep intestines) so the tone was quite weak, suitable for intimate recitals but barely adequate for concert or opera houses.

Violins in concert and opera dictated the keys composers chose. A large number of 18th-century symphonies and overtures are in D major, this key allowing the strongest tone from violins. Later modifications lengthened the neck and fingerboard and the body was strengthened to withstand the extra tension of all-metal strings. Violins then sounded strong in any key. Similar developments affected the

---

• BYGONE INSTRUMENTS •

➤ **Bible organ** This looked like an old Bible. When opened, it revealed bellows on one 'page' and a keyboard on the other. Reeds produced a sharp, grating sound like an electric alarm clock.

➤ **Cornett** A gracefully curved conical wooden trumpet with fingerholes. It produced a high, fluid, voice-like sound.

➤ **Garkleinflötlein** A tiny whistle instrument, scarcely longer than a fountain pen, with a piercing tone. The name means 'very little, little flute'.

➤ **Harpsichord** The workhorse for solo domestic playing and for orchestral continuo use. Its tone is bell-like and very penetrating.

➤ **Hurdy-gurdy** This resembles a broad violin with a handle which turned a circular 'bow' that sounded a drone. The player operated keys to bring other strings into contact with the 'bow'. It made a harsh sound, ideal for riotous dancing.

➤ **Lute** A guitar-like stringed instrument with a rounded-back. Its tone was more limited but purer than that of a guitar.

➤ **Nakers** Small drums held against the thighs and played by the hands or with sticks. The name rhymes with 'crackers'. The tone was high-pitched and penetrating.

➤ **Ophicleide** The 'keyed serpent', a large brass instrument somewhat resembling a saxophone. Its tone was rich and full.

➤ **Rebec** An early fiddle with a weak, scratchy sound.

➤ **Serpent** A woodwind instrument in the shape of a double 'S', conical and with fingerholes; later, it had keys. It was the lowest of the cornett family and was frequently used in military bands. Its tone is unlovely and its intonation unreliable.

➤ **Theorbo** A large member of the lute family, often employed as part of the basso continuo.

➤ **Tromba marina** Not connected either with the sea or a trumpet, as the name implies, this one-string instrument was the length of a man, triangular in cross-section and tapering to the top. Its bridge had one loose foot which vibrated against the soundboard, producing a noise of extreme harshness.

Old Traditions Revisited

IN THE EARLY 20TH CENTURY MUSIC-LOVERS failed to query the way in which music was presented. Was Bach really the bewigged dullard many performers made of him? Did Mozart benefit from inflated orchestras and pliable rhythms? Were Sir Hamilton Harty's arrangements of the *Fireworks Music* and a fraction of the *Water Music* really telling us all there was to know about Handel? When musicologists looked for answers in the composers' original manuscripts it became clear that the music was being changed significantly. Recent performance practices had gathered romantic excesses and many more, often superfluous, instruments.

The Dolmetsch family was the first to research ancient performing traditions and old instruments, and Wanda Landowska's courageous championing of the harpsichord created interest in that instrument. Dolmetsch's following was small, and Landowska's bravery was undermined by influential musicians who described the harpsichord's sound as "a birdcage being struck by a toasting-fork" and, in Sir Thomas Beecham's memorable phrase, "two skeletons copulating on a tin roof".

To the rescue came, first, the gramophone. In France, L'Oiseau-Lyre issued a series of 78rpm discs before World War II, presenting previously unrecorded rare ancient music; and in Germany in 1952 Deutsche Grammophon began an Archiv series which treated the exploration of old music like a military exercise, with repertoire divided into 'research periods' and severely practical and factual presentation of the LP records. Since then, research has revealed a great deal about early performance practices and instruments, and records have proliferated. From the early baroque researches of the Dolmetsch family and, later, of David Munrow, 'authenticity' has moved ever closer to the present, through the classical period of Mozart and Beethoven and up to

Arnold Dolmetsch (1858–1940), founder in 1925 of the Haslemere Festival of old music. He is seen here in 1936 with his third wife, Mabel, and daughter Cecile, who holds a viol. On the table in the foreground lies a treble lute.

Brahms. Performers are searching the scores of even more recent music in an effort to get at performance 'truth'.

Three quite different conductors may be cited in this connection. Nikolaus Harnoncourt began as an eager researcher, founding the Vienna Concentus Musicus to perform mainly baroque and early classical music. More recently he has become a world-renowned conductor of, for example, the Royal Concertgebouw Orchestra in Amsterdam, but his experience in research strongly colours his performances of standard classics with 'modern' orchestras. Sir Charles Mackerras, who rarely conducts 'period' bands, has taken research into early performing traditions seriously, with positive effect upon his readings. When Claudio Abbado, a conductor not known for his sympathy towards authenticity, recorded Schubert's symphonies with the Chamber Orchestra of Europe he included some of the composer's early sketches in the *Great* C major, which made at least two surprising changes to the familiar score.

It is the correct use of instruments, however, which makes the greater difference to how old music sounds. In Bach's *Brandenburg* Concerto No. 5 the anachronistic use of a piano for the harpsichord severely disrupts the balance of the music just as a standard trumpet in No. 2 damages Bach's intention when he wrote for high trumpet. Haydn's scores were once a veritable depository of errors (over 1,000 in the last 12 symphonies alone), and his requirements for horns were often ignored. In writing for C alto horns in, for example, Symphony No. 48, he envisaged horns at the same pitch as C trumpets, yet players still dropped the pitch by an octave until quite recently, thus completely destroying the intended effect. Use of cornet and ophicleide in Berlioz's *Symphonie fantastique* restores the bizarre effects he required for this semi-autobiographical work, and conductors such as Roger Norrington and John Eliot Gardiner have recorded the symphony in its correct scoring. Others such as Trevor Pinnock, Christopher Hogwood and Roy Goodman have rendered similar services to earlier music. ♪

MOZART'S *PRAGUE* SYMPHONY, THEN AND NOW

18TH-CENTURY ORCHESTRA (TYPICAL LAYOUT)

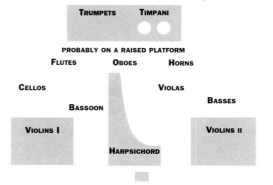

∞ An 'authentic' performance based on what is known of orchestral practice in Prague in Mozart's day, compared with a typical 'traditional' (between the wars) performance of Mozart's Symphony No. 38 in D, Prague.

AUTHENTIC

∞ **Strings** About 4 first violins to the left and 4 seconds to the right, 2 violas, 2 cellos and 2 double basses

   Woodwind As traditional

   Brass As traditional

   Timpani As traditional

   Director At the harpsichord

∞ The two small violin groups, playing without vibrato or portamento, would realize Mozart's antiphonal effects with great clarity. The proportionally much larger woodwind would strike through the textures, and brass would play out with full force, obeying Mozart's dynamic markings. Timpani would have a sharp, decisive impact. The director would hold the performance together with audible harpsichord signals, and if correct tempos were chosen there would be no need for mid-movement adjustments. The andante would move at a comfortable walking pace. All repeats would be played: this would give proper stature to the work and allow the key change in the finale its full effect.

TRADITIONAL

∞ **Strings** The band might comprise 20 first violins and 20 seconds, all grouped to the conductor's left, 10 violas in the centre, 10 cellos and 4 double basses, ranged right

   Woodwind 2 flutes, 2 oboes, 2 bassoons

   Brass 2 horns, 2 trumpets

   Timpani 1 pair

   Conductor

∞ Woodwind would often be submerged. Brass would be encouraged to blend, and timpani would add a slight boomy weight in loud passages. The conductor would 'mould' the music, perhaps slowing appreciably for second subjects. The andante would be slow, most or all repeats omitted, and the strings would play with vibrato and portamento.

TRADITIONAL ORCHESTRA (NB: VARIATIONS WERE COMMON)

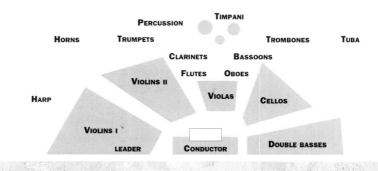

Strings: Types

UNTIL RECENTLY THE STRINGS WERE THE 'glue' of the orchestra. It was this section that usually carried the lead melodies and supplied the harmonic basis. If an 18th-century composer gave a difficult passage to woodwind or brass he would often double the part somewhere in the strings, since string players, and their instruments, were more reliable. The string section divides into five parts: first violins; second violins; violas; cellos; double basses. First and second violins are (usually) identical instruments: they are divided so that answering and echo effects may be obtained. Sadly, the division is often nominal, with all violins to the conductor's left, thus depriving the listener of such effects.

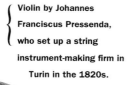

Violin by Johannes Franciscus Pressenda, who set up a string instrument-making firm in Turin in the 1820s.

THE VIOLIN FAMILY

Reduced to its basics, a stringed instrument of the violin family is simply two bows rubbed together, one with a soundbox attached. Experiments like this were probably made by cavemen after a hunt.

∞ **VIOLIN** The earliest violins, with three strings, appeared in northern Italy about 1505. They had evolved from viols ('violin' is the diminutive of 'viol'), alongside which they co-existed for half a century before the violin gradually assumed its accepted place as an accompaniment for dancers, acquiring a fourth string in the process. Amati, founder early in the 16th century of the violin-making school at Cremona, and Stradivari perfected the violin and other instruments for their own time.

Not until 1610 did G B Cima and, soon after that, B Marini, write sonatas for violin, accompanied by a basso continuo, but its very first real solo was a passacaglia by Biber, about 1675. By now its tone, more 'lively' and penetrating than that produced by even the smallest of the viol family, was attracting many composers and its place in operatic orchestras and chamber ensembles was established. Torelli's violin concertos appeared in 1698, the first in a long line of showpieces.

∞ **VIOLA** The violin family needed members to support its treble voice and by at least 1530 the viola had arrived as its tenor or alto voice. It was regarded only as a support instrument until Carl Stamitz, himself a viola player, composed concertos for it during the 1770s, since when it has received a symphony from Berlioz (*Harold in Italy*, 1834) and a concerto by Walton (1929), but little else. Its tone is much duller than the violin's and viola players talk of its excessive weight. Both factors militate against its use in a virtuoso context.

∞ **CELLO, OR VIOLONCELLO** 'Violone' is the old name for the large 'bass fiddle'; 'violoncello' its diminutive. Thus, a 'little big' instrument! A three-string cello (called 'bass violin') existed by 1529 and the word 'violoncello' came into use a century later still. A cello player, Domenico Gabrieli, wrote the first solos about 1675, and a cello-maker in Bologna, Giovanni Battista degli Antoni, contributed

some more in 1687. Its first concertos were by Jaccini in 1701.

∞ **DOUBLE BASS** As the 'bass' of the strings, the cello needed yet lower support, so a bigger instrument was conscripted from the viols to double it an octave below. Hence 'double bass', the only instrument to have retained the sloping shoulders of its viol cousins. Its deep voice is ideal as a foundation for the string section but unsuitable for long solos. Haydn attempted its first (now lost) concerto about 1761 and Vaňhal's of c.1765 is the earliest to have survived.

Violin of 1813 by Panormo. Born in Palermo, Sicily, Vincenzo Panormo moved to London, where he died about 1813. This violin may be the work of his son, Joseph.

OTHER STRINGED INSTRUMENTS

∞ **BARYTON** A rare oddity, remembered chiefly for Haydn's 125 trios, written for the baryton-playing Prince Esterházy. It is a six-stringed bass viol, with further strings (up to 40) running under, and sounding in sympathy with, the bowed strings. A hole in the back of the fingerboard allows the player to insert his left thumb and pluck the sympathetic strings to produce an 'invisible' effect that still tantalizes audiences.

∞ **CIMBALOM** A Hungarian folk instrument consisting of a flat wooden box of strings struck by sticks to produce a jangling, undamped, sound. Kodály used a cimbalom in *Háry János* (1926) and Stravinsky has also scored for it.

∞ **GUITAR** Apparently somewhat younger than the harp, but still emanating from folk roots, the guitar was first given respectability by Mudarra's books of guitar pieces in 1546. It makes rare concert appearances today – although concertos by Rodrigo and Castelnuovo-Tedesco are well known – but Paganini wrote for and played it, and Schumann included it in the first version (1841) of his Symphony No. 4.

∞ **HARP** Like the stringed instruments of the violin family this is probably a development of the hunter's bow, so its origin is undatable. An Egyptian 21-string angle harp, or 'triganon', from c. 1500 BC is preserved in the Louvre Museum, Paris, and pictures of harps date back to 3300 BC. As a folk instrument the harp is widespread and exists in many different designs, but it entered the concert hall only in 1736, when Handel included a concerto in *Alexander's Feast*. The modern 'double-action' Erard pedal harp, with as many as 47 strings, was invented in Paris in 1820.

∞ **LUTE** An obsolescent instrument of folk origin, usually plucked but sometimes bowed, widespread throughout Europe, Asia and Africa in hundreds of styles. Best-known in recitals of ancient music is the round-backed ten-string lute. Bach is the latest composer to have written substantially for it, but some obscure and inconsequential pieces appeared about 1800 and after.

∞ **MANDOLIN** A small lute, occasionally heard in recitals. A few concertos exist, including two by Vivaldi, one for a single mandolin, the other for two. A mandolin has eight strings tuned in pairs identically to the violin.

Strings: Sounds and Ranges

THE VIOLIN IS EASILY THE MOST POPULAR solo string instrument. Hundreds of works have been written for it and it has also been given important solos in such pieces as Rimsky-Korsakov's *Scheherazade* and *Caprice Espagnol* and Vaughan Williams's *The Lark Ascending*. An interesting association is that of the violin with things diabolical. Tartini's violin sonata *The Devil's Trill* is supposed to have been suggested to him by Satan in a dream; Paganini is reputed to have owed his incredible technique to the same figure, and in Saint-Saëns' *Danse Macabre* the Devil plays the violin. All these instances demonstrate the wide versatility of the instrument: from Scheherazade's erotic story-telling to Spanish fiddling; from the gentle song of the skylark to the evil tones

STRING INSTRUMENTS: • TUNING •

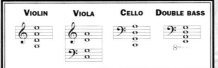

VIOLIN	VIOLA	CELLO	DOUBLE BASS

The above tunings are standard today but have not always been so. Vivaldi and others sometimes called for alternative tuning (*scordatura*) to make the instrument tonally more brilliant or in some other way more suitable for a special occasion, and the tuning of cello and double-bass has undergone many changes in the past. The 'sharp' keys, G, D, A, E, are particularly flattering to the violin because they allow prominent use of the open strings (that is, those not 'stopped' by the fingers).

The lowest note of each instrument of the string family is, of course, dictated by the lowest string (for example, G on the violin), unless the instrument is deliberately mistuned, but the upper limits are dependent upon a player's skill. The highest written violin note is B''''' (in Britten's Violin Concerto, 1939), though 'harmonics' (the gentle laying of a finger on the string to 'half-stop' it) produce a higher effect still. Viola players can in exceptional circumstances reach to about F'''', cellists to about A''' and double-bass players to about E''', though tonal quality is often compromised.

Stringed instruments produce their sound by vibration of the strings. The usual way of achieving this is to draw the resined hair of the bow across the string (*arco*) with the right arm. Steadiness of the arm is vital for even tone. An alternative way is to pluck the string with the fingertip (*pizzicato*), a technique which, if not overused, gives a charmingly light effect. A mute attached to the bridge produces a nasal sound, whether *arco* or *pizzicato*. Occasionally, to produce a grotesque rattling sound, a composer will call for 'col legno' ('with the wood' of the bow), unpopular with players because it can deposit paint from the bow on to the string. Haydn was the first to require *col legno*; Berlioz (*Symphonie fantastique*, 1830) and Holst (*The Planets*, 1916) the most famous. In his *La Battaglia*, Heinrich Biber required paper to be threaded between the strings of a bass viol to imitate the sound of a military drum.

READING THE NOTES

Notes of the chromatic scale are expressed in writing by using the piano keyboard as a reference and taking the octave from middle C to the B above as a starting point. The first C above middle C is noted as C', the next as C'' and so on. The octaves below middle C are noted as C, to B, and C,, to B,, following the same principle.

of Hades. An expert violinist can reproduce all these images by the varied speed and pressure of bow on string, by accent and attack, and by the judicious use or non-use of vibrato applied by the left hand. The instrument itself, in its power, responsiveness, tone colour and evenness

Andrea Amati of Cremona, who invented the modern violin.

The Devil appears to Tartini in a dream and inspires a violin sonata.

throughout its range is, of course, all-important.

Viola and double bass are less versatile, the first having been designed as a filling-in tone-producer between violin and cello in ensembles, the second existing as a necessary underpinning.

The cello is capable of a much wider variety of tone colour and attack. Its richness of tone is its great asset, and when *pizzicato glissando* is applied (the string plucked with the right hand while the left finger slides up or down the string), as in Kodály's Solo Cello Sonata, Op. 8, the effect can imitate a guitar. Earlier, Boccherini, himself a cellist, had directed that the cello be 'strummed' like a guitar to imitate the national instrument of Spain, where he spent much of his working life.

The only other string instrument regularly heard in orchestras is the harp. Its first sonata appeared in 1762, composed by C P E Bach, and Berlioz was the first to include it in a symphony, in 1830, the *Symphonie fantastique.* ♪

• THE VIOLIN MAKERS •

➤ The Amati brothers, Antonio (c. 1540–?) and Girolamo (1561–1630) were sons of the founder of the Cremonese violin-making school, Andrea Amati (b. by 1511–d. before 1580). It seems that Antonio had little to do with the firm after 1588. Girolamo worked on virtually alone and was in turn succeeded by his son Nicola (1596–1684). He refined his father's work, taking in pupils who later became famous, among them Andrea Guarneri (c. 1626–98), and producing his finest instruments during the 1650s and 1670s.

➤ Another pupil of Nicola Amati was Antonio Stradivari (1644–1737), who independently maintained the Cremona violin-making reputation from 1680, going on to produce what experts describe as the world's finest instruments. He made violins, violas, cellos and even a few guitars, of which about 650 instruments are extant, his greatest achievements being the violins he made around 1714. The 'Soil' of that year is owned by Itzhak Perlman and is said to be the finest of all. The 'Alard' of 1715 is hardly inferior to it. The secret of their perfection might lie in the maple or spruce, the water of the area, the varnish or – the latest theory – a paste 'filler' between wood and varnish.

Woodwind: Family Background

MOZART'S 'CLARINET' CONCERTO

∞In 1789 Mozart began a Concerto in G for basset horn but abandoned it, reusing the same material for the Clarinet Concerto in A. This latter was published in 1801 but in a spurious form, for the instrument Mozart wrote for went down to low A, four notes lower than the standard clarinet. Fortunately, a reviewer with access to the original itemized the alterations made to the score. This gave modern musicologists the means to reconstruct the 'Mozart' instrument. What to call it? 'Clarinet' is inaccurate, 'bass clarinet' refers to a different instrument, so 'basset clarinet' ('little bass clarinet') was coined.

APART FROM PERCUSSION, THE WOODWIND group has the longest history of all instruments and, furthermore, the ancestry of each can be traced back to a common origin: a prehistoric person experimenting with a piece of straw or bamboo. At a certain length it would produce a note when blown; cut, it would play a higher note, and the addition of fingerholes along its length would produce yet more.

BASSOON

In the 14th century a multi-folded wind instrument resembling a bundle of sticks was called 'faggot'. The bassoon is still called *fagotto* in Italy, but the early instrument has more recently acquired the unflattering name 'sausage bassoon'. From this inauspicious beginning the bassoon quickly established itself as a necessary foundation of the wind group.

Its development paralleled that of the oboe, but it did not readily lend itself to solo performance, being at first somewhat dull in tone. Vivaldi's 39 concertos represented its early coming of age, and a few years later works by Mozart, Devienne and Weber gave it the occasional chance to shine soloistically, but its main function in the 17th and 18th centuries was to provide sinew to the lower orchestral voices, strengthening the role of the bass viols and double basses.

Often described as the clown of the orchestra for its impressions of portly gentlemen or rude noises, the bassoon can also produce soulful and atmospheric effects. This instrument was made by the famous German firm Heckel.

CLARINET

Towards the end of the 17th century the firm of J C Denner in Nuremberg, experimenting with recorders and shawms, developed a new instrument to occupy a

The Japanese Yamaha company, which made these clarinets, is a relatively recent name in the West but was founded in Japan in 1887.

range above the shawm. Eventually this instrument with a tone like a small natural trumpet acquired the name 'clarinet' ('little clarino') and it is as a trumpet substitute that it may be heard in Vivaldi's oratorios and concertos, pitched in the trumpet key of C. By the end of the 18th century shawms had become obsolete, and larger (that is, lower-pitched) clarinets had been developed to replace them. The smooth lower notes of the clarinet are still referred to as the chalmeau register, chalmeau being an alternative name for the English word shawm.

By the mid-18th century clarinets were current throughout Europe and were in particular vogue in Paris, sometimes replacing oboes in orchestral works. Vivaldi's concertos had treated clarinets like trumpets, allowing them out only in pairs, but by about 1740 solo clarinet concertos were being written by, among others, J M Molter and J Stamitz. Mozart much admired the clarinet's tone ("If only we had clarinets in Salzburg!" he once lamented), wrote important solo works for it and included it in several orchestral pieces.

Steady advancement in the number of keys improved the clarinet's range and tone, and by about 1840 it was ripe for its final major stage of development. Basing his improvements upon Boehm's work on flutes, the instrument-maker Louis-August Buffet introduced many modifications which, with later refinements, resulted in the clarinet of today. Its range of tonal production is extraordinarily broad, a fact exploited by many recent composers. Karlheinz Stockhausen, for example, calls for a rasping flutter-tongue effect, a liquid percussive 'plopping' as the key pads are opened and closed during trills, near-inaudible notes, bird impressions, and so on. The range of the clarinet's family is also wide, from the tiny octave clarinet of the mid-19th century to the subcontrabass instrument of about 1930.

FLUTE

Latin has a word for an early flute made of an alternative material: 'tibia'. It is no accident that this is also the word for the shinbone. Less likely than wood to split or break, bone was an ideal medium for shaping and perforating early flutes. By at least 5,000 years ago it had become an artform, and the recorder is a direct descendant of these early experiments.

The crossflute (held across the mouth rather than vertically) was in existence in China by at least 3,000 years ago and was known in pre-dynastic Egypt; it evolved into the modern orchestral flute through a series of developments and refinements undertaken during a long period of folk use until it entered the orchestra in France in 1681. Within two decades it became widely accepted as a chamber instrument, and concertos began to appear during the 1720s. However, even with the popularity created by King Frederick the Great of Prussia's enthusiasm for the instrument, it was still relatively unsophisticated.

The German jeweller and flautist Theobald Boehm (1794–1881) completely rethought flute design, working from basic acoustic principles. Between 1832 and 1847 he repositioned and greatly enlarged the fingerholes and constructed an entirely new key system. Although Boehm's revolutionary reconstructions were slow to achieve adoption in his home country, they are now accepted worldwide.

A Yamaha flute, the sophisticated product of centuries of development from an instrument once fashioned from a bone.

OBOE

Some oboes may be regarded as imposters in the woodwind family if (like many 'woodwind') made of metal or plastic, but the name itself has a respectable ancestry, being derived from the French 'hautbois' ('high-' or 'loud-wood'). Developed during the Middle Ages from the shawms, the oboe has a plangent two-reed sound that carries over long distances and was used by shepherds and huntsmen before being admitted into the orchestra in France in 1657.

During the 18th century it was reported that the instrument was unduly harsh and "unlovely to the ear", but such stories may be attributed to inexpert handling of a still-developing instrument. A number of virtuoso-composers arose during this time, so the earlier problems (which included oboes so difficult to blow that cups were attached to the instrument to prevent the player's cheeks from bursting) were being overcome. Boehm, when not improving the flute, made changes to the oboe but these were not taken up and the transition to the modern oboe was made by the Trieberts, father and son, in the mid-19th century, and by the Frenchman Apollon Barret (1808–79), who played the oboe in London and published a Method in 1862. Even now there is a distinct difference in sound between the rich, thick tone of German oboes and the thinner, reedy quality favoured in France.

This oboe, made by Nippon Gakki, a division of the Yamaha company, typifies all that is best in modern woodwind design.

Woodwind: Sounds and Ranges

COMPOSERS ARE NOT EAGER TO WRITE concertos for wind soloists. If a gifted virtuoso commissions such a work it will emerge, receive a few playings, achieve a certain popularity, then sink into comparative oblivion. Wind instruments as solo voices do not provoke excitement in concert audiences to the same extent as do violin, cello and piano. They lack the spectacular dimension; more importantly, even the clarinet lacks the range and variety of expression sought by audiences, and solo wind instruments tend to sound insubstantial in a concert hall. For this reason they are much better suited to the chamber. Works such as Mozart's Oboe Quartet sound splendid in a small room. Paradoxically, serenades for all-wind groups (Haydn's wind sextets come to mind) make a most favourable impression in the open air, the medium for which they were originally written. ♪

WOODWIND RANGES

FLUTE The highest of the standard orchestral instruments, the wooden flute is, unlike the other woodwind, held across the player's mouth (hence the old term 'crossflute') and the air inside is set in vibration by the action of the airstream against the edge of the hole. There being no reed, the tone is pure and creamy and notes are selected by a system of keys.

OBOE Compared with the flute, the tone of an oboe is rasping, with a 'sawtooth' configuration to the sound when loud. This is due to the beating of the double reed through which the air travels as it leaves the player's mouth. However, the oboe can be made to produce a quiet and gentle sound when called for. An oboe's tone often approximates that of a human voice. Reeds made of cane were once fishtail-shaped but today are likely to be more straight-sided. A sophisticated key system produces the notes.

CLARINET Widest in both range and dynamics of all modern woodwind, the clarinet's single-reed tone can range from the most romantic cooing to a raucous wail. Constructed in the key of either A or B flat, the clarinet is a 'transposing' instrument (that is, a written C will sound as A on the one; B flat on the other) with a notorious 'break' between high and low registers which can affect tonal quality as the instrument traverses a scale. Skilful players overcome this; some can even produce chords. The clarinet reed is straight-sided and contained within the mouthpiece.

BASSOON The length of tubing necessitates folding the bassoon upon itself to allow the player access to the keys. A double-reed instrument, it has a tonal quality less rasping than that of the oboe because of its lower pitch, but it can produce high and delicate legato sounds, low and loud staccato notes, and much in between. Reeds of cane, with tips measuring only 0.1mm thick, modify the air column before it travels via a bent 'drinking-straw' pipe into the instrument, the notes being controlled by a key system. The player holds the bassoon across his body and to the side.

FLUTE	OBOE	CLARINET IN B FLAT	CLARINET IN A	BASSOON

The smallest woodwind instrument, the piccolo (Italian for 'small'). In common with the triangle, the smallest percussion, it can cut right through the heaviest sound an orchestra can make.

• RARER WIND, FROM HIGH TO LOW •

➤ **Piccolo** The top voice of the woodwind family, sounding an octave above the flute.

➤ **Alto flute** Known, incorrectly, as 'bass flute', this is a low-pitched flute in G which has occasionally been specified by composers. The true bass flute in C sounds an octave below the standard flute. Both instruments display their rich tones best in solo parts.

➤ **Basset horn** A low-pitched clarinet in F, used occasionally by Mozart for its subdued effect.

➤ **Cor anglais** This is neither a horn nor English in origin; the second component of the name probably means 'angled'. A lower relative of the oboe, it is pitched in F.

➤ **Cornett** Unrelated to the bugle-type brass cornet, the cornett is a gracefully curved wooden instrument of the Middle Ages with fingerholes. Its clear, woody tone has recently returned to fashion.

➤ **Saxophone** A brass instrument classified as woodwind due to its having keys rather than valves, a reed mouthpiece, and a bass clarinet-like shape. Developed about 1840 by Adolphe Sax, it entered the orchestra in 1844. Eric Coates's *Saxo Rhapsody* (1937) well displays its solo characteristics.

➤ **Contrabassoon** The elemental vibrations of this instrument were first heard in 18th-century opera to represent thunder, earthquake, and so forth. Its lowest note is an octave below that of the bassoon.

The contrabassoon entered the symphony orchestra only in 1808, when Beethoven included it in his Fifth Symphony.

Brass: Family Background

ACROSS THE BACK OF THE ORCHESTRA, behind woodwind but in front of percussion, sit the brass players, their shiny instruments giving colour contrast. 'Brass' instruments, originally of horn, cane or wood, are today made of several metals, but the golden sheen of many of them justifies maintenance of the group description.

The brass add weight and brilliance to the sound, trumpets and sometimes horns strengthening the higher notes, horns (at other times) and trombones filling the middle, and tuba supplying roughage in the foundations. The highest notes come from trumpets but historically the horns are placed at the top of the brass in musical scores so we shall examine horns first.

HORN AND TRUMPET

Short, slightly curved instruments derived from animal horns in ancient Egypt are referred to as both trumpets and horns, a confusion that continued until the 18th century; even now jazz musicians refer to anything from trumpet to clarinet, via trombone, flugelhorn and saxophone, as 'horn'. Orchestral horns are circular, trumpets are like a flattened 'O', although it was not always so. Generally, horns are at a lower pitch than trumpets. The French for hunting horn is 'tromp'; its diminutive is 'trompette' ('trumpet'), implying close relationship.

An early crescent-shaped horn had, by at least the 16th century, become hoop-shaped, ideal for mounted hunters to wear over their shoulders, while posthorns were tightly wound or long and straight. Horns were first used in opera in Venice in 1639: primitive instruments capable of playing in only one key. 'Crooks' were invented about 1703. These metal tubes were added to the horn, each to allow another key to sound, so a cornist changing key in mid-movement, even up to Beethoven's day, was a protracted and noisy procedure. Before then, the only way to escape from the basic key without changing crooks was to modify certain notes by placing a fist in the bell ('hand-stopping', attributed to A J Hampel about 1760), or by ascending to the top range where available notes were closer together. Realizing this, composers concentrated on the horn's high register and a school of horn virtuosos, many from Bohemia, emerged to play concertos and the breathtaking high parts in opera and symphony.

Various devices, some of amazing complexity, were tried to make the horn more versatile. The breakthrough came in 1815 when Silesian instrument-makers Stolzel and Bluhmel invented a piston valve horn. The double horn arrived in 1865, a design which has been refined to the modern F/B flat horn with four rotary valves.

The first trumpet was an animal horn or a conch shell used by prehistoric man as a signal. Developing in parallel with horns, trumpets became metal and by the 15th century had grown a tuning slide. Trumpets formed part of the very earliest orchestras. Their first sonatas appeared in 1638; their first concertos in 1665.

In 1796 Anton Weidinger added keys to allow chromatic playing (as heard in Haydn's Concerto of that year) and the first valve trumpet was built about 1816. This is virtually the design of today's orchestral trumpet. Traditionally, trumpets and drums were almost inseparable until well into the 19th century.

TROMBONE

When a particularly bright trumpeter devised a slide for his trumpet, some time during the 14th century, and then went on to enlarge the instrument, he invented a new one: the trombone (meaning 'large trumpet'). Meanwhile, the French invented

Alto, tenor and bass trombones, all from the Japanese instrument-makers Yamaha.

A Yamaha trumpet, above, and a modern 'French' horn, left, both capable of producing incisive effects.

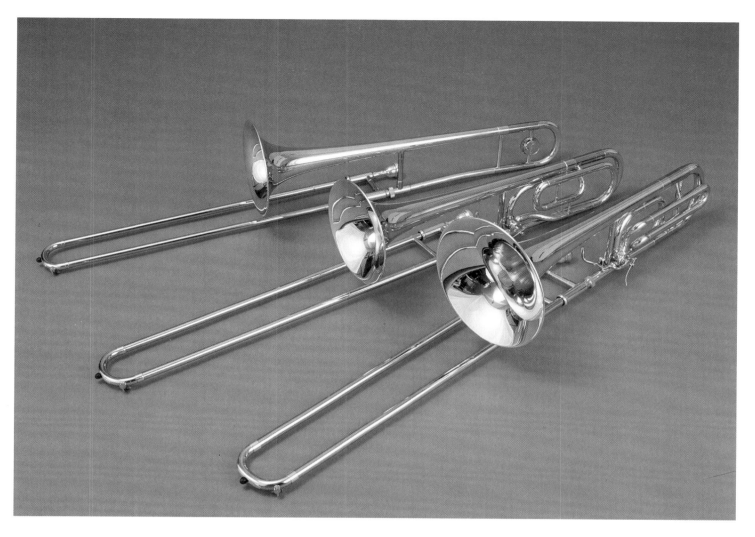

a word for it to describe the fascinating sliding action: *saqueboute* ('pull-push'), and, anglicized, this became the trombone's old name, 'sackbut'. Made in many sizes, some almost as small as trumpets, trombones were used first in church, where their resonant tones added to the gravity of solemn occasions and their tonal freedom meant that they could accompany the key of any anthem sung by the choir.

From church they moved, during the 17th century, to the Italian opera orchestra, providing a strong bassline, and in Bologna they served the same function in the stirring sonatas, symphonies and concertos for trumpets and orchestra in the last decade of that century. Although it was not the first concert symphony to use trombones (that had been in about 1766 in a *Pastoral Symphony* by Leopold Hoffmann), their most memorable early appearance is in the finale of Beethoven's Fifth Symphony (1808) where, together with piccolo and double bassoon, they add enormously to the range, weight and depth of the sound. The trombone was never a popular instrument among writers of concertos. Its first

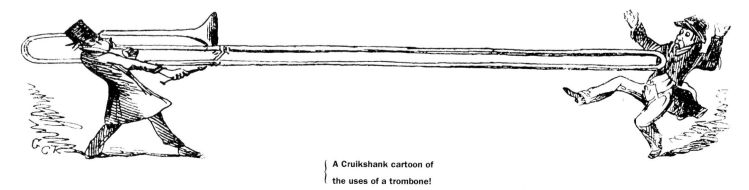

{ A Cruikshank cartoon of
{ the uses of a trombone!

SOUNDS AND RANGES OF THE BRASS FAMILY

HORN The player vibrates the air, using his lips as reeds. The depth of the mouthpiece has a bearing upon the tone, and as the vibrating air passes through the mainly conical tube and out through a large flared bell it is modified into a full and rounded sound. Valves direct the air through selected lengths of tubing to produce different notes, as in the trumpet. An authentic performance of a Mozart Horn Concerto played on a natural horn (that is, one without valves) will illustrate the different tones that are procured by 'hand-stopping'.

TRUMPET As in the rest of the brass, the trumpet's sound is produced by the player vibrating a column of air through a detachable cup-shaped mouthpiece and into the instrument. The trumpet's brilliant tone is the result of the tube being predominantly cylindrical, with a conical configuration only towards the outer end, and a relatively small diameter bell. Handel's *Water Music* Suite in D demonstrates the natural trumpet's sound, Haydn's Concerto in E flat the 'new' (in 1796) notes available on a keyed trumpet.

TROMBONE Sounding like an open-toned horn, the trombone's air column vibrates in a cylindrical tube that opens out conically only as it nears the bell. The player's spectacular push-pull action controls the tube length and therefore the note, and this arrangement of telescopic tubing allows complete harmonic freedom and the easy availability of *glissandi* (sliding from one note to another). For this reason there is no need for valves. Berlioz's *Symphonie funèbre et triomphale* includes a fine trombone solo in the middle movement.

TUBA The largest of the brass family, the tuba gains its deep tone from its wide-bore conical tubing and great size. Valves control the pitch. Because its bell faces upwards rather than towards the audience, a tuba sounds muffled; often it is 'felt' rather than heard, particularly when it is providing the bass notes in a loud orchestral passage. In Ravel's orchestration of Mussorgsky's *Pictures at an Exhibition* a solo tuba represents the approach and passing of a Polish ox-cart, 'bydlo', the instrument's tone ideally conveying the image of heavy solid wooden wheels on gravel.

HORN	TRUMPET	TUBA

TROMBONES	ALTO	TENOR	BASS

concerto was composed in about 1760 by Wagenseil. Nielsen's Flute Concerto (1926) has a prominent trombone solo part, and his Sixth Symphony (1925) exploits its glissando effects in a series of comical yawns. Made today in three sizes (alto, tenor and bass), the trombones have a forceful yet rich and sometimes romantic tone when playing in a group; when underpinned by tuba in an orchestra the effect can be particularly emphatic.

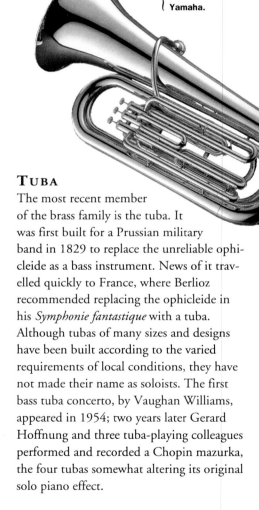

A modern tuba by Yamaha.

TUBA

The most recent member of the brass family is the tuba. It was first built for a Prussian military band in 1829 to replace the unreliable ophicleide as a bass instrument. News of it travelled quickly to France, where Berlioz recommended replacing the ophicleide in his *Symphonie fantastique* with a tuba. Although tubas of many sizes and designs have been built according to the varied requirements of local conditions, they have not made their name as soloists. The first bass tuba concerto, by Vaughan Williams, appeared in 1954; two years later Gerard Hoffnung and three tuba-playing colleagues performed and recorded a Chopin mazurka, the four tubas somewhat altering its original solo piano effect.

WAGNER TUBA

A related instrument to the tuba is the Wagner Tuba, made for that composer by the Parisian firm of Adolphe Sax for performances of *The Ring*. Wagner intended to fill a gap he perceived between horns and trombones, though the gap is not of notes but of tones, the new tubas being 'solemn, dignified and heroic' rather than having the lyrical quality he detected in ordinary tubas. Wagner Tubas have elliptical bodies and relatively small bells. Since Wagner, Richard Strauss and Stravinsky are among those who have written for the instrument.

Dennis Brain, an outstanding horn player who was killed in a motor accident, aged only 36.

RARE ORCHESTRAL BRASS

CORNET 'Authentic' performances of Berlioz's *Symphonie fantastique* include this valved posthorn, which appeared in Paris in 1828; it is also used in Tchaikovsky's *Swan Lake* and Stravinsky's *Petrushka*.

FLUGELHORN The large valved bugle, or flugelhorn (German for 'wing horn', once used by army signallers), is used mainly in jazz and brass bands but is sometimes encountered in the orchestra; for example in Vaughan Williams's Symphony No. 9 (1958).

GARDEN HOSEPIPE One of these made of rubber or perhaps plastic was substituted for an alphorn in Leopold Mozart's *Sinfonia Pastorale* at a Hoffnung Festival concert in 1956. Its inclusion as a brass instrument is justified by the artist who performed on that occasion: horn-player

Vom Kriegsschauplatze in Bayreuth.

Dennis Brain, who, in the interest of tonal quality, used a horn mouthpiece inserted in the hose.

POSTHORN This offshot of the trumpet/horn family was originally used by stage-coach guards to announce the mail. Usually circular, they were sometimes straight; an alternative name is coachhorn. The instrument can be heard in Mozart's *Posthorn* Serenade K320 (1778), and

Wagner, the noise-maker. His brass requirements were a gift for cartoonists.

elsewhere. Once completely 'natural', it has been keyed or valved since the early 19th century. Johann Beer (or Bähr, or Ursus, 1655–1700) wrote a Concerto in B flat for posthorn, hunting horn and strings.

TRUMPETS have been made in sizes ranging from a piccolo B flat instrument, built in Italy around 1960 (about 12 inches/30 cm long), to the large Wagner trumpets of a century earlier. Trumpeter David Mason supplied the obbligato to the Beatles' 'Penny Lane' on a piccolo G trumpet.

• MOZART AND THE CHEESEMONGER •

∞ Horn-player Joseph Leutgeb (1732–1811), with Leopold Mozart's financial aid, set up as a cheesemonger in Salzburg. Wolfgang Mozart met him in 1777 and between 1782 and 1791 wrote several concertos and a horn quintet for him. In the concertos he scattered insults in Italian and German which translate as 'Ass, ox, fool'; 'What a frightful din!'; 'Courage, idiot'; 'Alas!'; and 'It'll soon be over, thank Heaven'. He also instructed Leutgeb to play adagio while the orchestra played allegro, and added confusion by writing in different-coloured inks. One doubts whether Mozart would have written so much fine music for someone he apparently despised. Friendly leg-pulling is more likely.

Percussion

Cymbals, to be clashed together at climaxes or slid against each other for a hissing effect.

AS THE WORD IMPLIES, PERCUSSION instruments are struck. (Technically, hammers hit the strings of a piano but this instrument is treated separately.) Usually seated at the back of an orchestra, the percussionists play a very wide range of instruments, including various drums, gongs, bells, cymbals, triangle, xylophone and sometimes exotic objects such as wood blocks and whip. Percussionists are called upon for any extra effects such as wind machine (not strictly percussion) and glockenspiel, but the commonest percussion instruments, always present in pairs or more, are the timpani.

Percussion history is as long as man's. Cavemen would strike ringing rocks to signal to the tribe, beat rhythm on a log to accompany dancing, and stretch animal skin across the top of a pot to make a

pleasant resonance. This last is the direct ancestor of the kettledrum (hence its name) or timpano, and of the bass drum; also of many smaller drums including the sidedrum. Other than at sacred or solemn occasions, drums have been present at most musical gatherings, and even at wakes the funeral drum would attend. In Beethoven's *Eroica* Symphony slow movement the dragging rhythm of double basses at the start imitates the muffled sound of a funeral drum.

Asia has been the birthplace of countless percussion instruments and, distilled through the Middle East, they created a craze in 18th century Europe, where 'Turkish' instruments – triangle, cymbals,

bass drum – and Turkish accents occur in several Mozart, Haydn and Beethoven works. At this time, 'percussion' usually meant timpani, and their presence in an orchestra, invariably in company with trumpets, added weight to ceremonial pieces. Timpani parts were generally unadventurous, beating simple rhythms, and because the instruments were tuned to one note each, usually the tonic and the fourth below, and could be retuned only with difficulty, they played in the tonic key, contributing only occasional notes that fitted when the music modulated.

Haydn and Beethoven experimented to break free of this tyranny, Haydn by adventurous parts in his late works, Beethoven by allowing freedom to timpani from his First Symphony onwards but most memorably in the *Choral* Symphony (1823). They ram home the recapitulation of the first movement with 37 bars of fortissimo broken only by six sforzando markings, and in the scherzo they break tradition by being tuned in octaves, emphasizing this departure with four solo bars that confirm a new pulse.

Berlioz also experimented with percussion by laying bass drum horizontally, demanding tuned cymbals, calling for timpani to play chords or contradict an orchestra's rhythm. Since his day the 'kitchen department' has been increasingly liberated. Even concertos for percussion have appeared, but audience attention is quickly wearied by unbroken percussive sounds, necessitating the writing of short works with catchy rhythms, and calling on the relieving tones of melodic percussion such as bells, celesta and xylophone. Such attempts prove that percussion is far more effective used sparingly than excessively, a lesson Brahms learnt early in life.

The tubular resonators of this marimba lend the instrument a subtle, seductive tone.

{ Modern Yamaha pedal timpani, capable of wide tonal variety and glissandi. The triangular tuning controls are a refinement that replaces the hit-and-miss process of tuning by ear.

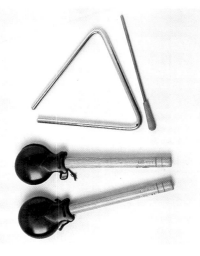

• ORCHESTRAL PERCUSSION •

➤ **Bass drum** A large vertical drum, a member of the so-called 'Turkish' bands but now a regular feature of large scores.

➤ **Castanets** (Spanish for 'chestnut') These are made of nut shells or wood but were originally of gourds. Now essentially Spanish, they contribute local colour in Bizet's *Carmen* (1875).

➤ **Cymbals** Two metal plates clashed together too often in many 19th-century overtures. Modern composers sometimes ask for cymbals to be played with a violin bow. The effect is ghostly.

➤ **Marimba** A xylophone with calabash resonators. The Italian-born American composer Paul Creston (born Giuseppe Guttoveggio) (1906–85) wrote a Marimba Concerto in 1940.

➤ **Sidedrum** A double-headed small drum with wires, or snares, against its lower skin. First used orchestrally by Handel (*Royal Fireworks Music*, 1749), its more recent employment by Carl Nielsen is mentioned elsewhere.

➤ **Temple blocks** Small skull-shaped wooden blocks which Walton used in *Façade* (1923). Related are the Chinese blocks, wooden oblongs whose dry rattle may be heard in Gershwin's Piano Concerto (1925).

➤ **Timpani** Originally with calf-hide heads tuned with keys, modern timpani have plastic heads and pedal tuning. Among works displaying their versatility are Dvořák's *New World* Symphony (1893), near the start, Beethoven's Fourth Symphony (1805), slow movement,

where timpani lead a quiet rhythm, Stravinsky's *Rite of Spring* (1913), with very prominent percussion, Nielsen's Fourth Symphony (*Inextinguishable*, 1916), where two sets do battle with the orchestra, and J C C Fischer's Symphony for Eight Tuned Timpani (c. 1790), a very early experiment.

➤ **Tam tam** A large gong of Pacific origin (hence its Chinese name) struck with soft or hard sticks, stroked with a metal object and so on, according to the composer's whim.

➤ **Triangle** The smallest but most incisive orchestral instrument, its three-sided metal ring struck with a metal beater in, for example, Brahms's Fourth Symphony (1885)

➤ **Tubular bells** Tubes hung from a frame and hit with beaters whose material depends upon the tone quality required. They feature in Tchaikovsky's *1812* Overture (1880), though the composer wanted something less practicable: "all the bells of Moscow".

➤ **Turkish crescent** A tall frame hung with bells and jingles, of Middle Eastern origin but heard in Berlioz's *Symphonie funèbre et triomphale* (1840).

➤ **Vibraphone** A xylophone with tube resonators and revolving flaps to produce the vibrant effect. Britten used one in his *Spring Symphony* (1949)

➤ **Xylophone** (from Greek 'xylon', 'phone', meaning 'woodsound') A framework of wooden slats strxuck with wooden beaters. Its dancing skeleton effect occurs in Saint-Saëns's *Danse macabre* (1874) and *Carnival of the Animals* (1886).

Keyboard: Family Background

BIBLICAL REFERENCES TO A TEN-STRING (one for each Commandment) plucked instrument designed to accompany the psaltery may refer to a harp, but the word psaltery came to be applied to a box of strings that were plucked by fingertips or plectra. Originally placed vertically like a harp, in time the psaltery was laid flat, and a keyboard was introduced which sounded the strings by an ingenious lift-and-release mechanism. These instruments became the virginals and harpsichord family. A related instrument is the clavichord, in which the strings are sounded by metal blades which stay in contact while the key is depressed.

HARPSICHORD

A study of acoustics shows that eight absolutely pure rising notes do not create a perfect octave, and, for example, B sharp in one scale does not precisely equate with C flat in another. To satisfy these scientific requirements keyboards would need at least 21 notes to each octave, so 'equal temperament' was introduced whereby slight adjustments were made in tuning to force B sharp to equal C flat, G sharp to equal A flat, and so on. That made seven basic notes (C to B, the white notes on the piano) and five 'accidental' notes (C sharp, E flat, F sharp, A flat, and B flat, the black notes), that is, 12 notes to the octave. Bach beautifully illustrated the principle in his *Wohltemperierte Clavier* ('Well-tempered Keyboard'). The keyboard he referred to was that of the harpsichord.

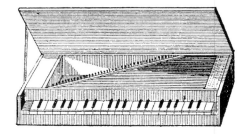

The earliest harpsichord (which would have sounded out of tune to today's 'tempered' ears) was an invention of Hermann Poll, active in Padua in 1397. From the beginning the harpsichord was a popular domestic instrument and manuscript music for it was soon in circulation. However, harpsichord music was considered too frivolous for the expenditure of the considerable skill that was required at the time for printing, this being reserved for sacred music. By the mid-17th century, though, printers and

• THE KEYBOARD FAMILY •

> **Celesta** Invented in Paris in 1886, this piano-type instrument replaces strings with metal plates and resonators.

> **Clavichord** An oblong box with internal strings running across and behind the keyboard. Sound is produced when a metal blade ('tangent') strikes a string from below, the point of impact determining the note. The non-sounding portion of the string is damped by a cloth pad. The extremely quiet and subtle sound may be modified by shaking the finger on the key.

> **Glockenspiel** Operated from a keyboard, hammers strike rows of metal plates. This older version has given way to an open type where the plates are struck with hand-held mallets; the latter is more properly a percussion instrument.

> **Harpsichord** Angular in shape but otherwise resembling a piano, the harpsichord has strings that are plucked by a rising quill which then drops back silently past the string. Early harpsichords had no control over the strings' bell-like tones but modern instruments have many refinements such as swell devices and electronic amplification. There may be one, two or three keyboards, and several stops to modify the tone quality.

> **Organ** Organs have up to five keyboards, plus pedals, and direct air streams into pipework to produce notes. Their tones are modified by

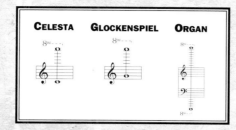

stops which can number over 100. An organ can produce the widest range of dynamic of any instrument, from whisper to thunder, plus many additional effects such as bells, whistles and even imitation percussion.

> **Spinet** A single-manual harpsichord, rectangular, triangular or perhaps pentangular in shape, usually with the strings running at an angle relative to the keyboard. Its harpsichord-like tone is small, making it well suited to domestic use.

> **Virginals** An early harpsichord with one keyboard set into the longer side of a rectangular box, the strings running from left to right. Its tone is less powerful and less varied than that of a harpsichord.

ORGAN

Probably the most dramatic evolution to have taken place in the world of musical instruments concerns the organ. In its most primitive form as the panpipes (derived from a bundle of humble oat stalks) it is a hand-held instrument blown from the lips. At the other end of the scale is a monster organ (built in the Wanamaker Store, Philadelphia, between 1911 and 1930) with 30,067 pipes, the longest of which measures 64 feet (19.5 m). Compared to the delicate, almost whispering, tones of the panpipe, an organ's volume can equal that of six American locomotive whistles, as may be experienced when the ophicleide stop is operated on the Auditorium Organ, Altantic City. This organ is said at one time to have been capable of equalling the volume of 25 brass bands.

Bach's massive volumes of organ works lend themselves to similarly massive treatment but still sound best on smallish baroque organs. Since then, Liszt, Franck and Widor have contributed valuable solo organ works, and Bruckner, an organist, allowed the organ's noble tones to invade his purely orchestral symphonies. Recent organ concertos are rare: of those that exist, Poulenc's (1938) is the best-known. ♪

composers were producing suites and dance music in abundance.

Domenico Scarlatti wrote at least 555 sonatas for harpsichord; meanwhile, it was entering opera house and concert hall as a continuo instrument. It was not given a concerto until Bach wrote a prominent part for it in his *Brandenburg* Concerto No. 5 (before 1721) and arranged a violin concerto for harpsichord in 1733. His son Carl Philipp Emanuel produced the first original harpsichord concerto that same year.

The harpsichord has enjoyed renewed exposure in the 20th century: De Falla (in 1926) and Frank Martin (1952) are among those who have written concertos for it. It also features in some recent symphonies.

{ Alexandre Guilmant at the Cavaillé-Coll organ of the Trocadéro, Paris, c. 1908. Aristide Cavaillé-Coll made great strides in organ development, and Guilmant composed eight organ sonatas.

{ The harpsichord, a workhorse instrument of the 18th century, seeing service for solo, chamber and concert use.

Keyboard: The Piano

AN INSTRUMENT CONSISTING OF A SQUARE, rectangular or trapeze-shaped flat wooden box of strings that were struck by sticks was in existence centuries ago – perhaps as early as the 12th century. It was called 'dulcimer' (from the Latin *dulce melos*, meaning 'sweet song') and was widely found from central Europe to Japan. In the 17th century, Bartolomeo Cristofori, working in his harpsichord workshop in Florence, was seeking ways to vary the volume of plucked harpsichord strings. He remembered the dulcimer's ability to vary its volume according to the force of the strike, and he experimented on his harpsichords.

By 1700 he had built his 'arpicimbalo'. Subsequent models, which could indeed

play both loud and soft ('forte' and 'piano') gave a name to the new invention: 'fortepiano', later 'pianoforte'. Unlike the harpsichord, the piano responded to varied

pressure of the fingers upon the keys.

Doubtful about its qualities, composers awaited the newcomer's success in a world where the harpsichord dominated instrumental music. In 1732 Lodovico Giustini published 12 *Sonate da Cimbalo . . . di martelletti*, literally 'Sonatas for harpsichord . . . with hammers', the very first music specifically for the piano. The first reference to a public performance of a piano concerto dates from 1763, when J B Schmidt played an unidentified work in Vienna. During that decade the piano became immensely popular in Britain.

To preserve the strings, the hammers were covered in a soft material (usually leather) which imparted a dull sound in the low and middle registers. Piano construction was constantly improving, and improvements accelerated as concert halls grew in size and composers became more demanding. By 1800 it was clear that composers much preferred the piano to the harpsichord for its wider range of expression and greater power. Beethoven's sonatas, written between about 1783 and 1822, illustrate not only his compositional development but also the ever-greater

A Steinway 'baby grand' piano, which was first introduced in spring 1879 so that an imposing horizontal piano to fit smaller rooms might replace the upright models.

An early 19th-century scene, *A Morning at Mrs Ingram's,* shows a typical parlour party with (presumably) Mrs Ingram at the piano.

refinements available on the piano, not least its widening range of notes.

In domestic situations the piano was proving popular, but small rooms demanded less space-greedy instruments. So-called 'square pianos' (actually rectangular) took less room, while the 'giraffe piano' needed even less floorspace but required much height because it resembled a grand piano stood on end. The first upright 'parlour piano' was made in Germany about 1770 and this became the chief means of providing home musical entertainment during the Victorian era and for several decades of the 20th century until the gramophone ousted it.

Meanwhile, the 'concert grand' acquired an iron frame for added strength and rigidity to withstand higher string tensions and temperature variations. The first iron frames appeared in America in 1825 and were universal by mid-century.

The popularity of the piano is reflected in its sales. In Britain, one of the most prolific piano manufacturing countries of the time, makers were selling 450 pianos of all types per week in 1850, many of them to private homes. From about 1930 the ratio of concert to domestic instruments was reversed. Bösendorfer, a leading maker which sold only four pianos in its first year (1828), sold 360 in 1900, mainly to private individuals; in 1990 the total was 600, mostly for concert and recital use. With prices topping £175,000 ($290,000) piano-selling continues to be big business.

Modern technology has made an impact on the piano, as on everything else. Optically connected computers can register every note and nuance, then replay it to the artist as it would be heard by the audience. This is of enormous help to both professional pianist and student. Furthermore, a live recital may be registered digitally and used for issue in a recording completely free of audience or traffic noise.

Early piano manufacture was far from standardized. There were many different 'actions' for striking the strings; hammers might be tipped with felt, leather or some other material; Viennese and German instruments were admired at first for their clear tone and delicate touch but became less favoured during the 19th century against advances elsewhere; and the Italian models are reported to have been heavy to play. In continental Europe there were more tone-varying devices than in England.

The modern piano still varies from maker to maker, while following similar specifications. Artists have their strong preferences: some will swear by Bechstein, others shun Steinway in favour of Bösendorfer or vice versa, and the relatively

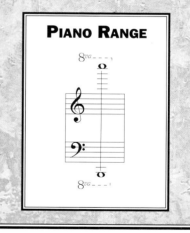

SOME PIANO TYPES

➤ **Baby grand** A small grand piano (that is, horizontal as opposed to upright) suitable mainly for domestic use.

➤ **Fortepiano** Early name for the pianoforte.

➤ **Grand piano** A large horizontal piano for concert performance. The first use of the word 'grand' in connection with pianos was in a Stodart instrument of 1777.

➤ **Pianino** A very small upright piano for use in small apartments. An even smaller version, the pianette, is sometimes encountered.

➤ **Player piano, or pianola** An automatic instrument in which holes in a roll of perforated paper control the hammers. The player-piano's greatest vogue occurred during the 1920s, mainly in America.

➤ **Square piano** A long rectangular instrument with the keyboard set in one long side. The strings run left to right. As 18th-century domestic instruments they were extremely popular, and in America they maintained their popularity into the 20th century, often growing to enormous sizes and with refinements similar to those of a grand piano.

PIANO RANGE

new Japanese instruments (such as Yamaha) also have their following. Furthermore, a piano that responds well to Beethoven's music may be unsuitable for Ravel, and some pianists choose to alternate between instruments depending on the repertoire they are playing. ♪

A modern Yamaha upright, descendant of countless instruments that were once to be found in every middle-class home.

New Waves: Electronics

ELECTRONICS ENTERED MUSIC AS EARLY AS 1906, when the Canadian inventor Thaddeus Cahill introduced his 200-ton Telharmonium to New York audiences. Then, in 1913, Luigi Russolo invented instruments to which he gave names such as cracklers, scapers and exploders, some of them being electrically operated. Russolo's first 'noise concert' was given in March 1914 to an audience noisier than the instruments. L S Termin's Etherophone (1920) produced noises when the operator waved his hands near an aerial, and several related instruments appeared prior to the notorious *musique concrète* movement of 1948. Pierre Schaeffer and Pierre Henry produced the ambitious *Symphonie pour un homme seul* two years later. It used taped sounds of footsteps, voices shouting, humming and conversing, locked-groove 78rpm records, prepared piano and so forth, and manipulated them into often unrecognizable effects. The idea was to produce sounds and effects for documentary and drama programmes for Schaeffer's employer, Radio-diffusion Télévision Française. Other broadcasting organizations followed in America, Italy, Japan and Poland, and in London the BBC's Radiophonic Workshop was founded by Desmond Briscoe, Dick Mills and Phil Young in 1958.

By this time the concept of producing music entirely by means of electronics was well established. Electronic music is more reliable and easier to work with than the bits of tape employed by *musique concrète*. In 1951 the first electronic music studio was founded by Cologne Radio and Herbert Eimert; music by Eimert, Krenek and Stockhausen was issued on commercial discs three years later.

Computers were still in their infancy but American research was proceeding apace. In association with Bell Telephone Laboratories, music by J R Pierce, M V Matthews and D Lewin, played by an IBM 7090 computer and digital-to-sound transducer, was issued on disc in 1962. This remarkable experiment proved that computers were capable of imitating musical instruments acceptably and the human voice comically, though the intention was serious.

Such music is carefully prepared in the studio before being presented to an audience. Risk is introduced in live electronics, as in Steve Reich's *Pendulum Music* (1968), in which three microphones are suspended above loudspeakers to which they are connected via an amplifier. By swinging

A Yamaha synthesizer. The tones produced when the keys are depressed are varied by the controls.

Lev Termin playing the etherophone or theremin, the instrument he invented.

• SWITCHED-ON BACH •

Sinette Martenot, sister of Maurice, inventor of the ondes martenot.

the microphones, unpredictable feedback is produced, ending only when the microphones cease to swing and the feedback is faded out. With the exercise of a little ingenuity anyone can play with such electro-acoustics, but it can hardly be said to advance the art of music.

Composer Malcolm Clarke collaborating with engineer Brian Hodgson of the BBC Radiophonic Workshop.

More promising are synthesizers, now extremely sophisticated. First introduced by Dr Robert Moog in the United States in 1965 and developed from earlier electronic instruments and the electronic organ, synthesizers can now convincingly reproduce any orchestral instrument through their digital circuitry, as well as creating any sound imaginable. Used extensively in the making of pop and rock recordings, such makes as Yamaha, Technics and Kurzweil machines even relieve the listener of the ruthless 'drum-machine' effects of early rock by introducing minimal variations of rhythm and touch to emulate human performance.

It seems that synthesizers are so versatile (though they are still, rather quaintly, advertised as 'electronic organ' or 'electronic piano') that musicians are in danger of being made redundant. Using a synthesizer, a composer can re-create the sound of any instrument or group, overlay it numerous times, then save and reproduce the result at will. Effects unobtainable by live musicians can be manufactured: extremely rapid note repetitions, unnatural instrumental ranges, 'impossible' combinations are all now possible. But for all the synthetic imitation of sounds and the 'human factor', the real human touch in performance, differences in interpretation between artists and between two performances by the same artist, and the feeling of spontaneity, will survive in serious music, if nowhere else. ♪

SOME ELECTRONIC INSTRUMENTS

Etherophone See theremin, below

Ondes martenot Maurice Martenot called his invention 'ondes musicales' (musical waves) when he introduced it in 1928. A successful and effective instrument consisting of a piano-type keyboard controlling an oscillator, it was memorably used by Messiaen in the *Turangalila* Symphony (1948); Varèse's *Equatorial* includes it, though it was originally scored for two theremins instead.

Synthesizer Morton Subotnik composed several works for synthesizer, notable among them being *Silver Apples of the Moon*, commissioned by Nonesuch Records, New York, in 1966.

Telharmonium An early instrument (1906) that used electromagnets to imitate musical tones.

Little else is known about it, apart from its extraordinary weight (200 tons), and the fact that it disappeared before World War I.

Theremin Invented in 1920 by Lev Termin and called at first the etherophone, its whip antenna induces amplified sounds when the player's hand approaches it, and pedals alter the volume. A F Pashchenko's *Symphonic Mystery* (1924) calls for the theremin but the instrument is better known for music-hall performances. Termin, who adopted the name Theremin, died in November 1993, aged 97.

Trautonium Invented by F A Trautwein in 1930, this produces notes by electrical contacts between wire and a metal rail. Hindemith wrote a *Konzertstück* for trautonium and strings in 1931.

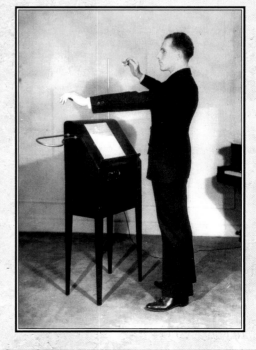

The Voice

Individual singers may get the loudest applause, but the most sublime moments in opera are often ensembles.

The sextet from Donizetti's *Anna Bolena*, with Joan Sutherland, or (below) the finale of Act IV of *Le nozze di Figaro*.

*V*OCAL TECHNIQUE HAS BEEN THE SUBJECT *of hundreds of books, and the ways and eccentricities of voice teachers the butt of jokes for centuries. Many great singers who have turned to coaching after their retirement from the stage or concert platform have been found wanting as teachers, generally only able to teach other people to sing in the same fashion that they did. Tuition for singers, like that for dancers and athletes, is mostly a matter of dedicated application of self-discipline, learning ways to sustain strength and regulate breathing, as well as undertaking general studies in music. Those singers who have also studied a musical instrument tend to find their careers easier to sustain. The Polish soprano Marcella Sembrich (1858–1935), whose career lasted over 40 years, was also an accomplished violinist and pianist. Singing is such an intensely personal activity that no two singers will take the same approach and the problems which each encounters will be slightly different.*

IN THE 19TH CENTURY, SEVERAL SCHOOLS of vocal training were widely held to be successful, especially those started by Manuel Garcia, a colleague of Rossini, whose pupils included his own daughters, the famous prima-donnas Maria Malibran (1808–36) and Pauline Viardot (1821–1910). The tenor Jean de Reszke (1850–1925) had a famous singing school in Paris. His 'method', which was mostly intense coaching based on certain arias from operas which he would encourage his pupils to sing day after day until they had perfected them, was augmented by exercises for basic technique in staccato, pianissimo, fortissimo and breathing exercises for the diaphragm. One of his most famous pupils was Dame Maggie Teyte (1888–1976), who maintained that stamina was the main gift of de Reszke's tuition: "How is the beautiful, natural quality to be developed and maintained?" she wrote. "How is it to survive the stress and worry of a professional career?"

It is often said that one damaging experience can ruin a singer's voice for life. An example of this is Dame Nellie Melba's unwise decision, never repeated, to sing the role of Brünnhilde in Wagner's *Siegfried*. Although the notes were well within her range, the power expected of a Wagnerian singer in this opera was outside her scope. She strained her vocal cords and later in life still suffered attacks of bleeding in the throat as a result of the vocal nodules she developed – like a recurring wound.

All the natural ills and stresses that befall a human body will automatically affect the voice. In particular the changes in a woman's body at the onset of the menopause can have a harmful effect on the voice, especially if they are ignored. Just as an older athlete has to judge a race very carefully, and conserve strength which was once there in plenty, so the older singer must learn how to avoid exhaustion, and especially to discard roles or songs that have a detrimental effect. ♪

RANGES OF VOICE TYPES

The following provide an indication only of the ranges found within each voice category. There are always voices that defy categorization by having a narrow or wider compass than the norm. The celebrated dramatic soprano Anja Silja, for example, at one point in her career claimed three whole octaves, a range exceeding that of most coloraturas.

BARITONE AND BASS

BASSO CANTANTE **BASSO PROFUNDO**

BASS-BARITONE **BARITONE**

TENOR

TENOR **HELDEN-TENOR**

COUNTER-TENOR

SOPRANO AND CONTRALTO

CONTRALTO **FALCON AND MEZZO-SOPRANO**

SOPRANO **COLORATURA**

• VOCAL TECHNIQUES •

➢ **Falsetto** The use of an exaggeratedly high voice, usually by a male singer, to achieve a comic or sometimes childish or effeminate effect. Counter-tenors are sometimes called falsettists.

➢ **Head voice** Whether applied to a male or female voice, this term generally refers to notes in the upper part of the voice, taken *piano* or as softly as possible. Certain notes are sometimes described as being 'floated', implying an effect in which the tone is extremely pure, using little air. The French soprano Emma Calvé had something she called her 'fourth voice', which can be heard on one or two of the recordings she made in the 1900s. The sound seems to come suddenly from nowhere; this technique was taught to Calvé by one of the last castrati, Domenico Mustapha.

➢ **Middle voice** The natural part of a singer's voice. The term *tessitura* applies generally to compositions, meaning that certain roles have a 'texture', and that they will therefore suit a particular voice whose middle range corresponds to that of the part.

➢ **Chest voice** The opposite of head voice, generally implying a note or phrase sung with full volume in the lowest part of the singer's range. Singers are referred to as 'abusing the chest register' when this vehement sound is used higher in the voice. The Italian *verismo* operas with melodramatic scenes often provide encouragement for sopranos to use these chest tones for exciting, dramatic purpose, but it is also considered detrimental to vocal health.

➢ **Mixed voice** Meaning the use of the chest voice in the upper range.

➢ **Vibrato** This literally means to vibrate the vocal cords to achieve an intense effect. An alternation of two distinct notes, achieved rapidly in succession, to produce a 'trill' is a separate part of the florid singer's technique. The vibrato or tremolo should generally only be used for effect, but since many voices are naturally produced with a vibrato, it can be accepted as part of the singer's personality. When it leads to an inability to hold the pitch, it is disparagingly referred to as a wobble. Traditionally, voices with no apparent vibrato, such as a boy treble, are taken to be 'pure' sounding, and those with a heavy vibrato are used to depict age and sometimes anger.

➢ **Half-voice** Sometimes called 'white voice', in which a singer deliberately blocks the flow of air to achieve a whispered or eerie effect. Sometimes, as in Schubert's song *Der Erlkönig*, this can prove unintentionally comic.

➢ **Sprechgesang** A German term, meaning speaking-singing. It is used in certain passages in opera, and especially in musical theatre works such as Brecht and Weill's *Threepenny Opera*, when a singer uses a speaking voice, although generally keeping within the rhythm of the song or musical accompaniment, and returns to the main melody without losing the musical thread.

➢ **Recitative** A term in Italian opera, implying the linking passages between arias and ensembles, where one or more characters may be singing, but generally in the middle of the voice. There is often an introductory recitative before an aria, which may well contain brilliant passages, with high notes and coloratura, but outside the main framework of the aria.

The Voice: Soprano

IN GREEK AND NORSE MYTHOLOGY IT IS the voice of a woman – singing soprano – which is capable of enticing and bewitching all who hear it. Though no music from these ancient times exists, such mythology tells us that it was the soprano voice that was valued above all.

This preference has remained more or less constant throughout history. Even in all-male religious communities, the boy soprano voice was so highly valued that it became necessary (because of the Vatican bar on women singing in church) and desirable to preserve it artificially (see page 203). With the flowering of opera in Italy in the 1600s, and especially because of the great roles written for sopranos by Monteverdi, the soprano became the most important vocal category in music for the theatre.

The term prima-donna, which merely means first lady, gradually grew to have overtones of characterful, often hysterical behaviour, as much because of the highly dramatic music written for the soprano voice as for the stories about the off-stage

Mirella Freni, the ideal lyric as Mimi in Puccini's *La bohème*. The heavy orchestral texture of Puccini's music makes this role potentially hazardous for the voice.

attitudes of the female stars. Until the Restoration, female performers on the stage had been greatly frowned upon in England (though never specifically outlawed), but in the era of Handel the cult of the prima-donna took control. Because many roles were written for male (castrato) sopranos, it also became fashionable for women to appear in male costume, a tradition which has continued in all theatre.

The majority of opera roles in the 18th and 19th centuries were written for specific artists, taking their particular abilities into consideration – for instance, Caterina Cavalieri, for whom Mozart composed the role of Constanze in *Die Entführung aus dem Serail*, and Rossini's favourite soprano (later his wife) Isabella Colbran, for whom he composed ten operas, were singers of great power and agility. Subsequent inter-preters of the roles written for them are often ill-equipped to attempt all the vocal feats of which the creators must have been capable.

The differentiation between soprano and mezzo-soprano was not acknowledged until later in the 19th century, so that many

Maria Callas (1923–77), the most famous dramatic soprano of modern times as Cherubini's *Medea*, a role which has had few great interpreters because of its extreme vocal demands. Callas was one of the few.

• SOPRANO VOICE TYPES •

The demands made upon the voice by different composers, usually taking into consideration the artists who were going to sing their music, can make some roles seem as if they were written for a lighter voice, when in fact it is only one passage that calls for the agility associated with a coloratura soprano. Examples of this are Verdi's Gilda in *Rigoletto* and Violetta in *La traviata*, both of whom have very florid music in places, but elsewhere are expected to sing in a dramatic, much fuller voice than the average coloratura can muster.

➤ **Coloratura** This literally means to colour the voice, and the music, with decorations. Traditionally coloraturas have lighter, thinner voices, and can sing ideally as high as F above the treble stave (as in the arias for the Queen of the Night in Mozart's *Die Zauberflöte*). There have been sopranos who can sing right up to the C above this, but they are often termed 'freak voices'. Famous coloratura roles include Donizetti's *Lucia di Lammermoor*, Bellini's Elvira in *I puritani* (both with celebrated 'mad scenes'), Marguerite de Valois in Meyerbeer's *Les Huguenots*, and Zerbinetta in Richard Strauss's *Ariadne auf Naxos*.

➤ **Lyric soprano** Perhaps the most 'natural' female voice. Many lyric sopranos have difficulty with the notorious higher notes C and B flat, with which composers are pleased to award them at climactic moments. Mimi in Puccini's *La bohème*, Pamina in Mozart's *Die Zauberflöte*, the title role in Massenet's *Manon*, and Marguerite in Gounod's *Faust* are all lyrical roles.

➤ **Soubrette** A lighter lyric soprano, sometimes with coloratura. Zerlina in Mozart's *Don Giovanni*, Despina in *Cosi fan tutte* (also by Mozart) and light roles such as Oscar in Verdi's *Un ballo in maschera* and Adele in Johann Strauss's operetta *Die Fledermaus* are usually termed soubrette parts.

➤ **Spinto** Although usually applied to Italian tenors, this term is often used for lyric sopranos who have extra power and can extend into dramatic roles. Examples would be the title role in *Madama Butterfly* (Puccini), Leonora in *La forza del destino* (Verdi) and some of the *bel canto* parts, such as Giulietta in Bellini's *I Capuletti e i Montecchi*.

➤ **Dramatic soprano** A full dramatic soprano who can take on the heaviest roles of Wagner, Verdi and Strauss is a rarity. Thus these roles are usually divided up, the heavier Verdi parts (the title role in *Aida*, Amelia in *Un ballo in maschera*, Elena in *Les vêpres siciliennes*) often going to lyric sopranos who can extend themselves, and the Wagner roles (Brünnhilde, Isolde, Kundry) sometimes being taken by mezzo-sopranos with extra power in their high notes. A few sopranos in the history of opera have confounded critics by singing everything from the highest coloratura to the heaviest Wagner roles (for example, Lilli Lehmann, Maria Callas and Anja Silja). Twentieth-century opera has made different demands on the soprano voice, and such roles as Marie in Alban Berg's *Wozzeck* and the title-role in the American composer Carlisle Floyd's *Susannah* (1955) pose new problems.

roles that were termed soprano before 1850 are now what we would call mezzo or even contralto roles. In the so-called *bel canto* repertory of operas by Bellini and Donizetti and many of the early roles in works by Verdi, a great deal of florid music, employing trills, runs, and the possibility of adding new variations and improvisation, led to the sharp division of sopranos into dramatic, lyric and coloratura.

With the influence of grand opera as it was performed in Paris during the 1840s and into the1860s, a fashion for larger orchestras and bigger choruses influenced composers such as Meyerbeer and later Berlioz, Gounod and, especially, Wagner to write for bigger, dramatic voices. Such parts as Fidés in Meyerbeer's *Le prophète* (1849), Cassandre in Berlioz's *Les Troyens* and Wagner's Brünnhilde in *Der Ring des Nibelungen* and Isolde in *Tristan und Isolde* are composed for dramatic sopranos of a type – to judge from the music written – not known before the 19th century.

By the end of the 19th century, though Verdi and later Puccini continued to compose soprano roles in operas for typically lyrical Italian voices, the fashion for Wagner's music encouraged singers to over-extend their range and led swiftly to an age of criticism in which the old *bel canto* operas were often dismissed. Even Puccini wrote for Wagnerian-style voices in *La fanciulla del West* (1910), and the operas of Richard Strauss, Berg and Korngold all call for *hoch-dramatische* voices. ♪

The great Wagnerian soprano Kirsten Flagstad (1895–1962), as Brünnhilde in *Die Walküre*.

The Voice: Mezzo and Contralto

THE CONTRALTO VOICE IS THE RAREST OF all female voice types and has thus at different times in musical history been the most valued – the equivalent of the high, heroic tenor, the rarest natural male voice. Strangely, this lower female voice has inspired composers to both sensual and sinister music. Although in many operas it is a low female voice that is used to depict an older woman or a villainess, in many cases the deeper-voiced female is taken to be the more erotic voice – Dalilah in Saint-Saëns' *Samson et Dalilah* is a good example.

Rossini, Berlioz, Brahms and 20th-century music-theatre composers such as Kurt Weill, Josef Kosma and Luciano Berio are among the composers who have valued the low female voice above others. The distinction between contralto, mezzo-soprano and low sopranos (singers who have begun their careers singing in the high soprano range but whose voices have 'shortened' with age so that they only use their low notes) has never been altogether clear. Before the 19th century the term mezzo-soprano does not appear to have been in use; as the century progressed composers seemed to demand a greater range from their singers and in late 19th century opera especially there are example of roles which were originally listed as soprano, but which seem much better suited to the voice of a true mezzo or even a contralto with a greater range.

The low female voice has been especially admired in England and Spain. Though it would be tempting to say that this has something to do with the way language is used, in Spain it seems more likely to derive from the influence of Moorish music, and in England from the great cathedral tradition of male alto singing. Handel's operas composed for London contain particularly rich music for the contralto voice, as can be heard in modern performances by singers such as Marilyn Horne and Janet Baker.

In Spain, to judge from contemporary accounts of singers like La Caramba (1751–87) who specialized in Spanish traditional songs (*seguidillas*) and dances (*tonadillas*), the lower part of the voice was particularly admired. Twentieth-century

• MEZZO AND CONTRALTO VOICE TYPES •

➤ **Contralto** Originally meaning a low female or male (castrato) voice, the word contralto has come to be applied to female singers, generally with a range going down to G below the stave. Few opera roles are designated specifically for contralto, but famous ones include Erda in Wagner's *Der Ring des Nibelungen*, Ulrica in Verdi's *Un ballo in maschera*, Klytemnestra in Strauss's *Elektra* and Lucretia in Britten's *The Rape of Lucretia*, the last composed for Kathleen Ferrier.

➤ **Mezzo-soprano** – a term not used in Mozart's time, although such roles as Dorabella in *Così fan tutte*, Cherubino in *Le nozze di Figaro* and Sesto in *La clemenza di Tito* (composed for the castrato Bedini) are always taken by mezzos today. Rossini composed many of his most famous roles for mezzos – Rosina in *Il barbiere di Siviglia*, Angelina in *La Cenerentola* and Isabella in *L'Italiana in Algeri* – and many operas of the mid-19th

century seem to have been composed for singers who today we would call mezzos, such as Maria Malibran, Rosine Stolz and Célestine Galli-Marié, the first Carmen.

➤ **Falcon** Named after the French singer Cornélie Falcon (1814–97), who created such roles as Rachel in Halévy's *La Juive* and Valentine in Meyerbeer's *Les Huguenots* ; a lower soprano, especially in French opera, is still called after her.

➤ **Diseuse** A term originally used for popular Parisian singers who mixed speech and song seamlessly in dramatic narrative *chansons* (two of the most famous being Yvette Guilbert and Eugénie Buffet), it has come to be used for any singer who employs spoken words within a piece, sometimes to avoid high notes that are out of reach, sometimes for dramatic effect. They are inevitably lower-voiced singers, for example Lemper and Milva, who consequently encounter problems in ensemble passages.

Brigitte Fassbaender as Octavian in Richard Strauss's *Der Rosenkavalier*, the best of all trouser roles. The role can be sung by soprano or mezzo. Few in either category have portrayed the character as affectingly as Fassbaender.

{ **Kathleen Ferrier (1912–53) as Lucretia in Britten's *The Rape of Lucretia*, a role she created in 1947.**

Spanish mezzos like Conchita Supervia (1895–1936) and Teresa Berganza have helped to revive interest in the vast literature of early Spanish song.

Because of the rarity of the contralto voice, composers have been slow to write music calling especially for it. Dame Clara Butt (1872–1936) was without question the most celebrated British contralto of her

time. Elgar composed *Sea Pictures* for her, and the image of her dressed as Britannia singing 'Land of Hope and Glory' has entered British folklore.

Mezzo-sopranos and sopranos have continued to vie for the position of prima-donna in operas such as Verdi's *Macbeth*, Bizet's *Carmen* and Strauss's *Der Rosenkavalier* in which the main soprano roles can be taken by mezzo or soprano. Generally, though, there are far fewer leading roles for mezzos and for this reason some singers will choose to push their voices

up in order to extend their repertoire and savour the rewards that come with soprano territory; the American mezzos Grace Bumbry and Shirley Verrett are two recent examples.

In the fields of music theatre and cabaret the free-form expression available to singers, and the comparative indifference of audiences to complete accuracy, has made such low-voiced singers as Lotte Lenya, Marlene Dietrich, Pearl Bailey, Juliette Greco, Ethel Merman and Lee Wiley among the most admired vocalists of the 20th century. ♪

The Voice: Tenor

THE WORD TENOR IS ADAPTED FROM THE Latin *tenere*, 'to hold', thus implying that it was the middle voice in early choral music that literally held the singing together, with the basses beneath and the male altos above. The earliest surviving opera that is still widely performed, Monteverdi's *Orfeo* (1607), was written for tenor and thus set the style for leading male roles to be taken by the tenor voice. During the era of the castrati, tenors were generally relegated to secondary roles, but Handel and later Gluck reinstated the tenor to his heroic place, and Mozart wrote such great parts as Idomeneo, Tamino in *Die Zauberflöte* and Ferrando in *Così fan tutte* for tenor voices.

In the 19th century, the developments of grand opera in France and the parallel growth of Romantic opera in Germany began to call for heavier tenor voices than had ever been used in Italian *opera seria* or *bel canto* works. In the operas of Rossini, Bellini and Donizetti, the high notes written for tenors were generally supposed to have been taken in a light 'head' voice, not with the full tones favoured by modern audiences. The first tenors to take the high

notes in full, or chest, tones were the Frenchman Duprez and the Italian Rubini. This more heroic Italianate voice led to such roles as Manrico in Verdi's *Il trovatore*, Raoul in Meyerbeer's *Les Huguenots* and John of Leyden in *Le prophète*, also by Meyerbeer.

Wagner's first successful work for the stage, *Rienzi* (1842) contains the first of his typically demanding roles for tenor, written in the most heroic fashion. The roles of

Tristan in *Tristan und Isolde*, Siegmund in *Die Walküre* and Siegfried in the eponymous opera as well as *Götterdämmerung* are the most demanding ever written for the tenor voice. The singers who can accomplish these Wagner roles are few and far between; indeed, it is generally supposed that the first Tristan, Ludwig Schnorr von Carolsfeld, died three weeks after the premiere as a direct result of the strains the music had put upon him.

In Italian opera, the trend towards writing more and more heroic music for a tenor voice that could accomplish high, trumpet-like tones has put great strain upon many voices not really cut out for the challenge, and curtailed many a promising career. Radames in Verdi's *Aida*, the title role in the same composer's *Otello* and Calaf in Puccini's *Turandot* are three of the heaviest Italian roles. Only in French opera did the fashion for lighter, more fluid tenor leading men continue, and the most stylish singing is demanded for parts like Chevalier des Grieux in Massenet's *Manon*, the title role in Offenbach's *Les contes d'Hoffmann* and that in Gounod's *Faust*.

In the 20th century, Richard Strauss was generally known to despise tenors and wrote fiendishly difficult parts such as Bacchus in

• TENOR TYPES •

➤ **Heldentenor** The most heroic male voice, as typified by the roles in Wagner's operas, and several in those of Verdi and composers of the *verismo* school, Puccini, Mascagni and Leoncavallo. The Italian term is *tenore robusto*.

➤ **Lyric tenor** In Italian, *tenore spinto* and in German *lyrischer Tenor*. Such roles as Rodolfo in Puccini's *La bohème*, Max in Weber's *Der Freischütz*, and most of the leading roles in French 19th-century opera (Romeo in Gounod's *Roméo et Juliette*, Don José in Bizet's *Carmen*) come into this category.

➤ **Tenore di grazia** Literally, graceful tenor (*Spieltenor* in German); such roles as Nemorino in Donizetti's *L'elisir d'amore* and Pedrillo in Mozart's *Die Entführung aus dem Serail* come into this category. The other Mozart roles, especially Don Ottavio in *Don Giovanni*, might

be taken by such a light tenor, but the term 'Mozart tenor' is recognized as denoting a lyric tenor with the facility to sing in a lighter fashion.

➤ **Ténor bouffe** An extra-light tenor voice, especially in French light operas of the mid-19th century, by composers such as Offenbach, Lecoq and Boieldieu.

➤ **Counter-tenor** Not strictly a tenor voice at all, since counter-tenors are often natural basses who have 'reversed their voices' to sing in the higher *tessitura* or reaches of the voice. Since the mid-20th century the new interest in this voice has led to revivals of much Renaissance music as well as modern composers writing for tenors singing falsetto or in counter-tenor fashion, for example Oberon in Britten's *A Midsummer Night's Dream*.

• THE CASTRATO •

The practice of removing the testes of young male choristers in order to preserve their childish high voices began in the latter half of the 16th century. The castrato voice could be either soprano or alto and it gained in strength as the singer matured and developed the physical capacity to exploit his instrument. In the 17th and 18th centuries much more music was written for the many famous castrato singers, whose amorous exploits were as much a talking point as their extraordinary vocal powers, despite or perhaps because of their lack of conventional virility. Such famous castrati as Senesino (c. 1680–1759), for whom Handel wrote many parts, Farinelli (1705–82), for over 20 years the favourite singer at the court of Philip V of Spain, and Domenico Bedini (c. 1745–95), for whom Mozart composed the role of Sesto in *La clemenza di Tito*, remain among the most important musical figures of their age.

Although both Rossini and Meyerbeer wrote parts for castrati in their earlier operas, by the mid-19th century the voice type had ceased to be part of the operatic scene. Even in the 18th century, the roles written for the castrati were sometimes taken by female singers *en travestie* (in male dress), and so it is today, although some counter-tenors have attempted castrato roles.

In Italy the Church continued to employ castrato singers until the early 20th century. The last famous castrato soloist at the Sistine Chapel was Alessandro Moreschi (1858–1922), who made 17 recordings. Although his voice was not necessarily typical of the castrati of the 18th century, and he was past his prime when these recordings were made, the unearthly quality that led to these singers gaining such special fame is discernible. It is easy to detect that Moreschi's voice was not like that of a counter-tenor.

Placido Domingo in the title-role of Verdi's *Otello*, with Katia Ricciarelli as Desdemona. The role of Otello is the most demanding of all tenor parts in the Italian operatic repertoire.

Ariadne auf Naxos and the Emperor in *Die Frau ohne Schatten*, which call for a combination of heroic timbre and florid singing almost unknown elsewhere in German opera.

Due to the efforts of Benjamin Britten and his main interpreter, Peter Pears (1910–86), a new fashion for a lighter, though dramatic, voice was ushered in after World War II. Coincidentally the revival of interest in the counter-tenor voice has led modern composers, mindful of the rarity of true heroic tenors in the German or Italian style, to write for lighter voices. Tippett, Henze, Penderecki, Glass, Reimann and Maxwell Davies have all written for the counter-tenor voice. ♪

The Danish Helden-tenor Lauritz Melchior (1890–1973) in one of his greatest roles, as Siegfried in Wagner's opera of the same name.

Like Domingo and several other famous tenors, Melchior began his career as a baritone. He ended it in musicals.

The Voice: Baritone and Bass

THE BARITONE VOICE IS THE 'NORMAL' range of the male voice. A man singing in his natural range will have a better chance of articulating words clearly than one who is in some way extending his voice, upwards or downwards, and therefore in danger of strain. For this reason, the majority of male concert singers and singing-actors in

• BASS AND BARITONE VOICE TYPES •

➤ **Baritone** The middle range of the male voice, corresponding roughly to the mezzo-soprano. In opera the two voices have often been 'paired' for characters, for example Dorabella and Guglielmo in Mozart's *Così fan tutte*, Fricka and Wotan in Wagner's *Das Rheingold*. In general, German opera demands an especially strong middle-range baritone, and Italian roles extend the voice further upwards. Several famous tenors have started their careers as baritones, among them Lauritz Melchior and Placido Domingo.

➤ **Baryton-Martin** A light baritone voice with especially fluent high notes, named after the French singer Jean-Blaise Martin (1768–1837). Although the roles he sang are not generally performed today (in operas by Dalayrac, Boieldieu among others), the style of singing he initiated can be followed through the history of French opera, culminating in the role of Pelléas in Debussy's *Pelléas et Mélisande*.

➤ **Basso cantante** Literally 'singing bass', the more usual type of bass voice. It is normally of similar quality to the 'Basso buffo', the two being distinguished more by the dramatic requirements of operatic roles than their vocal range.

➤ **Basso profundo** The lowest male voice, and the rarest, so that composers seldom write roles calling for it. The Grand Inquisitor in Verdi's *Don Carlos* is one exception. The term basso profundo is often misused for bass.

musical theatre are baritones. The sonorous basses and high-C tenors inevitably sacrifice clarity of diction to line, tone and volume on occasion.

In opera, the baritone voice was seldom used as the main role before the 19th century. Although there are many baritone roles in the operas of Handel, Lully, Rameau and other early 18th-century composers, when considering the baritone repertory in general, it is in Mozart's operas, with roles such as Count Almaviva in *Le nozze di Figaro*, Guglielmo in *Così fan tutte*, the title-role in *Don Giovanni* and Papageno in *Die Zauberflöte* that the baritone really comes into his own. The title-role in Rossini's *Guillaume Tell*, the King in Donizetti's *La favorite* and Riccardo in Bellini's *I puritani* are examples of roles from *bel canto* operas that show how the Italianate voice in the baritone range came to be regarded as equally expressive as the tenor during the early part of the 19th century.

Of all baritones in the 1800s, one of the most important was Schubert's friend Johann Michael Vogl (1768–1840), who encouraged the composer and gave the first performances of several important Schubert Lieder. Vogl can be said to be one of the inspiring figures for the great tradition of baritone singing on the concert platform. In the 20th century this tradition has been continued most notably by Dietrich Fischer-Dieskau and latterly by Olaf Bär, Thomas Hampson and Wolfgang Holzmair. Schumann, Brahms and Hugo Wolf all favoured the lower male voice in their songs.

If Schubert's song cycles (*Die schöne Müllerin*, *Winterreise*) are the pinnacle that baritones look towards in the concert hall, then the Verdi roles in opera are their equivalent. The title roles in *Nabucco*, *Rigoletto* and *Simon Boccanegra*, Renato in *Un ballo in maschera*, Rodrigo in *Don Carlos*, Iago in *Otello* provide rich material for the baritone to explore, both vocally and in terms of characterization. With maturity, the title role in *Falstaff* awaits like some special treat at the end of a long journey. No other composer of opera gave such opportunities to baritones. In the German repertory the baritone can look to the great Wagner roles – Wolfram in *Tannhäuser*, Wotan in *Der Ring des Nibelungen*, Kurwenal in *Tristan und Isolde* and Gurnemanz in *Parsifal* – in which such singers as Hans Hotter and George London have distinguished themselves.

In 20th-century opera, Strauss, Berg, Weill, Schoenberg, Britten and Birtwistle have all written major baritone parts, of

Tito Gobbi (1913–84) as Scarpia in Puccini's *Tosca*, one of his most famous roles.

Thomas Hampson, one of the most charismatic singers of the 1990s, as Figaro in Rossini's *Il barbiere di Siviglia*.

Fyodor Chaliapin (1873–1938) in the title-role of Mussorgsky's *Boris*

Fyodor Chaliapin (1873–1938) in the title-role of Mussorgsky's *Boris Godunov*. Chaliapin was as famous for his acting as for his voice.

BASS

Throughout the history of opera, the bass voice has been used as a vehicle to depict either father-figures, elder statesmen or the darkest villainy. Since all early operas were written for particular singers, one can judge that the comparative rarity of large roles for the bass voice coincides with the scarcity of accomplished bass singers. The lighter bass-baritone voice favoured by Mozart for his characters Figaro, Leporello and Don Alfonso gives us a fair idea of what his singers must have been like. Ludwig Fischer, who created the role of Osmin in *Die Entführung aus dem Serail*, had a long and distinguished career in Germany, and to some extent can be considered the founder of the tradition of comic-sinister bass singing.

Basses were accorded much more importance in 19th-century Italian opera, by Bellini, especially in *Norma* (Oroveso) and *I puritani* (Giorgio), and subsequently by Verdi, who though he provided one of the greatest scenes ever written for the bass voice, between Philip II and the Grand Inquisitor in *Don Carlos* (1867), and gave the title role to a bass in *Attila* (1845–46). The roles composed by Rossini for Filippo Galli (1783–1853), including Assur in *Semiramide*, with its famous 'mad scene', and those by Donizetti for Luigi Lablache (1794–1858), including Don Pasquale, established the bass as being on equal terms with sopranos, tenors and baritones.

The first internationally successful Russian opera, Glinka's *A Life for the Tsar* (1836), gave the main role to a bass singer, and thereafter, especially because of the success of Mussorgsky's opera *Boris Godunov* (1874), the dark, typically Russian bass voices have come to be especially prized. The performances of Fyodor Chaliapin (1873–1938) in this and many other Russian and French bass roles (Méphistophélès, Philip II, Don Quichotte among them), created a new style which has been continued by Boris Christoff, Nicolai Ghiaurov and most recently the American Samuel Ramey. ♪

which the most important is the title-role in Berg's *Wozzeck*, but it is the opportunities provided by the musical, in the works of Lehár, Kern, Romberg, Rodgers and Berlin, that have turned the 20th-century baritone into a star in his own right.

WORDS AND MUSIC

Choral
Plainsong to Polyphony

RATHER SURPRISINGLY, PLAINSONG HAS become a fairly popular type of music in recent years, sharing some features with the music of Górecki, Pärt and the minimalists. It could even be said to be a form of minimalism itself, because it is chanted by male voices, in unison (that is, without harmony), and with little sense of rhythm, and no kind of instrumental accompaniment. It is thus very austere, but by virtue of that fact, and its apparently unending melodic flow, it evokes a timelessness which is appealing in a world in which stress is a large part of life; up to a point, it once again serves one of the purposes for which it was originally designed.

Plainsong is the name given to the official chants of the Christian liturgy, that is to say the major services of the Church. It originated in synagogue chants, and in some varieties of pagan music. As the forms of Christian worship developed and were consolidated during the first centuries of the Christian era, some parts of them remained constant, others varied according to the season – Lent, for instance, or Christmastide.

THUS SUCH SERVICES AS THE MASS gradually took shape, in which the fixed elements included the opening appeal for God to have mercy, the celebration of God's glory, the Creed, in which the basic items of Christian belief are listed, and the closing of the service. In between came readings from the Bible, and prayers, which changed in part from one day to the next, for the cycle of the Christian year. The fixed parts were called the 'Ordinary', the changing ones the 'Proper' of the Mass. Some of each would be chanted, the rest spoken.

A number of differing chants were reduced to a manageable, though still large, collection, and though there was not yet any means of writing them down, we can assume that the first ones that were transcribed are substantially the same as those of several centuries before. That is why the terms 'Plainsong' and 'Gregorian Chant' are often used interchangeably. Since various parts of the Church – the Greek Orthodox, the Roman Catholic, for example, as well as regional parts of each of these – developed their own styles of singing, the great legacy of chant increased, and there are still striking differences between the way that it is performed in churches and monasteries in, for instance, Italy and France. However, the basic principles remain constant: one line of text and melody, the sense of which is easily understood, and which is sung by the priest and choir together, or by the priest alternating with the choir ('responsories'). The melodic line undulates and there are never any large leaps or dips in the flow. Some chants stick to one note per syllable, others become more flowery and give a single syllable, or even a single vowel, up to a dozen notes. The effect is hypnotic, and

The plainchant of the abbess Hildegard of Bingen was highly formulaic, and individual, like her poetry and paintings of mystical visions. The example shown here is from *Liber divinorum operum simplicimus hominus*.

an extremely effective way of expressing the confidence of the singers in their faith.

It was not until early in the 13th century that plainsong was written down with any degree of precision. Earlier attempts had merely consisted of sloping lines indicating the general direction of the melody, but with the invention of staves – a series of horizontal parallel lines – notes could be pitched exactly, and their length could be indicated, as it still is, by drawing them in different shapes. The books in which the chants are recorded, with elaborate illustra-

Plainchant and homophonic music are of their nature religious. The impression they leave on the senses is remarkably similar to that of a Fra Angelico painting.

tions in many colours, are in themselves among the masterpieces of Western art.

Over the centuries Gregorian chant has often developed into something far more florid, and there have been innumerable battles to bring it back to its pristine simplicity. With so much church music of a much more elaborate kind being written and performed from the late Middle Ages to the present time, the stark yet consoling character of the early chants comes as a refreshment, and it is not perhaps surprising that people who have no interest in religion as such are now listening to it, or perhaps simply using it as relaxing background music. It is less demanding even than the homophonic choral music which gradually emerged from it, and of which it is indeed the simplest form. 'Homophony' means simply 'same-sounding', and can be applied equally to vocal or instrumental music, but its original use was for unison singing, that is, plainchant. It was then extended to cover choral singing in which there is a melody that is clearly distinguishable from the accompanying harmony, and then to music in which all the parts move in the same rhythm, giving the effect of blocks of sound, which can be immensely impressive in a monolithic way. The next development is polyphony, which emerged in the late Middle Ages. Here the various voices move independently of one another, both melodically and rhythmically, so that the effect is less static.

Plainchant and homophonic music are of their very nature religious: they conjure up eternity, very much as the paintings of Fra Angelico do. Everything seems timelessly suspended. As soon as there is independent movement of the voices, and the addition of instruments, there is also the possibility of drama, and we are immediately brought down to earth, though the greatest writers of polyphonic music are capable of capturing a state of dynamic ecstasy which we can relate to more directly than to homophony. Only when polyphonic music got under way was it possible to use choral music for secular purposes. An obvious and

very celebrated example is 'Sumer is icumen in', composed around 1250, and not only a fine piece of music but a textbook case of early polyphony.

The Renaissance saw a great burgeoning of polyphonic music, mainly sacred but also secular, above all in Italy, the Netherlands, Great Britain and Spain. The greatest of Renaissance polyphonists are perhaps Palestrina, Lassus, Victoria and Byrd, but it is increasingly being realized that they are only the tip of an enormous iceberg, and their pre-eminence may be due to luck as well as merit. Palestrina (c. 1525–94) worked mainly in Rome, and was given the task of proving to the Council of Trent, bent on reforming the over-elaborate music of the time, that polypohony could still be verbally intelligible, to demonstrate which he wrote his most famous work, the *Missa Papae Marcelli* (1577). His music is serene, refined, and in notable contrast to that of

his Spanish contemporary Victoria (1548–1611), a kind of musical El Greco, who wrote intense, contorted and dramatic pieces. The Englishman William Byrd (1543–1623) was more versatile than either, and produced an immense quantity of music, both choral and instrumental, as well as many songs. Lassus (1532–94) was Franco-Flemish, and a cosmopolitan figure; his melodic qualities are Italian, his pointed setting of words French, and his rich polyphony Netherlandish. He wrote more than 2,000 works, and is considered by many to be the greatest of all Renaissance masters.

In the case of all these composers, and literally hundreds of others, there is a legacy so huge that it is in danger of being largely neglected because we hardly know where to begin. With a few exceptions, the music of these composers is not 'expressive' but rather a statement of universally-held belief.

In the latter half of the 16th century the Roman Catholic Church worked out its responses to the Reformation through the Council of Trent. The role of music in liturgical life was a major talking point. The Council's decision to demand a return to simpler musical values resulted in polyphony becoming more tightly organized.

Requiem

THE REQUIEM MASS IS THE NAME FOR the Roman Catholic Mass for the Dead. It takes its name from the first word of the entrance prayer, 'Requiem eternam dona eis, Domine' ('Give them eternal peace, O Lord!'). In its most characteristic form, and the one in which it is used for church services, it consists of 10 parts, most of them overlapping with the Mass as it is usually celebrated, but with the joyful 'Gloria' naturally omitted, and also the Creed, the statement of Christian beliefs. The medieval hymn 'Dies Irae' ('Day of Wrath') is usually added, besides the opening prayer.

The Requiem as a service maintains a balance between the elements of the orthodox Christian attitude towards death. On the one hand there is the lament of the living for having lost their friends or relations, on the other the celebration of the hoped-for entry of the departed into Heaven. Equally there is the awareness that we must all perish, and that some of us will end in Hell.

This makes the Requiem a naturally very dramatic as well as devotional affair. The heart of it is the very long hymn 'Dies Irae', which evokes the terrors of the Day of Judgement, when all our secrets will be revealed after we have all been summoned by the Last Trumpet. After an alarmingly graphic portrayal of God in His role as Judge rather than as Redeemer, references to the consuming flames and so on, it concludes with a cry for peace.

Not surprisingly, the words and mood of the Requiem have attracted an enormous number of composers to set it to music, though many of them have omitted one part or another. The first setting to employ sophisticated vocal means (with no instruments) is Ockeghem's, dating from 1470, though he only set four sections; they are still very powerful. About 40 settings from then to the end of the 16th century survive, including ones by Lassus and Palestrina, but they nearly all omit the 'Dies Irae', which really demands impressive orchestral forces not available to them to make a full impact. The mood is, on the whole, more elegiac than fearful in these often intensely beautiful works. It is only with Mozart's Requiem, written with his own death imminent (and indeed left incomplete by him), that alarm, even panic, predominate. It has a most lugubrious beginning and the 'Dies Irae' is a feverish, rending piece which suggests that Mozart no longer thought, as he had once expressed in a famous letter, that "death is mankind's truest friend".

During the 19th century, the Requiem gave composers the chance to demonstrate their mastery of ever-larger orchestral forces, and the most spectacular example of that is Berlioz's (fp1837), in which four brass bands are stationed around the church or concert hall, as well as there being a full symphony orchestra and a vast choir in the centre of the proceedings. Here the effect is almost wholly dramatic, hardly at all devotional; though there are many quiet sections, they too are expressive of awe rather than worship.

Alessandro Manzoni, in whose memory Verdi composed his *Requiem*.

A SHADOW CAST: VERDI'S *REQUIEM*

Interestingly, most modern Requiems have been written by non-believers. The greatest of these by far is Verdi's Requiem (1873), his most sustainedly inspired work. It was written as a tribute to Italy's greatest novelist, Alessandro Manzoni. Here everything is on a grand scale, as in the Berlioz, but Verdi manages to combine stunning theatrical effects with a strong and pervasive devotional tone, beginning with his agonized supplications for peace. His 'Dies Irae' is the most terrifying of all, and it erupts throughout the work, making sure that its listeners never forget their dread of the end. It concludes with a frightened whisper from the soprano soloist, and remains the work by which all subsequent writers of Requiems are influenced.

That applies even to Fauré, whose Requiem (1887) is determinedly comforting, omitting the 'Dies Irae' altogether, as if he realized that Verdi could never be matched. Fauré's work, with its cooing soprano soloist and insistent gentleness, is a sedative for an age without faith, as is that of his close follower Duruflé. Without the stimulus of belief, or its collapse, Requiems tend to be merely soothing. That does not apply to Britten's War Requiem, but that uses the Latin text as only one ingredient, juxtaposing it with the lacerating anti-war poems of Wilfred Owen. The dramatic effect is of irreconcilable attitudes towards death. ♪

Fantin-Latour's painting of Berlioz conducting his Requiem evokes the spirit of the music.

Masters of Tradition

FEW WOULD ARGUE THAT BACH IS THE greatest master of choral music who has ever lived. He wrote a prodigious amount of it, and even though large quantities are lost, there remains more than enough for even the most ardent devotee to explore in a lifetime. At the centre of his achievement in this area (and he is also one of the supreme keyboard composers) is the Mass in B minor and the two Passions.

'The Passion' was the name given to Christ's experiences on the Thursday and

Friday of Holy Week. Its central components were the Last Supper, the

betrayal by Judas, and the arrest, trial and crucifixion of Christ. Each of the four gospels gives a somewhat different account of these events, and Bach set at least three of them, of which the St John Passion and the St Matthew Passion have survived. In both the narrative is sung by the Evangelist, a tenor, and Christ is sung by a bass. The works are framed by vast choruses, with enormously elaborate counterpoint, interspersed with arias, in which the soloists reflect on the events, and chorales, originally sung by the congregation. In the St John Passion, the shorter of the two, the action proceeds quickly, there are fewer arias and dramatic effect is uppermost. In the St Matthew Passion the drama is still there, but the meditative element is much more pronounced, and it is Bach's largest work.

While the Passions are in German, the Mass is in Latin, and was written at different stages of Bach's life. It begins with a huge fugue on the opening words of the Mass, the only Greek ones: 'Kyrie eleison' ('Lord have mercy'), then a duet to 'Christe eleison' ('Christ have mercy') followed by a shorter fugue on 'Kyrie eleison.' The 'Gloria' which follows is on a similar scale. Then comes the Creed, much of which is despatched much faster, and the 'Sanctus', in which, as the critic Tovey said, Bach "conducts the heavenly choirs". More celebration follows, but the work ends with a profound supplication from the contralto soloist, 'Agnus Dei' ('Lamb of God') and a choral fugue, 'Dona nobis pacem' (Give us peace'). It is about two hours long, a work of staggering inspiration and grandeur. The contrast with the Passions is marked. In them, the individual human soul is led to repentance and hope through reliving the story of Christ's sufferings. In the Mass in

The two Passions, of St John and St Matthew, are among the greatest works of J S Bach and represent, with the same composer's Mass in B minor, the pinnacle of religious music. In them, the individual soul is led to salvation through Christ's suffering.

B minor, the whole church joins in affirming God's greatness, and imploring salvation. It is less obviously personal, though no less moving. The Passions and the Mass represent between them the pinnacle of religious music.

BACH'S CANTATAS

Bach wrote more than 200 church cantatas, which were performed on Sundays, each one reflecting the time of the Christian year, or the message of the day's Gospel. Some are for solo voice and orchestra, others for soloists, chorus and orchestra. The forces he used were undoubtedly quite small, the soloists being members of the choir. Among the finest solo cantatas are No. 56, 'Ich will den Kreuzstab gerne tragen' ('I will gladly take up the Cross') and above all No. 82, 'Ich habe genug' ('I have had enough'). The average length of these works is 20 minutes, though until recently they were performed more slowly than they are now, thanks to the 'authenticity' movement. There are a few duds, but with a little

luck any cantata chosen at random will be moving and memorable. The numbering of the cantatas is not even an approximate guide to the order of their composition, but that tends to matter less with Bach than with any other of the great composers.

BACH'S SECULAR WORKS

Bach also wrote a considerable amount of secular music for chorus, even attempting comic works, such as the 'Coffee' Cantata No. 211, 'Schweigt stille, plaudert nicht' ('Be quiet, don't chatter'), but that was not where his genius lay. In fact the division into religious and secular only rarely applies to Bach. Cantata No. 29, 'Wir danken dir, Gott, wir danken dir' ('We thank you, God we thank you'), was written for the inauguration of the Town Council of Leipzig, but serves equally well as part of a divine service. Some of his most magnificent choral writing is for unaccompanied chorus, and the six motets, including the sublime 'Jesu meine Freude' ('Jesus my joy'), are masterworks. ♪

Handel and the 19th-Century Tradition

HANDEL WAS BORN IN 1685, THE SAME YEAR as Bach. They have much less in common otherwise than is often thought. Handel's vocal music, religious or secular, is theatrical through and through; Bach, though he is capable of stupendous strokes of drama, belongs firmly in the church. Handel is essentially at home in this world, a celebrator of pleasure and beauty, though anxious about death; Bach meditates perpetually on the eternal. Handel's oratorios, written for concert performance, tend to take their stories from the satisfyingly bloodthirsty Old Testament; his one Passion is a bore. What he likes are plagues visited on Egyptians, giving him a chance to write vividly onomatopeic music; hymns of rejoicing over the downfall of the uncircumcized; lustiness and lustfulness. The division between his religious and secular compositions is as unclear as with Bach, but works the other

way round: he is almost always secular, whatever the subject matter. He marks, though under a smokescreen, the transition from faith in the beyond to concern with the visible world. The Victorians adored him because he seemed to be providing them with one thing while actually gratifying their worldly appetites. Such oratorios as *Israel in Egypt* and *Judas Maccabeus* are essentially unstaged operas in which the interest is in battle and victory.

Handel was almost as prolific as Bach, often borrowing from himself and other composers, again like Bach – such borrowing not being considered then, as it was in the Romantic age, to be an artistic crime. His greatest work, without question, is *Messiah*, but many of his other works, though they lack *Messiah's* fervour, depth and variety, make for highly enjoyable listening. Some of his most attractive works are allocated to the oratorio category, although operas in all but name; for example, *Alexander's Feast* (fp1736), *Saul* (fp1739), *Samson* (fp1743), *Israel in Egypt* (fp1739), *Judas Maccabeus* (fp1747), *Solomon* (fp1749), and *Jephtha* (fp1752). They tend to have the inbuilt deficiency of containing choral fugues, which are not conducive to drama however exciting they may be. Even the few da capo arias – in

which a character states an emotion, has a contrasting one, then returns to base – do not make for progress. Nevertheless, such is the brimming vitality of these works that they survive such flaws.

The 19th century strained for faith, but found it hard to achieve. In the case of Beethoven, a fanatical admirer of Handel but a man with a strongly religious temperament, his great *Missa Solemnis* (1818–23) is moving partly because it shows the strain. Where Bach celebrates the object of his worship, Beethoven has, with the enormous rhetorical force of his music, to create the object which he worships. Wonderful as the Benedictus of his Mass is, it is really the sublime slow movement of a violin concerto with the soloists and chorus providing exquisite decoration; and the cries for peace at the end are set against the evocation of warfare, not the fight within each of us between the Devil and God, but the Napoleonic Wars.

With Mendelssohn – second only to Handel in popularity with Victorian choral societies – whenever the transcendental makes an appearance, it is merely insipid. In his finest oratorio, *Elijah* (fp1846), the Handelian tradition is honourably continued; in *St Paul* (fp1836) we are in a dark and gloomy Gothic Revival church.

• THE *MESSIAH* •

∞ *Messiah* contradicts the claim above that Handel was essentially a man of the theatre. In Part 2 the evocation of Christ's sufferings has a profundity unique in Handel's work. He composed *Messiah* in three weeks in 1741, and it was originally performed in Dublin in 1742, with vast forces. As it was taken up elsewhere, Handel rewrote and reorganized it, so that there is no such thing as a definitive version, but its basic structure – the Nativity, the Crucifixion and Resurrection, and the hope of eternal life – is robust enough to withstand all kinds of tinkering. The level of inspiration is amazing, from the overture through to the great fugal Amen Chorus. However overexposed it may be, it is a work of inexhaustible vitality and inventiveness.

Increasingly oratorios became overtly national, either in subject matter – for example Elgar's *The Banner of St George* (fp1897) – or in idiom. By the end of the century anyone who wanted to write a genuinely religious work, and many did, had to create a new idiom. To draw, as still more did, on the tradition of Handel and Mendlessohn was a sure recipe for produc-ing works whose sell-by date preceded their composition.

Haydn, another man at peace with this world, wrote an abundance of fine Masses, and two of the most famous oratorios, *The Creation* (fp1798) and *The Seasons* (fp1801). They are the last great oratorios – Mozart wisely steered clear of the genre. The grandiosity almost inherent in them is negated in Berlioz's exquisite *The Childhood of Christ* (fp1854), which, like so much Berlioz, stands alone. There are countless works of the genre by distinguished com-posers who, in general, one feels should have known better, for instance Dvořák. This is not to say that choral works became anachronistic, but that a new departure was needed. ♪

{ An audience at the Royal Opera House, Covent Garden, listening to an oratorio in 1808, as depicted by Rowlandson and Pugin. Note Handel's Organ at the back of the stage. In September of the same year, the opera house was destroyed by fire.

A scene from the biblical story of the Maccabees: } Jonathan attacking the temple of Dagon. The heavily ornamental nature of this print shows, as Handel often does, that the artist is strongly attracted to what is being demolished.

The 20th Century: Sacred to Secular

AT THE BEGINNING OF THE 20TH CENTURY the tradition of massive oratorios was still going, if not strong, then ever more noisily. When Elgar visited Delius in France the latter, an atheist, asked Elgar if he had finshed setting the Bible to music, and one sees what he meant. Elgar's two-part work *The Apostles* (1902) and *The Kingdom* (1906) is a last kick of the old school, and though he intended to write a trilogy, he lost heart. Delius himself is one of the most original and instantly recognizable of choral composers, and in his *A Mass of Life* (1905) he threw down the gauntlet to traditional oratorio by setting words from *Thus Spake Zarathustra*, the prophetic book by the Antichristian Nietzsche. In typical late-Romantic mode, it celebrates the beauty of the earth and laments the brevity of man's life. Meanwhile Mahler, in his Eighth Symphony (1906), really a gigantic oratorio, set the hymn 'Veni Creator Spiritus' and the end of Part II of Goethe's *Faust*. It

Hans Pfitzner, the last great German conservative composer. His cantatas, including *Von Deutscher Seele*, are among his most impressive works

John Martin's painting of Belshazzar's Feast makes William Walton's oratorio on the same theme seem tame by comparison.

shows the danger of implosion from sheer oversize. Certainly before that ultimate watershed World War I, elephantiasis was severely afflicting Central European composers. Yet though few of them were believers in traditional Christianity, the desire to embody their profoundest beliefs and hopes in works that combined vocal and orchestral forces continued.

In the case of Hans Pfitzner, the arch-conservative among Germans, it found expression in *Von deutscher Seele* ('Of the German Soul') (1921), which distils an essence of seriousness and spirituality both German and – for those of us who regard it as a masterpiece – universal. The most progressive figures, Schoenberg and Stravinsky, also created their most ambitious works in something which could trace its roots to

oratorio. Schoenberg abandoned his *Die Jakobsleiter* ('Jacob's Ladder') (1922) but what survives of it is profoundly impressive, and in his unfinished opera *Moses und Aron* (1932) he really produced his statement of faith in semi-dramatic form: it hardly needs staging. Stravinsky actually called his *Oedipus Rex* (1927) an 'opera-oratorio', and also, in his *Symphony of Psalms* (1930), produced the most convincing expression of Christian belief that the 20th century has to show, in musical terms.

The English musical renaissance, represented by Elgar, Vaughan Williams, Britten, Tippett and Walton among others, has often resorted to traditional forms, even if, as with Tippett, they have become more determinedly wacky over the decades. Leonard Bernstein produced a Mass (1971) which is really a piece of ham theatre, and

• SOME GREAT STATEMENTS OF FAITH •

➤ **Janacek's** *Glagolithic Mass* (1926) is the most startling quasi-religious work of the century. A disciplined riot, with the organ, that sacred instrument, leading the pagan way, it is an immensely successful celebration, using the traditional words of the Mass, of life in its most earthy form.

➤ Beside it the works of **Delius**, master that he was, sound genteel, though his *Songs of Sunset* (1906–8) and infinitely poignant *Songs of Farewell* (1930) are works of refined genius.

➤ **Stravinsky** wrote a large number of religious works, including a rather forbidding Mass (1944–8), and what he called "the first

pocket Requiem' (1965–6). They stand in stark contrast to the highly subjective expressions of, for instance, Britten and Tippett.

➤ **Britten** was a Christian understandably repelled by Anglican cosiness, even if he failed completely to escape it. However, his *War Requiem* (1962) is taken by many to be a uniquely relevant work for our time.

➤ **Tippett's** *A Child of Our Time* (1939–41) more explicitly makes its bid for contemporaneity by narrating a harrowing, true story of persecution and interspersing it with negro spirituals. His utterly over-the-top *The Mask of Time* (1981–83) is the artistic equivalent of a 'theory of everything'.

GENESIS. Chap.XXVIII.V. 12.

Jacob's vision.

at its climax the priest announces 'Non credo' ('I don't believe'), before inciting the audience (not congregation) to indulge in an orgy of universal love. Choral music, large numbers of people singing of their common beliefs, has become large numbers of people announcing in harmony the importance of doing your own thing.

If God doesn't exist, the artist had better replace him; that is the message of many works of this century. However, the saddest are those which use the Christian texts to express a belief they don't share – it comes as a surprise to most people to learn that Vaughan Williams was an atheist. ♪

In Arnold Schoenberg's unfinished choral work *Die Jakobsleiter*, Jacob's dream was conceived as a symbol for limitless expression.

BELSHAZZAR'S FEAST

William Walton's *Belshazzar's Feast* (1929–31) is probably the most popular English choral work of the century. Its lineage is Handelian, with a sprinkling of wrong notes. As with Handel, it takes a biblical subject and gives it a technicolor treatment. The most affecting part is the opening, in which the Israelites bewail their captivity, in plangent dissonances. Once the celebration of the pagan gods sets in, on the part of the Babylonians, the brass of the orchestra have a whale of a time – that is the exciting core of the work. After the instant shock of the shout of 'Slain!' by the baritone soloist, taken up by the choir, there are the obligatory celebrations, always the most tiresome part of this kind of work. *Belshazzar's Feast* has achieved and maintained its place largely because it gives the impression of being daring, and thus flatters its audience, while in fact it is extremely conservative.

Art Songs

The Lied

THE TERM LIEDER (GERMAN FOR songs; singular, Lied) has over the last two centuries come to be applied only to art-songs to texts in German, so it is contrasted with, for instance, folk songs or popular songs. The first German art-songs were written during the 18th century, but they didn't really become established as a separate form of artistic expression until Haydn. J S Bach wrote at most five, including one about the pleasures of tobacco. Gluck was attracted to the Lied towards the end of his life, and in his Lieder the keyboard accompaniment develops some independence from the singing line. However it is Haydn, the great innovator, who truly put the Lied on the map, writing 24 German and 12 English songs, the earliest to remain in the repertoire. Mozart, supreme as a writer of arias in his operas, wrote rather few — he seems to have needed the inspiration of a dramatic situation. 'Das Veilchen' ('The violet'), a setting of Goethe, is his finest. Beethoven, not often a composer for the voice, nonetheless wrote many fine Lieder, and among them is the first song cycle, a series of songs linked by a common subject and, in this case, by musical cross-references: An die ferne Geliebte ('To the distant beloved') (1816) is a quarter-hour-long masterpiece.

ANY HISTORY OF THE LIED MUST centre around Schubert, and indeed he needs a section to himself. His enormous output, sustaining an amazingly high level, has never been equalled. However, Robert Schumann is surely a worthy successor, specializing in cycles in which passionate love is poured forth, often to be rejected or subject to hideous disappointment, as in *Frauenliebe und Leben* ('A woman's love and life') (1840), in which the songs move through love at first sight, marriage and motherhood to the husband's death. Like all German Lieder composers from the late 18th century onwards, he set many of Goethe's poems: some of the best-known of them have been set scores of times, and comparing the various settings is

Robert Schumann, introspective, vulnerable and mentally unstable.

Carl Loewe, a specialist in setting ballads to music.

{ Hugo Wolf produced his 200 songs in intensive, brief spells of creativity.

composer's second version of 'Kennst du das Land?' (Do you know the land?) (1856) is finer than Schubert's. His best known song, 'Die drei Zigeuner' (1860)('The three gypsies') has a permanent place in the repertoire, and avoids the over-elaboration of many of his accompaniments.

Two composers whose reputations are built solely on song are Carl Loewe, born in 1796 (the year before Schubert), who specialized in long ballads, many of them, such as 'Edward', highly dramatic; and the only composer who challenges Schubert as a song-writer, Hugo Wolf, who wrote more than 200 in short, intense creative bursts. He wrote no cycles, but he did write two 'books' of songs (*Liederbuch*), the Spanish and the Italian, which mix sacred and profane, passion and humour. Of all composers, Wolf paid the closest attention to the words of the poems he was setting, and his songs are less obviously melodic than expressive. Mahler, his contemporary, specialized in the orchestral Lied, and was followed in that by Schoenberg, Berg and Webern. The tradition of the German song has proved one of the most durable of all musical forms, and one of the most continuously, if subtly, rewarding. ♫

highly interesting, as with the Mignon and Harper songs from the novel *Wilhelm Meister*.

All the major German composers of the 19th century wrote fine songs, including Mendelssohn, Wagner, Brahms and the Hungarian-born Liszt. Liszt wrote 75 songs, in five languages: German, French, Italian, Hungarian and English, German

predominating. Not surprisingly, the piano parts are often more interesting than the vocal lines, but his seriousness as a song composer is demonstrated by his frequent revisions. He originally wrote the *3 Petrarch Sonnets* (1839) as songs, then turned them into piano pieces. In general, Goethe brought out the best in Liszt and the

A WAYFARER ❖ FOR ALL
~

*I*n Mahler's brief, early cycle *Lieder eines fahrenden Gesellen* ('Songs of a wayfaring lad') we get a kind of distillation of many of the topics and even words that have haunted the Lied throughout the century in which it was written. Mahler wrote the words to this cycle himself and originally composed it with piano accompaniment, scoring it for orchestra later.

The wayfarer begins in doleful mood, since his beloved is marrying someone else; there is the usual contrast between the happiness around him and his misery. The second song sets off in buoyant mood, as the lad walks through the fields and communes with Nature, cheerfully until the last line, when he insists his happiness will never bloom. The third is a passionate protest – he has a dagger in his breast. In the last he sets out in the night, finds peace under a linden tree – what else? – and the music lays him to rest.

The Supreme Exponent: Schubert

SCHUBERT IS A GREAT COMPOSER IN MANY genres, but it is in the Lied that he is supreme, even if a few listeners find Wolf more attentive to exact verbal shadings. However Schubert, as the greatest melodist who ever lived, was usually content to capture the overall meaning of the poems he set. The first triumphs of his song-writing career came astonishingly early, especially since he had no one on whom to model himself. When he was 17 he produced 'Erlkönig' ('Erl-king'), a terrifying ballad by Goethe, in which he characterizes vividly, through the song's headlong progress, the father riding through the night, his petrified son, and the hideously seductive erl-king himself, luring the boy to death. At the same age, in 'Gretchen am Spinnrade' ('Gretchen at the Spinning-Wheel') he evokes with infallible insight the longings of Gretchen as she thinks of Faust, the accompaniment evoking the whirring of the wheel, which comes to a temporary halt as she thinks of Faust's kiss, then resumes.

The range of his songs, throughout his pitifully short life, is amazing. He tackles profound philosophical issues, as in 'Grenzen der Menschheit' ('Limits of man'), vast ballads lasting up to half-an-hour, as in 'Der Taucher' ('The diver'), innumerable aspects of love, Nature, the whole realm of experience. He was not choosy about his poets, and some of his greatest songs are to very inferior lyrics. There are some duds among his output of over 600 songs, but remarkably few; often he composed several songs in a single day, writing in cafés. They were primarily intended for his circle of friends, and performed at what became known as 'Schubertiads', evenings at which he would accompany his friends on the piano and sometimes sing as well.

Schubert's imagination was mostly fired by a striking image, which would give him a melodic idea, forming the basis of the song. When he came to compose the two great song cycles *Die schöne Müllerin* ('The fair maid of the mill') (1823) and *Die Winterreise* ('The winter's journey') (1827), the poems, by Wilhelm Müller, were mainly undistinguished, but each of them contained a kernel which gave him what he needed: frozen tears, the mill-wheel, the

The title-page for *Die schöne Müllerin*, published in 1823.

linden-tree, the hurdy-gurdy man. Though he sometimes wrote strophic songs – that is, songs in which the melody remains the same for each verse – he came increasingly to vary the settings, especially harmonically; so that there will be a sudden heart-wrenching move from major to minor or – a speciality of his – an even more poignant shift from minor to major: past happiness recalled in present misery. As he explored the ultimate regions of pain, his friends became both bewildered and worried. He knew he was dying of syphilis, and although even in his last songs he is capable of being carefree, the torment of his existence led him to his deepest utterances, and to writing some of the greatest music there is.

THE SONG CYCLES

Schubert became fascinated by song cycles during the last five years of his life. They are in some ways easier to get to know than his individual Lieder, because there is a connecting link between the songs. Isolated songs, however impressive, tend to take longer to lodge in the mind.

His first cycle, of 20 songs, is *Die schöne Müllerin* and it tells (sometimes in the first person) of the love of a young miller for a girl and his succeeding with her in the eleventh song, 'Mein!', only to lose her to a green-clad huntsman. This cycle has a balance of bubbling energy and increasing low spirits. The cycle he wrote four years

later, *Die Winterreise*, is one of unrelieved gloom. It begins with the young man's rejection, and he leaves the town where his beloved lives, torn between hope and the knowledge that he is utterly alone. Only a crow accompanies him, hovering overhead. Every song in this series of 24 is a masterpiece, and the cumulative effect is devastating.

In their unity in variety, these two cycles are the biggest challenges faced by a Lieder singer; he or she has to characterize each song immediately, while leaving no doubt that it is part of an ongoing story. The

importance of the piano part is that it usually establishes the mood before the singer enters, so there is just as large a responsibility for the accompanist. In the case of *Die Winterreise*, it is crucial that something should be held in reserve for the last songs, even though the earlier ones are already incredibly intense.

Schwanengesang (Swansong) is often taken to be the name of a third cycle, but in fact it is the last 14 songs that Schubert wrote, opportunistically published under a suitably sentimental title, and making an unsatisfactory series if performed straight through, as it often is. Settings of seven poems by Rellstab, six by Heine and one by Seidl, ('Die Taubenpost', Schubert's last song), which has nothing in common with what precedes it, is not a recipe for integrated performance. ♪

Heinrich Heine, Romantic and ironic, inspired all the greatest Lieder composers with his poems. His *Buch der Lieder* is the volume on which his fame as a lyric poet is founded and was newly published when Schubert discovered it for the first time, in 1828. Schubert set only six of Heine's poems, but they are among his greatest songs. To each of Heine's untitled originals Schubert gave a title: 'Das Fischermädchen' ('The fisher girl'), 'Am Meer' ('By the sea'), 'Ihr Bild' ('Her picture'), 'Die Stadt' ('The town'), 'Der Doppelgänger' ('The ghostly double'), and 'Der Atlas' ('Atlas'). Among the composers the *Buch der Lieder* has inspired (in addition to Schubert) are Liszt, Schumann, Brahms, Mendelssohn, Wolf, Wagner and Richard Strauss.

For all the melancholy of many of his songs, Schubert revelled in playing them in convivial surroundings, usually with his friends. It was at a reading held by the circle of fellow musicians, writers and artists in which he moved that Schubert first came across the poems of Heine, in January 1828.

ANATOMY OF 'FRÜHLINGSTRAUM' (DREAM OF SPRING)

∞ The eleventh song of *Die Winterreise* encapsulates the typical Schubertian progression. It is in six verses, beginning with an artless melody on the piano which suggests blissful innocence, as the singer enters dreaming of May. Then there is an abrupt change to cold morning, and in the third verse the singer wonders who painted the icy leaves on the window, seeming to mock his dreams. The second set of three verses repeats the pattern: he dreams of love requited, wakes to find himself alone, and wonders when the leaves will be green and he will hold his love in his arms. What is astonishing is the compactness with which Schubert takes us through two sets of experiences in a few minutes, the contrasts and the unfailing beauty of the music; it is a microcosm of Schubert's world.

French Mélodie

THE FRENCH ART-SONG HAS NEVER achieved the heights or the popularity of the German, but it forms an equally strong tradition in French musical culture. The mélodie, as the French equivalent of the Lied is called, began at about the same time, but no more auspiciously. The earliest figure of any fame to write them was Jean-Jacques Rousseau, the philosopher, who composed about 100, which are today entirely forgotten. Meyerbeer, the once hugely popular composer of grand opera, wrote a fair number, some of which have a rather faded charm. However, the first major composer to create enduring mélodies was Berlioz. Since he was no pianist, his finest ones are for voice and

orchestra, and his cycle of six, *Les Nuits d'été* ('Summer nights') (1841) are among his most beautiful works. Each of them is haunting in a quite individual way, yet they make a most satisfying cycle, one never surpassed by later French composers. Gounod, Franck, Saint-Saëns, Bizet and

Massenet all composed mélodies, but all are rightly remembered primarily for other kinds of work. It is Gabriel Fauré who represents the peak of French song, writing them over a period of nearly 60 years.

The sensuousness of the French language compared with German has, in a way, militated against French song; the language itself already sounds so melodious that setting it to music seems superfluous. Certainly the relationship between words and instrument(s) in French song is very different from that of almost any Lieder. With the French, there is typically a much more intimate contact between the vocal line and the instrumental one. The voice tends to take up the piano's melody, or vice versa. Where the Lied seems to have the singer walking on the ground provided by the piano, the mélodie suggests that the piano is the element in which the singer is swimming or floating – a generalization, but very broadly accurate.

Henri Duparc, born in 1848, three years before Fauré, wrote only 16 songs before lapsing into permanent creative paralysis, but they are among the finest, and largely predate Fauré's. Duparc used a harmonic

---

Gabriel Fauré was the most refined and quintessentially French of song writers. Of his output of nearly 100 songs, 14 were to settings by Verlaine.

The two groups of Verlaine settings are *Cinq Mélodies* and *La Bonne Chanson*, the latter depicting the poet's wooing of his future wife.

language rooted in Wagner, but created an idiom of influential originality: he is the apogee of French sensitivity. Fauré worked a much richer vein, producing in *La Bonne Chanson* (1894), a cycle of nine songs to poems by Verlaine, his masterpiece of variety and subtlety. These, like nearly all his work, repay only careful repeated listening, but the rewards are extraordinary. In many ways he is the French equivalent of Hugo Wolf.

After Fauré come Debussy and Ravel, the inseparable yet very different pair, both producing much of their finest work in songs. With them the great tradition of the mélodie is consummated, though there are many other fine composers, most notably Poulenc. Indeed, with his wit, vigour, range and unexpected depth, he may be the most accessible of all composers in this elusive genre. ♪

Paul Verlaine in 1893. The poetry of this arch-Bohemian was widely exploited by French writers of mélodies, from **Fauré and Debussy (*Fêtes galantes* and *Ariettes oubliées*) to Chausson, Ravel and Reynaldo Hahn.**

DUPARC:
• 'L' INVITATION •
AU VOYAGE' (1870)

*I*f there is one song which can be called the greatest in French, this is it. Duparc took the first and third stanzas of Baudelaire's poem, which dreams of a journey to a mysterious land of love. The language of impressionism, floating, elusive, flecked with many colours, begins here. The song begins with slow, spread chords, evocative of rustling, which continue as the singer enters, inviting his child, his sister, to love and die in the land where 'everything is only order and beauty, luxurious, calm, voluptuous'. On those last three words the singer intones like a priest, while the piano plays widely spaced, hushed chords. In the second verse the original movement is repeated, until the piano begins to ripple, continuing to do so hypnotically to the end, as the magic formula at the close of the first verse is invoked once more. Apparently simple, this song is the most refined distillation of ineffable yearning for the beyond.

English Song

WHILE GERMAN AND FRENCH ART-SONG took some time to reach its full flowering, one of the finest English composers of song was also one of the earliest. John Dowland (1563?–1626) was a member of the greatest school of English musicians, who flourished in the reign of Elizabeth I and James I. He wrote 87 songs, to be accompanied by the lute. Though some famous ones are cheerful – 'Fine knacks for ladies', for instance – his art is characteristically melancholy; typical titles are 'Flow my tears' and 'In darkness let me dwell'. He was an innovator on the lute, writing complex harmonic progressions for it, and strikingly dissonant chords. Their impact is immediate and overpowering. He was followed by a distinguished series of song composers throughout the 17th century, among whom the brothers Lawes, Henry and William,

lead to John Blow, the teacher of another master, Henry Purcell. Like Dowland, Purcell had a fine voice himself. Among his more than 100 songs are many settings of Shakespeare, including 'If music be the food of love', though his literary taste was unreliable.

Though English music went into decline after Purcell the tradition of song-writing continued, perhaps because in some ways it is easier to write at least tolerable songs than any other form of composition. They are usually quite short, there is the text to give them structure, and they can succeed with a decent melody: nothing else in music makes so few demands, though of course the greatest songs need genius. Nevertheless, during what are normally regarded as the dead centuries of English music, there was a steady flow of songs which can still give pleasure; in the 18th century they came from Thomas Arne (who wrote 'Rule, Britannia') and William Boyce, in the 19th Edward Loder, whose 'The Brook' is one of the finest English songs, and Sullivan. Then there are the inseparables Hubert Parry and Charles Villiers Stanford, not innovative but enjoyable; whereas Elgar, great in so many genres, is comparatively weak in song. It was early in the 20th century that real distinction reappeared, in the songs of Arthur Somervell and Ivor Gurney, and

<table>
<tr><td colspan="2" align="center">ENGLISH CONTRIBUTIONS TO THE
SONG CYCLE</td></tr>
<tr><td>English composers have been especially attracted to the song cycle, at least during the last 100 years. Often they have drawn on English poets: John Ireland set a series by Blake, Shakespeare, Rossetti, Dowson and J V Blake, and called it Songs of a Wayfarer (c. 1905–11), as Mahler called his early cycle. Butterworth, another minor composer whose finest achievements are in song, set six of Housman's A Shropshire Lad poems, Housman being a special favourite for this highly national collection of composers.

➤ Britten alone is a flamboyantly international figure, though his compositional roots are deeply English. His magnificent early orchestral cycle Les Illuminations (1940) is to poems by the Frenchman Rimbaud, and mark a departure into modernism in English music.</td><td>However, he had a close creative relationship with W H Auden, whose 'Our Hunting Fathers' and 'On This Island' provided him with incitements to bold experimentation in what was basically a very conservative musical climate. With Blake, with the great German Hölderlin, with Donne, with Hardy and with Michelangelo he showed not only how wide-ranging his literary tastes were, but how versatile his idiom was; he even set Pushkin in the original Russian. In the marvellous orchestral cycles Serenade for tenor, horn and strings (1943) and its successor Nocturne (1958) he created two wide-ranging works united by an imagination in which dreams and terror, innocence and its loss, the abiding themes of his work, are given a colouring and tone appropriate to night music.</td></tr>
</table>

{ The young Benjamin Britten and his long-term partner Peter Pears, at Long Island, New York, in 1939. The distinctive tenor voice of Pears inspired many of Britten's vocal works.

then Vaughan Williams, whose cycle *On Wenlock Edge* (1909) is a major achievement. Peter Warlock, in his cycle to poems by Yeats, *The Curlew* (1922), as well as in his haunting last song 'The Fox', reached peaks which make his early death in 1930 still more painful.

However, the greatest figure in English song since Purcell is unquestionably Benjamin Britten, whose songs, often written with Peter Pears's distinctive tenor voice in mind, reach and sustain a superlative level. He wrote many cycles, often to poetry of great distinction, and also arranged many folk songs with a creative imagination that makes them into something new, and reveals a wit and depth that gives them an unexpected dimension. His contemporary Michael Tippett has also produced a series of cycles, most impressively *Boyhood's End* (1943) and *The Heart's Assurance* (1951), both also written for Pears. Their successors have not, in general, been particularly interested in song, but their achievement stands beside any in the century written in any country. ♪

ANATOMY OF DOWLAND'S 'IN DARKNESS LET ME DWELL'

In this astonishing masterpiece the doleful melody overrules rhythm and any sense of metre. The lute introduces the mood in plangent discords, until the voice creeps in, low and rising only with effort. 'Sorrow', 'despair', 'weep', 'woes' and 'tomb' are some of the keywords of this ineffably poignant song, and at its centre is the line 'My music hellish, hellish jarring sounds, jarring jarring sounds to banish, banish friendly sleep'. We are left in suspense by the repetition of the words as to whether the music itself is jarring, or whether it banishes hellish sounds. The last line is a repeat of the first, leaving us stranded on a dissonance.

On Wenlock Edge (1909), by Vaughan Williams, was originally set for tenor, string quartet and piano; he revised it in 1920 for tenor and orchestra. The cycle takes its name from the first song. The unity is of mood rather than subject, and is provided more by the distinctive flavour of Housman's poems than by musical means; but it remains the composer's most popular set of songs.

Russian/Slav and Scandinavian

THE NATURE OF EACH LANGUAGE DICTATES the kind of song written in it. Russian is notable for its huge clusters of consonants and its long vowels, but it took the Russian composers of the 19th century – and there are no important ones earlier – some time to realize the potential of their own language. Glinka, the father of Russian music, went to school with the Italians, whose language could hardly be more different. He met Bellini and Donizetti, and composed in an idiom derived from theirs. The result is not terrible, but it is only a start; the beauty of the tunes seems irrelevant to the language they are setting. It was really only when the so-called 'mighty handful' Borodin, Cui, Balakirev, Mussorgsky and Rimsky-Korsakov, born towards the middle of the century, began their conscious attempt to create a national music that the Russian song started to flourish. All of them wrote songs which are worth hearing, but Mussorgsky's achievement stands out as so much the greatest that the others are put in the shade by him.

Mussorgsky led a wretched, disorganized life which made the completion of any large-scale project virtually impossible. Neither of his two great operas exists in a properly finished state, but in song he was able to put into

practice his austere creed that art should tell the truth about life rather than offering consoling beauty, and in his finest songs he created wholly original, intense expressions of childhood, of the sovereignty of death,

ANATOMY OF TCHAIKOVSKY'S 'HAD I ONLY KNOWN'

This song, written in 1880, is not Tchaikovsky's most famous song – that is 'None But the Lonely Heart' (1869) – but it ranks with his best. It begins and concludes with the piano playing a fairly extended and cheerful passage which sets the scene of everyday undramatic living. Within that the drama of a country girl who has fallen in love with a dashing young officer and been jilted is played out from her point of view, while the piano drags on with intentional monotony as she expresses her pain. The centre of the song is a waltz, fevered with expectation, and a speciality of Tchaikovsky's. It leads to a climax which is the girl's cry of anguish at betrayal, and then the piano repeats the yearning, the girl's passion portrayed and denied – but what, the opening music suggests by its return, does that matter to anyone else? This is a consummate little drama, as real in its more glamorous way as Mussorgsky's.

{ **Mussorgsky, painted by Repin shortly before he died in 1881, at the age of 42, of alcoholic poisoning.**

and of solitude. He was capable of rollicking humour too, but he did that kind of thing less distinctively. Tchaikovsky, greatest of Russian composers, is also more eclectic than the nationalistic five, who viewed him with suspicion. Much more the professional than any of them except Rimsky-Korsakov, he turned out songs at a rate they could not have managed, even if they had wanted to. His output, as in other departments, is uneven, not surprising in view of the fact that he wrote more than 100, some of them very early in his career, but his finest songs are extraordinary in their lyrical and dramatic power, terse expressions of the same sensibility which created the great ballets, symphonies and operas.

Rachmaninov was in many respects a disciple of Tchaikovsky, not least in his song output, all of which was created before he left Russia in 1917. As a virtuoso pianist, he wrote accompaniments which have at least as much importance as the vocal line, and in this respect contributed something new. Prokofiev and Shostakovich were less copious in their song output than in some other respects, but towards the end of his life the latter produced some masterly orchestral songs.

Among other Slav composers, Chopin certainly needs mentioning; his 19 songs are his only substantial body of music outside the piano works. In Czechoslovakia Smetana and Dvořák were both prolific, Dvořák to much greater effect. The utterly original Janáček wrote a cycle, *The Diary of One who Disappeared* (1919), which ranks high among his masterworks.

In Scandinavia, though there have been many remarkable song-writers, two are outstanding: Grieg, whose song output is deservedly popular and his most significant achievement, his rich melodic gift being more ideally suited to song than to anything more extended. Sibelius, by contrast, has been neglected, but his best songs, a dozen or so, are utterly characteristic of his genius and deserve a central place in the repertoire. They also enlarge our view of his range. ♪

• MUSSORGSKY'S SONG CYCLES •

Mussorgsky can evoke, and invoke, Mother Russia with the best of them: witness his magnificent 'On the Dnieper' (1879), as sung by any fine Slav bass. His most personal works are the three cycles, and each has a quite different greatness.

➤ *The Nursery* (1868–72), set to his own words, enters into a child's mind and evokes his fantasies, fears and troubles with his nurse. As in *Songs and Dances of Death*, the semi-melodic content arises entirely from the rhythm and sound of the words, the piano commenting and giving shape to the whole.

➤ *Sunless* (1874) is as desolate as its title suggests; there is no concession to hope or the possibility of enjoyment, and it is hard to imagine a bleaker set of songs, inspired not so much by specific circumstances as the tedium of life.

➤ *Songs and Dances of Death* (1875–77) is the third and most famous of Mussorgsky's cycles. In this, Death appears as four different presences: he lures a baby from its mother's arms in the first, singing it a lullaby; in the second he appears as a seducer, serenading a maiden; in the third he offers consolation to a destitute and drunken peasant; and in the fourth, even more terrifying than those that precede it, he appears as the field marshal, the only victor at the end of a fearful battle. Mussorgsky had intended to write seven songs, but even as they stand these four constitute an overwhelming experience, not needing the orchestration they often receive.

Opera

OPERA IS AN INHERENTLY PROBLEMATIC *and unstable art-form as no other. Many people have trouble in coping with it at all, with being expected to believe that some-one who is starving to death might sing elo-quently about it. Yet that should not be a dif-ficulty, any more than Hamlet's expressing his anguish in magnificently metaphorical blank verse. The real problems concern the ingredi-ents of opera, varied as they are, and liable to come into conflict with one another. Those who were responsible for its creation could hardly have anticipated that singers would demand ever more florid music to show off their powers, utterly indifferent to the dra-matic demands of the work they were singing in, and often not able to combine singing and act-ing. Nor could they have envisaged the element of the spectacular which soon entered, opera often seeming to become a vehicle for the demon-stration of advanced technology rather than art. Then, too, with the increase in the size of the orchestra, especially in the 19th century, the whole issue of how much of the text the audience was expected to grasp while a soprano sang loud top notes over more than 100 musicians was raised, and has never been definitely settled.*

From 19th-century favourite to 20th-century museum piece: Meyerbeer's spectacular *Robert le diable.*

ORIGINALLY A COURT ENTERTAINMENT, opera was used from early on to demonstrate the wealth and splendour of a monarch or duke. That meant that it was forced into an association with display and pageantry which has proved surprisingly durable. In reaction to those excesses, serious-minded theorists, who have often also been the composers of opera, have insisted that it is primarily drama articulated through music. That has led, especially in recent times, to the hegemony of the producers, making points that seem to have scant connection with the music or the intended stage action. Their position has been strengthened by the fact that the number of operas that survive for more than a few years, and permanently enter the repertoire, is fairly small; the result is that there is claimed to be a need to reinterpret them, so that audiences do not become bored or complacent.

Should a production of an opera look and sound as much as possible as it did when it was first performed – or at least as much like its composer and librettist wanted it to be – or should it take account of subsequent developments in stage management, singing technique, the ever-increasing role of the conductor, and even contemporary social issues? Since these questions are probably unanswerable, this means that discussion of opera is lively, but that opera itself can often be relegated to the mere occasion for critical debate. There is also the unquestionable fact that time and again a given mode of writing opera has become decadent, and that the form itself is constantly in danger of falling into disrepute.

THE BEGINNINGS

Opera began abruptly at the end of the 16th century in the courts of Northern Italy. Of course there had been plays with music before – the Greek dramas were performed with music, but no one knows what it was like. As a Renaissance phenomenon, opera was concerned to go back to antiquity to justify itself, but with the advantage, probably, that it had scant idea of what classical antiquity was like. The high-society people who met in Florence to discuss the subject were ideally placed: they did not know exactly what they were talking about, but they knew what conclusions they wanted to reach.

They, and thus opera, had a stroke of miraculous luck. The first opera was produced in 1598: Jacopo Peri's *Dafne*, soon followed by his *Euridice* (1600), the first opera that survives, and very tedious it is. However, at the Court of Mantua the resident composer was Claudio Monteverdi, and he was the greatest composer of his time. His first opera, *Orfeo*, was produced in 1607, and it is a masterpiece which can be listened to and watched today with unaffected enjoyment. It was taken for granted that operas would have as their subject Greek mythological stories, which the audiences would know in advance. That would enable the composers to work within a narrative framework, while altering it interestingly and heightening expressive effects. It would also enable striking visual effects, such as gods appearing from on high. There could be lengthy diversions, so long as the drama remained the centre of attention. Singing would be a kind of heightened speech, called 'recitative', which at climactic moments could become more elaborate, 'arioso'. There would be a chorus, and whatever instruments happened to be available – but not such as to drown the

Ulysses wrestling with Iro in Act 3 of Monteverdi's *Il ritorno d'Ulisse in patria.*

singers. From this success Monteverdi went on to write many more operas, all but two of which are lost. Those two come from nearly 40 years later, at the end of his life. *Il ritorno d'Ulisse in patria* ('The Return Home of Ulysses') (1640) sticks to the classical formula, but by now opera was a popular entertainment, and Monteverdi had moved to Venice. Ulisse is a very long opera with comic diversions, but with the central figure, Penelope, developed with extraordinary psychological penetration, as a study in professional widowhood. Then, for his last work, Monteverdi turned to an historical subject: *L'incoronazione di Poppea* (1643) is the story of how Nero and his lover Poppea ruthlessly eliminate everyone who stands in the path of their union, and end singing a swooning love duet of shocking tenderness (it may not be by Monteverdi – these matters were treated

very casually at the time). *Poppea* is a scandalous masterpiece, and its reclamation over the last 30 years is the most valuable thing that musicology has achieved.

As soon as opera got under way, innumerable works were written, often cannibalizing one another. Most of the ones that survive strike us as very boring, as the majority of works in any form are bound to do; and genius in opera is especially rare. Opera remained for some time the preserve of the Italians, only gradually moving north-wards to France and Germany. Monteverdi remains the towering figure of the century, although his pupil Cavalli had a melodic gift which makes his many works inter-mittently attractive. *La Calisto* (1651), a complicated story of the goddess Diana in drag, has been revived recently and is good, dirty fun, but no more. He helped to standardize the form that opera took, with laments over a ground bass (that is, an orchestral figure repeated while the singer pours out his or her grief) as an essential ingredient: it reached its apogee in Purcell's *Dido and Aeneas* (1689), with Dido's Lament as one of the greatest pieces in the repertoire. Cavalli also made sure that there was a love duet at the end of each act. Monteverdi's music is gloriously free from conventions. That is fine in the hands of a genius, but dangerous for lesser men, whose works become shapeless if they lack formal structure, though often predictable if they possess it. The first period of decadence of opera arrived soon after its inauguration. ♪

• MONTEVERDI'S *ORFEO*: THE ACTION •

∞ The opera begins with an orchestral intro-duction, which is then varied and repeated throughout the first act (it is the same music which begins his *Vespers*). The first act and a half are devoted to celebrating Orfeo's and Eurydice's married bliss. Then – the first great dramatic coup in opera – a messenger arrives to announce that Eurydice has been stung to death by a serpent. Orfeo is inconsolable, but decides to go to Hades, where his eloquence in singing and accompanying himself is so great that he wins Eurydice back, so long as he does not turn round to look at her. At her insistence he does just that, but tragedy is forestalled, and they end up as constellations of stars – a pathetically weak ending, but prophetic of the reluctance of operatic composers not to let music rescue any situa-tion, however dire. *Orfeo* remains a masterpiece, even if a flawed one.

Life as Myth

THE FIRST OPERAS PERFORMED IN FRANCE were Italian, beginning in 1645, and it was Cavalli who wrote the opera which celebrated Louis XIV's wedding. However the French were, for the time being, more interested in ballet than in opera, and Cavalli flopped. The first major composer of French opera was Jean-Baptiste Lully, who collaborated with the great comic playwright Molière in a series of opera-ballets, the most enjoyable of which is *Le bourgeois gentilhomme* (1670), but once he got from the King the exclusive rights to opera production in Paris he produced a stream of somewhat more innovative pieces, working with the librettist Quinault in retelling classical myths: among their most distinguished collaborations are *Cadmus et Hermione* (1673) and *Atys* (1676); *Bellérophon* (1679) was Lully's most successful work, but Quinault was then in disgrace, and Lully used three other librettists for it.

Ballet still occupied an important position in his works, as did lavish spectacle. The singing is something between recitative and arioso, sometimes accompanied quite colourfully. Their ultimate point, though, was to glorify the Sun King, which can make for pretty tedious listening. It was not until Jean-Philippe Rameau began, late in life, to write operas that French opera took a marked step forward. He was adept at striking orchestration, unusual harmonies, and semi-melodic recitatives which are often almost memorable. The basic style, though, for all the frequent magnificence of Rameau's invention, is stiff, since it was still important to please the King (by now Louis XV). Nonetheless, his work has recently undergone a marked revival, and certainly *Hippolyte et Aricie* (1733, revised 1742, 1757), *Castor et Pollux* (1737, revised 1754, 1764) and *Dardanus* (1739, revised 1744, 1760) now seem assured of at least a

ENTERTAINMENT FIT FOR KINGS

Louis XIV's centralization of power in Versailles, which had such profound effects on every aspect of French society and culture, also had a lot to do with the form that French opera took. The King himself was an enthusiastic dancer, and the tradition of opera-ballets survived him. Since the plots were endlessly recycled versions of the ancient myths, variety was introduced by elaborate stage spectacles, and both the beginning and end of each work was expected to pay tribute to the King's magnanimity. This is opera as ritual and visual fantasy. Small demands are made on the attention-span of the audience, and larger ones would have been most unwelcome. The high-flown language of the libretti favoured a measured mode of singing, as opposed to the racy, idiomatic style of the Italians. In all respects emphasis was placed on decorum, even in the most harrowing situations.

against the singers in an entirely novel spirit. Thus when Oreste, in *Iphigénie en Tauride* (1779, revised 1781), sings that peace has returned to his heart, the orchestra continues to be agitated to show he is lying; and Gluck told one of his singers to scream as if his leg was being sawn off – the point being that dramatic truth was much more important than purely beautiful singing. Yet behind all this there is still a decorousness which shows that the values of the country which tirelessly congratulates itself on being civilized are upheld despite everything.

In opera, as in other respects, the 18th century in France ended in revolution. Classical tragedy gave way to so-called *opéra-comique*, in which spoken dialogue replaced recitative, and arias and ensembles took all the musical weight. Grétry and Méhul, hardly remembered today, were leading exponents of this new form, but the one who still holds the boards by dint of one fine work is an Italian much admired by Beethoven, Luigi Cherubini, whose *Médée* (1797) is quite often revived, if in a heavily revised version by Lachner, as *Medea.* ♪

marginal place in the repertoire. A battle was joined, of a characteristic French kind, between those such as Pergolesi and Rousseau, as well as the Queen, who favoured something lighter, in Italian style, and those who conservatively stuck to the *tragédies* in opera tradition, including the King and Madame de Pompadour.

Another battle of the same kind arose when Gluck arrived on the scene in the latter part of the 18th century. By far the most notable composer of French opera, and one of the supreme figures in the history of opera overall, Gluck took his role as creator of dramas with unprecedented seriousness. He himself was a convert to that cause, and even when his so-called 'reform operas' were being written he could still oblige with something less demanding. In his masterpieces, still on classical legends, there are great arias which are integrated into the dramatic structure of the work in a way which excited the devotion of such successors as Berlioz and

Wagner. With him, as with all his predecessors, we find an avoidance of tragedy which is typical of the 18th century, but also a willingness to use the orchestra

GLUCK'S MASTERPIECES: *ORFEO ED EURIDICE* AND *IPHIGENIE EN TAURIDE*

For all the beauties of many passages in Lully's operas, and many more in Rameau's, the constant holding up of the action by ballets makes the complete works a trial. Moving on to Gluck is an invigorating experience.

➤ *Orphée* is rightly one of the most performed of operas, if usually in its Italian form, *Orfeo ed Euridice* (1762). In this original version, the action is very compressed, and the opening tableau, in which the chorus laments Euridice's death while Orfeo cries her name repeatedly, is among the most affecting in opera. Act II, the first half of which consists of Orfeo taming the Furies, the second half taking place in the Elysian Fields, is a perfect balance, musically and dramatically. For the French version of 1774 Gluck added a bravura aria for Orphée, and a marvellous ballet sequence in Act II, including the central D minor section in the Dance of the Blessed Spirits, the loveliest flute

solo ever written. Once heard, the French version is hard to forego, despite the diffusion of dramatic interest. The compromise which Berlioz effected in 1859 is perhaps the best solution.

➤ Gluck's greatest work, and one which should have a central postion in the operatic repertoire, is *Iphigénie en Tauride*. The opening orchestral storm, into which Iphigénie launches her cries, is immediately overpowering, and the pace and intensity never let up. The plot centres round the choice which Iphigénie has to make between her unrecognized brother Oreste and his devoted friend Pylade, as a sacrifice to the gods; there are thus two conflicts, Iphigénie's and that between the friends, each of whom wants to sacrifice himself for the sake of the other. What is so remarkable is that with very limited resources of harmony and orchestration Gluck achieves such a wealth of varied dramatic effects.

Opera Seria

IN THE LATE 17TH AND EARLY 18TH centuries, Italy went through a period of extreme economic hardship. This meant that the expense which opera almost inevitably entails had to be curbed somehow: the results are in some respects predictable, in others not. Both orchestras and choruses had to be reduced in size, an expected consequence. Another, momentous for the development of opera, especially the variety of it which came to be known as *opera seria* (serious, as opposed to comic opera, in which the emotions were expressed at length), is more surprising. The seriousness takes what must strike us as odd forms: the more intense the feelings of a character in opera seria, the longer he or she is expected to carry on about them, in a display of vocal acrobatics which to us

---

• HANDEL'S OPERATIC MASTERPIECES •

The trouble with performing opera seria, apart from the difficulty of getting audiences to tolerate its static nature, is that there are no castratos, and it is not clear how different countertenors or contraltos sound from the original performers. Since the operas written for them depended so largely on their talents, we are only partially able to judge how impressive they were.

➤ Handel's operas, nonetheless, can be very effective, even if they are often more enjoyably listened to at home than seen in the theatre. His greatest may be *Giulio Cesare* (1724), which is about Julius Caesar's love for Cleopatra, and also about the widow and son of the murdered Pompey. The scene in which Cesare goes to contemplate Pompey's tomb, short though it is, and an arioso, shows

what depths of noble feeling Handel could plumb. It also tends, unfortunately, to make everything else in the opera seem less fine than it otherwise would. As with most of his operas, it is very long, about three hours. There are no ensembles, just a succession of arias and recitatives, a few choruses and a duet, yet once heard it cannot be forgotten.

➤ Nor, we are now finding, can *Rodelinda* (1725), *Tolomeo* (1728), *Ariodante* (1735), *Alcina* (1735), *Serse* (1738) and *Arminio* (1737), among a host of surprisingly dissimilar works, given the strict conventions which govern them. Handel was evidently a shrewd psychologist, and the thought of what he might have achieved with superior libretti is tormenting. As it is, his achievement is primarily musical rather than dramatic.

---

suggests high spirits or hysteria unless very carefully managed.

For assorted reasons both tenor and bass voices were regarded as unsuitable for the central figures in these works, so the potentialities of the castrato voice were

lavishly exploited. There were many such to hand, for many boys took it for granted that they would join the Church as priests or monks, both because that was the obvious respectable profession open to them, and because they could not afford to have

{ A caricature of the great height to which castratos often grew. In this scene from Handel's *Flavio*, the singers are Senesino, Cuzzoni and Berenstadt.

children. Since joining the Church meant that they would have to be celibate, and since they could earn money by singing in church choirs, they were not as reluctant as might be thought to submit to castration, which preserved their prepubescent voices. Then it was discovered that among the effects of the operation was considerable physical growth, so that they developed physiques which enabled them to sing prodigiously long passages without taking breath. This led them, if they were eager for wealth and celebrity, from the monastery to the theatre. The first great stars of opera were accidentally born, as it were. These castratos became the rage of western Europe, commanding vast fees and fanatical devotion.

The idea of opera seria was once more to celebrate the virtue of magnanimity on the part of a monarch (in the opera) who was plotted against in the most dastardly ways; a complicated set of conflicting love interests provided the main thrust of the plots, with the castratos as the desirable males, sopranos as the women in love with them, and tenors, who had previously been regarded as suitable for singing comic elderly roles, as the

{ Julius Caesar contemplates the head of his enemy, Pompey, in the profoundest moment in the eponymous opera.

all-forgiving king – hence the enormous proliferation of operas with the name 'La Clemenza di X'. The arch-purveyor of libretti for these operas was Metastasio, some of whose texts were used up to 70 times. The language is stilted and artificial, the sentiments conventional, the action implausibly involved. What they really did was serve the purpose of vocal display, especially of course for the castratos, who often had an amazing range and could sing coloratura as probably no one has since.

The greatest figure in opera during the first half of the 18th century was undoubtedly Handel, the master of opera seria. He is a complicated case: born and bred a German, then trained in Italian opera, he spent most of his composing life in England. He may be counted, all told, as an Italian composer for operatic purposes, though nearly all his operas were premiered in London. They are to Italian texts and often have the defects inherent in opera seria, though their enormous merits, still being rediscovered, are all his own. He did what he could within a straitjacketing form, but he was not sufficiently bold an innovator to break the mould and make a fresh start. Hence there will always be a certain effort in appreciating even his finest operatic creations, though they are being revised apace, especially on CD. ♪

OPERA TRADITIONS IN EUROPE

It is surely no coincidence that Italy was the country in which opera was born, and in which it has most continuously been cultivated, even if not always to good purpose. The fluidity of the language, its many liquid vowels and soft consonants, almost invite singing. Once it got under way, the traditions of Italian opera seemed to dictate that when a composer wrote to a certain pattern, Italian was the language that should inevitably be employed.

In Germany a quite different tradition grew up in the 18th century – that of the Singspiel, or sung play. The influences on this form came both from England, in the form of the ballad opera, and from France, in that of the opéra-comique. In the Singspiel the arias and choruses alternated not with the rapid recitative of Italian opera – rapidly sung German sounds clumsy – but with spoken dialogue, and the conventions of the time dictated that when there was a mixture of music and spoken language the subject matter should be comic, in a broad sense. Its leading exponent was Benda, who in *Das Jahrmarkt* (1770) produced one of its strongest pieces before Mozart took up the form.

The Human Heart Revealed

WITH MOZART WE REACH ONE OF THE two greatest operatic composers, one who produced works of such stupendous greatness that, once known, life is inconceivable without them. However,

The bird-catching Papageno represents the common man in Mozart's allegory *Die Zauberflöte*.

Mozart did not arrive at operatic maturity in one, or even several leaps; of his 17 operas, at the most generous count 10 can be discounted from having major stature, though lovers of Mozart will want to hear them occasionally. He began with a Singspiel, written when he was 12, and then spent much of his adolescence writing long opere serie. They never fall beneath a level of competence, it goes without saying, and there are delightful, touching, even moving moments in them, but these works of his pre-maturity are really only interesting because of what they led to, and also because they show Mozart's prodigious powers of assimilation. As a travelling prodigy from a very early age, he was able to sample the operatic wares of all the chief European states, and to learn from all of them – especially to learn what he could discard from the various traditions.

It was when he was 24 that Mozart produced his first masterpiece, *Idomeneo* (1781), an opera seria which transcends the form and culminates, in Act III, in a quartet which is by far the greatest ensemble written for an opera up to that time. Mozart, a man who understood the human heart with Shakespearean completeness, here managed to take the emotions characteristic of opera seria – love, jealousy, nobility, terror – and make them into something vivid and immediate, where before they had ossified into a series of conventional musical gestures.

Even so, his forte is as a comic opera composer. In his next opera, *Die Entführung aus dem Serail* ('The Abduction from the Seraglio') (1782), he reverted to the Singspiel, with a typical plot of an oriental despot capturing unfortunate Westerners.

However, as with *Idomeneo* he breathes life into them so that we care about their fate. None the less, compared to what he went on to produce, neither of these works has the stature which puts Mozart in a class apart. When he met Lorenzo da Ponte, that rarest of beings in the operatic world, a librettist of genius, he went on to write his three central masterpieces, *Le nozze di Figaro* ('The Marriage of Figaro') (1786), *Don Giovanni* (1787) and *Così fan tutte* ('Thus do all Women') (1790). Here, in a variety of ways, he portrays fully rounded human beings, using a flexible musical idiom which does away with standard forms when it needs to, and above all shows feeling flowing into action, and a set of people expressing emotion in entirely plausible ways. The triumphs of these very dissimilar works are their ensembles, which in the case of the finales last for up to 25 minutes, action-packed but lucid in their presentation of characters' reactions to situations fraught with anxiety and peril.

In the last year of his life Mozart went on to create his last two operas. One was *La clemenza di Tito* ('The Clemency of Titus') (1791), a return to opera seria, and a work which despite its constant beauty is ultimately a bore. The other was *Die Zauberflöte* ('The Magic Flute') (1791), a return to Singspiel, but at a level on which sublimity and low comedy alternate and merge to create something utterly new and unrepeatable. It is, fittingly, the climax of his operatic career.

It goes almost without saying that all these works were written to commissions, and that Mozart normally had an appallingly short time in which to write them. Among the miracles that he achieved in these works is the musical decorum which almost always prevails, effects such as the violently dissonant opening of the overture to *Don Giovanni* being very much the exception. This apparent well-manneredness makes the disruptive content of all three of the da Ponte works something that it took some time for listeners to realize. The catchiness of the melodies seems to have been what chiefly made for their immediate

Schinkel's set for Act I, scene I of *Die Zauberflöte*; Berlin production, 1816.

popular acceptance, together with a less puritanical view of human nature, especially the feminine variety, than was prevalent in the next century. The ease with which people can transfer their love, or at any rate their passion, from one object to another, which is the all too painful message of *Così*, seems to have been accepted at the time without demur – or maybe it is the uncanny, possibly unconscious skill with which subversiveness is encoded in these works that meant it was some time before their full impact was apparent.

With his unblinking view of humanity, Mozart could create works which later generations found shocking. The idea that two young women could indulge in fiancé-swapping was found so distasteful by Beethoven and Wagner, representative of their century, that *Così* was either unperformed or set to a different text, until Richard Strauss rescued it for our age. But now *Così*, and the other masterpieces, have been over-taken by a different, more subversive fate. Because they are so familiar, producers have updated them, placed

them in American diners, on space ships, Mediterranean cruises, anything to defamiliarize them. Faced with such 'concepts', discerning Mozart lovers may find it more rewarding to stay at home and listen to their CDs, for it is above all in listening to Mozart's music-dramas that we are able to appreciate the sometimes alarming gaps which open up between the conventional sentiments of many of the words and the disturbingly profound music;

for instance, in the sublime Farewell Quintet in Act I of *Così* the two men, who are collaborating with the cynical old philosopher Don Alfonso in his plot to test their girl-friends' fidelity, sing what would strike us, indeed does, as music of tragic power. Are they really fooling, or does their music indicate that more is going on inside them than either they know or understand? Mozart, unlike any other composer, leaves us with these conundrums unanswered. ♪

• ANATOMY OF A MOZART ARIA •

∾ Without being a conscious innovator like Gluck or Wagner, Mozart was happy to take the musical and dramatic idioms and conventions he found and manipulate them to his purposes, which were to be true to the human heart, understanding without judging, at the same time as adhering to musical decorum. In his mature operas he dispenses with the da capo aria, realizing the absurdity of taking his characters back to the emotional state in which they began: more typical of him is the Countess's second aria in *Figaro*, 'Dove sono'. She begins by recalling the happy days when her husband loved her, contrasts them with her present plight as a semi-deserted wife, goes back for a further recall, but then decides that she must do something about it, and in the last, quick section of the aria she makes her resolve to win her husband back. It is as psychologically convincing as it is musically satisfying. In the mature operas one never feels that any musical occurrence is merely the result of the demands of the form: it is always what the drama requires, and the more amazing for the wholeness with which every last character is drawn.

The Heyday of Italian Opera

THE MAINSTAY OF THE OPERATIC repertoire is, in large part, operas written by Italian composers during the 19th century. The earliest are a trio who are called *bel canto* composers, though the term merely means 'beautiful singing'. The justification for the name is that they were especially concerned with writing expressive vocal lines, accompanied by a strictly subordinate orchestra.

BEL CANTO: ROSSINI, DONIZETTI AND BELLINI

Rossini, the prodigy, early developed a gift for the hilarious, and in such eternal favourites as *Il barbiere di Siviglia* ('The Barber of Seville') (1816) and *La Cenerentola* ('Cinderella') (1817) wrote near-farces which occasionally reveal a heart, but mainly amuse through their beady near-brutality. However, they do more than amuse: Rossini is often thought of, particularly in contrast to Mozart, as a cynic. That suggests that he believed human feelings to be inevitably shallow, but in fact it is the villains in these works – and there are many more of them than the two mentioned above – who take that view, invariably prizing material possessions and appearances over desire. Everyone in his comedies, even the heroines, realizes that you will not get anywhere in this world without manipulation, but Cinderella's final aria shows how desperately important it is for her to gain her heart's object. Rossini's distinctive contribution to operatic form, the 'ensemble of confusion' in which the villains are gradually outwitted by a series of intrigues so complex that they lose their bearings, shows how close he can come to Mozart (for example in the finale to Act II of *Figaro*), while not quite making us feel the desperation on behalf of the characters

that Mozart can. Rossini was himself a manic-depressive, and his art at its finest is poised between hilarity and hysteria.

He moved on to grand operas, and his last, *Guillaume Tell* (1829), is his greatest work, a national epic with a huge sweep. His 'serious' works, most of which were forgotten for more than a century, are proving to be much more various than has been thought. He can achieve genuine grandeur, but the trouble is that the resolutions of even his most nearly tragic works do sound like those of his comedies, so that, in the last resort, the traditional view of him as primarily a mirth-maker may have more in it than his most ardent admirers wish to admit. For sundry reasons he abandoned opera composition at the age of 37, though he lived to be 76.

Both of Rossini's peers, Donizetti and Bellini, died early. Donizetti, too, was long famous for his comedies *Don Pasquale* (1843) and *L'elisir d'amore* ('The Elixir of Love') (1832). Their plots tend to be along Rossinian, traditional lines of scheming guardians trying to marry their young wards, who are in love with the tenor hero (by now the hero of an Italian opera was invariably a tenor), but they are less frenzied in mood, more lyrical and tender, and the laughs are affectionate rather than

vindictive. In sombre vein, *Lucia di Lammermoor* (1835) is the finest of his works, and the greatest of the innumerable operas inspired by the novels of Walter Scott. In recent decades, thanks largely to the exemplary genius of Maria Callas, some of his other tragic operas, often concerned with Tudor history (heavily doctored) have regained a place in the repertoire – in this respect his reputation has followed the same curve as Rossini's, at a respectful distance. They demand hair-raising virtuosity from their heroines, and sometimes from their heroes, and tend to conclude with protracted death scenes. The two most performed now, *Anna Bolena* (1830) and *Maria Stuarda* (1834) have scenes of great power alternating with much that is perfunctory and routine. Donizetti wrote so much so fast that he collapsed into insanity in his early forties, a painfully appropriate end for someone who had made mad scenes so much his own.

Bellini may have had the slenderest gift of the three (and was certainly the most painstaking and least productive), but did the most with it. He cultivated a vein of melancholic, early Romantic pathos which, given the right voices, is uniquely affecting, but was also capable of writing heroic music of vigour and conviction: in these respects

Costume designs for a 19th century production of Rossini's *Il barbiere.*

he is like Chopin, by whom he was greatly admired. Their enormous, sinuous melodies have a lot in common. Bellini's legacy is small but priceless. His masterpiece is *Norma* (1831), in which a Druid priestess who has had a long relationship with an enemy Roman proconsul dies on a pyre, having confessed all. It is the most taxing of all soprano roles, in a consistently inspired opera. Though its war music is staple 19th-century stuff, the rest could have been written by no one else. The orchestration is notable for its simplicity, which still manages to achieve many moments of poignant colouring. In more rustic vein, his *La sonnambula* ('The Sleepwalker')(1831) has many more of his long, Chopinesque melodies. His last opera, *I Puritani* ('The Puritans')(1835) shows yet further refinements in his art. Though the plot is less satisfactory than that of *Norma*, the expressiveness of the heroine's arias suggests that had Bellini not died so young, he would have created a vein of lyricism which might have placed him among the greatest masters of opera.

VERDI

The commanding figure of Italian opera is Verdi, born in 1813, and productive until he was 80. His early operas are Donizettian in idiom, but with a constant supercharged energy which he retained in his maturity. The central three works from his middle period, *La traviata* (1853), *Il trovatore* (1853) and *Rigoletto* (1851) show a genius for compression, memorable melody and the robust handling of strong situations which make them staples of any opera company. The latter two also show Verdi's poor literary taste, though he was exigent with his librettists; he seems to have been addicted to implausible, ramshackle plots and melodramatic situations which it needs all the verve of his music to justify.

His later works are sometimes on a larger scale, *Don Carlos* (1867, revised 1884) being a work of vast proportions, dealing with issues of the private and the public, love and duty, Church versus State, with a seriousness which was new to his art. Originally written for Paris, and thus in French, it was extensively cut even before its premiere, and further for its Italian version. Yet apart from its lamentable ballet music, opportunistically written to please the Parisian public, it is a work of almost continuously high inspiration.

After *Aida* (1871) Verdi felt his life's work was accomplished, but he was lured by the composer and librettist Arrigo Boito into writing his last works, *Otello* (1887) and *Falstaff* (1893), derived from Shakespeare but typical in their compression, newly free in their musical continuity. There was widespread chatter at the time that Verdi had been influenced by Wagner, but in fact these two incredibly contrasting masterpieces are purely Verdian. That he should have concluded his career with a gossamer-textured comedy remains a marvel.

All four of these composers, conscientious craftsmen as they were, wrote for a popular audience, and hardly expected their works to endure, though Verdi finally came

A poster advertising the first performance of *Otello*, in 1887, which was produced 16 years after the composer's previous opera, *Aida.*

to take a different attitude to that issue. For most of his life, as for that of all his predecessors, operas were something which lasted for a season and then disappeared; hence one of the reasons for the huge amount of self-borrowing which they all, except Bellini, went in for. Verdi was even prepared to adapt a whole opera to a different plot, time and place when the first version proved a flop. He was a shrewd businessman of musical genius. Oddly enough, although he was by far the finest of Italian opera composers of the last two centuries, he was less self-conscious about his art than his immediate successors, who made up in pretensions for what they lacked in musical substance. Apart from a superb melodic gift which rarely failed him, Verdi conveys a decency and genuine concern with 'family values' which have an enduring appeal. ♪

The 19th-Century Mainstream

OPERA FLOURISHED EVERYWHERE IN Europe except England and Spain during the 19th century. In Germany, Wagner aside, the Singspiel (see page 231) tradition continued, though no longer confined to comedy. Above all towers Beethoven's one opera, *Fidelio* (1805, revised 1814). A work about freedom, it features a woman disguised as a man rescuing her husband, a political prisoner. The libretto is naive, but the force of Beethoven's inspiration makes this perhaps the most exalting opera of all.

Weber, a master who was plagued by bad libretti and poor health, created in *Der Freischütz* ('The Free-shooter') (1821) the German folk opera *par excellence*, in which a village community has to come to terms with supernatural forces. His *Euryanthe* (1823) is more sophisticated musically, but this is one opera where the idiotic story manages to sabotage all the composer's efforts. For almost all the rest of the century Wagner's extraordinarily personality, let alone his music, eclipsed that of all other German operatic composers.

It was Giacomo Meyerbeer, a German by birth, who commanded the Parisian, and thus for a time the international, scene. His speciality was historical epics on the grandest possible scale, the most famous being *Les Huguenots* (1836) and *Le prophète* (1849). They were the equivalent of Hollywood's sonic and scenic spectaculars, and are no more durable, but they influenced everyone, including Verdi and Wagner. "Meyerbeer will be immortal in his lifetime and for 20 years afterwards," the shrewd Heinrich Heine remarked; and he was right – of which of our contemporaries might it also be true?

A composer whose greatest work was almost sunk by Meyerbeer's influence was Berlioz. In *Les Troyens* ('The Trojans') (1856–58) he created an epic of which the first part centres on Cassandra and the fall of Troy and the second on Dido and Aeneas. It has long stretches of music of unparalleled sublimity, especially the love duet with words from *The Merchant of Venice* (Virgil and Shakespeare were Berlioz's two heroes, and he was prepared to go to any lengths to unite them) and the finale, when Dido prepares to mount her funeral pyre; but many, too, of inert spectacle and irrelevant ballet. His other two operas are intermittently delightful: *Benvenuto Cellini* (1838), a ramshackle affair about the Italian sculptor's casting of his greatest work, with quirky episodes and grotesque figures; and *Béatrice et Bénédict* (1862), after *Much Ado About Nothing*.

The most successful French composer of

opera was Bizet, who in *Carmen* (1875) wrote a masterpiece which is inimitable, perfect and deservedly the world's most popular opera. Yet like many other enduring works, it was at first a flop, for reasons which remain obscure, and its failure helped to lead to Bizet's early death. Gounod purveyed love and piety, and in *Faust* (1859) wrote a work whose demise is often predicted, but which won't lie down. Just when the listener feels that he or she can take no more of its complacently sticky idiom, Gounod comes up with a melodic inspiration which disarms; and he does manage to cap it with a magnificent finale.

Slav opera has as its greatest achievements two national epics by Mussorgsky, scrappy but starkly powerful: *Boris Godunov* (1868–69, revised 1873) and *Khovanshchina* (1872–80). In them there are no heroes, not even the long-suffering Russian people; the central figures are portrayed with merciless realism, and a musical language to match. Tchaikovsky, not a nationalist, created in *Eugen Onegin* (1879) a fragile lyric work, and in *The Queen of Spades* (1890) one of

The programme cover of the Opera Russe's *Boris Godunov*; Paris, 1930.

the few genuinely scary operas; his other works in the genre are only intermittently interesting. In Czechoslovakia, Dvořák wrote a fairy-tale of bewitching beauty in *Rusalka* (1901), and Smetana a widely varied series of works, of which the incessantly tuneful *The Bartered Bride* (1866) is the most sturdy survivor. This was undoubtedly opera's most fertile, colourful period, in that there was an enormous amount of creative activity in many different styles, national and otherwise. The expansion of the symphony orchestra during the 19th century meant that in many operas it became an equal partner with the singers. Though there were still many works written to formulae, the number of formulae available was much larger, and because in

the 19th century the ambitions of art were greater than before, the climate was ideal for the creation of epics as well as for intimate pieces. Opera and the novel, so similar in so many ways, reached their highest points simultaneously.

The Gothic horrors of German Romantic opera before Wagner reach their climax in the Wolf's Glen scene in *Der Freischütz*, which can cause a frisson in even sophisticated spectators.

• SIGNIFICANT MINOR WORKS •

The century sported a host of operatic composers of genius; it was one of those periods when everything comes together for the production of at least interesting and at best magnificent works in a particular art-form. There are also many arresting figures who were supported by the artistic climate sufficiently to create works which still repay attention.

FRANCO-GERMAN

➤ **Halévy** managed in *La Juive* ('The Jewess') (1835) to work within the school of grand opera but to make something intimate and affecting of it.

➤ **Marschner**, colleague and devotee of Weber, gave contemporaries a thrill we can understand with *Der Vampyr* (1828); and his other major work, *Hans Heiling* (1833), treats the fashionable theme of a figure torn between the everyday and the supernatural world.

➤ **Lortzing** was of the same general disposition as Marschner, though he was at his best in comedy, for example *Zar und Zimmermann* ('Tsar and Carpenter') (1837).

➤ **Nicolai**, in *Die lustigen Weiber von Windsor* ('The Merry Wives of Windsor') (1849), created a minor masterpiece to the same plot as Verdi's *Falstaff*; had he not died in poverty, he might have become genuinely important.

➤ **Humperdinck** put Wagner's influence, generally swamping, to brilliant use in *Hänsel und Gretel* (1893), a gem which still attracts the finest talents so rewarding is it to sing and characterize.

RUSSIAN

Minor Russian composers contributed works which thrive best at home, but there are notable exceptions:

➤ **Glinka**, who founded Russian opera, sparkles

in *Ruslan and Ludmilla* (1842) and writes the first Russian epic in *A Life for the Tsar* (1836). Borodin's *Prince Igor* (produced 1890) is most famous for its Polotsvian Dances, but it has a good deal of dramatic life in it, too.

➤ **Rimsky-Korsakov**, a master-orchestrator, possessed limitless energy and facility, but for all his colour and verve his was fundamentally an empty talent. His operas continually threaten to make a comeback. Fairy-tale, taken broadly, is his preserve. In *Christmas Eve* (1895) he does a mildly amusing job, taking a fantastic story by Gogol and making it the pretext for comic-magic antics, but in such celebrated works as *The Golden Cockerel* (1909) and *The Snow Maiden* (1882, second version 1898) his inner vacuity is apparent; and in *The Invisible City of Kitezh* (1907) he attempts to deal with religious topics, with embarrassing results. His talent is essentially Hollywoodian.

Wagner, the Revolutionary

WITH RICHARD WAGNER WE REACH THE most controversial figure in the history of the arts, a man who divides opinion as fiercely today as he did thoughout the latter years of his life. The controversy stems partly from the nature of his music, partly from the ambitions of his works, and at least as much from the multifarious influence they have had, not only on artists but on every area of cultural life, and even on politicians, Hitler being a fervent disciple.

Wagner's beginnings, musically and otherwise, were humble. He was not precocious, and his first three operas, *Die Feen* ('The Fairies') (1833–34) *Das Liebesverbot* ('The Ban on Love') (1836) and *Rienzi* (1942), which have not remained in the repertoire, are skilful and often highly enjoyable imitations of German, Italian and French models respectively. Then at one bound he became fully himself in *Der fliegende Holländer* ('The Flying Dutchman') (1843). He took

a long-established legend, wrote his own libretto, as always, adapting it to his own highly Romantic view of the world, and set it to music which surges alarmingly from the opening chord: the strings rage in fortissimo open fifths, the horns blow the stark motif of the Dutchman himself, the whole effect being of violently unleashed energy. The subject matter, that of a man doomed to eternal roaming unless he is redeemed by a woman showing unconditional love for him, embodies his major themes: redemption removed from a specific religious context, and eroticism which always means more than it seems to.

He pursued this course in his next two operas, *Tannhäuser* (1845, revised 1860–61) and *Lohengrin* (1848) and then, in 1848–49, became a revolutionary and had to flee Germany with a price on his head. At this stage he theorized extensively about the need for a total reform of society, so that people could realize their potential in a kind of communist world, freed from greed and money. Exiled in Zurich, he planned the *Ring*

A sketch for the first Bayreuth production of the *Ring* in 1876; the Rheinmaidens were hoisted onto machines and moved around by (invisible) youths.

(first performance 1876), first as a single music-drama, as he came to call his works; then, in writing it, he expanded it into four, a work which, when it was finished 25 years later, lasted about 15 hours.

He broke off composition on *The Ring* two-thirds of the way through, and wrote *Tristan und Isolde* (1859), incidentally revolutionizing musical history. By now he had completed the tendency which he had begun as far back as *Holländer* to abolish the long-standing division into recitative, aria and ensemble; but now it was a matter of worked-out principle as well as practice, and he created what he called 'endless melody', welded together by leading themes which recur thoughout his works when the idea or object with which they are associated is mentioned, or anyway is relevant. As heir to the German symphonic tradition as well as opera, he expanded orchestral resources hugely, and finally had to build his own opera house, at Bayreuth, to mount *The Ring* and his last work, the seemingly Christian *Parsifal* (1882).

Every stage in Wagner's life was a battle, mainly against the complacent mediocrity which he saw triumphant in the operatic world, both in the works which it

Wotan takes his farewell of Brünnhilde, having kissed away her Godhood and surrounded her by fire, at the end of *Die Walküre*.

• WAGNERIAN LEITMOTIFS •

➤ *Tannhäuser* (1845) Here the theme is of a man torn between sensual and spiritual love.

➤ *Lohengrin* (1848) Wagner's most popular work during his lifetime deals with the issue of whether one person can make unconditional claims on another.

➤ *The Ring* After his period of deep reflection, Wagner achieved a wholly new level of operatic expression. This cycle is concerned with the issues of love and power, the compromises and betrayals which life seems necessarily to involve. He wrote the texts in reverse, beginning with the culminating *Götterdämmerung* and working backwards through *Siegfried* and *Die Walküre* to the music from the 'preliminary evening', *Das Rheingold*.

➤ *Tristan und Isolde* (1859) This is apparently the greatest of all love dramas, but as usual the concern is with finding salvation in a post-Christian world.

➤ *Die Meistersinger von Nürnberg* (1868) Surprisingly, this is the most enormous comedy ever written, though its underlying preoccupations remain the same.

➤ *Parsifal* (1882) Christianity itself as a myth, and thus one of the most audacious works of art we have.

The paradox in all this is that Wagner is the most intellectual of composers, dealing explicitly with fundamental human problems. Yet his music is unequalled in its sensuous appeal, and often gives rise to a state of ecstasy so extreme that some 'Wagnerians' survive on nothing else. Others find his music repulsive, cloying, oppressive.

was prepared to tolerate and its level of performance. As the first great conductor, he raised standards during the period when he was in charge of Dresden's musical life (1843–49) to a point that had never previously been attempted, let alone achieved. The radically new nature of his mature works meant that he had to train performers in a new style of singing, and, at least as important to him, of acting. There were many battles, and he won them all; that is why many people feel he is unforgivable. His works alone among operas give the impression that he is dealing with issues of cosmic importance, to which he may have the answer.

More than any other opera composer, Wagner is subject to the attentions of producers determined that he should mean what they would like him to. The tendency began with his grandson, Wieland, who de-Nazified Bayreuth after World War II by mounting abstract, symbolic and often very beautiful productions of the dramas. In recent years the tendency, especially in regard to the *Ring*, has been to see a Marxist message, which can only be realized by

updating it and having Wagner's primeval heroes in dinner jackets or lab coats. Tired of this reading, present-day producers will seemingly go to any lengths to defy Wagner's explicit stage instructions. Wagner's works are the ultimate playground for pretentious experimentation – a just fate, his detractors would claim. ♪

◆ BAYREUTH ◆

~

Wagner realized that in creating *The Ring*, with its unprecedentedly large orchestra (more than 100 players), its scenic demands, and the necessity of mounting four dramas on successive days, he would have to build his own theatre to cope with it. He finally chose the outskirts of Bayreuth, in northern Bavaria, as its location because it is a quiet place where people can concentrate only on the evening's performance. He had the theatre built on the lines of ancient Greek amphitheatres, with steeply raked seating, perfect sightlines for everyone, and no boxes. It was constructed largely out of wood, which resulted in its fabulous acoustics, full but clear, which can be detected even on records. Since Wagner found the sight of a full orchestra between the stage and the audience a distraction, he had the orchestra partly sitting under the stage, and a covering renders them wholly invisible to the audience. The stage is exceptionally deep, and the lighting and mechanical equipment has always been state of the art. Though the theatre has been rebuilt over the years since its inaugural opening in 1876, it retains all its original features, including acutely uncomfortable seats.

German Responses, Post-Wagner

WAGNER WAS A CATACLYSM, WHATEVER one thought about him. For many years after his death composers felt obliged to come to terms with him, either by continuing to do the same kind of thing that he had done – that is, producing works of huge ambition and correlative scale – or by fiercely rejecting his example and trying to give the impression that he had never existed. Of course, Wagner was unignorable, so 'non-Wagnerian' and 'anti-Wagnerian' tended to mean the same thing.

The most distinguished case of the first type of response was Richard Strauss, whose first opera, *Guntram* (1894, revised 1940) was a slavish imitation of the composer he always worshipped, even to the extent of writing his own libretto. However, Strauss had no real interest in cosmic issues, and he only hit form when he threw in his lot with decadence, and composed *Salome* (1905), Oscar Wilde's play providing the text. It is a deliberately shocking work, in which Salome spends the last 20 minutes in erotic inter-play with John the Baptist's severed head.

Strauss then moved on to Greek tragedy. *Elektra* (1909), his most advanced work, is unremittingly dissonant and intense and still makes a devastating impact, though more on the nerves than the feelings. Strauss, though, was basically an easy-going man of the world, and when his regular librettist Hugo von Hofmannsthal presented him with a mock 18th century comedy, *Der Rosenkavalier* ('The Rose-bearer') (1911), it suited him to perfection. It is sentimental, erotic, coarsely comic and very garrulous.

Strauss used many Wagnerian devices, but the effect of his works is quite different. His other idol was Mozart, so he was continually oscillating between mythological dramas, such as *Die aegyptische Helena* (1928) and small-scale pieces of mixed genre, such as *Ariadne auf Naxos* (1916) and the near-operetta *Arabella* (1933). He went on composing operas of assorted kinds until 1942, the last being *Capriccio*, a discussion of the relative importance of words and music in opera, set to charming music. It is another of his re-creations of the 18th century, with quotations from Gluck; but the luscious textures, the busyness of the action, and the passages of soaring soprano lyricism make it a quintessentially Straussian work. All his music gives the impression of coming at the end of a line.

Other German composers were more devout Wagnerians, none nearly so gifted as Strauss. They tended to use, or to write themselves, heavily symbolic and pretentious libretti, and to score very

thickly: Franz Schreker is a good example of this kind of thing.

Lear – Aribert Reimann's bid to reclaim opera as grand tragedy.

Among his six operas, perhaps *Der ferne Klang* ('The Distant Sound') (1912) is the most representative. It is, as so many operas of the period tended to be, about an artist; it is full of obscure and lofty symbolism, and it is laden with sexual overtones. The idiom is of thick, rich post-Wagnerian chromaticism, and it always seems as if a big tune is about to arrive.

The most successful post-Wagnerian opera is Hans Pfitzner's *Palestrina* (1917), a work about the difficulties of artistic creation. It contrasts the life of the solitary composer, searching for inspiration and finally being granted it, in the outer Acts, with the world of papal diplomacy and ruthlessness in the central Act, where the indebtedness to the Wagner of *Die Meistersinger* is especially clear. An unqualified masterpiece, it is almost never performed outside German-speaking countries.

The crisis which Wagner had precipitated was dealt with most drastically by Schoenberg, who abandoned tonality (that is, music in a key) altogether. He wrote several short operas, of which the half-hour long monodrama *Erwartung* ('Expectation') (1909) is the most powerful. In it a woman is searching in a forest for her lover, whose dead body she finds at the end. His major opera *Moses und Aron* (1930–32) was left incomplete, but what there is of it is magnificent, a profound expression of the composer's Jewishness. Though a Jew by birth, he was not one by religion until the Nazi persecution made him identify with his race much more closely. In this great torso of a work, Moses has his vision of God but is unable to communicate it, while his brother Aron is a fluent demagogue who fatally cheapens God's message to the Israelites. Moses is a speaking role, Aron a mellifluous tenor. The

Berg's Lulu: the ultimate vamp, she is responsible for the deaths of several men before herself being murdered by Jack the Ripper. Black farce? Sordid tragedy? It is impossible to say.

choral writing is of a surpassing eloquence.

Schoenberg's disciple Alban Berg wrote two operas which are among the 20th century's greatest musical achievements: *Wozzeck* (1925), a harrowing study of poverty, jealousy and madness, and *Lulu*, a kind of nightmarish comi-tragedy of sex and violence. *Lulu* was left incomplete at Berg's death in 1935. There was not a great deal to do to the score to make it performable, but when his widow discovered that the inspiration for some of it was a passionate affair Berg had been having, she forbad that the third act should ever be completed; fortunately her will has been posthumously overruled. These operas plead the case for their unattractive characters with desperate intensity. Indeed, the twelve-tone method of composing which Schoenberg invented is remarkable for the high emotional charge of the works he and his disciples composed in it, rather than for being cold and cerebral, as used to

be alleged and even now sometimes resurfaces.

German opera since World War II has tended, in the hands of such composers as Hans Werner Henze and Aribert Reimann, to be eclectic and derivative. They have scored many successes with the public, Henze notably in *Elegy for Young Lovers* (1961) and *The Bassarids* (1966), Reimann with *Lear* (1978), a vehicle for baritone Dietrich Fischer-Dieskau to show off in, but at the price of writing in a style, or series of styles, which initially sound advanced but are in fact easy to assimilate and to grow weary of. On the other hand, Stockhausen, with his plans for a work larger than Wagner's *Ring*, a vast cycle of works for each day of the week, has spawned an unfinished monster which by now may be making him feel like Frankenstein. The whole work is called *Licht* ('Light') and there are several days to go. It features Lucifer and St Michael, the latter portrayed by Stockhausen's son. ♪

New Directions

BETWEEN THE DEATH OF PURCELL IN 1695 and the early 20th century there was no indigenous opera of merit to come out of Britain, with the exception of John Gay's *The Beggar's Opera* (1728), which was a huge success for many decades, constantly being updated, with topical references and new popular songs; but none of its many imitators lasted. Sullivan wanted to be a serious opera composer, but never succeeded. Handel had, of course, been resident in England and had written his many operas in Italian primarily for an English public, but he exhausted the tradition of which he was the finest flower.

In the early years of the 20th century, as English music once again began to burgeon, there were various attempts to get a new tradition of opera started, including an English Bayreuth at Glastonbury, where Arthurian operas might be performed.

However, the first and second generations of significant English composers either had little inclination or no talent for opera. Vaughan Williams tried but failed; Holst was a bit better. It is widely agreed that English opera took off on 7 June 1945, with the premiere of Benjamin Britten's *Peter Grimes*. Concise, intense, tragic, even elemental, it has survived triumphantly for 50 years – a safe period. Britten followed it with a series of works in which he explored widely different idioms and kinds of drama, though his obsession with innocence lost was almost ubiquitous. He wrote a brilliantly effective thriller for chamber forces in *The Turn of the Screw* (1954); a coming-of-age comedy in *Albert Herring* (1947); his most powerful tragic work, one of injustice and pathetic violence, the homoeroticism of which is thinly disguised, in *Billy Budd* (1951); a pageant combined with a painful love story in *Gloriana* (1953), written for the Coronation of Elizabeth II and not wholly tactfully exploring the psyche of Elizabeth I; and still others, until his final *Death in Venice* (1973), written on the verge of fatal illness, in which he finally 'came out', in an idiom of such economy that it is possible to find it very tedious. Whatever the final verdict on Britten, he gave English composers confidence.

Tippett never lacked that quality, and was always as concerned to affirm as Britten was to query and doubt. Tippett's first opera, *The Midsummer Marriage* (1955) is an exuberant exploration of what would now be called personal growth, with exciting and relevant dance sequences. In *King Priam* (1962) he essayed Greek tragedy (he always wrote his own texts, often very gauche), and though it has embarrassing incongruities, its granitic musical idiom, with great bare brass chords, is wholly original and grimly effective. His later works in the form, though they are never uninteresting, tend to be too consciously trendy, and brevity is their chief virtue.

In Brussels' Théâtre de La Monnaie Adams' *The Death of Klinghoffer* appears to be taking place not so much on the stage as behind the scenes. Scenic brutalism and musical minimalism are for many a potent combination.

• TWO ORIGINALS IN A SEA OF • MEDIOCRITY

No doubt as many operas were being composed 200 or 100 years ago as now, but they have been winnowed out. Confronted with the vast majority of 20th-century operas, we may be bewildered by their profusion and dismayed by their quality; and it probably is true that for various reasons the greatest period for writing opera has passed. Nevertheless, there have been some originals, among whom the Czech Leoš Janáček is especially heartening.

➤ Janáček's operas are utterly personal. Influenced by Czech folk music, he also studied the rhythms of Czech speech which he rendered in jagged yet intensely lyrical music, setting terse and potent dramas. *Jenufa* (1904), *Katya Kabanova* (1921), *From the House of the Dead* (1930) and *The Makropoulos Case* (1926) have all gained a secure place in the world's opera houses, as has his delightful *The Cunning Little Vixen* (1924), which mixes human and animal characters without the least trace of coyness or sentimentality; far from it. He stands alone, the rarest kind of genius who has neither predecessors nor heirs.

➤ Gershwin, another original, was greatly admired by Schoenberg. His gift for popular songs, some of them masterly, was harnessed just once to a successful attempt to create a large-scale form, the result being *Porgy and Bess* (1935). It does what many American composers have tried to do before and since, without managing to pull it off: make a serious drama out of the happenings in the life of an impoverished urban community, and suffuse it all with the glow of a radiant lyricism. To distinguish it from the finest musicals of Jerome Kern, say, would be hard, yet for several reasons it does belong in the opera house and not in the theatres where today the works of Stephen Sondheim or the Bernstein of *West Side Story* are performed. It needs a fine symphony orchestra, a great conductor, and opera rather than show singers to do it justice.

Besides these two powerful figures, there have been a host of British composers writing works many of which have made more than a passing impression, but none has entered the repertoire. Indeed, the number of permanent additions to the regularly programmed works made during the 20th century anywhere has been small, and between them Richard Strauss and Puccini account for about half. There is one work which has cult status and is utterly unlike any other: Debussy's *Pelléas et Mélisande*. It exercises a curious spell over the susceptible spectator: it takes place in a mythical country of which the inhabitants are lost, unsure of who they are and what they are doing, but moving ineluctably towards poignant tragedy. The music is Debussy at his most elusive, both reacting fiercely against Wagner yet still evidently under his spell. The atrocious cruelty, harrowing jealousy, brief and bewildered love to which people are always prone here receives something like a final statement.

Another great composer who reacted against Wagner, but far more robustly, was Stravinsky. He spent much of his life skirting opera without quite assaulting it, but his 'opera-oratorio' *Oedipus Rex* (1927) is a terse masterpiece in which the Greek myth is sung in Latin, by figures wearing masks, interspersed with a narration in the language of the country where the work is being performed. It is the climax of his neo-Classical phase, spare of texture and all the more overwhelming for its concentration. In 1951 he produced a quasi-Mozartian full-length opera, *The Rake's Progress* (1848–51) the libretto of which is in English. Based on Hogarth's engravings, it is a curiously patchy work of genius, lacking in spontaneity but blossoming into a ravishingly lyrical final scene.

His compatriots Shostakovich and Prokofiev each made distinguished contributions, though Shostakovich's *Lady Macbeth of Mtsensk* (1934) so shocked Stalin with its raw sensuality that it was banned for many years. It moves uneasily between satire and anguish, but the final Janáček-like scene leaves the listener disturbed and wondering at the freedom of the composer's imagination. Prokofiev produced in *The Fiery Angel* (1923, revised 1927) a thoroughly over-the-top tale of sex, religion and witchcraft, in a sumptuously decadent style that is always his own; and in *War and Peace* a bid to write the ultimate Russian epic. The latter is, inevitably, a ramshackle and uneven work but in a lavish enough production it can seem to be a near-masterpiece, notable more for its luxuriant lyricism than for its self-conscious grandeur.

The history of opera to date ends on a strange and not very promising note. Though the form has often been thought of as elitist, a group of American composers has been thriving for the last 20 years attracting a young, trendy and even punkish audience in prodigious numbers. Known as the minimalists, these composers have operated on the principle that taking a weird text and setting it to music of an unprecedented simplicity, with the same series of notes or chords repeated exactly for up to half an hour at a stretch, will have a hypnotic effect: and for their admirers they can do no wrong. Philip Glass has been the most successful, with *Einstein on the Beach* (1976), *Satyagraha* (1980) and *Akhnaten* (1984) having world-wide productions. More recently, he has audaciously introduced elements of harmony and melody into his works, sometimes approaching conventionality. John Adams's *Nixon in China* (1987) is slightly more eclectic, and has the prestige of dealing with a contemporary political theme. Whether the brazenly limited means which they employ will have enabled them to produce works which will be heard in 200 years' time is an interesting speculation, though they would probably resent the idea that durability is important. For the time being, though, they seem to represent the cutting edge of a form that has survived many crises. ♪

The fisherman Grimes with his cowering apprentice and Ellen Orford, the school-mistress. In Britten's opera, emotional claustrophobia combines with stark settings.

Operetta

THE VIENNESE LINE

'OPERETTA' MEANS LITTLE OPERA, BUT AS A genre which thrived particularly in the second half of the 19th century and the first part of the 20th, it applies loosely to comedies with an overture, songs, dances and interludes, with a good deal of chatter. The Viennese line started with Franz von Suppé. Coming from a Belgian, Czech, Polish, Italian and Austro-Hungarian background, he was so cosmopolitan that he never learned German properly, though he was wholeheartedly adopted by the Viennese. He composed a parody of Wagner's Tannhäuser, Der Tannenhäuser *(1852),*

*and a portrait of Mozart (*Mozart*) (1854), and when the Theater an der Wien was unable to get the rights of one of Offenbach's operettas he wrote a clever pastiche,* Das Pensionnat *(1860), which marks the beginning of Viennese operetta.*

SUPPÉ HAS FALLEN INTO UNDESERVED neglect, and at least two of his operettas, *Die schöne Galathea* (1865) and *Boccaccio* (1879), deserve reviving. But like many innovators, he was put in the shade by his successor, in this case the irresistible Johann Strauss II. His first attempt at a large-scale

work – he was already responsible for innumerable waltzes, polkas and marches – was uncertain, but in 1874 he produced *Die Fledermaus* ('The Bat'), and no one, including its composer, has come near to equalling that flawless masterpiece since. Like all the greatest comedies, it has beneath its surface a serious theme: when do we mean what we say, and how often do we know what we are feeling? Most of the characters spend most of the time being insincere, and some of it in disguise. When Rosalinde sings her czárdás to convince the assembled company in Act II that she is a Hungarian countess, the depth of feeling in her opening melody makes one wonder if she does not believe it herself. This collection of pleasure-lovers, quaffing champagne and waxing ardent or sentimental, know that the fun will soon be

Parties are the meaning of life for Johann Strauss's characters in *Die Fledermaus.* **Here Rosalinde sings her czárdás in Act II.**

over and that, as in Strauss's finest waltzes, the cold light of dawn will show how transient their happiness is.

Strauss wrote many other operettas, and *Der Zigeunerbaron* ('The Gypsy Baron')(1885) and *Eine Nacht in Venedig* ('A Night in Venice') (1883) have wonderful things, but none carries conviction throughout. The most notable successor is *Die lustige Witwe* ('The Merry Widow') (1905), another flawless work, by Lehár, and that thrives on its indulgence of sentimentality. Lehár, Hitler's favourite composer after Wagner, was a specialist in gently tugging the heartstrings, making us pretend to feel more than we do. His example led to a riot of Viennese operetta, which gradually slithered into kitsch. Strauss had had satirical intentions, which give his best work an integrity that his

successors were happy to abandon as they thought of their bank accounts.

The Viennese rightly took the view that the best works in this genre deserved royal treatment: Bruno Walter, one of the finest conductors, was a *Fledermaus* specialist, and great singers like Lotte Lehmann and Elisabeth Schumann happily collaborated

with him. Richard Tauber, one of the century's most glorious tenor voices, performed and recorded a huge amount of operetta, including many written with him in mind. Today the best operetta is still receiving high-calibre treatment from top singers and conductors, among the latter Carlos Kleiber and John Eliot Gardiner.

Die lustige Witwe, Lehár's consummate evocation of a never-never world of romance, takes operetta to the end of its legitimate possibilities.

• A WALTZ TOO FAR •

The element of escapism in operetta is obvious: if it is to be art, as opposed to mere entertainment, there needs to be a perspective from which the escapism can be seen for what it is. That is provided in plenty by Suppé, and almost as much by Strauss in *Die Fledermaus* – the element of satire is as clear as it is in Mozart's *Così fan tutte*. However, Strauss increasingly abandoned himself to pure make-believe, the evocation of mere fantasy worlds, and his lack of conviction is plain in the correlative loss in musical substance. With Lehár we are into a diet of

meringues, though he tried something more substantial in *Giuditta* (1934). Heuberger, in *Der Opernball* (1898), which contains the delectable song 'En chambre separée', helps the progress towards Oscar Straus and his *Ein Waltzertraum* ('A Waltz Dream') (1907), and by the time Straus arrived at *Der letzte Waltz* ('The Last Waltz') (1920) one feels that is one too many. The end of the line is Kalmán, with his *Die Csárdásfürstin* (1913–15) and *Gräfin Maritza* (1924). He emigrated to North America and wrote there his last work, *Arizona Lady* (posthumously premiered, 1954).

Beyond the City of Dreams

JACQUES OFFENBACH WAS A GERMAN WHO spent most of his life in France, and is considered a French composer. He had a thorough training in classical composition at the Paris Conservatoire, which stood him in good stead throughout his life – he was an arch-professional. His career was slow to get going until he discovered his satirical bent,

and launched the series of operettas which are his claim to fame. Living in the exhausted Second Empire he had plenty of available targets, and his operettas, quite without the sentiment of the Viennese whom he inspired, are often almost savage in their treatment of contemporary realities.

However, they are more complex than that suggests. In taking stories from classical mythology and giving them contemporary reference

he makes fun of both sides: the gods and heroes of Ancient Greece are parodied, at the same time as they are used to poke fun at squalid and trivial goings-on in France. The cynicism is so comprehensive that it is hardly surprising that Offenbach founded no school, as Johann Strauss did. He pulls off yet a third trick. Well versed as he was in the history of music, he often ridicules aspects of that too, bel canto opera coming in for especially shrewd deflation. So familiar tunes from the classics make surprising guest appearances; it is a world in which nothing is sacred. It is all the sadder that, like many comedians, Offenbach harboured more serious aspirations, which he hoped to realize in his opera *Les contes d'Hoffmann* ('The Tales of Hoffmann') (1877–80), on which he worked very hard but which was a torso at his death, to be mauled over by many subsequent well-wishers who have never succeeded in making it into a satisfactory whole.

Offenbach's most brilliant satires are – besides *Orphée aux Enfers* ('Orpheus in the Underworld') (1858, revised 1874) – *La Belle Hélène* (1864), *Barbe-bleu* ('Bluebeard') (1866), *La Vie parisienne* (1866, revised 1873), *La Grande-duchesse de Gérolstein* (1866–7), *La Périchole* (1868,

Offenbach's *Orphée aux enfers* is timeless satire, and provides ample scope for modern directors to use it as a vehicle for poking fun at whichever social or political target they wish.

Jacques Offenbach in 1879. The sender-up of everything, he suffered from the traditional malaise of comedians, the desire to be serious.

revised 1874) and *La fille du Tambour-major* (1879). They are remarkably uninhibited in their observation of human nature, the Grand Duchess giving strong expression to how much she fancies her soldiers. The unflagging high spirits and the periodic bursts into dance, especially the can-can, serve to hide the extent to which Offenbach could not actually write many good tunes. The ones he did write are so memorable that their scarcity is overlooked.

Offenbach's influence was felt not only in Vienna, but in a very different way in London. There the satirical poet Gilbert and the would-be serious composer Sullivan joined forces to produce an English equivalent of Offenbach's biting satires. They actually produced something quite different, for their satire is genial and in the end complacent. The people and institutions which they make fun of are the object of their affections, and they have gratified audiences for the last hundred years by making them think they are seeing through the hypocrisies of English life while actually they are being seduced into affectionate collaboration with them. Even foreigners are delightful if quaint creatures in Gilbert and Sullivan's scheme of things. The brilliance of Gilbert's verses and the fertility of Sullivan's melodic gifts are in the end agents of smugness, and, although by comparison with Offenbach Sullivan is brimming with lyrical invention in *The Mikado* (1884–85), *HMS Pinafore* (1878), *The Pirates of Penzance* (1879) and *The Yeomen of the Guard* (1888), by the time Gilbert and Sullivan reached *The Gondoliers* (1889) the formula had gone stale, though it retains its popularity regardless.

A quite separate line of light opera is the *zarzuela*, a traditional kind of Spanish light opera, dating from the early 17th century. The form went into decline in the 18th century, but staged a revival in the 19th. The leading composer of the period, producing more than 60 examples of the genre, was Barbieri, with such enduring works as *Jugar con fuego* (1851) and *El barberillo de Lavapiés* (1874)to his credit. Many of these are still regularly performed in Spain, though like some good wines they do not travel well.

There is a thin line between operetta and the musical. To the extent that it exists at all, operetta tends to have its roots in opera and the light music of the last century, the musical in popular song of this century. However, as musicals have become more pretentious, especially in the hands of such crossover pioneers as Leonard Bernstein, the distinction between them and operetta has been by now virtually obliterated. There seems to be little doubt that the vitality of such classic musicals as Kern's *Showboat* (1927), or of the mid-1940s and early 1950s – Rodgers and Hammerstein's *Oklahoma*, Loesser's *Guys and Dolls* and Rodgers and Hart's *Pal Joey* – far exceeds anything that has followed, where there is too much effort to inject social significance and effect large-scale musical organization. ♪

BUILDING BLOCKS

*M*USIC IS A CONGLOMERATION OF sounds that can provide a deeply moving experience both for listeners and for performers. This section of the book explores the basic ingredients of music, the building blocks that composers use to make the sounds that together constitute our aesthetic experience of music. As wide a range of musical periods and styles as possible has been drawn upon to illustrate such elements as pitch, rhythm and dynamics, and to show that music —and in particular 'classical' music – is not just confined to a handful of works written over about two centuries, but a universal medium whose building blocks are common to all mankind, even though the buildings constructed with them may be different. Understanding the basic elements of music adds to the appreciation of its magnificent power.

Rhythm

THE WORD RHYTHM IS DERIVED FROM A Greek word meaning flow, so its broadest definition includes everything that refers to the passage of music through time. On its largest scale, rhythm is like the wind; often it can only be discerned by other factors, such as the stresses implicit in melodic shapes and the regularity of phrases. Even music such as plainsong or the long melismata of Arabic or Jewish cantilation can have rhythm, though it may not have a regular beat.

∾BEAT

Beat is the basic unit of time in music. It occurs at regular intervals, and is usually described in terms of its smallest regular unit, such as crotchet, minim or quaver. The largest beat that is currently used in Western music is the semibreve or whole note, but in the early Middle Ages it was the longa, which was four times the duration of the present semibreve. Later the breve (from the Latin word meaning short), or double whole note, became the largest basic unit, at half the length of the longa. Eventually this was replaced by the semibreve, which was half the duration of the breve. To guard against the danger of the music of Palestrina, Machaut or Josquin being performed too slowly, today's editors of music composed before about 1600 usually halve or quarter the value of the original notes so that this early music resembles modern scores on the page. The beat of a piece of music is indicated by the lower number which appears at the beginning just after the clef and (where appplicable) the key signature:

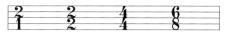

1 = SEMIBREVE OR WHOLE NOTE

2 = MINIM OR HALF-NOTE

4 = CROTCHET OR QUARTER-NOTE

8 = QUAVER OR EIGHTH NOTE

∾TIME (TEMPO)

Beats are usually grouped into regularly recurring patterns, and it is these which determine the 'time' of a piece of music. Thus three crotchets or quarter notes might form the regular grouping in a piece and this would be indicated at the beginning of a piece as 3/4. The time signature of the piece would be described as 3/4 and vertical lines would be inserted to show each grouping of three crotchets. The groupings and the lines between are called bars and bar-lines respectively. In the USA a bar is described as a measure.

The most common time-signatures are:

2/4 = two crotchets (quarter notes) in each bar. The quick-step and quick march are in this time.

3/4 = three crotchets (quarter notes) in each bar. The waltz and the minuet are in this time.

4/4 = four crotchets (quarter notes) in each bar. This is sometimes called 'common time' because of its regular occurrence. It is the time-signature of most marches and hymn-tunes and many other kinds of music.

2/2 = two minims (half notes) per bar. Mathematically this is the same as 4/4 since there are four crotchets in each bar, but 2/2 is sometimes referred to as 'alla breve' and is faster, implying a feeling of two beats in a bar rather than four.

∾PHRASES

Just as a bar is made up of beats regularly grouped, so much Western music, particularly dance and folk-music, is made up of phrases which comprise the regular grouping of bars. A waltz is just as much characterized by its regular four-bar phrases as its 3/4 rhythm.

∾RUBATO

One of the most important skills a performer has to develop is the ability to inflect regular rhythms very slightly to bring out such things as melodic nuances or harmonic colouring. This technique is called rubato, and one composer whose music is particularly associated with it is Chopin, whose own performances were apparently remarkable for their subtle rhythmic inflexions.

∾SIMPLE AND COMPOUND TIME

In modern notation beats are divided into two to arrive at the next smaller unit: that is, two minims (half notes) = one semibreve (whole note), two crotchets (quarter notes) = one minim, two quavers (eighth notes)= one crotchet, two semiquavers (sixteenth notes) = one quaver and so on. However, in the earliest Western European notation, from the 9th to the 16th century, most beat-units were subdivided by three. This was because three was a divine number, like the Trinity, and the subdivision into three was described as 'tempus perfectum' (perfect time). Notation did not have bar-lines and the duration of a particular note depended on its context. In modern notation much medieval music thus sounds as though it is in some kind of triple time, but not all the beat-units are subdivided into three. As a result two kinds of 'time' are current today: simple time and compound time.

Simple time is where each larger beat is divided by two to arrive at the next shortest beat-unit unless special indications such as a triplet sign indicate something different. Examples of simple time are 2/4, 3/4, 4/4, 2/2; 2/4 and 2/2 can be referred to as simple duple, 3/4 as simple triple and 4/4 as simple quadruple time.

Compound time is where the main beat-unit is subdivided into three, expressed as a time-signature in the shorter note values. So 6/8, which is a compound time, is effectively a duple time, but the crotchet (quarter note)-beat is divided into three semiquavers (sixteenth notes) not two. In modern notation, the crotchet beat is now expressed as a dotted crotchet and the time signature is expressed as six quavers or eighth notes; but a bar of 6/8 should not be heard as having six quavers but as having two dotted crotchets divided into three quavers each.

Of course, mathematically a bar of 3/4 contains six quavers just as a bar of 6/8 does, but the different time signatures reflect the different beat units. In a bar of 3/4 there are three crotchets which can be subdivided into three groups of two quavers, whereas in a bar of 6/8 there are two dotted crotchets which can be subdivided into two groups of three quavers. The two sound quite different – so different that their juxtaposition became a favourite device in French *courantes* of the 17th century (where the main beat was usually a minim or dotted minim rather than a crotchet, so the time-signatures were 3/2 alternating with 6/4). On the same principle, a favourite device of the 17th and 18th century was a 'hemiola', in which two bars of a passage in 3/4 might suddenly be regrouped to form three bars of 2/4, thus creating a cross-beat effect. Composers such as Handel and Corelli favoured this at cadences.

Some 19th-century composers were very fond of cross-rhythms: Schumann, for instance, as in the beginning of his *Rhenish* Symphony or in the orchestral tune in the last movement of his Piano Concerto, where the melody is notated completely off the beat.

∾ UNUSUAL TIME SIGNATURES

The great majority of music written between 1600 and the end of the 19th century uses the time signatures listed above. However, a great deal of Eastern European folk music does not. In countries such as Bulgaria, Romania, Hungary and some of the Russian republics, it is quite common to find time-signatures such as 5/4 or 7/4. Bartók, in his *Six Dances in Bulgarian Rhythm* (1940) which conclude his teaching series *Mikrokosmos*, uses folk rhythms that include bars where the accents fall irregularly. For instance:

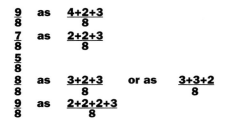

Earlier in the century Stravinsky had used compound rhythms in his *Rite of Spring* (1913), but had notated these as a succession of bars with different time signatures (for example, 2/16, 3/16, 5/16, 3/4 all follow in quick succession). Stravinsky was not the first Russian composer to experiment with unusual time signatures. In his piano-work *Pictures at an Exhibition* (1874), Mussorgsky juxtaposed 5/4 and 6/4 in the opening promenade, and Tchaikovsky wrote a 'waltz' in 5/4 as the second movement of his Symphony No. 6 (*Pathétique*) (1893).

The 20th century is commonly considered to be the age with the most complex rhythms in music, but it is closely rivalled by the late medieval period, which, just before the end of the 14th century, developed a courtly art in Avignon whose rhythmic intricacies are extremely difficult to perform and frequently almost defy modern notation.

Rhythm in the 16th century was also complex. The works of Palestrina, for instance, achieve their fluidity while maintaining musical momentum by having each voice-part use an individual series of accents resulting from the melodic shapes which subtly counteract the main 'pulse' of the music. More ostentatious cross-rhythms were also employed, as in the motet 'Haec Dies' by the English composer William Byrd, in which the opening free-flowing polyphony is interrupted by a joyful passage of alternating and sometimes simultaneous 3/4 and 6/8.

On balance, however, the 20th century has

been more experimental with rhythm than almost any previous age. The French composer Messiaen has used a technique of 'additive rhythm' in which small extensions of particular notes remove the traditional accentuation and achieve a sort of measured rubato. The American composer Elliott Carter subtly transforms the pace of his music by making successive passages in a particular rhythm proportionally altered. He calls this technique 'metrical modulation'. Many composers have also been influenced by the much more complex rhythms of Africa and Asia, and some composers have experimented with leaving the rhythm of a piece of music up to the performer. This, however, has a precedent in the preludes of 17th-century French harpsichord music which were notated completely without rhythm.

∾ CHARACTERISTIC RHYTHMS

Apart from the speed and time signature of a piece, rhythm can also determine the character of music. The lilting 'oom -pah-pah' of 3/4 can immediately suggest not only a waltz but its home, Vienna.

The proud rhythm of a polonaise as used by Chopin, such as the one in A flat major, can conjure up images of Poles in national costume or fighting for the country's existence.

Though rhythm is an important part of suggesting

THE RHYTHM OF A POLONAISE

the character of a piece, it cannot do it alone. The polonaise rhythm is not very different from the Spanish but it is recognizably different when combined with the characteristic melodic pattern, as Rodrigo used it at the beginning of his guitar concerto *Concierto di Aranjuez* (1939):

Tempo

THIS IS AN ITALIAN TERM MEANING TIME, USED universally to refer to the speed at which a piece of music is performed. Often the speed is employed to establish a mood for a piece, such as a fast dance for a happy piece (for example the saltarello which concludes Mendelssohn's *Italian* Symphony) or a slow march for a funeral (for example the Dead March from Handel's *Saul*). Amongst the fastest pieces ever written are Rimsky-Korsakov's *Flight of the Bumble Bee* and Chopin's so-called 'Minute Waltz', which very few performers can actually play in a minute. One of the fastest modern pieces is György Ligeti's *Continuum* (1968) for harpsichord.

The speed of a piece does not just depend on how fast the notes are played; it is also affected by

• SOME FAMOUS RHYTHMS •

*A*ll dances depend on regular rhythm to help dancers keep in time and in step, so phrases and bars have to be audibly repetitive. This is usually aided by the melodic patterns. Thus most dances have immediately recognizable rhythms, and since the national origins of many dances are well known, these rhythms can often be a shorthand way for a composer to evoke a particular country or mood.

➤ **Jig** Originally an English dance, but often found in Ireland and as the final movement of 17th- and 18th-century suites. From the early 17th century the jig spread to northern Europe via the tours of English comic actors. It has a regularly repeated pattern of 6/8 (sometimes 9/8).

➤ **Ländler** – see Waltz

➤ **March** A musical accompaniment to military parades, of very old origin. At its simplest the march is merely a repetition of a basic beat in 4/4 and in successive four-bar phrases, but early commentators noted the effect of slightly varying the rhythm to include rests and sometimes dotted variations. A typical march phrase might be:

➤ **Mazurka** A Polish dance (originating from the Warsaw area) made particularly famous by Chopin though found earlier and later, notably in the music of fellow-Pole Karol Szymanowksi. Though in 3/4 it has a characteristic accent on the final beat of each bar:

➤ **Minuet** Originally a French rustic dance which employed small steps (from 'menu', meaning small). It was later taken up by 17th-century French composers (for example Lully) in their suites and ballets, and in the 18th century it became, with a trio, a standard movement in most symphonies. In the 19th century it was often replaced by the faster scherzo.

➤ **Polka** A Bohemian dance dating from the early 19th century and resembling the Schottische. An early use in opera was in Smetana's *The Bartered Bride*.

➤ **Polonaise** A festive dance of the Polish aristocracy and used by some 18th-century Polish symphonists as an alternative to the minuet. Chopin popularized it.

➤ **Quadrille** A duple-time 19th-century Napoleonic dance in five figures, usually based on favourite tunes and operatic airs of the day, performed by foursomes or eightsomes moving in a square. It was popularized by the Strausses.

➤ **Ragtime** A duple-time dance-song which came out of the bordellos, pool halls and vaudeville can-can shows of the Mississippi Valley and flourished in both Europe and the United States at the turn of the 20th century. Distinguished by simple harmony and captivating syncopation, it was made famous by Scott Joplin. Stravinsky sophisticated the style in *Piano-rag music* (1919).

➤ **Rumba** A Cuban dance in 8/8 divided into:

➤ **Samba** An Afro-Brazilian dance, which originally included an introductory 'navel touching' ceremony and singing. Though in duple rhythm, it often obscured this with elaborate syncopation. Out of the samba evolved a more urban cousin, the bossa-nova.

Samba rhythms   Bossa-Nova rhythms

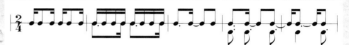

➤ **Sarabande** Originally from Spain and Latin America, this was one of the most popular dances of the late Renaissance and Baroque periods. Though there was a fast version, a wild love-dance condemned for being too suggestive and banned by Philip II, by far the commonest form was a slow, stately dance in triple time with a characteristic emphasis on the second beat. It is found in the instrumental suites of Bach and Handel, and in some Romantic works where its stately character is given even greater emphasis.

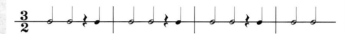

➤ **Tango** A syncopated, sexually suggestive Argentinian dance, though possibly imported originally from Africa by slaves, related to the Andalusian tango and Cuban habañera. The dancers move slowly and exaggeratedly to a striking rhythm in 2/4 time. Post-First World War Europe echoed nightly to the tango steps and songs of Gardel and Rodriquez. Walton used a tango in *Façade* (1921).

Tarantella
POSSIBLE RHYTHMS OF MELODY

➤ A lively Neapolitan dance in 6/8. According to legend, dancing the tarantella was a cure for the poisonous bite of the tarantula spider. Chopin, Liszt, Auber and Thalberg were the composers who did it most justice.

➤ **Waltz** This originated in Upper Austria from the ländler and became very popular in Vienna as a flirtatious dance. It is notable for its 3/4 rhythm with a characteristic Viennese inflection of the first beat which is not notatable. The most prolific composer of waltzes was Johann Strauss Jnr, who wrote over 500 and introduced them into his operettas.The ländler was used by Mozart, Beethoven, Schubert and Lanner, and was given symphonic significance by Bruckner and Mahler.

POSSIBLE RHYTHMS OF MELODY

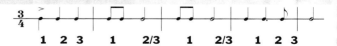

1   2   3   1   2/3   1   2/3   1   2   3

◆ ～ ◆

how fast harmonies change or how often accents can be heard. So a piece with very fast notes can sometimes sound relatively slow if the fast notes appear only as a decoration of the principal beats, as in the very rapid violin passages in the first movement of Bach's *Brandenburg* Concerto No.4.

Tempo is one of the hardest things to gauge, and a perfomer will often vary the tempo of a piece from one performance to another. In the late 19th century and early 20th centuries performers frequently changed the tempo mid-piece, varying the regular accents by as much 20 to 30 per cent. In a recording of *La Cathédrale engloutie* Debussy doubled the printed tempo – whether by accident or by design being the subject of a good deal of debate. Nowadays performers do not tend to deviate from the printed page as much as they once did; it is much more common for a performer to

feel he or she should be faithful to the composer's intentions as expressed on the printed page.

∿The Metronome

Notation is a notoriously ambiguous matter, and tempo indications are very vague. How fast is allegro, for instance? Is it necessarily fast at all? In an attempt to make sure that exact tempo was as communicable as exact pitch, Johann Nepomuk Maelzel (1772–1838) patented the metronome in 1816, having taken the idea from a Dutch inventor who had improved on the devices for measuring tempo which had appeared in France in the 17th century. Maelzel's metronome is a clockwork machine for measuring the number of beats per minute. Thus = 60 means there are 60 crotchets per minute, thus 15 bars of 4/4.

Maelzel's metronomes were not always accurate

and it is thought the one Beethoven possessed was faulty, so his metronome speeds are not to be trusted. Nowadays electronic metronomes have largely replaced Maelzel's clockwork apparatus, but metronome markings are by no means universally observed. Some composers either do not use them, or only suggest an approximate metronome speed; and some performers steadfastly refuse to be ruled by a metronome speed.

Some composers, however, have been almost fanatical metronome users. Bartók, for instance, was meticulous about how long his music should last, and even prefaced individual sections of movements with metronome markings, frequently concluding them with timings for the duration of the sections.

• TEMPOS •

> **Lentissimo** Very slow.

> **Lento** Slow. An example is Mahler's 'Nun will die Sonn' from *Kindertotenlieder* (1902).

> **Largo** Slow and with dignity. The most famous piece supposedly described as 'largo' was Handel's 'Ombra mai fu' from his opera *Serse* (1738), which often used to be played at funerals. However, Handel's actual marking is larghetto, and in the 18th century largo did not mean slow so much as broad; more a character than a speed. In the 19th century it came increasingly to indicate speed. Mussorgsky's 'Catacombae' from *Pictures at an Exhibition* (1874) is marked largo.

> **Larghetto** Faster than largo, and the original tempo-marking of 'Ombra mai fu'. Another example is the slow movement of Mozart's Piano Concerto No. 24 in C minor, K 491 (1786).

> **Adagissimo** Very slow.

> **Adagio** Slow (literally, 'at ease') but not as slow as largo, for example Samuel Barber's *Adagio for Strings* (1938).

> **Adagietto** Slow, but not as slow as adagio. The fourth movement of Mahler's Symphony No. 5 (1901–2) (used in the film *Death in Venice*) is marked adagietto.

> **Andante** Flowing at a relaxed but not too slow pace (literally, at a walking pace), for example the slow movement of Tchaikovsky's String Quartet No.1, which is coupled with cantabile (in a singing style).

> **Moderato** At a moderate pace. One of the commonest tempo markings, but also one of the least precise, it is best described as not too fast, not too slow. Debussy's *L'Après-midi*

d'un faune (1894) is marked 'très modéré', which might be considered a contradiction in terms!

> **A tempo ordinario** A commonly used 18th-century term which meant 'at a normal tempo', a definition which was as vague then as now.

> **Tempo giusto** At just the right speed. An example is Stravinsky's 'Danses des Adolescentes' from *Le Sacre du Printemps* (1913).

> **Allegro** Nowadays allegro means fast, but in the 18th century it described more the mood than the speed (its literal meaning is happy). Handel sometimes marked scores 'andante allegro' meaning happily at a relaxed pace. It took on its present meaning in the 19th century. The third movement of Tchaikovsky's Symphony No. 6 (1893) is marked 'allegro molto vivace'.

> **Allegretto** A term derived from allegro which now indicates a little slower than allegro, though in the 18th century, when it was first used, it sometimes meant a little faster. Probably the best-known movement that is marked 'allegretto' is the slow movement of Beethoven's Symphony No. 7, whose very varied interpretations indicate how imprecise the term 'allegretto' can be.

> **Vivace** Though it literally means lively it most often refers to speed. Beethoven's scherzo from the Symphony No. 9 is marked 'molto vivave' (very lively).

> **Presto** Fast, for example the last movement of Mozart's Piano Concerto No. 23 in A, K488 (1786).

> **Prestissimo** Very fast.

𝒟 y n a m i c s

An important aspect of music is how loud or soft it is. Dynamic range can vary from the extremely soft sound of a clavichord to a large symphony orchestra, from a brass band to the massive sound of a large organ. Some sounds are too soft for the human ear to hear, such as the flapping of butterfly wings; other sounds are so loud the ear cannot distinguish their constituents ('white noise').

∿Dynamic markings

All music is loud or soft, but composers do not always specify how loud or soft with any great precision, nor has a set of signs emerged which can do this. The first dynamic markings occur in 15th-century lute music, though it was not until the 17th century that they became used with any frequency. The exploitation of the dynamic contrasts between different groups of singers and instrumentalists in St Mark's, Venice led to some composers requiring particular dynamics. Giovanni Gabrieli called one of his *Symphoniae Sacrae* (1597) 'Sonata pian e forte' and indicated what should be loud and soft.

The growth in quantity and importance of instrumental music during the 17th century led to more music having dynamic markings, though they are by no means universal. By and large the approach to dynamic shadings in music between about 1600 and 1730 was terraced; that is to say a passage was either loud or soft, but how loud or

• DYNAMIC TERMS •

> **pp Pianissimo** – very soft. The last movement of Vaughan Williams's Symphony No. 6 (1948) is marked *pp* throughout. Sometimes composers used *ppp* or more to indicate extremes of quietness.

> **p Piano** – soft. The commonest indication of soft. The opening of Beethoven's String Quartet No. 3, Op. 18 is marked *p*.

> **mp Mezzo piano** – half soft. The opening of Brahms's Violin Concerto in D, Op. 77 (1878) is marked *mp*.

> **mf Mezzo forte** – half loud. By far the commonest indication of a dynamic somewhere between loud and soft. Sometimes composers have used it to make one orchestral section of the orchestra play less loudly than another (though not softly) to ensure the predominance of something more important, for example when the full orchestra (especially brass) is accompanying a soloist.

> **f Forte** – loud.

> **ff Fortissimo** – very loud. For a long time this was the loudest dynamic, but with the general increase in composers trying to specify exactly the dynamic required, so fortissimo became increased to *fff*, and even *fffff*.

> **crescendo** Literally 'growing', means getting louder. The term was seldom used before the late 18th century, but since has become common. Sometimes it is indicated by *crescendo* or *cresc.*; sometimes by the sign < .

> **diminuendo** Literally 'getting smaller'. Its history and use is exactly similar to the crescendo, and it is sometimes indicated by *dim.* or the sign > .

> **sotto voce** Literally 'below the voice', in effect like a dramatic aside, almost as though not articulated. It can be found in vocal and instrumental music.

> **sf Sforzando**, literally 'reinforced'. This is a direction that applies to one note or chord at a time to indicate that it should be very strongly accented. Sometimes it is used to upset the regular beat of a piece with strong cross-accents. It is prevalent in the first movement of Beethoven's Symphony No. 9 (1823). An alternative to sforzando is rinforzando (*rinf*, *rf*) which, like sf, indicates a sudden stress.

soft was left to the discretion of the performer.

The mid-18th century saw a change, initially at the court of Mannheim, which had built up a good court orchestra and developed a style of playing and composing. Among the special Mannheim features was an orchestral crescendo (marked as *crescendo* on the score). So popular did this become that Haydn's Symphony No.1 (1759?) opens with a Mannheim crescendo.

One interesting use of dynamics in the 18th century was its description of a new keyboard instrument which could play loudly or softly according to the touch of the player. Originally the instrument was called fortepiano but in time this became reversed and today it is called the pianoforte. Later in the 18th century the number and use of dynamics markings developed. The opening adagio of Haydn's Symphony No. 100 (*Military*) (1794) contains the following markings: p, fz, < >, f, ff in the space of 23 bars.

Rossini made an orchestral crescendo one of his hallmarks, and Shostakovich used a very long orchestral crescendo to represent the inexorable advance of military forces in his Symphony No. 7.

In the last 200 years there has been a marked increase in the use of dynamics as composers have become more anxious to make sure performers understood exactly what dynamics are required. In the 'adagio, ma non troppo e semplice' variation from the fourth movement of Beethoven's String

Quartet in C sharp minor Op. 131 the following dynamic instructions appear: *sotto voce, accent, crescendo, p cantabile, non troppo marcato, < >, p, poco cresc, pp, f, dim, più p, morendo, ppp*.

At the beginning of the 20th century composers such as Anton Webern might often give each note a different dynamic; and in his piano study *Mode de Valeurs et d'Intensités* (1949) the French composer Olivier Messiaen used a set of dynamics as a repeating series.

Despite composers' attempts to communicate exactly the dynamic they want, their indications are always vague; it is impossible to say exactly how loud *mezzo forte* is except that it is louder than piano and quieter than *forte*. The loudness or softness of a sound can be accurately measured and recorded as a number of decibels (dB), but while this might have been useful for electronic composers others have not tried to employ it, maybe because it would prove impossible in live performance where dynamics are always relative to each other. There is no absolute *piano*; some passages are quieter than others.

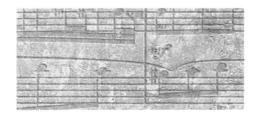

Notes and Pitch

THE PITCH OF A NOTE IS ITS LOCATION ON A TONAL scale. It can be measured accurately by using an oscilloscope, which detects exactly the number of frequencies a note is generating. Sound travels through the air in waves, and the pitch of a note is measured by the number of regularly repeating waves it produces each second. 'Middle' C on the piano, for instance, vibrates at 261.6 vibrations per second, and anything that vibrates at this speed will sound middle C. In the central octave of the piano the following vibrations constitute the scale of C major:

$$c = 261 \cdot 6$$
$$d = 293 \cdot 6$$
$$e = 329 \cdot 6$$
$$f = 349 \cdot 2$$
$$g = 392$$
$$a = 440$$
$$b = 493 \cdot 9$$
$$c' = 523 \cdot 2$$

The descriptions of the vibrations were standardized by the German physicist Heinrich Rudolph Hertz (1857–94), after whom the unit of frequency of sound waves is named.

∽ CHANGES IN PITCH THROUGH THE CENTURIES

A common pitch was agreed internationally in 1939 (an agreement renewed in 1960), so that in any part of the world the A above middle C = 440 Hz, and all the other pitches are calculated from this agreed basis. A was chosen as the note to calculate from as it is the note to which orchestras tune up before they start playing. More recently pitch can be guaranteed on recordings, since CDs are able to reproduce pitches exactly, unlike LPs which could vary as much as a quarter-tone either side of A440.

Standardization became necessary for wind and brass soloists travelling throughout the world, as playing to widely varying pitch standards made the manufacture of internationally usable instruments impossible. Concert halls with organs that are used with the orchestra can now guarantee that the orchestra and the organ are in tune, whereas before the 1930s (and in many churches since) organs were often so sharp that wind and brass instruments found it very hard to tune to them.

∾PITCH CHANGES

The first international agreement about pitch was made in Paris in 1859, when 'diapason normal' was settled on A=435 Hz. This replaced a multitude of different pitches to be found in different countries. In the Elizabethan period, for instance, the pitch of keyboards was probably about a tone and a half lower than present-day pitch, though vocal music was almost certainly sung higher than today, possibly by as much as a tone. Some modern recordings of Purcell's church music, for example, have used the research into the pitch of the contemporary Chapel Royal organ (see below) and performed the works a semitone higher than printed.

One of the ways of telling the pitches of past centuries is from surviving instruments. Sir James Jeans in *Science and Music* (Cambridge, 1937) listed some surprising differences of pitch in the following organs:

ORGAN BUILDER	LOCATION	DATE OF BUILDING	PITCH
Silbermann	Strasburg Cathedral	1713	a=393
Schnitger	St Jakobi, Hamburg	1688	a=489
Father Smith	Trinity College, Cambridge	1759	a=395
Schmidt's	Durham Cathedral		
	Chapel Royal		a=474.1

∾ THE HARMONIC SERIES

The above cycles show a 'pure pitch' or fundamental, but no naturally produced pitch is pure – it has overtones, and the overtones are as much part of its nature as the fundamental pitch. The first notes of the overtone or 'harmonic' series are:

fundamental [X] These notes are slightly 'out-of-tune' with the tuning of the modern piano

If a brass instrument is in B flat this means its lowest note is B flat and all its other notes are achieved by selecting one of its overtones. Up to J S Bach's day brass instruments could only use the notes available from the fundamental note of the instrument. In the later 18th century a system of lengthening the tubes of several brass instruments, notably the horn, was evolved so that other fundamentals and thus different overtones were available, but this was very cumbersome. The

additional lengths of piping were called 'crooks'. In the 19th century all brass instruments acquired valves, so that the length of tubing through which air is blown could be altered with the single depression of a valve. As a result brass instruments can now play all the notes of the chromatic scale in their middle and higher registers.

Even in a modern orchestra some instruments do not play the notated pitch of notes in front of them, but transpose them. This is a residue from the days when the fundamental (for example, B flat on the clarinet, or F on the horn) was taken to be the note "c" on that instrument so all the music intended for it was transposed when it was written out. Modern scores, and many modern players, are now quite happy not to play from transposed parts.

∾PERFECT PITCH

Some people can recognize any pitch they hear, or sing a pitch accurately without playing it first. This is called perfect pitch. Being able to reproduce a note from another by working out the relation between the two is called relative pitch. It used to be thought that perfect pitch was an innate ability, but modern psychology and aural training have shown that it is only very highly developed pitch memory and that with the right training and practice many people can acquire it.

∾NOTATION OF PITCH

When Western notation first appeared in the 9th

---

century it employed little signs called neumes which were placed above the text being sung. At first these neumes only indicated whether a melody went up or down; they did not specify a pitch.

In a 9th-century treatise called *Musica Enchiriades* the neumes were placed above or below a single line whose pitch was specified, which was a step in the direction of establishing the relation between pitches. Then, a monk called Guido d'Arezzo popularized (and may even have invented) a system called Solmization. Solmization was a method of labelling particular notes in a scale by an aide-memoire derived from a Latin hymn ('Ut queant laxis'), whose initial notes for each line began on the next note higher in the scale. The six notes (hexachord) were labelled UT RE MI FA SOL LA.

These names survive to the present day in the Tonic Sol-fa system of notation and in the way some European countries refer to the names of keys. In Britain these have been replaced by letters of the alphabet: Ut=C, RE=D, Mi=E and so on.

∾THE STAFF

This is a set of parallel lines corresponding to individual pitches determined by a clef. Since the early 13th century this has most commonly been of five lines, though plainchant has continued to be notated on four lines from the 12th century to the present day. Some instrumental tablatures used six- or seven-line staves and in the case of lute, guitar and similar plucked instruments the notational letters on the staff referred to the position on the string to be plucked rather than the pitch to be heard.

In his treatise *Aliae regulae* (1030), Guido d'Arezzo recommended using a three-line staff. He suggested that the lines should be placed a third apart, and that one or more should be prefaced with a letter indicating its pitch.

*M*odes

THE WORD 'MODE' COMES FROM THE LATIN WORD *modus* meaning 'measure', 'manner' or 'way'. In Western music it has had several different meanings. Between about 1000 and 1300 mode could refer to the rhythmic proportion between two notes. There were six rhythmic modes, which governed the rhythm of plainsong (which was probably never sung freely in the way we know

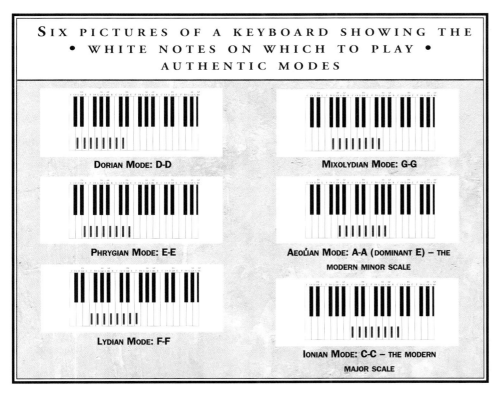

SIX PICTURES OF A KEYBOARD SHOWING THE • WHITE NOTES ON WHICH TO PLAY • AUTHENTIC MODES

DORIAN MODE: D-D

MIXOLYDIAN MODE: G-G

PHRYGIAN MODE: E-E

AEOLIAN MODE: A-A (DOMINANT E) – THE MODERN MINOR SCALE

LYDIAN MODE: F-F

IONIAN MODE: C-C – THE MODERN MAJOR SCALE

A mode can be transposed so that it starts on another note, but what remains fixed is its arrangement of tones and semitones. Thus the Dorian mode, which on the white notes of the piano is D–D, could be A–A provided that it follows the pattern of tone, semitone, tone, tone, tone, semitone, tone.

In 16th-century music the presence of an accidental (that is, a sharp or a flat) in the key signature indicates a transposed mode; and notes which were foreign to the mode but appeared for ease of singing, for avoiding unpleasant harmonic clashes or to make a cadence more defined, were called *musica ficta*. Sometimes modern editors add the *musica ficta* notes they think would have been sung above the notes in the music.

∾MODES AND FOLK MUSIC

Another large body of music that uses modes rather than the major and minor scale is folk music. The carol 'God Rest You Merry Gentlemen' is modal, which is most easily detected by the absence of a sharpened leading-note in the tune. If it is sung starting on E, this means there are no D sharps in the tune as you would expect in a key ending on E.

Folk music sometimes uses modes that are different from the so-called church modes. Some employ the pentatonic scale (see Keys, page 256), which is really just another mode. An example of this is 'Auld Lang Syne'.

Some folk music in Eastern Europe uses modes that are very different from those of Western Europe, and these appear in the music of composers such as Bartók and Kodály.

∾MODERN USE OF MODES

In the 19th century modes were used for archaic effect by Beethoven in his String Quartet in A minor, Op. 132, where he wrote the 'Hymn of Thanksgiving' in the Lydian mode. Later in the century Fauré used modal moments to refresh the prevailing tonality in his songs and in the opening of his Piano Quartet No. 1 in C minor.

In the 20th century renewed interest in folk music and 16th-century counterpoint has led to a number of uses of modes. In England, Vaughan Williams and Holst consciously used modal melodies and harmony in such works as *Fantasia on a theme of Thomas Tallis* and *The Planets*; and Bartók and Kodály used different modes drawn from the music they discovered on their researches into folk song.

today till the Solesmes monks sung it that way in the 19th century), the rhythm of early polyphony (for example Léonin and Pérotin) and the rhythm of the monodies of the 11th- and 12th-century troubadours and trouvères.

∾COMMON USES

The most common use of the term mode refers to a scale, but even here there is some confusion. The Ancient Greeks used mode to refer to mood or style rather than scale, so they applied area names to the styles of music: Dorian, Ionian, Lydian, Aeolian, Phrygian. The Roman orator Cicero told a story about a famous general on the eve of battle who was 'relaxing' with a lady to the sound of a lascivious mode. His staff, hearing that the battle hour had been brought forward but fearing to disturb him directly, bribed the musicians to play some music in a martial mode. Whereupon, as if by magic, the general was up and ready for battle!

In the Middle Ages, which were much influenced by Greek theories (especially those of Pythagoras) about the categorization of musical pitches, modes wre most commonly used in plainsong. In their attempts to categorize the scales, medieval theorists identified at first four modes (5th century), then, around 600 AD, as a result of the modifications made by singers, added four more.

The modes were merely numbered I–VIII until a Swiss theorist, Glareanus (1488–1563), added

four more modes and applied what he mistakenly thought were the original Greek names to them. The oldest modes were called the Authentic modes: Dorian, Phrygian, Lydian and Mixolydian. To these were added so-called Plagal modes: HypoDorian, HypoPhrygian, HypoLydian and HypoMixolydian. Glareanus added Aeolian, HypoAeolian, Ionian and HypoIonian. These last were considered most suitable for harmony and the Aeolian corresponds to the present-day minor scale and the Ionian to the major scale.

∾THE MODES IN PRACTICE

The easiest way to hear what the modes sound like is to play scales on the piano only using the white notes. For instance, the Phrygian mode is E–E.

1= semitone; 2= tone

The mode begins with a semitone, E–F, which gives it its characteristic flavour. In the late 17th and 18th centuries a cadence (closing sentence) using this semitone was used as an alternative to the normal minor one for special effect. This cadence was known as the Phrygian cadence. Handel uses a Phrygian touch just before the final cadence of the first chorus of 'Dixit Dominus', though he does not end with a Phrygian cadence.

Keys

THE WORD KEY CAN MEAN SEVERAL THINGS IN music. It can refer to the keys on a keyboard or a woodwind instrument – the means by which notes are played – or someone can be said to sing off-key, meaning out of tune. However, the commonest meaning refers to pitches and scales and their use in pieces of music. The term key came to be used increasingly as most of the modes disappeared, leaving only the Ionian and Aeolian, which became the present-day major and minor keys.

The simplest form of the key of a piece is the scale, which is an arrangement of tones [T] and semitones [S])

Major scale: T T S T T T S

Melodic minor scale: (up) T S T T T T S (down) T T S T T S T

Harmonic minor scale: T S T T S augmented T S

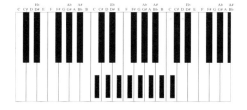

SCALE OF C MAJOR

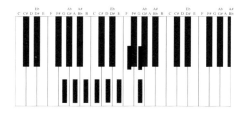

SCALE OF G MAJOR

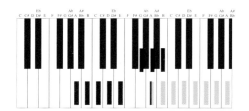

Melodic Minor Scale (in A), ascending and descending

NOTES FOR MELODIC MINOR – A MINOR – ASCENDING

NOTES FOR MELODIC MINOR – A MINOR – DESCENDING

HARMONIC MINOR SCALE (IN A, WITH G SHARP AS LEADING NOTE)

In Western music the major and minor scales have seven pitches – in the case of C major, for instance, C,D,E,F,G,A,B,[C]. The span of C to the next C is known as the octave, because in Western music major and minor scales are divided into eight degrees – seven in fact, as the octave C is the beginning of the next C-C pattern. The Western chromatic scale has 12 subdivisions, all of which are equal semitones: C, C sharp, D, D sharp, E, F, F sharp, G, G sharp, A, A sharp, B [C].

CHROMATIC SCALE: SIMPLE FORM

CHROMATIC SCALE IN PRACTICE: OPENING OF LISZT'S _FAUST_ SYMPHONY

Of course, the interval between C and C can be divided differently. The pentatonic scale, for instance, which is found in many folk tunes (for example 'Auld Lang Syne') divides the octave into five degrees: for example C, D, E, G, A, [C]. The whole tone scale, which has become increasingly popular in 20th-century music since Debussy used it so frequently is C, D, E, F sharp, G sharp, A sharp [C].

PENATONIC SCALE: SIMPLE FORM

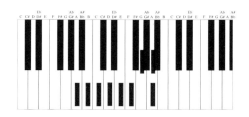

PENATONIC SCALE IN PRACTICE: 'AULD LANG SYNE'

In non-Western music the interval between C and C has been divided in many other ways, frequently using more intervals than just 12. Indian music, for instance, with its very subtle melodic inflexions, frequently uses notes that lie between the notes of the Western chromatic scale. These have also been used by Western composers, such as Bartók. In the West they are known as quarter-tones.

The notes of the scale show which notes are 'in the key'. A simple melody, such as 'Three Blind Mice', is all in one key.

Not many long (nor even short) pieces remain in one key throughout their duration as this would make them very dull listening. However, for special effect some do – Ravel's _Bolero_ , for example, which remains in the same key for a long time until a very dramatic key-shift occurs.

ACCIDENTALS AND MODULATION

All notes not included in the scale of a particular key are chromatic notes, and are indicated by the use of accidentals (sharp, flat or natural) on the printed page. Originally the word 'chromatic' meant 'coloured' and came to refer to a note that 'coloured' the original key, or inflected it, but did not change it. To change key, a piece needs to modulate. This means that by a variety of harmonic processes the key of a piece can change away from the fundamental tonic. The change from one key (or key-centre) to another is known as modulation. Thus, a simple tune such as the second movement of Haydn's Symphony No. 94 (_Surprise_) begins in C major, but modulates after a while to G major. This is achieved by introducing a note that is 'chromatic' to C, namely F sharp, which effectively shifts the key-centre for a short while to the dominant key, G major.

Modulation to dominant in Haydn's Surprise Symphony:

A work such as Beethoven's *Eroica* Symphony is described as being in E flat major, but for variety and length it contains many modulations and key shifts. In fact, it could be said that the first movement, for example, is about the journey away from the tonic and the return to it.

Some modern theorists have questioned the idea of modulation, claiming that all the notes in a piece of music (or a movement) are in the key of the piece and that there are no modulations but merely passing emphases on important notes of the prevailing key. This idea certainly helps to make sense of the phrase 'in a key' and explains why a tonal piece needs to return to its original key at its end no matter how many excursions away from the key there have been. No intermediate key-centres rival the main key, though many popular music theory books often imply that they do.

∾RELATIVE VALUES

Not all the notes in a scale are of equal importance when they are used in a piece of music. For instance, the chief note is the foundation note of the scale, the so-called 'key-note', and every other note is described in reference to it. The fifth degree of the scale is called the dominant, the fourth, the sub-dominant, and so on, as can be seen from the table in the next section, Tonality and Harmony. The relative importance of notes depends on the harmonic series (see page 254). The most important notes are those closest to the tonic in this naturally occurring series of pitches.

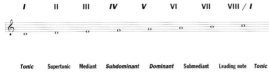

I	II	III	*IV*	*V*	VI	VII	VIII / *I*
Tonic	Supertonic	Mediant	*Subdominant*	*Dominant*	Submediant	Leading note	Tonic

PRINCIPAL NOTES IN THE SCALE

NB: Bold italic type indicates important notes

∾KEY ASSOCIATIONS

Keys first became common in the 17th century but it was not until well into the 18th century that they began to carry aesthetic characteristics. Handel, for instance, wrote his very sad 'Dead March' from *Saul* in a major key, whereas J S Bach wrote his very jolly Suite No. 2 for Flute and Strings in a minor key. However, by the time of Haydn and Mozart composers more frequently used minor keys for anxious or sorrowful music and major keys for the reverse. Haydn's Symphony No. 49 (*La Passione*) is in F minor; Mozart's two most 'gloomy and anxious' piano concertos are in D minor and C minor. Mozart was particularly fond of G minor for certain sad moods (for example the Symphony No. 40, the G minor String Quintet and G minor Piano Quartet).

It is not possible to say that all pieces in a minor key are gloomy, or that all pieces in a major key are 'happy', but there is no mistaking how often composers up to the end of the 19th century did use major and minor keys in this way. There is nothing intrinsically 'sad' about a minor key, or 'happy' about a major key, though minor keys are less tonally stable since, as can be seen above, they allow more variables with the result that they are more able to suggest shifting emotions by employing different versions of different notes.

Some keys have become associated with certain types of music, often because at the time they were written the instruments used could only play in those keys. In Handel's day, for instance, the fundamental note of the trumpet was D, so a great deal of martial and ceremonial music is in D major.

An interesting sideline on keys is the fact that some composers and theorists have associated particular keys not only with moods but with colours. This is highly contentious, and it is impossible to prove scientifically that there is any correspondence between music and colours, even though some composers have argued strongly for it. Hearing C major, or the note C, one person may equate it with red and another with green, but whether they are consciously or unconsciously making parallels or are in fact passively responding to similar stimuli is almost impossible to state.

Equating colour with music is not new. The Greek philosopher Aristotle drew parallels, and the English physicist Sir Isaac Newton noted analogies between the colour spectrum and the musical scale. Various methods of playing a 'scale of colours' on a colour organ were devised in the 18th century, and the idea of parallels between colour and music gathered momentum in the late 19th century when subliminal connections between the arts were part of much current thinking.

Probably the most significant composer to be convinced about the parallels between colours and keys was the Russian Alexander Scriabin, whose *Prométhée: le poème du feu* (1908–10) uses a colour organ, and which requires different colours to be projected on a screen according to the prevailing harmonic centre of particular moments. More recently, the French composer Olivier Messiaen assigned colours to particular notes and chords.

∾CONSONANCE AND DISSONANCE

These terms are synonymous with concord and discord but, since what has been described as a concord or a discord has changed over the centuries, they are hard to define exactly. By and large, the concord describes any two intervals played simultaneously which together make a satisfactory harmony. In practice this means an octave, a fifth, a third and a sixth are concordant intervals, and chords in which these intervals predominate are described as consonant or concordant. The term discord usually describes a second, a fourth and a seventh; and a chord in which any of these intervals predominates is called a dissonance or discord. The fourth is the only interval which bridges the divide between concord and discord, as in some circumstances it is concordant, for example when it is the upper interval of a chord consisting of a third and a fourth.

In tonal music a discord has to be handled as part of a sequence of chords, and the dissonant note (that is, the one forming the dissonance with the bass) has to be prepared and resolved with care. However, increasingly mild dissonances, such as minor sevenths and ninths, became treated as pseudo-consonances by composers such as Debussy, and in the works of Schoenberg, for example, dissonances have been freed of having to be prepared and resolved by consonances. Consequently, much 20th-century music has become freely dissonant.

Tonality and Harmony

A TONAL PIECE OF MUSIC IS ONE WHICH HAS A fundamental tone from which the significance of all the other tones derives and to which the piece returns at its conclusion. For example, a piece in A major has the note A as its fundamental tone, so E major is its dominant, D major its subdominant and F sharp minor its relative minor. Though E major is a key in its own right, in a piece in A major it can never be the fundamental key, so it is described in its relation to A major.

NAMES OF DEGREES OF SCALE

The note A in a piece in A major is called the tonic. The other degrees of the scale are as follows:

DEGREE OF SCALE	NAME
FIRST	**TONIC**
SECOND	**SUPERTONIC**
THIRD	**MEDIANT**
FOURTH	**SUBDOMINANT**
FIFTH	**DOMINANT**
SIXTH	**SUBMEDIANT**
SEVENTH	**LEADING NOTE**
(EIGHTH=OCTAVE)	**TONIC**

I = Tonic; II= Supertonic; III= Mediant; IV= Subdominant;

V= Dominant; VI= Submediant; VII= Leading note;

VIII/I= Tonic

However, describing a piece as tonal usually means more than its just having a fundamental note from which all other notes are derived. After all, a mode has a fundamental note, but a modal piece is not usually described as tonal. More confusingly, a good deal of very dissonant, or highly chromatic, 20th-century music is tonal, but is not commonly described as such. This is in order to differentiate the kind of music, mostly written between the mid-17th century and the early 20th century, in which the tonal centre is clear and the deviations to other keys are audible. A Corelli concerto, a Mozart symphony or a Brahms piano work would be described as tonal, as would a neo-Classical movement by Stravinsky. On the other hand, works which go beyond the chromaticism of Wagner's *Tristan*, while technically being tonal, are often referred to as chromatic or hyperchromatic. Works without a tonal centre are referred to either as pan-tonal or atonal; and Schoenberg's post-1920

serial music is described as twelve-tonal, though it is not strictly speaking tonal music at all. Other variants are bi-tonal, which means written in two keys at once (a technique used by, among others, Darius Milhaud and Gustav Holst) and poly-tonal, which is the use of several keys at once.

∞TONALITY

Tonality describes the use of a structure based on the tonal hierarchy of the above table. For instance, a piece might begin in A major (the tonic), modulate to E major (the dominant), return to A major on the way to F sharp minor (the relative minor) and return finally to A major to conclude.

∞HARMONY

Harmony is the simultaneous sounding of several notes. This could be said to be synonymous with the word chord, but in practice chord usually refers solely to a simple simultaneous sound, while harmony implies a much wider-ranging set of musical associations and practices.

'Harmony' comes from a Greek word that not only meant concord but also the means by which planks of a ship were bound together. Ancient Greek philosophy believed in the Harmony of the Spheres as the means by which the sun and the planets were kept in place. This implies balance and order and a relationship between the heavenly bodies.

In the Middle Ages, when the prime concern was the linear direction of several individual contrapuntal lines, composers were aware of the effect they had when sounding together. During the 16th century composers increasingly used powerful dissonances to illustrate words (for example, in Italian madrigals) and from the 17th century the arrival of the *basso continuo* encouraged composers to write their music less as a collection of independent melodic lines and more as a series of harmonies. From the middle of the 17th century until about the 1920s Western composers have for the most part considered harmony the basis of their music – so much so that the French 18th-century composer Jean-Philippe Rameau wrote, "melody is but the surface of harmony".

Harmony, however, has never lost its contrapuntal roots, and many harmonic terms and procedures derive from them. For instance, the terms concord and discord imply notes in a harmony that form, respectively, pleasing or displeasing notes; and certain harmonies need particular preparation and resolution because one or more of their constituent notes expects to move in a particular direction. The

chord, C–E–G–B flat, for instance, expects the B flat to resolve down to A and the C to resolve to an F. It is called a 'dominant seventh' not only because the addition of the B flat to the chord of C makes it a seventh on the dominant chord of F major, but also

---

SOME MELODIC • TYPES •

> A melody that does not imply harmonic support: Plainchant ('Te lucis ante terminum')

F major   modulates to dominant – C major

modulates back   hints at relative   ends with a clear
to F major   minor-D minor   cadence in F major,
                                            the tonic

> A simple melody in regular phrases with clearly implied harmonic direction and roots: Hymn tune ('While shepherds watched')

> An embellished melody. The first example shows the principal notes; the second, the embellishments

> A folk melody – modal showing irregular phrases: 'Joseph and Mary' (collected by Ralph Vaughan Williams)

> An open-ended melody: *Romeo and Juliet* (Berlioz)

> An exotic melody showing the use of microtones and an unusual scale: Bartók's Fourth Quartet

because it implies a resolution onto a chord of F major. The word 'dominant' comes from the Latin meaning a 'leader' – and it is helpful to think of the dominant seventh not only as the most important seventh chord, but also one that leads to the tonic.

Over the centuries composers have, of course, increased the tension and forward movement of their music by delaying and embellishing resolutions. J S Bach tended to delay the resolution of his harmonic progressions (cadences) by making one dissonant chord resolve into another. Mozart was particularly fond of exploring the far-flung resolutions of discords and finding himself in keys quite foreign to the prevailing tonic. In the 19th century harmonic experiments were rife. Chopin, for instance, increasingly explored how far he could delay cadences by using chromatic harmonies, and this trend was developed much further by Wagner, particularly in the period after he wrote his music-drama *Tristan und Isolde*.

Harmony in which the role of different chords is clearly defined as part of a tonal context is said to be functional harmony. In the years following Wagner's experiments, many composers (for example, Debussy) have used harmonies just for their individual sounds and have not attempted to resolve discords, thus robbing them of their function. One notable example of this is in atonal and twelve-tone music.

∾MELODY

The most basic definition of a melody is a sequence of notes, but the term means more than this; it also implies a shape and a relationship between the notes. The earliest Western melodies, plainchant and folk tunes, are elaborations of a single tonic note, so their shape and direction derive from their need to conclude on a tonic note.

Since the time when harmony dominated Western music, melodies have always been written with harmonic implications; even if they are played with no harmony, harmonies are implied and their presence gives direction to the melodies. This has not prevented melodies from becoming highly sophisticated, and more often than not they are the most immediately accessible part of harmonic music. Many people find themselves remembering a melody (or tune) rather than the harmony on which it is based.

Before the widespread use of harmony in the West, and in the non-Western cultures where harmony plays no part, melodies have often become freer, more elaborate and capable of highly

sophisticated expressiveness. Indian music, for instance, has melodic flights of fancy that explore microtones, a wide variety of shapes and patterns, as well as multi-octave ranges.

Twelve-tone Music

A TWELVE-TONE (OR TWELVE-NOTE) PIECE OF music is one which uses all 12 notes of the piano's chromatic scale. These are organized into a particular sequence, which is called a 'series' or a 'row', or sometimes tone-row or note-row. The series of notes can be used in different ways throughout the piece, but it is important that no one note emerges as more important than any other and thus becomes a tonic.

Because the 12 notes of the chromatic scale are organized into a repeated series of notes, twelve-note music is sometimes called 'serial'. It is also known as 'dodecaphonic'.

∾DEVELOPMENT

By the end of the 19th century many composers had explored such rich chromatic harmony that the chords they used could often not be confidently related to any particular key. Consequently, much music consisted of dissonances (albeit relatively mild) which previously had been prepared and resolved, but which now could be used freely for their colour alone.

One of the effects of this weakening of the

harmonic foundation of musical structure was to create music of considerable fluidity, in which gestures, textures and motivic cross-references held the music together. This 'atonal' style was ideal for expressing some of the current artistic and philosophical ideas, particularly the often illogical and disturbing images of dreams and insanity.

Arnold Schoenberg dispensed with tonality after a brief period of writing hyperchromatic compositions, such as *Verklärte Nacht*. Between 1908 and 1910 he wrote works that used a consistently dissonant language in a burst of highly expressive pieces, often of nightmare visions (*Erwartung* (1909) and *Pierrot Lunaire* (1912), for example), which were also highly compacted structurally.

By 1915 Schoenberg was interested in exploring whether dissonance could be organized to support musical structures as consonances had been. Could there be an equivalent of a key-centre or scale to which every further harmony was related? By taking all the notes of the chromatic scale (that is, merely extending the range notes of the same harmonic series that had formed the basis of tonal harmony) he arrived at the solution of organizing the 12 notes of the scale into a particular order, or series. This series would be repeated in various ways throughout the piece, rather in the way a scale had been used by Beethoven – that is, the series was not the theme of the piece, but more like the underlying 'scale' of the work.

Schoenberg's first twelve-tone piece was *Five Pieces for Piano* (1921), and between then and his death in 1951 he wrote many more, including Serenade, Op. 24 (1923), Variations for Orchestra, Op. 31 (1928), *Ode to Napoleon Buonaparte* (1942)

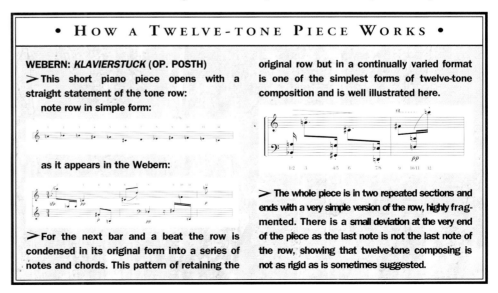

and String Quartets Nos 3 and 4 (1927 and 1936).

∾ANTECEDENTS OF TWELVE-NOTE WRITING

A number of composers accidentally anticipated Schoenberg's thematic use of all the notes of the chromatic scale. Some Baroque composers used it in their most chromatic fugues, as did some late 18th-century composers. More importantly and less accidentally, the opening of Liszt's *Faust* Symphony uses a chromatic series which has no harmonic implications; but as the work proceeds its harmonic foundation becomes clearer.

Around the turn of the 20th century Alexander Scriabin with his 'mystic chord' came close, as did Josef Matthias Hauer shortly before Schoenberg. But it is really Schoenberg who thought through the implications of using a method of composing that used all the 12 notes of the chromatic scale equally.

∾TWELVE-TONE MUSIC IN THE 20TH CENTURY

Schoenberg was a very influential composer and teacher. His two most distinguished pupils, Alban Berg and Anton Webern (the New or Second Viennese School) adopted the 12-tone technique in the 1920s, and both demonstrated the range and fruitfulness of the new style. In his Violin Concerto (1935), Berg reconciled the rich chromaticism of the late 19th century with the new dissonance by devising a 'tone-row' that largely consists of major and minor triads. Webern, on the other hand, in his Symphony, Op.21 (1928), showed how deriving every note of his music from the row in a succession of contrapuntal devices could not only produce a new kind of brevity and intensity, but could also link the new style with Renaissance and earlier techniques.

After 1945 Webern's serialism became very influential, especially on Pierre Boulez and Karlheinz Stockhausen, both of whom extended the serialization of pitches to include rhythm, dynamics and duration.

Other composers, such as Hans Werner Henze and Luigi Dallapiccola, explored the lyrical side of Berg's writing to draw serial music away from Schoenberg's abiding Expressionism. In his opera *The Turn of the Screw* (1954), Benjamin Britten used a note-row that was not chromatic but which could be in several keys. It was tonal, not atonal, thus further divorcing serialism from Schoenberg's dissonance.

Fugue

A FUGUE IS CONTRAPUNTAL COMPOSITION, meaning that its dominating characteristic is its use of 'counterpoint'. Counterpoint describes music in which two or more independent musical lines are combined; in Tudor music an initial melody sung, or played, by one part was called a 'point', to which another was subsequently added and called a 'counterpoint'. When several voices (or parts) are combined contrapuntally, music is sometimes described as polyphonic (from two Greek words meaning 'many voices'). The opposite of polyphonic is homophonic, meaning all the voices move together.

A simple harmonized hymn-tune might be described as homophonic, whereas a Bach fugue or a motet by Palestrina can be described both as polyphonic (having more than one voice-part) and contrapuntal (describing the way they are combined). The words 'parts', or 'voices', are here taken to refer to the musical lines on the page, not to what instruments or singing voices would perform them.

The musicologist Sir Donald Tovey said that fugue is a texture, to emphasize the fact that it is not a pre-existing form but a way of giving a piece of music a particular kind of texture in which the individual voices, or parts, interweave contrapuntally to give a closely argued effect. That said, one or two things do fairly consistently occur in fugues.

∾WHAT HAPPENS IN A FUGUE?

The most important element in a fugue is the subject. This is heard alone in one voice at the beginning of a fugue. Sometimes in choral fugues it is accompanied, and in so-called double fugues there may be two subjects heard simultaneously. Fugue subjects vary greatly in length, some being almost 'good tunes', such as 'He trusted in God' from Handel's *Messiah*. Others have only a few notes, such as Bach's C sharp minor fugue (*The Well-Tempered Clavier*, Book 1). The character of a fugue subject strongly influences the subsequent events of the fugue.

The subject is replied to by an 'answer' which is the subject repeated in another part and in another key, sometimes exactly (real answer), sometimes modified (tonal). While the answer is being played the first voice accompanies it with a counter-subject. To bring the music back to the original key there then follows a short contrapuntal episode, sometimes called a codetta.

This procedure of answer following subject is repeated until all the voices or parts have played or sung the subject once. When the last note of the subject has been played by the last voice to enter the first section of the fugue is complete. This section is called the exposition, and some fugues stop being fugues from that moment. Sometimes this truncated form is called a fughetta.

The middle section of the fugue goes through a number of keys and in many cases the arrival at a key is marked by the return of the subject, with or without its countersubject(s). The passage in between consists of material from the codetta

---

• SIX FAMOUS FUGUES •

➤ **Bach** – *The Art of Fugue* The most exhaustive example of fugal procedures . Bach died before he could finish it.

➤ **Mozart** – *Finale of String Quartet in G, K387* This is a fugue combined with a sonata structure. Mozart achieves a remarkable 'stretto maestrale' at the end: all four voices enter before the first has finished.

➤ **Beethoven** – *Grosse Fuge* This started life as the finale of his String Quartet Op.130, but became so large it was separated. It is now a three-movement quartet in its own right.

➤ **Brahms** – *Requiem* This work contains a number of fugues, but perhaps the most remarkable is 'Der Gerechten Seelen sind in Gottes hand' ('But the souls of the righteous are in the hands of God'), which is entirely constructed over a held D in the bass.

➤ **Britten** – *Young Person's Guide to the Orchestra* The subtitle of this work is *Variations and Fugue on a Theme of Purcell*. Purcell's theme comes from his incidental music to the play *Abeldazer*. The fugue which ends Britten's work is outstanding. Britten not only writes a dazzlingly virtuoso fugue for the whole orchestra on a theme loosely derived from the Purcell original, but brings the work to a climax by grandly quoting the Purcell theme in its original form as a countersubject.

➤ **Shostakovich** – *Preludes and Fugues* This is probably the greatest set of preludes and fugues written in the 20th century, paying homage to, but not imitating, J S Bach. They cover a wide emotional and technical range.

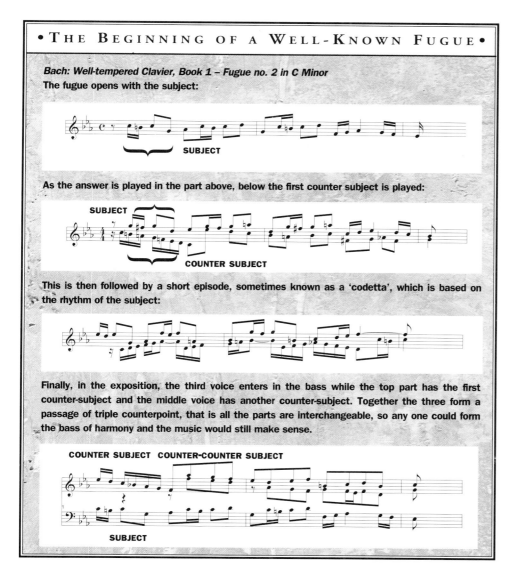

• THE BEGINNING OF A WELL-KNOWN FUGUE •

Bach: Well-tempered Clavier, Book 1 – Fugue no. 2 in C Minor
The fugue opens with the subject:

SUBJECT

As the answer is played in the part above, below the first counter subject is played:

SUBJECT

COUNTER SUBJECT

This is then followed by a short episode, sometimes known as a 'codetta', which is based on the rhythm of the subject:

Finally, in the exposition, the third voice enters in the bass while the top part has the first counter-subject and the middle voice has another counter-subject. Together the three form a passage of triple counterpoint, that is all the parts are interchangeable, so any one could form the bass of harmony and the music would still make sense.

COUNTER SUBJECT   COUNTER-COUNTER SUBJECT

SUBJECT

played with any one of the parts forming the bass line (invertible counterpoint). Sometimes, however, these bridging passages (known as episodes) are not related to any previous material.

The final section of the fugue is in the tonic and usually has a last entry of the subject and a concluding cadence that may include the subject.

∽ USES OF THE FUGUE

The difficulty of writing a fugue lies not so much in making the music fit the design, as making it flow as though it was not being forced. This is the supreme gift of the great contrapuntalists like Bach, Mozart, Brahms, Shostakovich and Britten.

Composers have used fugue for a variety of reasons. In Bach's day fugal writing was an everyday way of musical thinking. By the end of the century fugal writing was more often used as a special set-piece, such as the Amens at the end of choral movements. However, fugal passages crept

into longer works, especially the development sections of symphonic and sonata movements, to give greater depth and a sense of the music being argued over more deeply. Some composers, like Brahms, used complex contrapuntal techniques in pieces that are not outwardly fugues at all.

∽ DIFFERENT KINDS OF FUGUE

A canon is a special kind of fugue in which each of the parts imitates the subject exactly and for its entire duration. A round is the same thing as a canon. The original name for a canon was *Fuga ad canonem* – fugue according to the rules. Among the most famous canons are 'Three Blind Mice', 'Frère Jacques' and Tallis's canon which is sung to 'Glory to thee, my God, this night'.

Rondo

THE TERM RONDO LITERALLY MEANS A ROUND, AND is probably derived from a form of dance. Its most essential feature is a regularly repeated passage of music that is returned to, after contrasted episodes, throughout the piece of music. The term is sometimes used in 18th-century vocal music to refer to an aria in which a slow section is followed by a fast section, but by far its commonest use is in reference to instrumental music. There were medieval and Renaissance rondeaux (usually spelt in the French way), but these had little connection with the later developments. The medieval rondeau was one of three song-forms (the others being a virelai and a ballade) which had a fixed pattern for the words and the music. The words had a regular rhyming scheme, and the music a fixed pattern of repetition. Though the form of the medieval rondeau was established by the 13th century, its heyday was the 15th century, when it was a favourite form of Burgundian composers such as Dufay and Binchois.

∽ THE MODERN RONDO

The rondeau's first 'modern' appearance was in France in the 17th century, where it figures in the ballets of Lully and the harpsichord music of François Couperin. Though the pattern was not standard, one of its most frequent forms was:

A EIGHT BAR IDEA IN THE TONIC KEY
B FIRST EPISODE (= 'COUPLET'). THE
   OPENING MATERIAL (A) IN ANOTHER KEY
A REPEAT OF A
C SECOND EPISODE (= 'COUPLET') –
   INVERSION OF A
A REPEATED TO CONCLUDE

The French rondeau became much imitated elsewhere in Europe during the 18th century, but in time a new kind of rondo emerged that was more openly tuneful than the French had been. The rondo thus became a much more deliberately popular form, and a suitable ending for large-scale works. In England, for instance, a particularly light-textured melodious kind emerged in the works of James Hook and others which was nicknamed the 'Vauxhall rondo' because of its frequent use in the instrumental music performed in the Vauxhall Pleasure Gardens.

One of the most prolific and interesting writers of rondos on the 18th century was CPE Bach. He confessed to writing rondos in his later keyboard works to meet with modern taste, although the structure of his fascinating rondos is very individual and met modern taste only in their search for expressiveness. Essentially his rondos mix improvisatory passages with rapid virtuoso passages, often juxtaposing these highly contrasted types in an almost wilful way. The two most famous 18th-century writers of large numbers of more conventional rondos were Mozart and Beethoven. The former wrote a number of independent rondos for piano, including the famous one in A minor, K511 (1787). In this Mozart showed that the rondo form was capable of sustaining deeply reflective and structurally adventurous music.

However, by far the largest number of rondos by Mozart are of the popular variety, for instance, the finale of his piano sonata in A minor, K331 (1778), the so-called *Rondo alla Turca*. The structure of this is slightly unusual (A, B, A, short B and Coda) and it is a good example of how flexible composers were in treating forms. Mozart also invented a blend of sonata and rondo for the finales of his concertos, symphonies and other works. The first example is the finale of his String Quartet, K157 in C (1772–73). Haydn sporadically adopted this from his Symphony No. 77 (1782) onwards, and by the end of the century the structural pattern for the sonata-rondo finale was as above.

Beethoven adopted this pattern for the finales

A	**MAIN THEME**
B	**FIRST EPISODE – CONTRASTED KEY AND MELODIC MATERIAL**
A	**FIRST RETURN**
C	**SOMETIMES CONTRASTING MATERIAL, BUT INCREASINGLY MORE OFTEN A DEVELOPMENT OF A**
A	**SECOND RETURN – THOUGH IN PRACTICE THIS WAS OFTEN LEFT OUT**
B	**A RECAPITULATION OF THE FIRST EPISODE IN THE TONIC KEY**
A	**THIRD (OR SECOND) RETURN, WHICH SOMETIMES CONTAINS CHANGES CODA OF VARYING LENGTH AND COMPLEXITY TO END.**

of his concertos, including the Violin Concerto and Piano Concertos Nos 4 and 5.

In the 19th century composers found the rondo a good form for independent compositions. Typical rondos are Weber's *Rondo brillant* for piano (1819) and Chopin's *Krakowiak Rondo*, Op. 14 (1828), in which the main theme is based on a Polish national melody. Some composers modified the rondo form slightly, but by and large composers as varied as Tchaikovsky and Mendelssohn were happy to take the Mozart mould and fill it with their own music.

In the 20th century the rondo is still found. Mahler used a *Rondo Burlesca* in his Symphony No. 9 , and the finale of his Symphony No. 5 (1901–2) is also a rondo. In his two-piano *Introduction and Rondo alla Burlesca* (1940), Britten treated the form in a characteristically individual way.

• STRUCTURE OF A FAMILIAR RONDO • (HAYDN: RONDO ALL'ONGARESE FROM PIANO TRIO NO. 25)

➤ **A** Piano opens with the main Rondo theme (A) in the tonic key, G major. It is then joined by the violin in a repeat. After cadencing in the tonic there is a brief development of the idea before the piano and violin repeat A to finish the first section.

➤ **B** The violin introduces a new theme (B) in the tonic. The theme is characterized by a rapid sighing phrase. It is played three times before hints of A are heard in the first violin as an extension of B. They form a modified return to A.

➤ **C** The piano introduces a new idea in the tonic minor (G minor). It is a more folk-dance type idea with the piano playing strongly rhyth-

mic repeated chords. After four playings of C the piano plays it loudly in thirds.

➤ **A** Piano and violin join in a return of the main idea (A) in the tonic major.

➤ **D** The music goes back to the tonic minor. Again the minor key suggests a folk idiom to Haydn, who as in C uses repeated chords in the piano left-hand. This episode contains one or two stronger dissonances.

➤ **A** A returns in the tonic key and includes the little passage of development heard earlier in the first section. The closing moments of the Rondo form a coda based on the rapid figuration of A.

• BASIC SONATA • PRINCIPLE

By the mid to late 18th century the classic features of sonata principle had taken shape, but few composers treated it as a formula. Each piece was different depending on the musical material from which the music was constructed. By and large the format was as follows:

FIRST SECTION – *called* EXPOSITION

A First musical ideas in the tonic key. Often these outlined the tonic chord and had a strong definitive rhythm.

After perhaps two contrasted statements of A the music moves away from the tonic. Some books describe this shift as the transition, but the term is confusing as the music often sounds like a continuation and development of A.

B Second set of musical ideas. In the earliest examples this was usually made up of just short cadential phrases, and Haydn until the end of his life often preferred this approach. Mozart usually had a more defined set of second ideas which often took up much more time in the First Section of the work.

Short cadential phrases to round off the First Section.

DOUBLE BAR – FIRST SECTION
REPEATED SECOND SECTION
– *First part – Development*

This is the least predictable part of sonata principle. Usually the composer began in the dominant key and found his way back to the tonic through a variety of contrasting keys. This passage was articulated by showing a number of ways that the opening material could be treated and transformed, hence the term 'development'. Some composers hardly used their B material, some invented new material. Sometimes this section was short; in Beethoven's *Eroica* Symphony it was very long.

– *Second part – Recapitulation*

A The return of the opening material in the tonic key usually marked the opening of this section. In the 19th century composers often tried to disguise the opening by beginning in an unexpected key or continuing developing material.

The modulating section no longer being required as far as the keys were concerned, but being necessary for the balance of the structure, composers often explored some richer harmonies as a way of reapproaching the tonic and the re-presentation of B

B The second material returns in the tonic key. and leads into the final cadences – CODA

Sonata Forms

EVER SINCE THE EARLY 18TH CENTURY, SONATA form has been the most commonly used musical form. Most first movements, and a good many others, of symphonies, string quartets, solo sonatas and of many other works are cast in this form. Even some operatic scenes (such as the Act 2 finale of Mozart's *Le nozze di Figaro* (1786) are in a modified sonata form. Given the huge variety of differences between the various examples, it is better to think of sonata form as a way of musical thinking rather than a specific form.

∾THE DEVELOPMENT OF SONATA FORM

Sonata form or principle acquired its name from Italian keyboard sonatas at the end of the 17th century. These sonatas increasingly broke with the classic Baroque features of counterpoint and a single permeating mood, and started using more fragmented and emotionally evocative melodic material played over much simpler basses. Bit by bit each new section of the opening half was marked by new melodic material and a dramatic tension emerged between the characterization of the tonic and that of the dominant. The dramatic tension and the working out of this became an essential feature of sonata principle, as opposed to Baroque music, which had been expository.

In the early to mid-18th century two great exponents of the earliest sonata idea appeared: Domenico Scarlatti and C P E Bach. The latter had a profound influence on Haydn, Mozart and Beethoven, the three composers who represent the first classic phase of sonata principle.

In the 19th and 20th centuries many developments took place. Liszt in his Piano Sonata in B minor and Schoenberg in his Chamber Symphony No.1 combined four movements into one sonata movement. The concert overture and its successors the symphonic poem and the tone poem were frequently indebted to sonata structures.

It was in the 19th century that theorists first started to describe sonata principle as sonata form, and to lay down its procedures, but their stress on first and second subjects frequently obscured the fact that sonata principle is essentially a dramatic struggle between keys.

Sonata principle remained a favourite form for composers until at least the early 20th century because highly contrasted musical material and styles can be worked out in a coherent overall structure. As in a novel, different characters can appear in many different situations but they are held together by the overall storyline, which in music is the constant need for the music to return confidently to the tonic.

With the disappearance of tonality as an automatic ingredient of music many composers have had to evolve new formal procedures, and others have consciously wanted to return to the unfolding quality of the Baroque. But there are still many who use tonality and enjoy the perennial challenges of sonata principle. ♪

A TYPICAL SONATA MOVEMENT
(MOZART: SONATA IN C, K545)

~

THE FIRST SECTION: EXPOSITION

A Mozart begins the sonata with the first idea A in the tonic key – C major. After a four-bar phrase consisting of two playings of the same rhythm, the music introduces a section of running scales. These lead to a modulation to the dominant.

B After a rest the left hand plays an oscillating figure which leads to the second idea B, which begins rather like the first idea turned upside down. Once again the idea is two bars long but this time it is followed by a passage of semiquavers in which the hands have a dialogue with one another.

CODA After a trill there is a short coda, C, rounding off the exposition which Mozart indicates should be repeated.

THE SECOND SECTION: DEVELOPMENT AND RECAPITULATION

This starts with the coda idea, C, in the minor key, which gives the music a more determined mood. The music then follows a cycle of fifths from G minor to D minor but avoids settling in A minor, finding its way instead to F major, in which the A is repeated.

A The repeat of A brings the recapitulation of the main idea, but as often in sonata principle movements the composer avoids making the return of thematic ideas coincide with that of keys.

B B returns in the tonic key and appears almost exactly the same as in the first section except it is transposed into the tonic. Once again after the trill the music has a short CODA with which to end.

INDEX

Page numbers in bold refer to principal topics; those in italic to illustration captions

Abbado, Claudio 175
Abel, Carl Friedrich 70, 138
Academic Festival overture (Brahms) **106**, 107
Academy of St Martin-in-the-Fields 162-3
accidentals 256-7
Adagio (Barber) 163, **163**
Adam, Adolphe Charles 70, 83
Adams, John 40, 70
    Grand Pianola Music **127**
    operas 147, 242, **243**
Addinsell, Richard 70, 123
Adler, Larry 127
Agoult, Marie d' *29*
Aho, Kalevi 70, 151
Aida (Verdi) 202, 235
Al Santo Sepolcro sonata (Vivaldi) **98**
Albéniz, Isaac 33, *52*, **52**
Albert Hall, London **167**
Albert Herring (Britten) 242
Albinoni, Tomaso Giovanni 19, 70, 115, 133
Albrechtsberger, Antonius 98
Albrechtsberger, Johann Georg 70, 138
Alkan, Charles 70, 87, **87**
Allegri, Gregorio 19, 70
alphorn concertos 126
Amadeus (film) 55
Amati family *178*, 179
American quartet (Dvořák) 100
Andriessen, Hendrik 70
Andriessen, Louis 40, *41*, 70
Anna Bolena (Donizetti) 234
Années de Pelèrinage (Liszt) 26, 31
Antheil, George 70
Appalachian Spring (Copland) 66, 85
Après-midi d'un faune (Debussy) 85, 109, 252
Archduke trio (Beethoven) 156, **157**
Arensky, Anton Stepanovich 70, 156, 158
Ariadne auf Naxos (Richard Strauss) 199, 203
Arlésienne (Bizet) **111**
Arne, Thomas 70, 135, 222
Arnold, Malcolm 70, 107, *126*, 150
    Concerto for Phyllis and Cyril **127**
'Ars Antiqua' 9
Ars Nova (Philippe de Vitry) 10
Art of Fugue (J S Bach) 18, 260
art songs **216-25**
Art of the Violin (Locatelli) 116
atonality 36, **38-9**, 124, 150-1, 241
    see also tonality; twelve-tone music
Attaignant, Pierre 11
Auber, Daniel-François-Esprit 70, 251

Auden, W H 222
Auric, Georges 33, 70
'authenticity' and tradition **174-5**

Babbitt, Milton 70
Bach, C P E 20, *21*, 23, 70, 92, 115, *135*, 179, 262, 263
    concertos, harpsichord 118, 191
    symphonies **135**
    in F 135
Bach, Johann Christian 70, 118-19, 137, 138
Bach, Johann Sebastian 15, 16, 18, 19, 20, 50, **53-4**, *54*, *114*, 177, *211*
    cantatas 18, **211**
    concertos 115
    Brandenburg 18, 115, **162**, 163, 175, 191, 252
    fugue, *Art of Fugue* 18, **260**
    Mass in B minor 54, **211**
    Passions 53, **210-11**, *211*
    preludes/fugues *Well-Tempered Clavier* ('the 48') 18, **89**, 190
    sonatas
        flute 155
        No.3 for Unaccompanied violin (BWV 1005) **95**
    songs 216
    suites 128, **129**
        No.2 for Flute and Strings 257
    variation form, *Goldberg* Variations 18, **103**
Bach, W F 70, **133**
Bachianas Brasileiras (Villa-Lobos) 67
Badinage (Godowsky) 87
Badings, Henk 70, 126
Bagatelle sans tonalité (Liszt) 60
Bailey, Pearl 201
Baker, Janet 200
Bakst, Léon 85, *85*
Balakirev, Mily 33, **63**, 109, 224
Balanchine, George 83, 84
Balfe, Michael 70
ballet 15, 33, 36, 37, **82-5**, 228
Ballo in Maschera (Verdi) 199, 200, 204
Bär, Olaf 204
Barber, Samuel 70, 122, 149, 252
    Adagio 163, **163**
    Summer Music 159
Barber of Seville (Rossini) **105**, 200, *204*, 234
Barbieri, Lucio 70, 247
Barbirolli, John 48
baritone voice 197, **204-5**
Baroque **14-19**, 81, 96, 153, *155*, 163, *165*, 170
Barraqué, Jean 70
Barret, Apollon 181
Barshai, Rudolph 163

Bartered Bride (Smetana) 60, 237, 251
Bartók, Béla 33, *34*, *35*, 61, 87, *125*, 252, 255
    Mikrokosmos 250
    Music for Strings, Percussion and Celesta 91, 162
    ballet, Miraculous Mandarin **85**
    concertos 124, 125
    Concerto for Orchestra 61, **165**
        piano, No.3 91, **125**
        violin, No.2 **125**
    quartets 100, *101*, *101*, 258
    sonata, for Unaccompanied Violin **95**
    suites
        Dance Suite **131**
        Out of Doors 91
barytons **177**
Basle Chamber Orchestra 162, *163*
bass clarinets 166
bass voice 197, **204-5**
basset horns 183
bassoons 115, 126, 165, 169, 173, *180*, **180**, **182**, 185
Batalla Imperial (Cabanilles) 112
Battle symphony (Beethoven) **139**
Baudelaire, Charles 36, *221*
Bax, Arnold 70, 109
Bayreuth and Wagner 57, **239**
BBC Radiophonic Workshop 194, *195*
Beach, Amy 70
beat (rhythm) 249
Beatrice et Bénédict (Berlioz) 236
Bedini, Domenico 203
Beer, Johann 187
Beethoven, Ludwig van 24, 25, *55*, **55**, 81, *138*, 170, 251
    ballet *Prometheus* 103
    choral, *Missa Solemnis* 138, 212
    concertos 120, 126, 262
        piano, No.5/E flat (Op.73 *Emperor*) **120**
    duos
        Sonata/A (Op.47 *Kreutzer*) **97**, 155
        Sonata/D major (Op.40, cello/piano) **155**
    fantasias 92
    incidental music *Egmont* **111**
    Lieder **216**
    opera, *Fidelio* 55, 236
    overtures 105, 106
    piano sonatas 94, 192-3
        B flat (Op.106 *Hammerklavier*) **95**
        C sharp minor (Op.27 No.2 *Moonlight*) 90, 92, *94*, **95**
    quartets 100, 153, 158
        No.3 (Op.18) 253
        No.13/B flat (Op.130) 100
        C sharp minor (Op.131) 253
        A minor (op.132) 255
        Grosse Fuge (Op.133) **260**
    quintets, string (Op.29) 159
    septet/E flat (Op.20) 160, **161**
    symphonies 26, *27*, **138-9**, 165
        No.3/E flat (*Eroica*) 26, *27*, 55, 103, 138, *139*, **139**, 188, 257, 262

No.4/B flat 55, 138, **139**, 189
No.5/C minor 26, 55, 138, **139**, **165**, 183, 185
No.6/F (*Pastoral*) 26, **112**, 113, 138, **139**, 142, 165
No.7/A 138, **139**, 252
No.9/D minor ('Choral') 25, 26, 29, **139**, 165, 166, 189, 252, 253
    trios 157
        B flat major *Archduke* (Op.97) 156, **157**
        C major (Op.87, two oboes/cor anglais) **156**
    variation form 102-3
        Diabelli variations **103**
    violin sonatas, /A major (Op.47) 97
Beggar's Opera (Gay) 19, *19*, 242
bel canto 199, 204, 234-5
Bellini, Vincenzo 51, **51**, 199, 202, 204, 205, **234-5**
Belshazzar's Feast (Walton) 214, **215**
Benda, Georg Anton 70, 135, 231
Benjamin, Arthur 70
Benjamin, George 41
Bennett, William Sterndale 70, 130, *131*
Benvenuto Cellini (Berlioz) 236
Berg, Alban 38, 39, *58*, **58**, 124, 131, 217, 260
    operas 58, 199, 204, 205, **241**
    Violin Concerto 58
Berganza, Teresa 201
Berio, Luciano 41, 70, 200
Berkeley, Lennox 70-1, 163
Berlin, Irving 205
Berlioz, Hector 26, 29, *43*, **43-4**, *113*, *166*, 170, 189, 199, 200
    'Virtuoso of the Orchestra' 166
    choral
        Childhood of Christ 213
        Requiem 166, 209, *209*
    operas 43-4, 236
    voice/orchestra, *Nuits d'été* 220
        Harold in Italy 29, 121, 141, 176
        Romeo and Juliet 141, 258
    Symphonie Fantastique 26, 29, 43, **113**, **140**, 141, **165**, 166, 175, 178, 179, 186, 187
    Symphonie funèbre et triomphale 141, 186, 189
Bernstein, Leonard *67*, 214-5, 243, 247
Bertini, Henri-Jérôme 71
Berwald, Franz **58**, 100
Biber, Heinrich 19, 71, 176, *178*
Billy Budd (Britten) 242
Birtwistle, Harrison 71, 161, 204
Bizet, Georges 35, **44**
    Arlésienne **111**
    Carmen 35, 44, 130, 201, 202, 237
    Jeux d'enfants 155
    Symphony in C **140**
Black Angels (Crumb) 100
Black Mass piano sonata (Scriabin) **95**
Bloch, Ernst 71, 124
Blow, John 17, 19, 71, 222
Boccherini, Luigi 71, 138, 159, 179

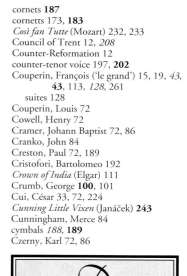

ACKNOWLEDGEMENTS

Rob Ainsley would like to thank Victoria, Neil, Daniel, Kate, Nick and Andy at *Classic CD* for making work so much fun; Apple, for making Macs cheap enough to buy and prepare this book on; the lady who found my contact lens on 18 March 1995; Shostakovich, Vaughan Williams, Bach, Blur; Mum and Dad; Angharad; Rebecca.

The Publisher would like to thank the following individuals for their generosity in contributing to the making of this book: Rachel and Nicholas Bush, Simon Farnhell, Frank Haskins, Impact Percussion, The London Philharmonic Orchestra, David Weir and Richard Wigmore.

PICTURE CREDITS